ACT Alliance and the Refugee Crisis

Dissertationes Theologicae Holmienses

Dissertations from University College Stockholm

www.ehs.se/dth

Main editor:

Thomas Kazen

Editors:

Petra Carlsson Redell

Joel Halldorf

Jonas Ideström

Susanne Wigorts Yngvesson

No. 10

Torbjörn Toll

ACT Alliance
and the Refugee Crisis

Ecclesiology and Tensions in Refugee Assistance

Enskilda Högskolan Stockholm

2025

ACT Alliance and the Refugee Crisis: Ecclesiology and Tensions in Refugee Assistance

Dissertation presented at University College Stockholm to be publicly examined in Room 219–220 at Åkeshovsvägen 29, Bromma, January 31, 2025, at 13:00, for the degree of Doctor of Philosophy in Theology (Practical Theology with Church History: Church History). The examination will be held in Swedish.

Faculty examiner: Klas Lundström, Associate Professor of Missiology, Johannelund School of Theology.
Supervisor: Sune Fahlgren, Associate Professor of Practical Theology, University College Stockholm.
Assist. supervisors: Mika Vähäkangas, Director, Polin Institute, Åbo Akademi University, and Extraordinary Professor, Stellenbosch University; and Hans Engdahl, Associate Professor of Systematic Theology, Uppsala University.

Abstract

The thesis attends to ecclesial matters of aid by analysing the ecclesiological problem of identity and meaning of ACT Alliance. African churches are participating in aid, and Ethiopia is a good case with its intensity of church-based aid work. ACT Alliance was an ecumenical initiative to act in solidarity with people in need through coordination and collaboration. ACT, i.e. *Action by Churches Together*, expresses the churches growing together in *koinonia*. In theory, this ecclesiologically informed idea was conceptualised as *ecumenical diakonia*. Christian aid agencies may suffer a mission drift and loss of identity causing inner secularisation in the churches thus endangering Christian commitment to the poor. Tensions in the study signify an ambiguity that this thesis investigates through the case of *the ETH141 ACT Appeal* to support South Sudanese refugees in Ethiopia in 2014 with two churches in Ethiopia shedding light on the issue. The ACT forum failed to attract church funding and mobilised state funding by a consortium with a principled humanitarian approach appropriate for refugee assistance. The *Maedot* of 1983 from the Ethiopian Orthodox Tewahido Church and *the ECMY letter* of 1972 from the Ethiopian Evangelical Church Mekane Yesus supported integral human development while criticising a donor-based approach, based on a sense of Ethiopian ownership, Christian anthropology, and the gospel. The ETH141 resembles an international crisis model, i.e. relief assistance by ecumenical specialised agencies coordinating with other stakeholders without being: integrated with the churches, intended as intra-church aid, or set up for Christian mission. Tensions indicate superficial conflict but deep concord between aid and church, and deep conflict between *exclusive humanism* and the churches' mission to reach every person with the gospel and life of the church.

ACT-alliansen och flyktingkrisen: Ecklesiologi och spänningar i flyktinghjälp

Akademisk avhandling presenterad vid Enskilda Högskolan Stockholm för disputation i sal 219–220, Åkeshovsvägen 29, Bromma, 31 januari, 2025 kl. 13.00, för teologie doktorsexamen i praktisk teologi med kyrkohistoria med inriktning mot kyrkohistoria. Disputationen kommer att äga rum på svenska.

Opponent: Klas Lundström, docent och högskolelektor i missionsvetenskap, Johannelunds Teologiska Högskola.

Handledare: docent och högskolelektor i praktisk teologi, Enskilda Högskolan Stockholm.

Bitr. handledare: Mika Vähäkangas, forskningschef, Polin-institutet, Åbo Akademi, och extraordinarie professor, Stellenbosch University; och Hans Engdahl, docent i systematisk teologi, Uppsala universitet.

Sammanfattning

Studien uppmärksammar den kyrkliga sidan av bistånd genom att analysera det ecklesiologiska problemet om ACT-alliansens innebörd och identitet. Kyrkor i Afrika behöver beforskas på egna villkor. Studien utgår från Etiopien: ett fokus för kyrkligt bistånd. ACT-alliansen är ett ekumeniskt initiativ för att samordna och koordinera stöd till människor i nöd. Tanken, uttryckt som *ekumenisk diakoni*, var att *Kyrkornas gemensamma arbete* (dvs. ACT) visar att kyrkorna växer samman i *koinonia*. Kristna biståndsorganisationer kan förlora identitet och mission över tid och orsaka inre sekularisering i kyrkorna, vilket hotar kristnas engagemang för de fattiga. De spänningar som beforskas innebär en tvetydighet om vad detta *kyrkornas gemensamma arbete* innebär, vilket denna avhandling undersöker genom ett fallstudium – *ETH141 ACT-appellen* att stödja sydsudanesiska flyktingar i Etiopien 2014 – med två kyrkor i Etiopien som belyser frågan. ETH141 ACT-appellen lyckades inte samla in medel från kyrkorna och därför mobiliserades statliga medel genom ett konsortium med en principiellt humanitär hållning avpassad för flyktinghjälp. *Maedot* 1983 från den Etiopiska ortodoxa tewahido-kyrkan och ECMY-brevet från 1972 från den Etiopiskevangeliska Mekane Yesus-kyrkan stödde *integrerad mänsklig utveckling* men riktade kritik mot statligt bistånd. Kritiken var baserad på en uppfattning om ett etiopiskt huvudmannaskap, kristen antropologi och det kristna evangeliet. Fallet kan beskrivas som *en internationell krismodell*, dvs. katastrofbistånd från ekumeniska specialiserade organ som samarbetar med alla berörda parter utan att arbetet integreras i kyrkorna, är avsett som inomkyrkligt bistånd, eller utformas för kristen mission. Spänningarna pekar på en ytlig konflikt och djup samstämmighet mellan bistånd och kyrka och en djup konflikt mellan *exklusiv humanism* och kyrkans mission att nå varje människa med evangelium och ett sakramentalt liv i kyrkan.

Enskilda Högskolan Stockholm

Enskilda Högskolan Stockholm erbjuder utbildningsprogram i mänskliga rättigheter och demokrati, samt i teologi/religionsvetenskap. Högskolan grundades 1993 genom en sammanslagning av utbildningsinstitutioner med rötter från 1866, hette tidigare Teologiska högskolan, Stockholm, och har tre avdelningar: Avdelningen för mänskliga rättigheter och demokrati, Avdelningen för religionsvetenskap och teologi, samt Avdelningen för östkyrkliga studier. Forskarutbildningen i Praktisk teologi med kyrkohistoria bedrivs inom inriktningarna Praktisk teologi respektive Kyrkohistoria. Utbildningen fokuserar på den kristna kyrkans utveckling och den kristna trons praktiska gestaltning, i ett konstruktivt samspel mellan empiriska metoder och teori. Utbildningen innefattar bland annat historiska, hermeneutiska, filosofiska, teologiska, sociologiska och etnologiska perspektiv.

University College Stockholm

University College Stockholm offers programmes in Human Rights and Democracy and in Theology / Religious Studies. The university college was founded in 1993 through a merger of educational institutions with roots dating back to 1866, is also known as Stockholm School of Theology, and has three departments: the Department of Human Rights and Democracy, the Department of Religious Studies and Theology, and the Department of Eastern Christian Studies. The doctoral programme in Practical Theology with Church History provides specialisations in Practical Theology and Church History respectively. It focuses on the development of the Christian church and practical expressions of Christian faith, in a constructive interplay between empirical methods and theory. The programme includes historical, hermeneutical, philosophical, theological, sociological, and ethnological perspectives.

© 2025 Torbjörn Toll
ISBN: 978-91-88906-28-1
Page and cover design by Carl Johan Berglund. Typeset in EB Garamond.
Printed by Libri Plureos GmbH, Hamburg, Tyskland
University College Stockholm
Åkeshovsvägen 29, 168 39 Bromma, Sweden
www.ehs.se

Preface

The questions raised in this dissertation arose from the curiosity and bewilderment stemming from my brief involvement in refugee assistance. By the end of 2013, I had been asked to chair the ACT Ethiopia Forum. Almost immediately, conflict broke out in South Sudan and the ACT members in Ethiopia started to prepare for being able to assist asylum seekers in case people would seek refuge in Ethiopia. So they did, and the ETH141 ACT Appeal and its follow-ups were put in motion. I therefore had the privilege and duty to follow the appeal close at hand. I learnt much from that experience but was also perplexed at how different practical relief was from my expectations. Things did not always turn out as planned. For me, this raised my scholarly interest.

There are many aspects of interest: My prime interest lies in what could be called *church-in-aid*, i.e. simply the fact that churches are both engaging in and living in a context shaped by humanitarian and development aid. Therefore, life in the church is thoroughly impacted by whatever "aid" is. I believe a combination of studies of church and aid is a fruitful area for further research. Ecclesiology, as a comprehensive approach to the study of the Christian church, would be able to shed light on matters that other disciplines may not see, and yet learn, from other disciplines, matters that are part of the same historical dynamics.

The research went into a difficult phase under the COVID-19 pandemic. The whole world went under humanitarian regimes, some more benign than others. The experience showed many that the stakes are high in such a situation – lives are at risk – but other values, such as the ordinary lives of people and the basic rule of law, are also at risk. The pandemic would entail that field research in refugee camps, interviews with key people, and studies in archives had to be abandoned. The dissertation was thus delayed in the process.

I wish it would have been possible to write some of the sections with a pencil, indicating the tentative nature of some of my writing. The intent is to open up for more research, not to close the debate. I raise questions that are more important than the answers I indicate. I welcome others to take up the torch and carry it on.

Thank you to all who supported this project with ideas, critical questions, and encouragement over the years in Europe and Africa. Sadly, only some will be mentioned by name, but others have also given significant contributions.

The academic seminars in ecclesiology, missiology, practical theology, and church history have all been invaluable. From Uppsala University, Professors Sven Erik Brodd and Hans Engdahl, Rt Rev. Dr Erik Eckerdal, Dr Erik Egeland, Rev. Dr Ezra Gebremedhin, Rev. Dr Staffan Grenstedt, Dr Agne Nordlander, and Mr Rickard Lind helped to form the project during its long process. The staff and faculty at Johannelund School of Theology and Swedish Evangelical Mission supported the project from its inception.

From Lund University, Professors Mika Vähäkangas, Stephan Borgehammar, and Samuel Rubenson and participants of higher seminars brought critical questions and valuable input. *Lunds missionssällskap* enabled this research through a generous stipend.

The University College Stockholm with its leadership, faculty, and academic seminars made this project possible: Professors Joel Halldorf, Jonas Ideström, Tone Stangeland Kaufman, and Kjell-Åke Nordquist, the *Church and Society* members: Hanna Alenius, Joel Appelfeldt, Björn Asserhed, Anki Falk, Simon Hallonsten, Elin Lockneus, Pernilla Myrelid, Daniel Strömner, Ellen Vingren, as well as Rev. Dr Abate Gobena. A special thanks to Professors Thomas Kazen and Carl Johan Berglund for the assistance in turning the written manuscript into a printed dissertation. Professor Sune Fahlgren, you remained my patient supervisor during all the ups and downs, and your encouragement has helped me through.

From the Ethiopian Graduate School of Theology, a special thanks to Professors Desta Heliso, Lidetu Alemu, Misgana Mathewos, and Seblewengel Daniel, and Hanna Bekele, colleagues, and students. Respect and gratitude to former colleagues at the ACT Ethiopia Forum and Church of Sweden Mission, in particular: Commissioners Girma Borishie and Agidew Redie *in memoriam*, Representatives Ingunn Brandvoll, Bob Hedley, Sophie Gebreyes, and Else Berglund, and Dr Rebecca Horn. Thank you, *Ingeniera* Sam Vander Ende and Dr Joachim Persoon!

All mistakes remain my own. Finally, thank you to my parents, Ulla and Per, and parents-in-law, Mrs Gunnel and Professor Fasil Nahum, and my wife Hanna, and our children David, Jonatan, and Rebecka for joy, patience & encouragement. እወዳችኋለሁ። እንኳን፡ አደረሰን፡ To all who share the burdens of refugees: Gal 6:2.

Addis Ababa in December 2024 / ታኅሣሥ 2017
Torbjörn Toll

Contents

Preface 7

Contents 9

Abbreviations 13

1. The Ecclesiology of Acting Together 15
1.1 Earlier Research and Background to ACT Alliance...........................17
    African Churches, Ecumenical Movement, and ACT Alliance....................17
    Aid, Secularism, and Inner Secularisation of Churches....................19
    A Renewed Focus on Churches.. 23
    The Problem of Identity and Meaning of a Christian Organisation 35
1.2 Research Problem, Questions, and Material.....................................41
    Research Problem 41
    Research Questions... 44
    Research Material...48
1.3 A Historical and Theological Approach 50
    Terms and Acronyms...53
    Researching a Familiar Setting.. 54
1.4 ETH141 ACT Appeal and Research Limitations 58
    Research Limitations – Sketches from the Church-In-Aid 60
1.5 Outline 62

2. The ETH141 ACT Appeal: Assisting Refugees 67
2.1 Sources to the Appeal.. 69
    Raising Relief Support to a Crisis Situation 70
    The Study of the Primary Sources of the Appeal 72
2.2 Emergency Preparedness 75
2.3 ACT Response to the Refugee Crisis 81
    An ACT Alert December 20, 2013 81
    Four Preliminary ACT Appeals.. 83

ETH141 ACT Appeal February 12, 2014 91
2.4 A Silent Crisis Is Rapidly Evolving 109
    Challenges to the Refugee Response 109
2.5 Funding Tension: The Ideal and the Practical 114
    The Problem of Funding 115
    Shifting Focus from Problems to Symptoms 121
    Tension between the Ideal and the Practical 122
    End of Appeal – End of Engagement? 122

3. International Framework and Stakeholders **125**
3.1 A Commitment to High Standards 127
    Sphere, Quality Standards and Principled Humanitarian Action 128
    Rwanda and Do No Harm 132
    An NGO Code of Conduct 134
    Humane, Impartial, Neutral, and Independent Agencies 134
    ACT and Principled Humanitarian Action 142
    Standards and Subsidiarity 146
    Accountability and Moral Responsibility 148
3.2 The Humanitarian Moral Argument 149
    The Question of Why and an Evolutionary Explanation 150
    The Humanitarian Moral Argument 154
3.3 Action Based on International Law 165
    International Humanitarian Law 167
    International Refugee Law 170
    International Human Rights Law 172
3.4 African Gate Keeper States and Stakeholders 173
    The Gate Keeper States 173
    Crossing African Borders 176
    Promotion of Civil Society and Tensions with the State 177
    Stakeholders 179
3.5 Morality, Principled Action, and the Church 182
    A Moral Argument for Refugee Assistance 183
    An Objective Moral Law 183
    A Principled Approach 184
    Do No Harm 185
    Ethics and Ecclesiology 185
    Narrow Agencies and Broader Mission of the Church 186

4. Ethiopian Churches: Ecumenical Engagement 189
4.1 A Letter from Mekane Yesus 1972 191
   Earlier Research on the ECMY Letter.........................191
   Proclamation of the Gospel and Human Development.........193
   Material versus Holistic Anthropology....................195
   Integral Human Development...............................197
4.2 Passover Message 1983 from the Ethiopian Orthodox 202
   The Maedot Journal of 1983...............................205
   Church in Context..211
4.3 Gospel and Liturgy Form the Christian 213
   The Voice of the Gospel..................................213
   Secularity and Exclusive Humanism........................216
   The Liturgy Forms the Christian..........................217
4.4 Voluntary Societies and Church Contributions...............221
   Voluntary Societies......................................222
   Church Contributions.....................................222
   The Problem of Voluntary Funding.........................224
4.5 Ethiopian Church Basis for Ecumenical Engagement 225

5. Ecumenical Models: For Acting Together 229
5.1 The Mission Model and the Integrated Church 230
   Holistic Mission...231
   Respect for the Orthodox Church..........................231
   General Unity Among Missions.............................232
   Ethiopian State Coordination.............................233
   Solidarity Among Evangelical Christians..................233
   The Ideal of the Integrated Church.......................235
   Discussion on the Mission Model..........................237
5.2 The Inter-Church Aid Model 237
   Ecumenical Initiatives...................................237
   Ethiopian Initiatives....................................238
   An Orthodox Ecumenical Commitment........................239
   Inter-Church Aid...240
   Sovereignty, Modernity and Unity.........................241
   Discussion on the Inter-Church Aid Model.................242
5.3 The International Crisis Model 243
   1960s Radical Student Movement...........................243
   The Revolution of 1974...................................244

Civil War as the Context...247
Ecumenical Coordination and Collaboration...............................248
The Christian Relief and Development Association (CRDA)......................248
The Joint Relief Partnership (JRP) 249
Discussion on the International Crisis Model and the Issue of Solidarity....251
5.4 ACT in Ethiopia 252
ACT Ethiopia Forum...253
European ACT Members: "Six Agencies Group" or "E8"................. 254
ACT Appeals...255
5.5 Comparing Historical Models and ACT Alliance.........................258
ACT Comparison with the Mission Model................................ 258
ACT Comparison with the Inter-Church Aid Model................................264
ACT Comparison with the International Crisis Model........................... 266
Discussion on Ecumenical Models.. 270
ACT Alliance Informed by Ecclesiology..271

6. Action by Churches Together **273**
6.1 The ETH141 ACT Appeal and Its Standards 275
6.2 The Churches and Ecumenical Models..280
6.3 What "Action by Churches Together" Is and Is Not 288
Predicated Attributes of Action by Churches Together in ETH141..............289
Attributes Not Predicated of Action by Churches Together in ETH141........290
Correlation between the Idea of ACT and its Operation................................291
ACT as a Model of Ecumenical Diakonia..294
6.4 Beyond ACT Alliance..295
Church Ministry Beyond Humanitarian Relief Work.........................296
The Mission of Church-Based Aid Agencies.....................................296
6.5 Concluding Discussion 298

Appendix A: Primary Sources to ETH141 303

Appendix B: ACT Ethiopia Forum Activities 2014................................307

Bibliography 311

Index of Ancient Literature 331

Index of Modern Authors..333

Index of Subjects 337

Abbreviations

AACC	All Africa Conference of Churches, est. (1963) in Kampala
ACT	Action by Churches Together (1994) pronounced like Eng. "act"
ACT International	(1994), ACT Development (2007), merged to create ACT Alliance in 2011
ACT Alliance	see ACT, Alliance of organisations and churches set up by WCC and LWF
AEF	ACT Ethiopia Forum, the forum of ACT members in Ethiopia
ARRA	Administration for Refugee and Returnee Affairs of FDRE
BftW	Bread for the World (1959), BftW/PADD see PADD
CA	the Christian Aid
CBO	Community Based Organisation
CBPS	Community Based Psychosocial Support as defined by IASC
CCCE	Council for Cooperation of Churches in Ethiopia (1976)
CDAA/E	Churches Drought Action Africa/Ethiopia (1984 developed into JRP)
CEEC	Conference of Ethiopian Evangelical Churches (1944–1963)
CRDA/CCRDA	(Consortium of) Christian Relief and Development Association (1973)
CHS	Core Humanitarian Standard (replacing the HAP Standard)
CHS Alliance	The organisations behind CHS
CMCR	Committee of Mutual Christian Responsibility of EECMY and partners
CMS	Church Missionary Society
CoS	Church of Sweden formerly Church of Sweden Aid and Mission
CRS	Catholic Relief Services (1941)
CWME	WCC Commission on World Mission and Evangelism
DASSC	short for EECMY-DASSC, (pronounced like Eng. Dusk)
DCA	Dan Church Aid
DICAC	short for EOC-DICAC (pronounced *daikak)
E8	a development of SAG to include 8 European ACT members
ECFE	Evangelical Churches Fellowship of Ethiopia
ECHO	European Community Humanitarian Aid Office (1992)
ECS	Ethiopian Catholic Secretariat
EECMY or ECMY	Ethiopian Evangelical Church Mekane Yesus (1959)
EECMY-DASSC	EECMY Development and Social Service Commission
EECMY-IMS	EECMY International Missionary Society, (2008)
EED	Evangelischer Entwicklungsdienst (1999), merged in 2012 with BftW
EFFORT	Endowment Fund for the Rehabilitation of Tigray
EGST	Ethiopian Graduate School of Theology
EKHC	Ethiopian Kale Heywet Church

EOC-DICAC   EOC Development and Inter-Church Aid Commission
EOTC/EOC   Ethiopian Orthodox Tewahido Church
EPLF   Eritrean People's Liberation Front
EPRDF   Ethiopian People's Revolutionary Democratic Front
ERA   Eritrean Relief Agency
ERD   Emergency Relief Desk (1975–1992)
ETH141   an ACT emergency appeal to support South Sudanese refugees 2014
FAO   Food and Agricultural Organization, est. 1945
FDRE   Federal Democratic Republic of Ethiopia
FO   Faith and Order Commission of the World Council of Churches
HAP   Humanitarian Accountability Partnership (replaced by CHS Alliance)
HAP International accrediting organisation of the HAP Standard
HEKS   Swiss InterChurch Aid (pronounced like Eng. Hex)
IASC   Inter Agency Standard Committee, (setting humanitarian standards)
ICCO   Dutch InterChurch Aid (pronounced *ikko)
IRCE   Inter-Religious Council of Ethiopia (2010)
IFRC   International Federation of the Red Cross
IOCC   International Orthodox Christian Charities, American based
JRP   Joint Relief Partnership (1984–2005)
KdK   "KdK-group", "Kontakt der Kontinenten" (1985–2010), network
LWF   Lutheran World Federation (1947)
LWF-WS E   LWF Department for World Service Ethiopia Programme
LWF Ethiopia   short form for LWF-WS E
LWR   Lutheran World Relief (1945), American relief association
NCA   Norwegian Church Aid
NGO   Non-Governmental Organisation, synonym INGO, International NGO
UN-OCHA   United Nations Office for Coordination of Humanitarian Affairs (1991)
OECD   Organisation for Economic Co-operation and Development (1961)
OLF   Oromo Liberation Front
ORA   Oromo Relief Agency
PADD   Protestant Agency for Development and Diakonia (BftW and EED 2012)
REST   Relief Society of Tigray
RRAD   Refugees and Returnees Affairs Department of EOC-DICAC
RRC   Relief and Rehabilitation Commission (1974)
SAG   Six Agencies Group, European ACT members working in Ethiopia (2006)
SEM   Swedish Evangelical Mission (1866)
SCC   Sudan Council of Churches
SCHR   Steering Committee for Humanitarian Response, (1972) (ACT member)
SIM   Sudan Interior Mission (1927), later Serving In Mission
Sphere   Sphere project (1997) est. by non-governmental organisations
TPLF   Tigrayan People's Liberation Front
UNHCR   United Nation High Commission for Refugees (1950)
UN-OCHA   Office for the Coordination of Humanitarian Affairs (1997)
WCC   World Council of Churches (1948)

1. The Ecclesiology of Acting Together

This dissertation is a study of ACT Alliance, the aid organisation established in 2011, built upon the idea of *Action by Churches Together*. The main purpose is to draw attention to ecclesial issues of aid built into its very name, as an abbreviation. The aim is to analyse the ecclesiological problem of the meaning and identity of action by churches together. Ecclesiology here refers to the study of the Christian church as church, and ecclesial here to that which concerns actual Christian churches, as distinct from that which concerns other social bodies such as the state. A secondary purpose of the thesis is to highlight the plight of asylum seekers and the challenges in addressing their needs through a case of refugee assistance in Ethiopia. The thesis may be of interest to students of both church and society.

The topic has special relevance to African churches that are both engaging in aid and affected by it. The aim is to centre on questions of ecclesial identity by studying tensions arising when the ecclesiologically informed idea, *action by churches together*, is put into practice in the actual work and organisation of ACT Alliance. As such, it is a study of ecclesiality, features of the church that are visible in practice. ACT Alliance as an expression of *ecumenical diakonia* exhibits overt tensions when put into practice. The study investigates a historical case of refugee assistance in Ethiopia, 2014, set in a larger historical context in which two Ethiopian churches are shedding light on the subject matter. The thesis asks questions about what it means for ACT Alliance to be, in some sense, an *action by churches together*, in respect to: the refugee assistance of an ACT Appeal and its stated principles, an ecclesial self-understanding, a Christian worldview, and the churches' mission to reach every person with the gospel and the sacramental life of the church. The ambition is not to close the debate but to open up research on the intersection of ecclesiological and social studies. When violence in Juba, South Sudan began on December 19, 2013, the ACT members in Ethiopia started preparing for an international humanitarian appeal. The purpose was to raise financial support for the expected arrival of South Sudanese asylum seekers in Gambella, located in the Western corner of Ethiopia. The *ACT ETH141 ACT Appeal*, requesting 2.3M USD, was posted on February 12, 2014, on the ACT Alliance website.

The ACT members in Ethiopia are not exclusively dedicated to working with refugees but are rather so-called "multi-mandated organisations": raising humanitarian relief appeals for drought responses,[1] working with long-term development projects, and providing social services such as running clinics and schools.[2] Several members are also working in different countries, not only Ethiopia.[3] This meant that the influx of refugees,[4] with its implicit moral demand for a response, created challenges for the different ACT members in how to prepare for and execute an appropriate and coordinated response to the new situation. This research project intends to analyse the Ethiopian ACT response to the South Sudanese refugee crisis as a historical and theological case study with an emphasis on what *action by churches together* means in the practical context of refugee relief response and the larger context of Ethiopian Christianity.

This first chapter introduces the ecclesiological problem and the topic of the refugee crisis and assistance in Ethiopia starting with a brief overview of the ETH141 appeal of refugee assistance. Section (1.1) *Earlier Research and Background to ACT Alliance* motivates the research problem and shows that scholarly inquiries have ignored the ecclesial questions of church and aid. (1.2) *Research Problem, Questions, and Material* formulates the research problem, raises some fundamental issues, and describes the primary sources the thesis is built upon. (1.3) *A Historical and Theological Approach* elaborates on the research approach the thesis will take. (1.4) *ETH141 ACT Appeal and Research Limitations* describes the historical case of the South Sudanese refugee response, the ETH141 ACT Appeal, and research limitations. The final section, (1.5) *Outline*, gives the general structure of the thesis.

---

[1] 2014 02 12 ETH141 Asylum Seekers South Sudan 12 Feb 2014. The ACT Ethiopia Forum raised humanitarian appeals, in 2011, 2012, 2014, 2016 and 2017; ACT Appeal ETH111, ETH121, ETH141, ETH161 and ETH171. These humanitarian appeals were mainly targeting drought response with components of refugee assistance. The growing unrest in the Horn of Africa presented a developing humanitarian crisis to which the ACT members responded by serving members of all the four main refugee populations: Somalis in 2011, Sudanese in 2012, South-Sudanese in 2014, and the ongoing support to Eritrean, and other diverse populations in the EOC-DICAC Urban Refugee Programme in Addis Ababa.

[2] Both the Ethiopian Orthodox Church and the Mekane Yesus Church, with their development wings, are running various education and health institutions in Ethiopia.

[3] The European members of ACT Alliance working in Ethiopia work in different countries.

[4] As of July 2008, there were some 76 000 registered refugees in Ethiopia. Droughts and conflicts led more than 700 000 people to seek refuge in Ethiopia between 2009–2017 creating a total of 811 000 refugees in the country by the end of February 2017. UNHCR Global Appeal 2009 Update and UNHCR Infographics-Ethiopia as of 28 February 2017.

1.1 Earlier Research and Background to ACT Alliance

ACT Alliance, originally *Action by Churches Together* (ACT), expresses the necessity of churches acting together as a consequence of mutually growing together in *koinonia* through participation in the ecumenical movement. ACT Alliance was established by the World Council of Churches (WCC) and the Lutheran World Federation (LWF), as an ecumenical initiative for ACT members to act in solidarity with people in need through collaboration and coordination with the intent of raising the quality of the churches' humanitarian relief response.[5] The ecclesiological problem of the meaning of *action by churches together* will be refined through this review of historical developments and scholarly debates on the importance for churches to act together and the concept of *ecumenical diakonia*. It also raises the concern of inner secularisation of the church and how it may impact church and society. As such, this section of earlier research gives the theological background that motivates the research problem.

African Churches, Ecumenical Movement, and ACT Alliance

There is little research on ACT Alliance which was set up through an ecumenical relief initiative in 1995 as *Action by Churches Together* (ACT), for its members to act in solidarity with people in need through coordination and collaboration, and as ACT Alliance in 2011. The question of why churches should work together on societal issues has been explored in the World Council of Churches' and the Lutheran World Federation's deliberations on *ecumenical diakonia* and *ethics and ecclesiology*. Earlier research has largely ignored how this question pertains to ACT Alliance and to the ecclesiological discussions that preceded its establishment. The asking of this question is not an abstract issue, but it directly relates to African churches that are both actively engaged in aid and passively affected by it. If ACT Alliance truly is an *action by churches together,* then it is crucial to study other churches than in the West. The Second Vatican Council gave two reasons to study churches of the Eastern tradition: "for the faithful preservation of the fullness of christian tradition, and for bringing about reconciliation between eastern and western Christians."[6] As this literature review and historical background will show, African churches also need to be studied in their own right. Ethiopia would be a good place to start such investigations because of the intensity of church-based aid work.

---

[5] John Nduna "Launch speech of the ACT Alliance" 2010, held in Geneva Jan 2011.

[6] RCC 1964b: *Unitatis Redintegratio*, n. 15. Tanner 1990, 917. See Wojcichowsky 2013, 231.

The literature on the ecumenical movement is extensive, with publications coming from the ecumenical institutions themselves. That being said, even though practical societal engagement and inter-church aid have been part of the ecumenical movement from its inception, not much research has been conducted about the establishment of ACT Alliance as an expression of the idea of *action by churches together* and as an organ for relief, development and advocacy efforts. In the aid practices of churches, research has rarely been able to highlight the complexities of inter-church matters, which is surprising given the importance of aid in general and the commitment of African churches to social issues in particular.[7]

John Baur states in *Two Thousand Years of Christianity in Africa* that there has never been a century for the last two thousand years without Christianity in Africa: "Christianity in Africa is not a recent happening, nor is it a by-product of colonialism – its roots go back to the very time of the Apostles."[8] African Churches do engage in development issues, human rights, and humanitarian relief, and they belong to societies where faith plays a major role in life. Despite this, current research on churches in Africa has been preoccupied with African Theology, mission heritage, prophetical traits, and local expressions of faith.[9] Churches in Africa are not necessarily best analysed according to traditional confessional lines, but according to their respective historical conditions, traits, and traditions.[10]

In this respect, the church scene in Ethiopia is unique: with an unbroken presence and tradition of an Oriental Orthodox Church; a long history of co-existence with Islam; a relatively small but significant Roman Catholic Church; a growing Evangelical and Pentecostal Christianity; and a particular meeting point of imperialism and Marxism in the not-too-distant past. All of this during decades in which churches and their organisations have been heavily involved in relief and development works. This gives justification for ecclesiological studies on ecumenical aid work built on historical and contemporary research of the Ethiopian church scene.[11]

---

[7] Visser't Hooft 1982, 89. Taylor 2002. Shivute 1980, 12 on ecumenical aid in Vietnam and Biafra. Ager 2011; Deneulin and Banu 2009; Engelsviken 2001; Goulet 2006; LenkaBula 2008; Narayan et al 2000; Nordstokke 2008; Padilha 1994; Sanneh 2011; and WCC 2012.

[8] Bauer 1994, 17. Cf. Atiya 1968; Bediako 1999, 2001; Isichei 1995; Sundkler and Steed 2000.

[9] Eide 1997; Eshete 2009; Gaillardetz 2008; Gifford 2008; Kwame 2001; Okure and Engdahl 2008; Onsrud 1999; and Sæverås 1974. Negussie 2010, on ecclesiology of churches in Ethiopia.

[10] Grenstedt 2000.

[11] Bakke 1986; Eide 2000; EOC 1996; Getnet Tamene 1998; Grenstedt 2000; Jonsson 1998; Misgana Mathewos 2010; Sæverås 1974; Tibebe Eshete 2009. See Grenstedt 2000 on the development of independent African churches.

A theological approach can take the theology and experience of African churches seriously into account in a study of ecumenical aid work. Such an approach may contribute to academic discussions in a context in which the distinction between the secular and the religious in the modern West may be seen as fraught with controversies.

Aid, Secularism, and Inner Secularisation of Churches

Current scholarship on aid gives more attention to the role of religion and faith in relief and development than before, but there are still many issues to sort out, particularly with regard to church and aid. Existing research shows the need for the study of ecumenical aid work with a theological approach to the churches for a better understanding of both the complexity of the work and its principal actors.[12]

Traditionally, scholarship on relief work has been influenced by a secularist agenda. According to Alastair Ager and Joey Ager, there is often a collision between the secular ideal of humanitarian work and the ideals of the local community affected by the humanitarian crisis. Ager and Ager problematize the functional secularism in humanitarian action. Intending to be ideologically neutral, it becomes a functional framework with a materialist character: "Materialism – generally in the form of liberal materialism – thus becomes the determining ideology of functional secularism. Indeed, it may be represented as a *fundamentalist* ideology to the extent that its users assume its universality and self-evidence."[13]

The background is the marginal place of "faith" in humanitarian and development debates despite the major role played by "faith-based actors". It shows that the ambiguity behind words like "secular" and "religion" may foster a situation in which secular humanism is taken for granted as the default position.[14] Nineteenth-century thinkers like "August Comte, Herbert Spencer, Émile Durkheim, Max Weber, Karl Marx and Sigmund Freud – all believed that religion would gradually fade in importance and cease to be significant with the advent of the industrial society."[15] The secularisation thesis, however, and its prediction, was based on the unproven philosophical assumption that Christianity was false based on anti-

---

[12] Axelsson 2006. Marshall and Van Saanen 2007 initiated a new dialogue on faith and development. On faith-based humanitarianism, Fiddian-Qasmiyeh 2011.

[13] Ager and Ager 2011, 462. Ager and Ager 2011, 459.

[14] Holmefur 2016 on such a state ideology of "development" and humanitarian aid.

[15] Norris and Inglehart 2011, 3.

realism concerning religious truth.[16] This, in turn, was based on scientism, the belief that all knowledge is scientific knowledge,[17] and a commitment to philosophical naturalism.[18] The philosopher Alvin Plantinga categorises naturalism, not as a religion, but as a worldview that functions like a religion.[19]

Such predispositions explain part of the ignorance of and hostility toward "religion" in social theories. The late nineteenth-century warfare thesis, that there is a conflict between science and religion, was formulated in this intellectual context.[20] What scholars like Pippa Norris and Ronald Inglehart have missed in secularisation studies is the shift in the centre of gravity of Christianity from the global north to the south due to the growth of churches across the globe. The growth shows the vitality of Christianity as a global phenomenon.[21]

Some scholars argue that deeper cultural and philosophical changes have occurred in the Latin West which lies behind the marginalisation of religion, the Christian faith, and the church in scholarship and state policies during the twentieth century. For the Orthodox theologian Alexander Schmemann (1921–1983), secularism is "the progressive and rapid alienation of our culture, of its very foundations, from the Christian experience and 'world view' which initially shaped that culture – and the deep polarization which secularism has provoked among Christians themselves."[22] This is entirely different from a clear distinction between church and state. In the classical account *A Secular Age*, Charles Taylor wrote that secular humanism adopted an exclusive stance – an *exclusive humanism* – in which the world is perceived as "secular" and "natural" and man[23] as an irreligious being.

---

[16] Insole analyses and rejects influential forms of anti-realism over the last two centuries and provides a reasonable defence of religious discourse. Insole 2006a, 2.

[17] Lennox 2019. McGrath 2005, 91–92 on "Clifford's rule".

[18] Plantinga 2011. Plantinga's definition of naturalism as the idea that "there is no such person as God, or anything like God" is helpful in this context.

[19] Plantinga 2011, Preface. See also Milbank 2006, critiqued by Andrea 2013.

[20] On warfare thesis, Harrison 2019; McGrath 2005; Meyer 2021; and Plantinga 2011.

[21] Norris and Inglehart 2011. Jenkins 2002 and Walls 2002.

[22] Schmemann 1973, 7.

[23] Charles Taylor uses the larger definition of "man", in which the term refers to both men and women equally as it signifies one common human nature, one kind of being, male and female. This affirms the equal intelligence and dignity of women and men, the basis for gender equality. A current trend is to use "humanity" to designate both males and females. However, "humanity" is an abstract term, while man is a concrete term. Compare abstract nouns such as "humanity" and "divinity" that designate a quality with concrete nouns such as "animal," "man," and "God" that designate beings and their nature. In this thesis, both "man" and "humanity" will be used in this inclusive sense. Kreeft 2014:186. Cf. The Ethiopian Constitution art. 7.

This "new man" feeds on classical sources, such as stoicism and Christianity, but understands atheist secular humanism, based on modern philosophy and science, as a superior replacement for Christianity as the moral force in society.[24]

If these anthropological presuppositions of man as irreligious and science as the only guide in society become appropriated by the churches, inner secularisation may occur. Attempts to integrate development organisations with the institutional church may therefore lead to unintended consequences for the life of the churches. The organisational study of Eskil Jonsson on the development work of the Ethiopian Evangelical Church Mekane Yesus showed how donor requirements may lead to an inner secularisation of churches since the work was integrated into the organisational structure of the church itself. This may lead to an ecclesiology of the church as a welfare institution which alienates its members and paradoxically endangers their commitment to the poor.[25]

Consequently, the mobilisation of external financial support may in the long run be detrimental to the "moral impulse" that lead to social engagement in the first place. Studies on ecumenical, or church-based aid work, need to be able to discern other forces at work than ecclesial – not the least of ideological or political kinds[26] – for which the churches and their organisations may become convenient instruments for other ends endangering a Christian identity and the goal to work for the good of the neighbour.[27] Cooperation with others is not the issue, assessing how to work with different actors with other agendas is. Christian aid agencies may suffer a mission drift and loss of Christian identity over time.[28]

Several scholars have shown the importance of a theological lens to the role of governments in aid. For Holmefur, religion is often invisible in the principles guiding state action, at best religion is seen as facilitating development and at worst acting as a hindrance to foreign policy objectives.[29] Holmefur's research points to the problem of Western state aid, that state action is not necessarily religiously neutral or benign. This is in line with the scholarship of William Cavanaugh. In his *Migration of the Holy: God, State, and the Political Meaning of the Church,*

---

[24] Taylor 2007 on "buffered self". Blomberg 1999, 188 on St. Paul's teaching in 1 Cor 13:3. Jacobs 2018 on Christian humanists like W. H. Auden, C. S. Lewis, Jacque Maritain, and Simone Weil who, after WWII, sought "a renewal of Christian thought and practice". Jacobs 2018, xii.

[25] Jonsson 1998, 201 on resource dependence, church disintegration, and loss of morality.

[26] For a historical critique of the 68-movement within the Church of Sweden, Sundeen 2017.

[27] On Rwanda, Anderson 1999. On solidarity and SIDA, Nilsson 2008 and 2017.

[28] Sundqvist 2018. Jonsson 1998. Ager 2011.

[29] Holmefur 2016. On misrepresentation of Muslims, Fiddian-Qasmiyeh, and Qasmiyeh 2010. Also Fowden 2014 on the importance of Islam for Western Civilisation.

Cavanaugh critiques the modern state itself by analysing its claims theologically.[30] Historically, he argues that "the kinds of public devotion formerly associated with Christianity in the West never did go away, but largely migrated to a new realm defined by the nation-state."[31] If this is true, the secular state may be far from secular in the sense of being non-religious.[32] The state may in effect operate as a secular church, substituting and marginalising the Christian Church in the public sphere.[33]

In a critique of Cavanaugh, Christoper Insole sees weakness in a simplified analysis that does not recognise that "a principled neutrality on theological matters [for the state] need not arise from an indifference to religious truth", but for the sake of the protection of individuals from the enthusiasms of others and to "preserve freedom of conscience, toleration and the right of free association." [34] Cavanaugh, however, has no intention to reject secularisation in the sense of a separation of church and state, but stresses that the church ought "not simply rely on the nation state to be its social presence" and put its hope in the state.[35] Instead of invoking the state "as a kind of savior, the *deus ex machina* to be invoked whenever crisis hits",[36] Christians should "demystify the nation-state and treat it like the telephone company."[37] The church may still cooperate with the government,[38] but ought to consider the state as something akin to a "a large bureaucratic provider of goods and services that never quite provides value for money."[39]

The kind of "migration of the holy" that Cavanaugh is writing about is not exclusively the domain of state politics. Stephen Hopgood argues in *The Endtimes of Human Rights* that the development of "humanitarianism" is far from secular. Hopgood uses the expression "secular church" to identify what is elsewhere

---

[30] Cavanaugh 2011.

[31] Cavanaugh 2011, 37.

[32] Cavanaugh 2011, 37. On the modern myth, Howard 1969.

[33] Cavanaugh 2011, 21: "What Hobbes accomplished by absorbing the church into the state, Locke accomplished by privatizing the church."

[34] Insole 2004, 237. Insole 2004 and Insole 2006b, 323–35.

[35] Cavanaugh 2011, 37. For an Orthodox critique of the same matter, Deleskmap-Hayes 2009.

[36] Cavanaugh 2011, 2 At a deeper level, the challenge that Cavanaugh sees is that "we want the state to absorb the risk involved in living a mortal human life", Cavanaugh 2011, 3.

[37] Cavanaugh 2011, 42.

[38] Cavanaugh 2011, 41–42.

[39] Cavanaugh 2011, 42.

described as purely secular institutions and agencies, showing the extensive use of religious symbols and language in these seemingly "secular" institutions.[40]

A Renewed Focus on Churches

There has not been much scholarly work on ACT Alliance, the subject matter of this enquiry, which was established in 1995 as *Action by Churches Together*, (ACT), or *ACT International*, as the aid organisation of the members of the World Council of Churches and the Lutheran World Federation.[41] A brief overview of the early history of inter-church aid in the World Council of Churches was offered by Martin Robra in 1994 using the concept of *ecumenical diakonia* in the context of the ecumenical movement. Using Robra's article as a foundation, Alexander Belopopsky edited an updated article on ecumenical diakonia. It included *ACT International*, but naturally enough not the later developments of *ACT Development* (2007) and *ACT Alliance* (2011) since it was published in 2002.[42]

This relates to historical research on *the diakonal movement* which provided significant societal contributions by establishing clinics and hospitals. Contemporary medical services owe foundational values to this movement and the practices it developed. The deaconesses of this diakonal movement gave rise to nursing as a medical profession and opened the opportunity for women to participate as professionals in society. The movement was an evangelical reform movement that took inspiration from Roman Catholic monasteries and nunneries and spread far beyond its German origins. Because of its integral connection with the modern mission movement, it may be considered a constitutive part of the ecumenical movement. The *Diakonie* of the nineteenth-century diakonal and mission movements focused on Christian voluntary associations and the establishment of diakonal institutions.[43] It needs to be examined whether it is this latter sense of *Diakonie,* as dedicated service of Christians in church and society and the establishment of institutions, that has found its continuation in the ecumenical diakonia of ACT Alliance.[44]

---

[40] Hopgood 2013. For secular church, pp. 22, 33, 63.

[41] Robra, Martin 1994.

[42] Belopopsky 2002.

[43] See Brodd 2005a, "Diaconia through Church History: Five Ecclesiological Models."

[44] Shivute 1980, 15 identifies the origin of the missionary movement "in the Pietism of Central Europe, the Evangelical movements of England and the religious revivals of North America."

The establishment of ACT Alliance was the fruit of years of practical collaboration and ecumenical deliberations in the second half of the twentieth century.[45] There is however an earlier historical parallel. After a century dominated by free associations in the mission movement, there was an attempt in the early twentieth century to focus on the churches as seen in the *International Mission Council, Life and Work,* and *Faith and Order.*[46] Seen from the experiences of the international mission movement, Christian unity was required with regard to Christian missions. J.H. Oldham had predicted that the cooperation of mission societies would lead to a world league of churches. Oldham spoke to thirty-nine mission delegates about collaboration after the First World War as the secretary of the continuation committee of the World Missionary Conference of Edinburgh 1905.[47] Mission co-operation was thus set in the context of collaboration among the churches. Oldham gave three reasons for working directly with the churches: to fit existing conditions, to account for new churches on the mission fields, and to be more effective in matters of public opinion by involving church authorities. As such, the motivation was mainly pragmatic, with the work of the missions being the primary focus, but Oldham also recognised the significance of the new churches, and therefore the primacy of the Christian church in relation to mission societies.[48]

The World Council of Churches was formed through the merging of *Life and Work* and *Faith and Order* in 1948.[49] The assembly of gathered churches from around the world and across confessions became a focal point for the ecumenical movement. As such, "the Church and the churches" is a major issue in the movement:

> The whole problem arises from the fact that Christendom is divided into a number of "Churches", which are separated more or less widely from each other in faith and order, doctrine and practice, history and tradition, but which nevertheless (though there are

---

[45] Belopopsky 2002, 20; Forrester 2002, 348–49; Van Beek 2002, 382–83; White 2002, 305–10.

[46] Brodd 1990, 14–18.

[47] Edinburgh 1910 was the starting point of the twentieth-century ecumenical movement.

[48] Visser't Hooft 1982, 10. Later mission theology would claim that the Christian church itself is missionary. Lundström 2006, 28–29. Bosch 2011, 415. John Stott saw "reconciliation with man is not reconciliation with God, nor is social action evangelism, nor is political liberation salvation", but "the actual commission itself must be understood to include social as well as evangelistic responsibility." Bosch 2011, 415, quoting from Stott 1975, 23.

[49] Visser't Hooft 1982.

exceptions) recognise each other as "Churches", i.e. as truly parts of the Church of Christ.[50]

This naturally put focus on churches, including "younger churches" across the world. It also inspired the *International Missionary Council* to merge with the World Council of Churches in 1961.[51] These developments gave a new impetus for churches to work together under an ecumenical umbrella. Visser't Hooft commenting on "the mandate" of the World Council of Churches wrote:

> It was an attempt to encourage the churches to cooperate in service to each other and to the world. When churches come together, the fact of their common relationship to the one and the same Lord Jesus Christ becomes decisive, and it becomes difficult for them to continue to live their separate lives. The second aspect of the ecumenical task is therefore to attempt to give expression to their unity.[52]

It is in this context of bringing the Christian concerns for societal life and welfare – "alliance mission" – into "church ecumenism"[53] that *The Lutheran World Federation (LWF)* and *The World Council of Churches* (WCC) have held discussions on societal issues and the question of how the member churches may work together as churches.[54] *Faith and Order* is the part of the ecumenical movement which took up the challenge of dealing with the contrary teachings and differences in church structures. During the twentieth century, progress has been made towards convergence and consensus on theological controversies such as the

---

[50] WCC FO 5 1952, 20–21: "The problem exists only for those who recognise that within the one Church of Christ there are *Churches*, not in a merely local or regional sense (as in the New Testament) but in the sense of denominations which make conflicting claims, and therefore in certain situations find themselves in actual competition with each other." On Vatican II, Dulles 1972. See also Hovorun 2017, 162ff. who in his chapter on "Frontiers: the Boundaries of the Church" discusses the concept of frontiers as "an alternative to the mentality of sharp-cut borderlines" regarding the boundaries of church jurisdiction and their relation to church communion. Hovorun (2017, 176) is quoting Georges Florovsky (1893–1979), "one should not draw the line of the Church body only through the dots of canon law" and "[t]hrough its practice, the Church witnesses that beyond its canonical threshold there is a continuation of its mystical territory, and the 'external world' does not begin immediately." The importance lies on whether communities confess the same faith, perform the same sacraments, and preserve communion with each other. If one of these criteria fail, communities "cease partaking in the common ecclesial nature and become schismatic or heretical". Hovorun 2017, 183. Rodopoulos 2007, 1–18.

[51] Shivute 1980 gives a vivid account on the dynamics which resembles church - aid relations.

[52] Visser't Hooft 1982, 89.

[53] Brodd 1990, 15–18. See later on Brodd's discussion on those terms.

[54] Forrester 2002, 348–49.

doctrine of justification as well as church structures such as the ordained minis-try.[55] Lorelei Fuchs, in her study on *Koinonia and the Quest for an Ecumenical Ecclesiology*, quotes from the "Lund Principle" 1952 with regard to an ecclesial im-petus to work together as churches:[56]

> Should not our Churches ask themselves whether they are showing sufficient eagerness to enter into conversation with other Churches and whether they should not act to-gether in all matters except those in which deep differences of conviction compel them to act separately?

This and similar calls within the ecumenical movement spurred the consultations on ecclesiology and ethics[57] "Costly [Ecclesial] Unity",[58] "Costly Commitment",[59] and "Costly obedience."[60] "These texts pointed out the close link between ethics and ecclesiological reflection and named 'the ethical dimension as a datum of ec-clesiology'."[61] These deliberations were related to the concurrent "discussion on the nature of the World Council of Churches."[62] The main message was to refocus on churches rather than mission and developmental agencies and liberation move-ments by seeing the church as a "moral community" and church unity and moral conviction as "two sides of the same coin."[63] Thus the work of Faith and Order on the visible unity of the churches was linked with the *Justice, Peace, and Creation Team* on moral and societal issues. The discussion represented a move towards recognition of the social value of churches.

The background, according to the first consultation was "the cleft" between forces committed to "visible church unity" and those committed to "witness, ser-vice and moral struggle" through "the length of the modern ecumenical move-ment."[64] The 1960s had seen a turn in the ecumenical movement in which atten-tion turned away from churches towards concern for societies. The missiologist

---

[55] Cf. LWF-Roman Catholic agreement of the justification in 1999, and *BEM*, WCC 1982.

[56] Fuchs 2008, 169n.

[57] Best and Robra 1997 reporting on 1992–1996 consultations by WCC Unit I and Unit III. The fifth FO conference recommended the study, WCC 2013, 7 "which should be directly linked to local experiences of the interconnectedness of faith and action and move between an investi-gation of the moral substance of traditions and the moral experience of the people of God today."

[58] Best and Robra 1997, 2–23. WCC consultation, Ronde, Denmark, Feb. 1993.

[59] Best and Robra 1997, 22–49. WCC consultation, Tantur, Israel, Nov. 1994.

[60] Best and Robra 1997, 50–91. WCC consultation in Johannesburg, South Africa, June 1996.

[61] WCC 2013, 7 FO 215.

[62] Best and Robra 1997, 82. Cf. Forrester 2002, 348–49.

[63] Best and Robra 1997, 2. The church as a moral community can be traced to Albert Ritschl.

[64] Best and Robra 1997, 2.

David Bosch writes: "The uncritical acclamation of every manifestation of renewal, change, and liberation, so called, during the sixties and early seventies ... was
the last almost convulsive illustration of the West's inability to believe that an era,
the era of its hegemony, had passed."[65]

The high point of the secularisation of the movement was the two reports to
the World Council of Churches assembly in Uppsala in 1968 on *the Structures for
Missionary Congregations* from a European and a North American delegation[66]
which had little to do with churches and congregations[67] and all to do with civil
society developments such as the Civil Rights Movement[68] in the USA.[69] As the
Zimbabwean theologian Mavuto Jambulosi points out in his dissertation on the
missiological developments of the World Council of Churches and the Lausanne
movement, the Uppsala 1968 assembly was more balanced than the report *The
Church for Others*, but secularised enough in its emphasis on salvation as humanisation[70] that mission societies created the independent Lausanne Movement to
safeguard Christian mission from secularisation.[71] The World Council of
Churches had thus failed to keep the movement together under one organisation
and the mission endeavour had lost its evangelical flavour and become a civil mission.[72] The radicalness of the Uppsala report on mission lay in its proposals which
located mission in society and putting "the church in danger of not being relevant

---

[65] Bosch 2011, 369 (1991, 361 1st Ed.) references several ecumenical meetings with this trend:
WSCF conference, 1960; Church and Society Conference, 1966; Uppsala Assembly of the WCC,
1968; Catholic Bishops Conference in Medellín, 1968; CWME Conference in Bangkok, 1973.

[66] Theologians like Harvey G. Cox and Johannes C. Hoekendijk marginalised other theologians in the group to the extent that some left the group as the project deviated from historical
theological patterns of the church, WCC 1968, 63–65. Harvey Cox's *The Secular City* was at the
very forefront of the "God is dead" theologians and "the theologians who were then claiming
that they could be Christian without believing in the living God." Braaten 2010, 76.

[67] On pastoral reorientation towards an urban environment, Brodd 1989.

[68] This is true of the American report in which the civil rights movement as contrasted to
churches becomes "the basic normative form of the church's life", WCC 1968, 61.

[69] WCC 1968. Cf. Bosch 2011 and Jambulosi 2021. On civil society, Axelson 2006.

[70] See Bosch 2011, 392: "The goal of mission was identified as *shalom* by the European team
and as *humanization* by the North Americans." See Bosch 2011, 402–10. Cf. Björk 2014 (diss.).

[71] Jambulosi 2021, 121. Jambulosi 2021, 134 quotes the Bolivian Bishop Mortimer Arias to the
Nairobi WCC Assembly (WCC 1976, 15): "We have not always been worthy of our predecessors
from Edinburgh 1910 to Mexico 1963; And we have not always fulfilled the hopes which gave rise to
the WCC and its merging with the IMC." On civil mission, Björk 2014; Benedict XVI 2007, 15–16.

[72] Jambulosi 2021, 376: in 2005, "the idea of the world setting the agenda for mission still
informed ecumenical mission", resulting in a disconnect between "kingdom" language and the
faith of the church, identifying political agendas with the Holy Spirit. Jambulosi 2021, 233.

as an ecclesial community since the locus of ministry now lay in the *secular world*."[73] According to Jambulosi, this represented, a paradigm shift in Christian mission from "Christianisation to humanization."[74] The issue is not Christian engagement in society,[75] nor political engagement by Christians.[76]

What was at stake in missiology was a shift in eschatology. The *Parousia* was overshadowed with the liberal idea of "the realization of the kingdom within history" working to bring about utopia by human effort,[77] as a gospel of social salvation.[78] For Schmemann, the church, in a secular age, is reduced to a religion, in which the criteria is not truth but "help." For Christians, this is an issue since truth is the criterion, and practical service gives witness to the truth of the gospel.[79] Schmemann offers a background:

> Christianity, with its message offering fullness of life, has contributed more than anything else to the liberation of man from the fears and the pessimism of religion. Secularism, in this sense, is a phenomenon within the Christian world, a phenomenon impossible without Christianity. Secularism rejects Christianity insofar as Christianity has identified itself with the "old religion."[80]

In some scholarly critiques of secularism, the "secular" should not be understood as in contrast to "religious" in the context of the modern world.[81] Rather

---

[73] Jambulosi 2021, 120.

[74] Jambulosi 2021, 121.

[75] Jambulosi 2021, 167 asserts the importance of work for peace, humanization, and peace.

[76] Cf. Jambulosi 2021, 159–60 on the revivalism, evangelicalism, and social action.

[77] Jambulosi 2021, 313. Cf. 2021, 349: In Hoekendijk's *missio Dei*, "God was considered to be at work in the world first and not the church. This approach established humanization and *shalom* as missiological paradigms", splitting the WCC and Lausanne movements.

[78] Jambulosi 2021, 349: Bangkok 1973 "defined salvation in socio-political terms of liberation and social justice and lacked a clear biblical exposition of salvation as a working basis." Instead, people in social and political movements represented salvific themes. The kingdom of God was associated with struggle for justice and liberation of the oppressed in history. Cf. Benedict XVI 2007, 53–54.

[79] Schmemann 1973, 99–100: "Christianity is not reconciliation with death. It is the revelation of death, and it reveals death because it is the revelation of Life. Christ is this Life. And only if Christ is Life is death what Christianity proclaims it to be, namely the enemy to be destroyed, and not a 'mystery' to be explained." Cf. Cooper 2021.

[80] Schmemann 1973, 98. On reducing the church to religion, Benedict XVI 2023, 40: "Christianity did not conceive of itself as a religion but, rather, in the first place as a continuation of philosophical thought, in other words, of man's search for truth."

[81] Schmemann 1973, 99: "Secularism is a religion because it has a faith, it has its own eschatology and its own ethics. And it 'works' and it 'helps.' Quite frankly, if 'help' were the criterion, one would have to admit that life-centered secularism helps actually more than religion."

secularism may be seen as the loss of a Christian worldview[82] and secularisation may become a method for bringing about an earthly Kingdom of God.[83] The Christian church is not the focus of such a conception of the kingdom, society is, and with society, the state.[84] As Cavanaugh writes: "The story of the death of the sovereign God and his rebirth in the sovereign state is not a story of the progressive stripping of the sacred from some secular remainder. It is instead the transfer of care for the holy from church to state."[85] Theologically, in the ecumenical movement, this brings up the question of how the church, the world, and the kingdom relate to one another in the οἰκονομία (*oikonomīa*), household ordering of God, or as it is phrased in ecumenical mission theology: *Missio Dei*, Latin for God's mission.[86] This discussion is linked to issues of philosophical method,[87] social trinitarianism,[88] natural law morality,[89] and philosophical trends in modern theology[90]

---

[82] Zizioulas, 1985, 162. The alternative to a secular or a religious view is the catholic worldview.

[83] Jambulosi 2021, 130. Jambulosi 2021, 139. Jambulosi sees the WCC Assembly in Nairobi 1975 and CWME meeting in Melbourne 1980 as theological turning points away from millennial connotations of utopia, and CWME in San Antonio 1989 trying "to correct the one sided view of mission espoused by Bangkok and Melbourne", Jambulosi 2021, 141. Svenungsson 2014, VIII–XII traces utopian visions back to the this-worldly millennial vision of the mystic Joachim of Fiori (ca. 1135–1202) condemned by the fourth Lateran Council in 1215. With Kant, Hegel and Marx messianic conceptions and an idealised view of human society takes the centre stage.

[84] Kant's Kingdom of God becomes an idea separated from its Augustinian denotation of the church, Hull 2020, 226–27. Cf. WCC 1968, 15 "Since God is constantly active in the world and since it is his purpose to establish *shalom*, it is the Church's task to recognize and point to the signs of this taking place", i.e. signs in movements, academies, business, and governments.

[85] Cavanaugh 2011, 3.

[86] Eph 1:10 and 1 Tim 1:4. Both *oikonomīa* and *Missio Dei* expresses primarily the active work of God, cf. Benedict XVI 2007, 55 on the Kingdom of heaven and the Kingdom of God with primary reference to God. WCC 1968, 69–71. Schmemann 1979. WCC 1986 FO 130.

[87] Hull 2020; Liederbach 2008; and Cooper 2018 on scholastic, modern, and postmodern epistemology. For problems regarding analogical predication and classical categories when replacing Aristotelian logic with symbolic logic, Cooper 2023, 86–94 and Kreeft 2014, 15–25.

[88] Kilby 2000, 1741–2005 critiques social trinitarian theories for circular thinking.

[89] Braaten 2007. With Karl Barth's rejection of natural law, the ecumenical movement lost the default position of the Reformation churches. Braaten had been at the forefront of a theology of hope with ideas such as a "theology of revolution", and "the future of God *in* history and the future *of* history in God." Braaten 2010, 75. Cf. Cooper 2021.

[90] See Halldorf 2018; Benedict XVI 2007, 52–53; and Cooper 2021.

with its dependence on Kant, Hegel, and Marx.[91] Particularly in the 1960s these were vexed questions due to the historical context.[92]

Ecumenical Diakonia and Other Key Terms

One question to face in a study ACT Alliance is how to understand the key theological concepts discussed in the ecumenical literature, such as *oikoumene, apostolicity, catholicity, church ecumenism*, and *ecumenical diakonia*.

The Greek word οἰκουμένη (*oikoumene*), which signified the civilised world, may be used ambiguously. Sven-Erik Brodd clarifies that when used in an ecclesial setting the words derived from the Greek original, such as ecumenical and ecumenism,[93] may have five basic meanings to be distinguished. That which is ecumenical may refer to a) an ecclesiological category, b) a process to restore the historical unity of the church, c) a form of all-Christian collaboration, d) a mode of theology, and e) a research and study discipline.[94] As an ecclesiological category, ecumenical refers to a characteristic attributed to the church as such.[95] *Oikoumene* describes how the church is related to the world through its mission in the world as an instrument for Christ and as Christ's continuing presence in the world.

The ecumenical as an attribute of the church thus shows the missionary character of the church: the church is "missio-logically" related to the world as corresponding to its *apostolicity*.[96] Mission means that the church is charged with the unique mission to reach every person with the gospel and the sacramental life of the church.[97] In a secondary sense ecumenical connotes the unity of the church, in

---

[91] See Hull 2020 and Insole 2019, 473, 481–83 for dependence on Kantian thinking.

[92] On the Cold War context, Sundeen 2017; Sjöström 2019; Karltun 2020.

[93] Brodd 1990, 10–12. Brodd uses the word *ekumenik* (n.) in Swedish.

[94] Brodd 1990, 10–12.

[95] Brodd 1990.

[96] "Missiological" here in the sense of *following the integral the logic of mission*. AG 6 based on 1 Pet 2:9 declares the church to be missionary by nature, see Bosch 2011, 381. Bevans and Schroeder, 2006; Kirk 1999. *Missio Dei*, i.e. God's bringing this world to its end goal and creating a New Heaven and Earth dictates the nature of the presence of the church in this world on its way to become the heavenly Jerusalem in the *Parousia*. Schmemann 1973, 20 "The Church itself was the new and heavenly Jerusalem: the Church in Jerusalem was by contrast unimportant."

[97] WCC 2009 FO 198.

relation to its mission in the world.[98] The church also lives in the world,[99] and often copies patterns of "the world, where it is called to go and preach."[100]

The Christian church understands itself as *Catholic,* the attribute that refers to *catholicity* – the universal nature of the church.[101] Therefore the Catholic nature of the Christian church also implies its unity. It requires that the unity of the Christian church is expressed in the visible unity of the churches in the eyes of the world.[102] As Nathan Söderblom expressed the matter in 1925: "We need an evangelical catholicity which will not demand uniformity but serve and strengthen the cause of spiritual unity."[103] It is because of the goal in the ecumenical movement for ecclesial unity (meaning b) that ecumenical becomes linked to the historical unity of the churches.[104]

Given that the Lutheran World Federation and the World Council of Churches have from their initiation been involved in the tasks of ecclesial unity and social services, the word ecumenical has been strongly associated with these types of inter-church institutions and their specialised ministries such as the World Council of Churches Department of Refugee and Inter-Church Aid and the Lutheran World Federation World Service.[105]

Brodd clarifies that ecumenical action can refer to two main types: *church ecumenism* or *alliance mission.*[106] If the common action is aimed at accomplishing a

---

[98] Cf. the ecumenical patriarch as the bishop of Constantinople, the capital. Visser't Hooft 1982, 91 "The definition that the word 'ecumenical' embraces 'everything that relates to the whole task of the whole Church to bring the Gospel to the whole world' was first used in a statement of the World Council's Central Committee on 'The Calling of the Church to Mission and Unity,' issued in 1951, but the idea contained in that definition was present from the beginning."

[99] Dulles 2002, 85–86: Vatican II "asserts that the Church should consider itself as part of the total human family, sharing the same concerns as the rest of men." Cf. Brodd 1992:63–65.

[100] Hovorun 2017, 163.

[101] Brodd 1990, 10–12. Catholic refers to the one of the marks of the Christian church in the Nicene Creed of being *una sancta ecclesia*, something that both the church in the East and the West attributed to itself for example the Roman church as *Sancta Catholica Apostolica Romana Ecclesia.* Hovorun 2017, 165.

[102] Brodd 1990, 10–12. Cf. Staples 2002, 151–54.

[103] Visser't Hooft 1982, 13.

[104] Brodd 1990, 10–12.

[105] Taylor 2002, 583–86. For the WCC: the World Council of Churches Department of Refugee and Inter-Church Aid (1945); the WCC Department and then Division of Inter-Church Aid and Service to Refugees (DICASR 1949), the WCC Division of Inter-Church Aid, Refugee, and World Service (DICARWS 1960), the WCC Commission on Inter-Church Aid, Refugee, and World Service (CICARWS 1971), and the WCC Unit IV: Sharing and Service (1992).

[106] Brodd 1990, 10. Brodd, in Swedish, uses the terms *kyrkoekumenik* and *alliansverksamhet.*

greater unity between the churches, or to be an expression of a unity that has been realised, one may speak of church ecumenism. If individual Christians from different churches act together, or if churches act together, without the expressed purpose of bringing the churches together towards a visible unity, it is referred to as an alliance mission. Thus, it needs to be clarified whether the ecumenical diakonia in ACT Alliance refers to church ecumenism or alliance mission.[107]

In the concept of ecumenical diakonia, the service, or diakonia, is situated primarily in a socio-political world. It is thus the third meaning of ecumenical – as a form of all-Christian collaboration in society – that the joined concept of ecumenical diakonia is formed as an expression of the Christian churches' concern for and life in the world, rendered as Christian service. This concern for the common good in society does not set the churches apart from other societal bodies but is rather something shared with all people of good will.[108]

The debate on ecumenical diakonia should be set in the context of the lexicographical scholarship of John Collins whose research offered a critical view on the theological concept of *diakonia*. The Greek concept, διακονία (*diaconía*), was reinterpreted in the nineteenth and early twentieth centuries. This was shown in Kittel's Theological Dictionary of the New Testament in 1935 where H.W. Beyer wrote an article describing diakonia as "any loving assistance rendered to the neighbour... the very essence of service, of being for others, whether in life or death."[109] Beyer's concept of diakonia has no basis in ancient Greek or its use in the New Testament. This misunderstanding of diakonia has been important for the ecclesiological model of the "church as servant",[110] a Christology that emphasises Christ's service without reference to his atoning work, and church ministry as equated with the vocation of every Christian. In the context of the early church, the Greek word would primarily refer to the office bearers and the ministry in the

---

[107] Brodd 1990, 10. Brodd mentioned the evangelistic work of the Evangelical Alliance 1846 as example of alliance mission.

[108] The idea of "people of good will" is there in *Lumen Gentium*, but the actual expression comes first in later documents. Cf. WCC Uppsala 1968, 29 "a more open and humble partnership with all who work for these goals even when they do not share the same assumptions as ourselves." The expression "good will" is tied to a concept of the objective good as based on natural law morality. People who "work for these goals" may contain the same basic idea.

[109] Collins 2014, 13.

[110] WCC 1968, 81 "[T]he church in mission is a *servant* church. WCC 1968, 18 "[The Church] is called to service of mankind, of the world", WCC 1968, 20. For the ecclesiological view of the Church as Servant, Dulles 2002. Dulles critiques the model of the Church as Servant for lacking a biblical foundation.

church with its apostolic origin. This usage would be in continuity with the word ministry in English, from Latin *Ministerium*.

In light of Collin's scholarship, I propose a distinction between *diakonia* as a biblical term and *diakonie* (ending with "e" from the German *Diakonie*) as a historical term. Diakonia as a biblical term cannot, in light of Collin's research, be limited to charitable work, but is rather integrated into questions of the three-fold ministry of the church, and the ministry of the whole church.[111] The biblical sense of diakonia, in the ecumenical context, would therefore refer to the *Baptism, Eucharist, and Ministry* process and the continuing theological discussions on *The Nature and Mission of the Church*.[112]

Diakonie as a historical term can be understood as a development stemming largely from the nineteenth-century German diakonal movement. *Diakonie* was a way to give expression to Christian life as a life of charity, solidarity, and selfless service.[113] This service could be rendered by laypeople and the ordained alike. Theologically, it is to be considered in the light of Christian ethics – a practical application of the love of neighbour[114] – rather than as the ministry of the church.

The challenge in the ecumenical movement has been to keep together the *diakonia* and the *diakonie*, the ministry of the church with the service of Christians in the world (*saeculum*). In ecumenical discussions, witness and service are therefore often joined to prevent an inner secularisation of the church. Witness is derived from Greek μαρτυρία (*martyria*), meaning witness in the legal sense.[115] It refers primarily to the apostles as first-hand witnesses, as seen in Acts chapter one 1 Cor 15, and in St. Paul's explication of the κήρυγμα (*kerygma*), the proclamation of the Christian gospel, as Christ's death, burial, and resurrection according to the scriptures, and as testified by many people. The witness of the church, therefore,

---

[111] For a critical discussion on the biblical terms related to *diakonia*, see the works of John N. Collins, e.g. *Diakonia Studies: Critical Issues in Ministry*, 2014.

[112] *BEM* FO 111 (1982) and FO 198 (2009) for the main documents. Both the accumulated documents and the literature is extensive. Cf. White 2002, 305–10.

[113] White, 2002, 303–5, states that Collin's critique has challenged deacons to "eliminate hints of servility from their roles and to emphasize that their high-skilled and community-focused ministry involves training and leading the laity in their own diakonia." That misses the point that *Diakonie*, modern diakonia, diverts from the Greek biblical terms and that its theological meaning probably originates elsewhere.

[114] See the sermons of Martin Luther, who stresses serving the neighbour as a practical expression of loving the neighbour. Also *Freedom of a Christian,* Luther 1999 *LW* vol. 31, in which Luther clarifies the position that a Christian through faith in God is free to serve his neighbour.

[115] *Martyria* also denotes the suffering of Christians as witnesses to the truth. Cf. Cahill 1995.

concerns the identity of the gospel with the apostolic tradition, παράδοσις (*paradosis*), received once and for all. Witness, in this sense, does not necessarily imply targeted evangelisation, however, it does suggest that the uniqueness of the Christian church, among other human societies, is that it stands for the Christian gospel of Jesus Christ.[116]

Related to the issue of the gospel concerns the nature of the church. In ecumenical discussion, *koinonia* ecclesiology is frequently used, but the Greek word κοινωνία (*koinonia*), is ambiguous and its ecclesiological meaning needs to be made clear.[117] One meaning is private association. It is a meaning that fits into a modern political public–private distinction in which the state is public and the church private. It also fits into the historical trend in which ecclesial movements and Christian associations become "churches."[118] There is an issue, however, with applying "association" to the Christian church, as Cavanaugh writes:

> In calling itself *ekklesia*, the church was identifying itself as fully public, refusing the available able language for private associations (*koinon* or *collegium*). The church was not gathered like a koinon around particular interests but was concerned with the interests of the whole city, because it was the witness of God's activity in history. At the same time, the church was not simply another polis; instead, it was an anticipation of the heavenly city on earth, in a way that complexified the bipolar calculus of public and private.[119]

So *koinonia* as civil association when applied to the Christian church clashes with the church's apostolic self-understanding as *ekklesia,* meaning a public assembly, akin to that of the Roman Republic. Similarly, any easy identification of the Christian Church, and churches, with civil society associations ought to raise the same concerns. What does *koinonia* refer to in the context of the Christian Church? It refers primarily to the sacramental *participation* in the life of Christ,[120] through word and sacrament,[121] and it also refers to the sacramental *community* that the

---

[116] On the use of "gospel" as an extended term in WCC and Lausanne, Lundström 2006. Witness, in aid, refers to aid workers witnessing atrocities in the line of work. Cf. WCC, Pontifical Council for Interreligious Dialogue, and World Evangelical Alliance 2011.

[117] Dulles 2002, 53 Dulles differentiates between "the church as a network of friendly interpersonal relationships" and "the Church as a mystical communion of grace".

[118] Brodd 2005b.

[119] Cavanaugh 2011, 42–43.

[120] 1 Cor. 10:16.

[121] For Borgehammar 2007, 32, *ekklēsia* refers to the eucharistic congregation.

Holy Spirit give rise to and sustains by the same means.[122] The *sharing* in the sacred gifts and the *participation* in the mystical body of Christ bring the moral obligations to behave towards one another in Christ accordingly. The New Testament apostolic writings, which move from a theology of land to one of the body of Christ,[123] is filled with references to implications of being a member of the church,[124] as in Matt 25:42–43,[125] Acts 9:4–5, and Gal 3:27–28.

It is in light of the secular turn of the ecumenical movement that the discussions on "Costly [Ecclesial] Unity", "Costly Commitment", and "Costly Obedience" moved its attention to societal progress from mass movements, such as the civil rights movement, and political liberation fronts, such as *the African National Congress* (ANC) and *the South West Africa People's Organisation* (SWAPO), to giving weight to actual churches. This gave rise to *ACT International*, and later *ACT Alliance*, conceived as an *action by churches together*. The Robra and Belopopsky articles wrote on this development without explicitly arguing how ACT as an organisation would fill the perceived gap as an *action by churches together*.[126]

The Problem of Identity and Meaning of a Christian Organisation

The relative silence in the scholarly literature on ACT Alliance, its member organisations, and their participation in and contribution to the ecumenical discussion as institutions is part of a general problem in the sources and literature on the ecumenical movement. Though Christian relief and development agencies have been a significant part of the movement – their presence is seldom overt and distinct from "churches."[127] Even in the latest publication from the World Council of Churches on the matter *Called to Transformation: Ecumenical Diakonia* from

---

[122] Nygren 1945, 19: "we cannot create our religion. We may conjure a surrogate, but not true religion because religion does not consist in feelings, but community with God and such community is beyond human capabilities to produce at will."

[123] See Blomberg 1999, 187; 161–63, 174; 191–99. Benedict XVI 2007, 50 for the Kingdom of God not to be found on any map, but "located in man's inner being".

[124] E.g. 1 Cor 11:21; Acts 2:44–46; and διακονίαν, assistance, i.e. famine relief, in Acts 11:27–30.

[125] The biblical scholar Blomberg (1999, 125–26) comments that the "least" in Matthew without exception refers to the disciples of Christ and that the obligation to assist people in need "whether or not they are Christian" is an important biblical theme but, not likely the focus in this passage.

[126] Robra 1994 and Belopopsky 2002.

[127] Barrow 1998. Bernander 1968 for the links between relief and mission during WWII; Ryman 1997 and Wejryd 2021 for Church of Sweden Aid (Lutherhjälpen); Taylor 2002 "Inter-Church Aid"; Taylor 1995 on ecumenical aid in the context of Christian Aid.

2022 which seeks to reconcile the standing tradition in the council to talk about *ecumenical diakonia* with the *faith-based* and *rights-based* approach of ACT Alliance, the relationship between these two ecumenical organisations is not clear and the similarities and differences in their respective approaches have not been researched.[128] Though the World Council of Churches and ACT Alliance are part of the same movement, they also operate according to the logic, dynamics, and direction of their respective missions, therefore and ACT Alliance deserve a study in its own right which includes understanding its ecclesial, or faith-based, identity.

In one of his articles, Brodd turns his attention to the theoretical problem of Christian faith-based organisations. His thoughts are preliminary, his purpose being more to draw out the question and to set some fundamental parameters rather than an attempt to deal with the issue itself. Brodd's question regards "how to grasp the identity and thereby the meaning of a Christian organisation and more specifically what is called a 'church related development organisation'."[129] The theological problem is that such a concept is "based on an institutional view of the church that in this case identifies the church with its governing bodies."[130] At the end of the article, Brodd gives his thesis that "Christian organisations cannot exist outside the Church; that they actually are expressions of what is the Church." The argument is using the concept of the church as a sacrament to the world. The church, following this ecclesiological model[131] may "give rise to organisations", and these in turn may express something of what the church is.[132] The argument presupposes a distinction between the concept of the church and the concept of organisation.[133] The church is not an organisation, since:

> [t]here is no organizational theory about the sacrifice of Christ with which the Church stands or falls. There is no way of organising that love which is the centre of Christian life, and there is no organization, which takes into consideration that the Church consists of all the faithful in heaven and on earth.[134]

---

[128] WCC 2022. Mission agencies are more visible in the ecumenical movement.

[129] Brodd 2005b, 245.

[130] Brodd 2005b, 252.

[131] Dulles 2002. Ecclesiological models was first used by Cardinal Avery Dulles (1918–2008) in an article "The Church, The Churches, The Catholic Church" *re* Second Vatican Council, Dulles 1972. Dulles enlarged the scope in *Models of the Church* from 1974, last edition from 2002.

[132] Brodd 2005b, 248. Brodd reformulates his initial question as "how to grasp the identity and thereby the meaning of a Christian organisations from an ecclesiological perspective".

[133] Brodd 2005b, 250–53.

[134] Brodd 2005b, 258–59.

This implies not identifying organisational structures such as Christian aid agencies with the nature of the church and yet not separating them. The church makes use of organisations to express itself and its mission, but there is a need to integrate practices theologically.[135] Otherwise there is a risk that these organisations bring about an internal secularisation.[136] This is being said with direct reference to the already mentioned study of Eskil Jonsson on the Ethiopian Evangelical Church Mekane Yesus and the difficulty for its church officers to keep together the church as a result of donor requirements.[137] "If the way of being church does not bear witness about what the church is", a discrepancy arises. It shows a gap "between what a church claims to be and what it is in reality."[138] The model of the church as a sacrament, in contemporary theological discussion, thus indicates that it is possible to talk of Christian organisations as being expressions of the Christian church without necessarily being part of the institutional church.

Cyril Hovorun uses the post-structural thinking of Michael Foucault, Gilles Deleuze, and Roland Barthes to talk about some ecclesial structures often identified with the church as relating to the church as "scaffolding to an edifice" rather than being part of its "nature" in the Aristotelian sense. [139] Whereas communities, baptism, eucharist, and ministry have always been part of every church community without disruption, historical forms of the church ministry, such as canonical territory and autocephaly, particularly on the "supra-communal level" have varied according to need.[140] The "scaffolding" is meant to "serve communities and facilitate their partaking in the nature of the church, they accord to this nature", as Maximus the Confessor put it. [141] Thus if they fail to fulfil their supporting mission "or begin to serve themselves, they harm the church and go against its nature."[142]

Sacramental language, applied to Christ and the Christian church, was used in Vatican II documents, explicitly in *Lumen Gentium* (n. 48):[143]

---

[135] Brodd 2005b, 259–61.

[136] Brodd 2005b, 248.

[137] Jonsson 1998.

[138] Brodd 2005b, 261.

[139] Hovorun 2017, 181–98.

[140] Hovorun 2017, 182.

[141] Hovorun 2017, 183. Cf. Brodd 1992, 86–87 on sacramentality vs. non-sacramentality.

[142] Hovorun 2017, 183. Corruption and despotism may appear "holy" when ecclesiastical order turns into hierarchism, a problem related to the reality of the church, Hovorun 2017, 188.

[143] Dulles 2002, 56 referring to *Lumen Gentium* (LG 9 and 48), *Sacrosanctum Concilium* (SC 26), *Ad Gentes* (AD 5) and *Gaudium et Spes* (GS 42).

> Christus quidem exaltatus a terra omnes traxit ad Seipsum (cfr. *Io.* 12, 32 gr.); resurgens
> ex mortuis (cfr. *Rom.* 6, 9) Spiritum suum vivificantem in discipulos immisit *et per eum*
> *Corpus suum quod est Ecclesia ut universale salutis sacramentum constituit* [added
> stress]; sedens ad dexteram Patris continuo operatur in mundo ut homines ad Ecclesiam
> perducat arctiusque per eam Sibi coniungat ac proprio Corpore et Sanguine illos
> nutriendo gloriosae vitae suae faciat esse participes.[144]

This development ought to be understood as a rediscovery of sacramentality in the
ressourcement movement at the beginning of the twentieth century.[145] As Hans Boersma in his systematic study of *La Nouvelle Théologie*[146] stresses, it was a return to
mystery, as seen in the theology of the fathers and a sacramental view of reality
beyond traditional Aristotelian metaphysics and its modern rationalist or roman-
tic alternatives.[147] Henri de Lubac had shown that the neo-Thomist idea of "pure

---

[144] RCC 1964a *Lumen Gentium* (LG 48). In English translation: "Christ, when he was lifted up
from the earth, drew all people to himself (see Jn 12, 32 Greek text); rising from the dead (see Rm 6, 9),
he sent his lifegiving Spirit down on his disciples and through him he constituted his body which is the
church as the universal sacrament of salvation; sitting at the right hand of the Father he is continuously
at work in the world to lead people to the church and through it to join them more closely to himself;
and he nourishes them with his own body and blood to make them sharers in his glorious life." LG
continues, "The promised restoration, therefore, which we await, has already begun in Christ, is ad-
vanced through the mission of the holy Spirit and by means of the Spirit continues in the church in
which, through faith, we are instructed concerning the meaning of our temporal life, while we, as we
hope for the benefits that are to come, bring to its conclusion the work entrusted to us in the world by
the Father and work out our salvation (see Ph 2, 12)." (RCC 1964a: Tanner 1990, 887–88. Cf. DS 4168).

[145] Significant literature is published in French and German. A standard work in English is
Vorgrimler 1992, the English translation of *Sacramententtheologie* from 1987 which sets the sacraments in the context of a sacramental theology. Another resource in English is Boersma and
Levering (eds.) 2015 *The Oxford Handbook of Sacramental Theology* which deals with sacramental roots in scripture, patristic sacramental theology, medieval sacramental theology, modern developments from the Reformation onwards, dogmatic approaches, and philosophical and theological matters by a range of scholars from different church traditions. In Swedish, Bexell 1997
links the fundamental ecclesiological analysis of de Lubac with issues of fundamental theology
and essential questions of man and the origin and destiny of mankind.

[146] Boersma 2009.

[147] On the philosophical presuppositions of modern theology with the rationalist traditions
of French, British and German Enlightenment thinkers and the abandonment of classical metaphysical positions, see Hull 2020. Hull demonstrates the similarity of secularists and fundamen-
talists in metaphysical and epistemological positions, Hull 2020, 19 "both the secular humanist
and the religious fundamentalist are convinced that what we find in the Enlightenment's age of
reason is a total antithesis to what had been there before. For what was there before was the dom-
inance of the church, the prevalence of faith and its theological systems of thought, the very opposite of an age of reason, its veritable antithesis."

nature" had contributed to the rise of naturalism and secularism by considering nature apart from grace and a supernatural end. This led later Thomists to think in line with one natural and one supernatural order each leading to its τέλος (*telos*), its integrated end.[148] As in Aristotelian thinking, every being would be able to fulfil its nature by its own powers, man would thus have no *desiderium naturale* (natural desire) for God. This, de Lubac saw was a deviation from the church fathers whose biblical distinction in Genesis 1:26 between εἰκών (the image) and ὁμοίωσις (likeness) was not the same as the relationship between Aristotelian "nature" and Christian "grace."[149]

Thus the idea of "a self-enclosed natural realm" and the subsequent denial of a natural desire beyond this world had been promoted by influential scholars[150] as if these ideas were in line with Thomas Aquinas himself. Once the idea of human nature without a supernatural end had taken hold "two unconnected parallel outcomes to human life" could be posited. Aquinas' subordinated ends of earthly happiness thus ended up with neo-Thomists courting secularism because the idea of two parallel tracks in life implied an autonomous realm of nature unrelated to a vision of God and the Christian life. The supernatural could then be marginalised and life could be pursued as a pursuit of goods based on a "natural order." In contrast, de Lubac,[151]

> believed it was necessary to hold together two paradoxical notions: on the one hand, human beings had an innate natural desire for God; on the other hand, this natural desire was unable of itself to attain the beatific vision, so that the human interior aptitude in no way obliged God to give sanctifying grace. The Aristotelian principle of

---

[148] Greek τέλος, for end, termination, or conclusion. In philosophy, the *telos* points to the integral fulfilment that everything strives.

[149] Boersma 2009, 91–93 The Aristotelian "nature" was not the same as the Father's "image", the first restricting human beings to a closed natural realm and the latter opening up to a supernatural horizon obtainable only by God's grace.

[150] Boersma 2009, 94. Robert Bellarmine (1542–1621) had used the term *pura natura* to protect the free gift of grace in his controversy with the followers of Michael Baius (1513–1589). It was Denys the Cartusian (1402–1471) and Thomas Cardinal Cajetan (1469–1534) who had, by applying the Aristotelian principle of connaturality denied an innate *desiderium naturale* which had hitherto been accepted by the church fathers as well as the medieval schools of thought including Duns Scotus (1265–1308). The denial became influential due to Francisco Suárez (1548–1617) book *De fine ultimo* (1592). These thinkers also impacted people in the reformation churches despite the schism. Boersma 2009, 93–94.

[151] Boersma 2009, 90–98.

connaturality was, in de Lubac's mind, an unfortunate rejection of paradox and mystery in favour of common sense.[152]

What de Lubac describes above is the surprising discovery that neo-Thomism had contributed to the rise of naturalism – the worldview that gave rise to secularism, a social realm devoid of religion.[153]

Brodd's article suggests making distinctions between the concept of the church, church organisation, and church institutions,[154] As such, it may be helpful, in light of the ecclesiological language used in the ecumenical discussion and made explicit in the name ACT Alliance as "Action by Churches Together", to be able to discuss "church matters" outside of the strict purview of the institutional church. Borgehammar uses a distinction from Dietrich Rössler:

> Rössler has suggested distinguishing between three central forms of contemporary Christianity: the ecclesial, the public – consisting of the Christian heritage of society in the form of traditions, education, art, politics, culture, morals, and institutions – and the private,[155] with varying degrees of participation in the ecclesial form and varying degrees of identification with the public. In our time, these forms tend to drift apart, presenting the Church and ecclesial action with a complex task. The Church is accountable for all the baptised, not only the church-active, but she is co-responsible for public Christianity, and she has to deal with the individual types of piety that are formed in relation to both church and public Christianity.[156]

Such distinctions between the ecclesial, public Christianity, and private forms of Christian life would make it possible to research Christian practices – such as the ecumenical diakonia or diakonie of ACT Alliance – as a form of life in the church. It would be doing justice to the integral nature of the institution and its action as such, and the ecclesial framework from which the action originates and under whose name the assistance is performed.[157]

---

[152] Boersma 2009, 98.

[153] Boersma 2009, 97. The alternative vision was to integrate history and faith as well as nature and the supernatural "with a sacramental ontology that regarded nature as innately or inherently oriented to the supernatural."

[154] Brodd 2005b.

[155] Borgehammar 2021, 86. Cf. the distinctions of *ecclesia, politia*, and *oeconomia*, Brodd 1992, 64. Within the church, as Brodd points out, Brodd 2005, 251, the idea of *koinonia*, entails "that the Christian community is always personal but can never be individualistic. The difference is that a person always is defined based on the identity-giving community, whilst an individual is defined by what is unique in relation to other individuals."

[156] Borgehammar 2021, 86.

[157] Borgehammar 2021, 86.

1.2 Research Problem, Questions, and Material

The purpose is to draw attention to ecclesial issues of aid with special reference to African churches. *Earlier research* (1.1) has drawn attention to the lack of research on ACT Alliance in general and the significance of the meaning of ACT Alliance as an *action by churches together* in particular. In ecumenical theory, the idea, conceptualised as *ecumenical diakonia*, was for ACT to express *action by churches together* in consequence of a sense of churches growing together in *koinonia*.

By approaching this theoretical issue from the practical angle of discussing tensions in a historical case of refugee assistance, the plight of asylum seekers and challenges in addressing their needs constitutes a secondary purpose for the thesis. By addressing the matter from a historical angle with Ethiopian churches in the centre, the intent is for the research to open up for discussion on ecclesial and theological matters for those primarily interested in aid, and issues of aid and refugee response for those more concerned with theological and ecclesial matters. The aim is not to close the debate but to open up for further research.

Research Problem

The research deals with the theoretical problem of the meaning and identity of ACT Alliance as it is understood to be, in some sense, an *action by churches together*. The relationship between church and aid can be conceptualised in differing ways and more questions can be asked than one dissertation may answer. The thesis is therefore limited to the ecclesiological problem meaning and identity of ACT Alliance and its implication for Ethiopian churches and their refugee assistance.

Brodd in bringing attention to the problem of the identity of Christian organisation[s], with specific reference to "church related development organisation[s]", showed that a distinction but not a separation between the Christian Church and such organisations needs to be drawn.[158] At the same time, as these organisations are not churches, they still may be expressions of churches, as "no Christian organisation can exist outside of the Church."[159] These two statements, the first a quote and the second a summary, appear to be contradictory: "Christian organisations cannot exist outside the Church."[160] Christian organisations are not "ecclesial entities."[161]

---

[158] Brodd 2005b, 245.
[159] Brodd 2005b, 248.
[160] Brodd 2005b, 248.
[161] Brodd 2005b, 247.

If these organisations are considered ecclesial entities, i.e. "churches",[162] then they act like sects in relation to the churches. If not, then they may complement the work of the churches "by establishing means for their responsibilities for the world." The second statement gives the reason why it was important for mission agencies not to bypass the indigenous churches in the Lausanne movement.[163] The reason why these statements are not contradictory is that: "The Church is not an organisation."[164] Although the Christian Church "has to be institutional",[165] the institutions of the church are not to be confused with the church itself, which is something more than and different from an institution or organisation. The church may contain organisations, but an organisation cannot contain the church.

Following Aristotelian logic,[166] there are four options[167] for the relationship between Christian organisations (Subject: S) and the Christian Church (Predicate: P). There are four propositions, A, E, I, and O. (A) universal yes: All S are P. (E) universal no: No S are P. (I) particular yes: Some S are P. (O) particular no: Some S are not P.

(A) All Christian organisations, S, are a part of what is the Christian Church, P.

(E) No Christian organisations, S, are a part of what is the Christian Church, P.

(I) Some Christian organisations, S, are a part of what is the Christian Church, P.

(O) Some Christian organisations, S, are not a part of what is the Christian Church, P.

---

[162] By being called "religious organisations" in part of the aid literature – that seems to be one interpretation. Brodd 2005b, 253, relates how the idea of organisation eventually was integrated into the self-understanding of some churches as associations that were founded, such as Bible and Missionary Societies, impacted the ecclesiological views also of the old churches.

[163] Brodd 2005b, 247–48. As was shown in the literature review of earlier research, This issue appeared in the modern missionary movement and was a significant impetus for the rise of the ecumenical movement and its concern with churches as well as mission. Visser't Hooft 1982.

[164] Brodd 2005b, 253 clarifies that the idea of organisation is relatively new, based on 17th C, natural law theories, and the nineteenth-century idea of association, which by the rise of ideologies "gave to organisations their meanings and status in society."

[165] Brodd 2005b, 252.

[166] Kreeft 2014.

[167] (A) All S are P. (E) No S are P. (I) Some S are P. (O) Some S are not P. "A" and "I" are the first two vowels in the Latin word *affirmo* (from the verb "to affirm") and "E" and "O" are the first two vowels in the Latin word *nego* (from the verb "to deny"). Kreeft 2014, 145–51.

This exercise can be done also with Aid organisations (S1) and the Christian Church (P),[168] or with ACT organisations (S2) and the Christian Church (P).[169]

These alternatives can be visually illustrated and conceptually clarified using Euler's Circles.[170]

Proposition A:  **E:** **I:** **O:**

Figure 1.1: *Euler's Circles with the differing propositions A, E, I, and O.*

Proposition A, universal affirmation asserts that all S is P. In terms of comprehension (A) means that P, i.e. church, is part of the meaning of S (S1: Christian organisation, S2: aid organisation, S3: ACT organisation). In terms of extension, (A) asserts that the whole class of S's is included in the class of P's (church). Example: *All Christian organisations are a part of what is the Christian Church.* This is the position of Brodd: no Christian organisation can exist outside of the church.

Proposition E, universal negation would represent the opposite view: In terms of comprehension (E) means that P, i.e. church, is no part of the meaning of S. In terms of extension, (E) asserts that the populations of S's and P's exclude each other. So, there is nothing that is a member of both S and P. S is not included in the class of P's. Example: *No secular aid organisation is a part of what is the Christian Church.* It is a common claim.

Proposition I, particular affirmation asserts that some S is P: In terms of comprehension (I) means that P, church, is part of the meaning of some S's. In terms of extension, (I) means that some S's are in the class of P. Example: *Some aid organisations are a part of what is the Christian Church.*

Finally, proposition O, particular negation asserts that some (S) is not (P): An O puts part of the class of S outside P (i.e. it is "not-P") but leaves the other part unknown. If we know that some S is not P, then we do not know whether some S

---

[168] (A) All Aid organisations, S1, are a part of what is the Christian Church, P. (E) No Aid organisations, S1, are a part of what is the Christian Church, P. (I) Some Aid organisations, S1, are a part of what is the Christian Church, P. (O) Some Aid organisations, S1, are not a part of what is the Christian Church, P.

[169] (A) All ACT organisations, S2, are a part of what is the Christian Church, P. (E) No ACT organisations, S2, are a part of what is the Christian Church, P. (I): Some ACT organisations, S2, are a part of what is the Christian Church, P. (O) Some ACT organisations, S2, are not a part of what is the Christian Church, P.

[170] Kreeft 2014, 152–55.

is P. Example: *Some aid organisations are not a part of what is the Christian Church, but we do not know whether some are part of the church.*

Brodd's thesis therefore corresponds to proposition A, but it is formulated in the negative: "no Christian organisation can exist outside of the Church."[171] It means that if an organisation is outside the reality of the Christian Church, then by definition, it is not Christian. At this point, it is important to note that when Brodd speaks of the church, he does not refer only to the institutional church, but to the whole reality of the Christian Church. This thesis will take seriously that ACT Alliance claims to be, in some sense, an *action by churches together*, by using Brodd's thesis as a starting hypothesis treating ACT Alliance as if it is part of the reality of the Christian Church.

Research Questions

Building upon that fundamental analysis, this thesis explores and clarifies the issue further by starting from a practical point of view, i.e. investigating the ACT appeal to support refugees from South Sudan in Ethiopia by ACT Alliance in 2014. If ACT Alliance is considered an *action by churches together*, what does it mean conceptually and what does it entail practically? The aim is to centre on questions of ecclesial identity by studying tensions arising when the idea, *action by churches together*, is put into practice in the actual work and organisation of ACT Alliance. In this thesis, tension is defined as practical challenges that may, or may not, show a discrepancy "between what a church claims to be and what it is in reality."[172]

Tensions may be an indication that Christian aid agencies are suffering from a mission drift and loss of Christian identity. As Jonsson showed, such a loss of identity may cause inner secularisation in the churches endangering the moral life of Christians and their commitment to the poor.[173] ACT Alliance contains tensions that appear in practice. The study deals with the ecclesiological problem of meaning and identity by investigating a historical case of refugee assistance in Ethiopia, 2014, the ETH141 ACT Appeal. The appeal is situated in a historical context. The two Ethiopian churches that are members of ACT Alliance will be shedding light on the problem of the ecclesial identity of ACT Alliance. The thesis asks questions about what it means for the refugee assistance of ACT Alliance to be, in some sense, an *action by churches together*, with regard to the refugee assistance of an ACT Appeal and its stated principles, an ecclesial self-understanding, a Christian

---

[171] Brodd 2005b, 248.
[172] Brodd 2005b, 259–61.
[173] Jonsson 1998. Brodd 2005b.

worldview, and the churches' mission to reach every person with the gospel and the sacramental life of the church.

This research project proceeds from several questions: If the refugee assistance by the ACT Ethiopia Forum, as a national expression of ACT Alliance, is, in some sense an *action by churches together*, what does that entail? Does it mean that there are recognisable "Christian" or "ecclesial" characteristics in the work? In that case, how would these features influence the work? If the refugee assistance of ACT Alliance is not to be "church" in name only, the work needs to be grounded in the Christian Church, its faith, and Christian practices. If ACT Alliance is genuinely part of the Christian church, one might reasonably expect that it would show in the way the refugee assistance is done. In other words, it's important to establish in what sense ACT Alliance is representing an *action by churches together*.

From an epistemological point of view, problems of meaning and identity are difficult. It would, however, be possible to narrow the gap by asking what the work (the appeal) and its principles (the international framework) say about the purpose of the work and the identity of the organisations involved in the appeal. What do the actual work, the refugee assistance, and the stated principles say about the meaning and extension of the *action by churches together* of ACT Alliance?

There is also another angle from which to ask questions, the ecclesial side. ACT members are related to churches, and these churches have a stake in the work. What churches think about the work and its organisation matters and may show how ACT Alliance is of Christian and ecclesial concern. How have Ethiopian churches motivated, understood, and critiqued the ecumenical engagement they are part of? The answers may shed light on how the work corresponds to an ecclesial self-understanding, a Christian worldview and the churches' mission. As such those answers will finally contribute to answering in what sense the refugee assistance of ACT Alliance is an *action by churches together*.

The societal issue at stake in the thesis concerns the South Sudanese refugee crisis beginning in 2014 and the response in Ethiopia to which Ethiopian churches and churches from other parts of the world participated through their respective aid agencies, coordinated by ACT Alliance. I aim to explore and analyse the implications of ecumenical refugee assistance at a time when the number of refugees across the world is growing. Taken as a global crisis, the movements of asylum seekers constitute one of the most significant humanitarian issues in modern times, raising concerns for all those involved, including churches. There is nothing new about refugees, but the scale of the crisis has risen to an unprecedented level which is disconcerting and political solutions are not always forthcoming.[174] Christian churches have used different vehicles for the coordination and collaboration of their efforts. Refugee assistance has been one such area for Christian intervention in the global arena. The societal and humanitarian issues at stake concern civil conflict, refugee movements, and the safety and welfare of asylum seekers. Altogether, this kind of social crisis raises ethical and moral questions to Christians as they seek to pursue life in the church.

The ecclesial issue at stake concerns the involvement of churches, and Christian aid agencies, as they support refugees and seek the common good together as part of life in the church. The churches see themselves in the Nicene Creed as rooted in the self-revelation of God the Father, the Son, and the Holy Spirit, which includes the nature and mission of the Christian Church. It raises the question of the sense in which the work of ACT Alliance corresponds to an ecclesial self-understanding, a Christian worldview, and the mission to reach every person. These ecclesial aspects have an ecumenical dimension made explicit as the assistance is coordinated through an ecumenical organ, ACT Alliance, and as the common action is directed towards society.

ACT Alliance will be the research subject of this thesis. The ACT Ethiopia Forum is the main national structure for the eleven ACT Alliance members working in Ethiopia.[175] This includes the aid agencies of two Ethiopian churches: the Ethiopian Orthodox Tewahido Church and the Ethiopian Evangelical Church Mekane Yesus. The *Action by Churches Together*, ACT, was founded in 1995 for

---

[174] UN 2016 02 02 Ban Ki-Moon 2016.

[175] 13 ACT members have signed the MoU of the ACT Ethiopia Forum from Oct 2012: Bread for the World (BftW), Ethiopian Orthodox Church - Development and Inter Church Aid Commission (EOC / DICAC), Ethiopian Evangelical Church Mekane Yesus - Development and Social Service Commission (EECMY / DASSC), Christian Aid (CA), Church of Sweden (CoS), Dan Church Aid (DCA), *Evangelischer Entwicklungsdienst* (EED), Finn Church Aid (FCA), *Hilfswerk der Evangelischen Kirchen* Schweiz (HEKS), Interchurch Organization for Development Co-operation (ICCO - *Kerk in Actie*), International Orthodox Christian Charities (IOCC), Lutheran World Federation - Department for World Service (LWF/DWS) and Norwegian Church Aid (NCA). FCA later left the forum. BftW and EED merged as organisations and created the Protestant Agency for Development and Diakonia (PADD). The emergency wing of the German churches, *Diakonie Katastrofenhilfe* (DKH) is represented by PADD in the forum. The Anglican Church is an ACT member, and the church is present in the country, but is not as such a forum member. Other local churches, notably the Ethiopian Catholic Church, the Ethiopian Kale Heywet Church (EKHC) and the Evangelical Churches Fellowship of Ethiopia (ECFE), are not members of the WCC and hence not eligible to become ACT members according to the statutes of ACT Alliance.

the coordination of the humanitarian response of the churches, with the intent of raising the overall quality. Later, in addition to relief assistance, development work and advocacy of Christian faith-based and church-based agencies were added, and ACT would develop into *ACT Alliance.* It was established by the World Council of Churches (WCC) and the Lutheran World Federation (LWF) as part of the wider ecumenical movement of the twentieth century.[176]

The research objects, therefore, are not churches, but ACT Alliance and its member agencies, dedicated to social services, not church services. The local forum, the ACT Ethiopia Forum, in 2014 had eleven active ACT members in Ethiopia. Of these organisations, two represent Ethiopian churches: *the Ethiopian Evangelical Church Mekane Yesus Development and Social Service Commission* (EECMY-DASSC), and *the Ethiopian Orthodox Church Development and Social Service Commission* (EOC-DICAC). A third, *the Lutheran World Federation World Service Ethiopia* (LWF-WS), the international aid branch of the Lutheran World Federation (LWF), has a close relationship to *the Ethiopian Evangelical Church Mekane Yesus* (EECMY). A fourth organisation, *the International Orthodox Christian Charities* (IOCC) has a strong link with *the Ethiopian Orthodox Tewahido Church* (EOTC). These are four of the implementing organisations giving refugee assistance among the ACT members in Ethiopia. Of interest, however, is also the other seven European ACT members and particularly the role of the so-called "E8 group."[177]

The thesis is concerned first with the meaning and applicability of the idea of ACT and second with the way the case study and its principles are related to the Ethiopian Churches and the nature and mission of the Christian church. Does the refugee assistance of ETH141 correspond to an ecclesial self-understanding, a Christian understanding of reality, and the mission to reach every person with the gospel and the sacramental life of the church? All this leads to questions regarding in what sense ACT Alliance is an *action by churches together.*

---

[176] John Nduna *"Launch speech of the ACT Alliance"* 2010, held in Geneva Jan 2011.
[177] E8 consists of BftW/PADD, CA, CoS, DCA, FCA, HEKS, ICCO, and NCA.

The Research Problem of Ecclesiological Tensions in ACT Alliance			
Chapter two	*Chapter three*	*Chapter four*	*Chapter five*
ETH 141 Appeal	International Framework	Ethiopian Churches	Ecumenical Models
Primary material "The Societal Side"	Primary material	Primary material "The Ecclesial Side"	(Primary material)

Figure 1.2. *The research on ecclesiological tensions in ACT Alliance begins in the ETH141 ACT Appeal and spans across the chapters. Chapters two to five contain primary material used to deal with the ecclesiological problem and its two sides: the societal and the ecclesial.*

In this thesis, the societal and ecclesial issues will be analysed in two ways. First, chapters two and three are concerned with organisational and ethical matters in the case of the ETH141 ACT Appeal, and the international principles guiding the work. This may give a functional understanding of the refugee assistance by the ACT Ethiopia Forum as an *action by churches together*. Second, chapters four and five situate the case study in the longer historical context of church and aid in Ethiopia. The latter concern is with Ethiopian Churches and their relation to ACT Alliance. The idea is to take seriously that ACT Alliance sees itself as an *action by churches together*, hence churches must be relevant in one way or another. What the connection is between ACT Alliance and churches, however, cannot be taken for granted, as seen in the visible tensions in the literature study. Does the refugee assistance of ETH141 correspond to an ecclesial self-understanding, a Christian understanding of reality, and the mission to reach every person with the gospel and the sacramental life of the church?

Research Material

The thesis is built primarily on written primary material with complementary interviews.[178] See the bibliography for a list of primary sources. Humanitarian relief work produces documents which may be used as primary sources in research.

In this case, *the ETH141 ACT Appeal document* with its preceding forms, *the ACT Alert,* and *the Preliminary Appeal,* constitute the primary documents in chapter two which create a paper trail to follow in the investigation into this specific work of refugee assistance. Other primary documents from ACT Alliance

---

[178] For qualitative interviews, Kvale 1997. On research with refugees, Hugman 2011.

and its Ethiopian forum related to the appeal have also been studied to bring the appeal into its textual and historical context.

Most documents have been collected by the author from the Dropbox folder of the ACT Ethiopia Forum. The folder is still present, but inactive. Other primary documents have been acquired by email from ACT members. ACT documents can be found in the archives of the ACT members in Ethiopia and ACT Alliance in Geneva. Norwegian Church Aid is responsible for the archive of ACT Ethiopia Forum.

The ETH141 appeal cites international standards used in the work of refugee assistance. Different organisations produced these documents that may be requested from those organisations or found online. There are earlier and later documents of the same kind in the relief sector, the selection criterion has been to use the standards cited in the appeal.

The following documents will therefore be analysed in chapter three: ACT Alliance. 2011. *ACT Alliance Code of Conduct: For the prevention of sexual exploitation and abuse, fraud and corruption and abuse of power.* HAP. 2010. *The 2010 HAP Standard in Accountability and Quality Management.* 2nd ed. ICRC. 1994. *The Code of Conduct for the International Red Cross and Red Crescent Movement and NGOs in Disaster Relief.* Inter-Agency Standing Committee. 2007. *IASC Guidelines on Mental Health and Psychosocial Support in Emergency Settings.* Sphere Project. 2011. *Humanitarian Charter and Minimum Standards in Humanitarian Response.* 3rd ed.

Chapter four relies on primary sources from the two Ethiopian Churches and their development wings. The Ethiopian Evangelical Church Mekane Yesus Development and Social Service Commission (EECMY-DASSC), and The Ethiopian Orthodox Church Development and Social Service Commission (EOC-DICAC) both produce project documents and annual reports. There are, however, fewer documents explicating the views of the Ethiopian Evangelical Church Mekane Yesus and the Ethiopian Orthodox Tewahido Church on issues of aid and ecumenical engagements. As such, it is hard to come by contemporary sources that may speak with authority on these types of issues. The first issue of *the Maedot* (1983) is such a source from the Orthodox Church and *On the Interrelation between the Proclamation of the Gospel and Human Development* (*the ECMY Letter* 1972) is a relevant source from the Mekane Yesus Church. There is therefore a time gap between the texts from the churches and the refugee assistance in the case study. The criteria for the selection of these two written sources will be described in chapter four.

Chapter Five on Models for Ecumenical Action is partially based on some archival primary source material from the ACT Ethiopia Forum. Still, most of the chapter's historical account is built upon previous research.

1.3 A Historical and Theological Approach

This is a study of how churches support refugees through ACT Alliance and its member agencies.[179] As two Ethiopian churches, the Ethiopian Orthodox Tewahido Church and the Ethiopian Evangelical Church Mekane Yesus are members of ACT Alliance and its Ethiopia forum, they are given a larger space than the churches in the global north that are represented through their northern ACT agencies.[180]

The research is not primarily about these churches *per se*, as the thesis focuses on ACT Alliance as an ecclesial phenomenon and its work with refugees through ACT-affiliated aid agencies, but their inclusion in a separate chapter is crucial in this study of ACT Alliance and its ecumenical refugee assistance in order to answer the main research question regarding the identity of ACT Alliance.

Relief work and relief organisations have developed historically. ACT-affiliated organisations are theologically motivated as can be seen from their historical development. Chapter five will offer a glimpse of this. A church historical approach, focusing on modern Ethiopian and African church history, has been part of the background work of the thesis. These historical findings are embedded in the textual study in chapter four. ACT organisations and their churches relate to each other and to the rest of the world ecumenically as seen in the literature review with its focus on the ecumenical movement. Therefore, the ecumenical movement and its issues enter the analysis.

The whole thesis may be seen as a study of ecumenism: a study of *diakonie*, in the sense of service or assistance, to refugees. Hence the foundational study of the primary documents of the ETH141 ACT Appeal, in 2014, a study of contemporary history. In addition, the project has considered issues of church and state, *International Human Rights Law* (IRHL), *International Humanitarian Law* (IHL),

---

[179] The ecumenical movement widened due to the Second Vatican Council, but the thesis will be limited to ACT Alliance associated with WCC and LWF. The Roman Catholic Church has similar organs for the coordination of relief and development services, such as the American-based Catholic Relief Services *et al.* and a comparison would be worth future research.

[180] The Porvoo Community or the North European Catholic Church is the ecclesial background of the E8. A significant ecclesiological study of the majority of the churches behind the E8 churches is Eckerdal, Erik 2017. See also Fagerli, Nathaniel, and Karttunen 2016.

and *International Refugee Law* (IRL) from the perspective of ecumenical collaboration of churches. This is in connection to the textual study of the international standards analysed in chapter four.

As these standards, and indeed international law, have historically developed, chapter four studies them as they were in 2014. This study entails some incursions into ethics and moral theology[181] – particularly in the chapter dealing with international standards – to show how a principled ethical approach may be related to the Christian faith and the Christian church.

The theological approach provides the overall approach, with the study of the Christian practices within the framework of the Christian church at its core. This is not a study of ecclesiology in the strict sense of a deductive study of the doctrine of the church, but a study of ecclesial practices from the viewpoint of the Christian Church with its nature and mission.[182] The study can therefore also belong to practical theology as traditionally conceived with the practical aim of contributing to the contemporary life of the church by dealing with "the tension between academic theology and ecclesial praxis."[183] It entails a study of historical sources and processes of significance for the church as it appears in history in the form of the church itself, public Christianity, and private forms of Christian life.[184] The sources of theological knowledge in practical theology are philosophical and historical theology.[185] Whereas the state begins from ideas of politics and statecraft, the Christian church is a theological concept drawn from biblical and theological sources. Research in theology therefore considers the Christian tradition as the main reference point to the church practices it studies.[186]

---

[181] Mannion 2015, XIII, "Foreword" in Fahlgren and Ideström 2015 *Ecclesiology in the Trenches* states: "Bridging ecclesiology and ethics in a consistent fashion is *the* challenge for the church in our times. Even ecumenism is, ultimately, as such a moral challenge (and thus an obligation) as it is a theological and sacramental calling." Bexell and Grenholm 2003 on ethics.

[182] See Brodd 2005b, 248–49 On ecclesiology as the theological discipline that studies the Christian Church: "ecclesiology, for a long time was a term for the doctrinal statements of the Church about itself with a locus in dogmatics. Nowadays ecclesiology embraces the total reality of what it means to be Church, not only in doctrine but also in practice." Eckerdal, Erik 2017; Eckerdal, Jan 2012; Fahlgren 2006a; 2006b; 2015; Ideström 2009; 2015; Öljarstrand 2011, 11–13; Padilha 1994, 287; Watkins 1991; 1993.

[183] Borgehammar 2021, 74, 86. This project belongs to a larger research project on *Church and Society* at *the Stockholm School of Theology*, with several dissertations coming out of the research school and its focus on Practical Theology.

[184] Borgehammar 2021, 79.

[185] Borgehammar 2021, 79.

[186] Brodd 2005b, 251.

As churches – through their specialised agencies – call for and are involved in refugee assistance, it is important to analyse the work, not only to assess the efficiency and effectiveness, or even long-term impact of the assistance but also to develop and use analytical models for understanding and theologically consider the aid agencies of the churches and the way they operate. This means that it is imperative not to remain at the level of operative assessment, which in aid-terms often focuses on efficacy – regarding the question of whether the aims set for the project were met – and efficiency – whether the time spent, and the human and material resources used were handled in such a way that there was little "waste" and that the resources contributed well to the set objectives serving the overall aims.

Beyond these measurables, it is important to analyse meta-level questions of why efficacy and efficiency matter and whether focus on means-to-end rationality may make people overlook other issues of human relations, power, and human ends beyond survival. This includes the theoretical and methodological problem of how to do research on organisations with a claim to be "faith-based", "Christian", or "church-based" aid organisations and pay attention to other stakeholders such as state agencies, international organisations, refugee and host communities.

The emphasis of this research will be on organisational and ethical aspects.[187] This research is not overly concerned about the effectiveness or efficiency of the operation, or to what extent the work had a measurable impact. It is more focused on asking about truth than "what works." G.E. Moore proved in "William James's Pragmatism" that the pragmatic theory of truth is based on linguistic confusion. There are several words for "what works" such as *efficient*, *effective*, or *practical*. Truth cannot mean "what works" because "what is true is always practical" while "what is practical is not always true", such as a lie. The thesis is practical, in the sense of dealing with Christian practices within the framework of the church.[188]

This includes bringing in critical voices concerning the possibility of an "inner secularisation" of Christian practices by ideologies of secularism.[189] The concrete cooperation and work with refugees is analysed based on its integral conditions, challenges and ideas and reviewed against the Christian tradition of two Ethiopian churches. The purpose is to understand what it means when churches engage in concrete refugee work in a network of organisations created by states rather than churches. Theologically, therefore, this needs to be analysed.

---

[187] Bakka, Fivelsdal and Lindkvist 2006; Esaiasson et al 2012; Gustavsson and Tallberg 2014; de Vylder 2013.

[188] Kreeft and Tacelli 2009, 382–404, chapter 15 "Objective Truth."

[189] Jonsson 1998, 201. Schmemann 1973.

Terms and Acronyms

The eleven member organisations of the ACT Ethiopia Forum are legally registered as autonomous charity organisations, and not as churches, but at the same
time they are all self-identifying as Christian, relate to the World Council of
Churches, and act on behalf of the churches as implied by the acronym *ACT*; *Action by Churches Together*. These organisations are not churches, but they still may
be expressions of churches, as "no Christian organisation can exist outside of the
Church."[190] "Church" as a concept is not per se limited to only institutional aspects such as local congregations, church polity or organisational structure, rather
it is a theological concept, and thus theologically structured.[191]

Literature may refer to relief and development organisations as non-governmental organisations (NGOs). It comes from a classification of international organisations into governmental, non-governmental, and public corporations.[192]

The term "refugee assistance" will be used as a broad term as support rendered
to people who seek refuge. A refugee or a migrant is not another kind of person;
any one of us may end up as a refugee or migrant, and some of us have that experience and others may experience it yet.[193] Being a refugee is a historical condition
that may change, not an essential quality of a person. The term assistance does not
set a time limit, such as "emergency response," nor does it limit the nature of the
assistance in terms of "relief," "development," or "advocacy".[194]

There is a proliferation of abbreviations and acronyms in relief and development works. A habit which may intimidate newcomers to the world of relief and
development and make these "NGOs" anonymous, lacking personality. Some organisations have long names that inhibit the usage of their full names; thus, they
are abbreviated. The Ethiopian Evangelical Church Mekane Yesus Development
and Social Service Commission is abbreviated EECMY-DASSC, or DASSC for
short. The Refugees and Returnees Affairs Department of the Ethiopian

---

[190] Brodd 2005b, 248.

[191] Brodd 2015, 18.

[192] Abass 2012, 194. International organisations may refer to public intergovernmental organisations (such as UN, represented by governments), private international organisations (NGOs),
and international public corporations (IPCs).

[193] Cf. 2016 02 02 Ban Ki-Moon 2016 in which the general secretary of the UN narrated his
experience as refugee from the conflict in Korea.

[194] George and Adeney 2018, 34 deliberate on the meaning of several relevant terms: *aliens,
asylum seekers, diaspora, displaced people, ethnic minority, expatriate, foreigners, forced or invol-
untary migrants, illegals, immigrants, refugees, stateless, trafficked, undocumented,* and *uprooted
people.*

Orthodox Church Development and Inter-Church Aid Commission is abbreviated RRAD, and the commission, EOC-DICAC, and the Ethiopian Orthodox Church, or the Ethiopian Orthodox Tewahido Church as it is also referred to is abbreviated EOC or EOTC respectively. The Lutheran World Federation World Service Ethiopia Program is abbreviated LWF WS-E. For those familiar with these organisations, the abbreviations become acronyms. ACT Alliance, becomes *act*, not A C T Alliance. EECMY-DASSC, becomes **dassc*, pronounced like English *dusk*, or simply *Mekane Yesus* as the church itself. Similarly, EOC-DICAC becomes **dicac* or **daicac,* not D I C A C. Alternatively, within the church, EOC-DICAC may be referred to as the *lemat commission,* ልማት (*lemat*) being the Amharic word for development, derived from መልማት (*mälmat*) to thrive.

To open my research to readers who are unfamiliar with both the Ethiopian church context and the world of relief and development, I will avoid the usage of both long names and abbreviations when possible. I will refer to "Mekane Yesus" or "the Mekane Yesus Church" instead of the Ethiopian Evangelical Church Mekane Yesus (or EECMY), to the "Orthodox Church" or the "Ethiopian Orthodox Church" rather than the Ethiopian Orthodox Tewahido Church (or EOTC). Similarly, I will refer to the "refugee department" and the "development commission" of the Orthodox Church or the Mekane Yesus instead of the RADD, EOC-DICAC and EECMY-DASSC respectively. "LWF World Service" will be used for the relief organisation and "Lutheran World Federation" will be spelt out for the whole federation with its departments and agencies. In footnotes, abbreviations will be used.

Researching a Familiar Setting

This thesis, in its analysis of primary documents of the ETH141 ACT appeal to support South Sudanese refugees in Western parts of Ethiopia in 2014, starts on a personal note. In 2014, as the chair of ACT Ethiopia Forum, I followed the progress of *the ETH141 refugee emergency appeal* and was intrigued by the complexities and challenges of humanitarian relief assistance to refugees. My PhD research grew out of a desire to know more about aid-based refugee assistance and seeking to explore explanations as to why things turned out the way they did and in what ways the complex interactions that we were involved in were related to the faith and life of the churches; the Christian or church-based aspects of the aid initiative.[195]

---

[195] After several years of work and research in Ethiopia, teaching at theological institutions (from 2006), serving as the local contact person for Church of Sweden (2010–2015), and writing

The practical challenges ACT Alliance faced in the relief work, raised theoretical questions about church-based aid work, and the principles behind the actual work, a line of questioning I am now pursuing as a researcher. The personal involvement allowed for the collection of primary sources and raised my interest in questions arising from the work of ACT Ethiopia Forum. Without this experience, the thesis would not be.

There is however a heightened risk that personal participation would also entail prejudice and a clouded judgement and reasoning. As a researcher of ACT Alliance and its Ethiopian forum, I have dealt with the dual dilemma of closeness and distance.[196]

As a scholar, I need to distance myself from my personal experiences and opinions to consider other academic perspectives, and simultaneously re-engage with the primary sources to come to a comprehensive understanding of its integral structures, processes, and actors. I recognise the danger of bias, and I have taken several measures to challenge my own presuppositions,[197] and engage in a more

---

a Master Thesis (2013–2014), I began thinking about research topics for Ph-D after a year as chair of the ACT Ethiopia Forum (Oct 2013 – Nov 2014). For the reader, it may be relevant that the church office in Uppsala, built to house the voluntary national organisations of the Church of Sweden – Church of Sweden Abroad (old Seaman Mission), the Church of Sweden Mission, and Church of Sweden Aid, was in constant organisational change while I was employed there 2006–2015. The former collaborative model with Church of Sweden Aid, Church of Sweden Mission, and Swedish Evangelical Mission (est. 1855) collapsed as it was decided to dismantle the Church of Sweden Aid (est. 1947), the Church of Sweden Mission (est. 1874), and Church of Sweden Aid (est. 1947) to give place for a new organisation. See Wejryd 2021.

[196] Alvesson 2003, 176. The terms closeness and distance are from the field of Ethnographical studies in which the researcher aims to come very close to the research subject. Wejryd 2021 for an example of self-ethnography. Cf. Engdahl (2006, 7–15) who uses the terms system transcendence, system immanence and system conformity referencing Bischofberger, *Svenska Dagbladet,* September 17, 2003. Historians customarily study past events from a larger distance, but historical studies of contemporary events do not have this advantage. For this thesis, the fact that the future developments in South Sudan are unknown emphasises the difference between the study of contemporary history and closed historical events.

[197] There are risks involved in studying a context in which you are familiar. In ethnographical research they call part of this issue "going native", Alvesson 2003, 172. I have used several strategies of defamiliarizations, such as exposing myself to different theories, technical terms of related disciplines, and new experiences to challenge my preliminary understanding of the subject matters involved in the project. I consciously disengaged from the ACT context between 2015–2018 to create a critical distance and re-engaged as a researcher by the end of 2018. By taking up consultancy work within ACT Alliance, but in other projects and other contexts (Tanzania, Zimbabwe

detached way with the research questions to come to a more considerate under-standing of the issues at hand.[198] The research topic is not about my person, or my former work, but about ecumenical organisations working to promote the wellbe-ing of asylum seekers. I have utilised insights from self-ethnography "to draw at-tention to one's own cultural context, what goes on around oneself rather than putting oneself and one's experiences in the centre."[199]

These insights have helped me to reflect on my closeness to the research topic. The approach used is textual studies of primary sources, using the historical method, combining an initial *benevolentia* to the subject matter, sources, and main actors, and *critical thinking* of the complex relations of causes and reasons for events. In chapter two, it is unavoidable that I use some personal knowledge of the events, with the risks it entails, combined with the written sources available.

---

and Bangladesh), new insights and perspectives have been gained. The character of the project has also led me to use a logbook to reflect on everything from personal feelings to theoretical perspectives in relation to the project as the main tool for reflexivity. I have also read broadly and taken courses in missiology, church history, Orthodox theology, human rights, and humanitar-ian relief to be able to confront the issues from different theoretical perspectives and not get stuck with preconceived ideas. I have also presented texts in different research seminars in Lund and Stockholm, using the seminars as a context in which the critique acts as a distancing from the community being studied.

[198] Alvesson, and Sköldberg 2006, 486–89; Toll 2014.

[199] Alvesson 2003, 175. Self-ethnography, as described by Alvesson, is to be distinguished from autoethnography, where "the deeply personal experiences of the researcher are in focus". Alvesson argues for self-ethnography as an approach to study "settings which the researcher is highly familiar with, and has direct access to" and highlights the advantages and disadvantages of "utilizing closeness to empirically rich situations and avoid the closure following being (staying) native". In this approach, the researcher works within a familiar cultural setting and not as "a professional stranger". The researcher then aims at "breaking out" of that which is taken for granted to be able to think through issues and to bring valuable insights both to those who are and who are not familiar with that setting. There are several general reasons for this approach according to Alvesson, such as the capacity to bring rich and interesting research material, the potential for theoretical knowledge well-grounded in experience, and the opportunity to study prestigious groups such as professionals within a field, "thereby reducing the political-ethical problem of solely doing research 'downwards'." It also avoids treating the people involved as "the Other". The challenges include the problems of taking things for granted, missing and omission of blind spots and difficult aspects of the home culture, and "the potential opposite problem of motivation coming from negative experiences and an urge to get 'even'." Alvesson 2003, 167.

An initial *benevolentia*,[200] as distinct from *a hermeneutics of suspicion* aims at avoiding what C.S. Lewis called *Bulverism*, a type of *ad hominem* fallacy that combines circular reasoning and the genetic fallacy by assuming that an argument is false or invalid and then explaining why by attacking the person rather than critiquing the argument.[201] An approach of *benevolentia* by contrast is aiming at a precise description of an event or a person (historical research) and an accurate depiction of a view, or philosophical (or theological) position. The idea – as in historical research – is to get a historical event, a person, or a philosophical position right and thus to distinguish the work of description from the work of criticism.

With critical reasoning, I mainly refer to the philosophical method of examining terms, premises, and arguments of a position.[202] With critical reasoning, it is possible to point out internal inconsistencies showing flaws in an argument. As such, I may offer a critical discussion after careful consideration of the primary sources and the literature on the subject. It does not mean that I am critical of the idea of aid or believe that I would do better in other people's shoes. After studying the aid sector, however, I have grown to appreciate the insights of a *do no harm* approach to aid (see chapter three). I also believe that actual churches on the ground have valid things to say about aid in their context, and aid done in the name of the churches.

Furthermore, critical thinking may be used to compare a particular viewpoint against a standard. In an evangelical understanding of Christian theology, Scripture is the *norma normans* against which other norms are evaluated. It is read in light of the whole tradition of the Christian Church.[203]

---

[200] Such a *benevolentia* does not preclude but presupposes a source critical method, but not of the cut and paste kind that dictates to the sources to tell a predetermined story, but one used in literary and historical context.

[201] Lewis 1970, 271–77. First published in *Time and Tide* 1941. Lewis 1970, 273 "You must show *that* a man is wrong before you start explaining *why* he is wrong. The modern method is to assume without discussion *that* he is wrong and then distract his attention from this (the only real issue) by busily explaining how he became so silly. In the course of the last fifteen years I have found this vice so common that I have had to invent a name for it. I call it 'Bulverism'."

[202] Bradley and Muller 1995, 25 In the ecumenical environment of academic research, Bradley and Muller write an "author cannot write today… without consulting what is being said by Catholic and Orthodox scholars both in relation to history and among themselves."

[203] As this is a study of other ecclesial and theological traditions than the one, I belong to, I have done much reading to understand these traditions, particularly the Ethiopian Orthodox Tewahido Church and the Ethiopian Evangelical Church Mekane Yesus tradition, in their own right, and to present their views as accurately as possible. My ideal follows what I learnt during

As ACT Alliance is an ecumenical project within the framework of the whole ecumenical movement – beyond the World Council of Churches, I have utilised theological resources both from the movement and philosophers and theologians of different traditions. The aim is for the Church "to learn to breathe again with its two lungs: its Eastern one and its Western one", as Cardinal Yves Congar phrased it in words that were often quoted by Pope John Paul II.[204]

The criteria of intersubjective verifiability and reliability are met by the use of written primary sources so that the results can be scrutinised; this means, among other things, observing good citation practice. The issue of being part of the historical process is related to the ACT Appeal in chapter two. The methodology in chapters three, four, and five serves to limit the harmful effects of subjective experience by the use of primary sources unrelated to my person. The historical review of ecumenical models also serves to ground contemporary events in a longer historical context.[205]

1.4 ETH141 ACT Appeal and Research Limitations

To answer the main research question, the thesis will explore and analyse the so-called *ETH141 ACT Appeal* as a case study (chapter two). The ACT appeal was launched during the initial year of intervention, 2014, to support the asylum seekers from South Sudan who ended up in Gambella region, Ethiopia. The case includes the international standards on which the appeal is based (chapter three). Both chapters two and three will be limited to the year 2014. The civil war in South Sudan, attempts at reconciliation and resolution, and continuous efforts at catering for the needs of refugees is a historical process that, since we are dealing with contemporary and not past history, remains to be written.

---

an exchange year at the Roman Catholic Heythrop College in London (1998–99). The lecturers modelled how to present a problem accurately along with different positions and presented the pros and cons of each position. The lecturers were also able to inform of their positions without imposing their views on the diverse class of students.

[204] Wojcichowsky 2013, 229, cf. quote from Protopresbyter Georges Florovsky, the Orthodox patristic scholar, that "the authentic catholicity of the Church must include both the West and the East", and "the centuries-old experience of the Catholic West must be studied and diagnosed by Orthodox theology with greater care and sympathy than has been the case up to now."

[205] Borgehammar 2021, 83 outlines six points on the benefits of historical thinking: to be able to distinguish between the description and the described, be sceptical of the apparently unambiguous, recognise that everything is subject to change, think more independently, reject absolutism, and recognise things belonging together without separating them. Borgehammar refers to Christian Albrecht, *Enzyklopädische Probleme der Praktischen Theologie*, Tübingen 2011.

The refugee assistance in the case will be discussed in relation to the ecclesial context of the two Ethiopian churches of ACT Alliance in the study and previous models for ecumenical collaboration in Ethiopia (chapter four and part of chapter five). The ETH141 will generate questions such as: What is refugee assistance in the form of an ACT response? What sort of assistance is rendered? What are the aims and conditions for the assistance? In what senses are the ACT members working together? What are the principles of the assistance? What does it mean to use international standards as guidelines for the work? What are the basic ideas and principles of the international standards ACT is committed to? The answers to these kinds of questions will specify *the what*: what is the action, in this case, the refugee assistance, of ACT Alliance, defining the genus and specificity of the work. It will also answer part of the *how* with particular reference to how ACT works together. This is the first part of the thesis: chapters two and three.

Chapter four will begin the process of analysing the meaning of churches in *action by churches together* by asking questions about the reasons for and meaning of the assistance and ACT Alliance itself. It should be possible, for example, to find indications that the refugee assistance of ACT Ethiopia Forum carries a Christian understanding of reality. Questions such as: How is the ecumenical engagement motivated and understood by Ethiopian churches? What recognisable signs are there that the refugee assistance of ACT Ethiopia Forum carries a Christian understanding of reality (Christian worldview), the human person, and the mission of the Christian church?

If the research object, ACT Alliance, is neither a super-church, nor an alliance of churches, but of social service organisations, then it needs to be understood what *action by churches together* means, if anything, in that context. If indeed there is some kind of ecclesiality in ACT Alliance and its work. It cannot be assumed from the outset that the ecclesial and theological meaning of the refugee assistance of ACT Alliance is clear. It means that refugee assistance and the principles upon which it is based could show signs of a Christian worldview and a Christian anthropology. By studying how Ethiopian churches historically have been speaking on their commitments to ecumenical collaboration, it should be possible to find indications of the relationship between ACT Alliance and the Christian churches, and the practical sense to which *action by churches together* corresponds. This is the second part of the thesis: chapters four and five.

Research Limitations – Sketches from the Church-In-Aid

The Christian church is present in different forms in the context of aid: There are churches in South Sudan that are impacted by the political crisis and the consequent refugee crisis. There are also church communities in the refugee camps. Furthermore, there are churches in the areas to which refugees seek refuge. Church communities do not visit, but rather live the realities of aid, and seek to serve both their own members and others. Since this research is aimed at ACT Alliance as a manifestation of the church and ecumenical diakonia, other expressions of the life of the *church-in-aid* lie either on the outskirts or outside my research.

The research was initially conceptualised as including a small-scale ethnographical field study in a camp setting in Gambella, with key informant interviews with South Sudanese refugees, field staff and local church communities. It would have allowed refugees, and field staff confined to refugee camps, to reflect the assistance of the ACT members. It would also have allowed local churches to share views on church-based relief assistance. The field study was excluded for three main reasons: To begin with, the primary documents warrant a study of their own. Second, a major field study requires a separate study based on research questions, which documents may not answer, to motivate the intrusion into the privacy of asylum seekers that a field study implies. Third, the risk of spreading COVID-19 made even a smaller field study questionable, and it was subsequently dropped.

For the same reasons, considerations of local church communities in Gambella are left out unless specifically of concern to the ACT appeal. There are therefore opportunities for further research with local field studies.

The thesis leaves out the dynamics of South Sudan, including the civil war, the situation of the churches and the South Sudan Christian Council's efforts of peacebuilding and peace negotiation, except when the ACT Ethiopia Forum is directly concerned. There is a growing literature on the civil war in South Sudan which also relates to the dynamics of aid and civil war and the atrocities taking place despite aid.[206]

I have sketched below some of the forms in which the church is present in the aid context besides the refugee assistance of ACT Alliance. These sketches, which I will now mention, are based on interviews in Addis Ababa with church leaders and refugees and lie outside the proper purview of the thesis. Mentioning these aspects is important as it relates to ACT Alliance as a church institution.

---

[206] Johnson 2016; Perry 2014; Pinaud 2021; de Waal 2014; de Waal 2018 (chapter ten).

There is the life and ministry of the "sending" churches, the churches in South Sudan, who are impacted by the political strife, the violence, and the dispersal of their parishioners. Many South Sudanese Christians have become internally displaced or refugees in neighbouring countries. This may be referred to as *the church in civil crisis*, connoting the challenge of church leadership to handle such a crisis. This may be called *the church in exile* connoting the disintegration and dispersal of the church communities.

There are church communities in the refugee camps. Christians who are refugees are striving to come to grips with what it means to be a Christian and live as a church community in a camp. They worship, teach the Christian faith, set up self-help groups, and contribute to the work of aid organisations as incentive workers, community organisers, and refugee representatives. Christians also share their faith with others, giving hope and light in extreme circumstances. This may be referred to as *the refugee church*.

There are also local church communities, that are impacted by the sudden influx of asylum seekers, whether Christians or not. The churches in the Gambella region attempt to welcome, serve, and integrate the newcomers into the churches. Pastors, priests, catechists, evangelists, and mature Christians serve the Christian communities in the camp. Local churches may send mission teams into the camps to capacitate the refugee churches. Church leaders attempt to bring Christians among the refugees into already existing structures of the local churches and to create new structures to cater for their needs. I will refer to this as *the pastoral life of the local churches* in a refugee crisis.

There are also church communities spread out across Ethiopia bound together by the commonalities of the Christian church but divided into separate churches for historical reasons. Many of these communities are unaware of the refugee influx into Ethiopia or the response by the ACT members and various other bodies. At the national level, those who are part of the relief work are engaged, but on the whole, national churches in Ethiopia are neither aware nor mobilised for a common response. This follows a historical pattern of externalising support systems.

The choice of ACT Alliance as the research object entails that in terms of churches, since only the Ethiopian Orthodox Tewahido Church and the Ethiopian Evangelical Church Mekane Yesus are members of the World Council of Churches and ACT Alliance, only these churches will be looked at in chapter four leaving out a broad spectrum of churches and ecclesial communities in Ethiopia from the Roman Catholic Church to Pentecostal Churches. The same goes with ecumenical organs and Christian aid organisations and similar types of organisations that are not directly involved in ACT Alliance. The exception is chapter five which, for historical reasons and relevance to the research subject, will mention other ecumenical collaborative schemes. Still, chapter five will not give the full picture. The churches' engagement in society is so broad and deep that it is difficult for any researcher to do justice to it.

The thesis analyses *ecumenical diakonia* (*diakonie*) as conceived by the World Council of Churches, set in motion by ACT Alliance as an *action by churches together*, and operationalised in the ACT appeal system. This thesis will therefore not be able to discuss properly the church in crisis in South Sudan, the church in exile as parishes are split apart, the refugee church as the church members become asylum seekers and live in refugee camps, or the pastoral church of the host communities that are affected by the refugee influx. This pastoral concern of the churches is protected by Human Rights specifically within article 4 of the 1967 Protocol Relating to the Status of Refugees that was built upon and improved the original and time-limited United Nations Refugee Convention from 1951.

These reflect different aspects of *diakonia as church ministry*, which is important for a more comprehensive understanding of the church in aid than what one thesis may deal with. The "national churches" will be discussed in chapter four with their ecumenical commitments and in chapter five concerning earlier models of ecumenical collaboration.

Also, regarding ACT Alliance, not all the issues relating to the ecumenical diakonia will be covered. The research is limited to analysing the refugee assistance of the ACT Ethiopia Forum members using the primary material of the ETH141 appeal and the international standards used in the appeal in the light of the main research question. This study is thus limited by its primary research question, the case study of the ETH141 appeal and its primary documents, the Ethiopian side of the ACT response, and ACT Alliance in the form of its Ethiopian forum. Aspects of the historical context will not be comprehensive but aim to deepen the understanding of the case study of the refugee appeal and the principles of refugee assistance and its significance for a deeper understanding of ACT Alliance.

1.5 Outline

This first chapter, *the Ecclesiology of Acting Together,* has introduced the ecclesial problem of church and aid built into ACT Alliance, the topic of the refugee crisis and assistance in Ethiopia, and the case of the ETH141 ACT Appeal. In *Earlier Research and Background to ACT Alliance* (1.1), it was stated that research on aid in general and African churches, in particular, have largely ignored the ecclesial questions of church and aid despite the fact that churches and their agencies are both involved in aid and affected by aid and its potentially harmful effects. In *Research Problem, Questions, and Material* (1.2), the research problem was formulated, and some fundamental issues were posed: In what sense is ACT Alliance and *action by churches together*? And how does the refugee assistance of ACT Alliance correspond to a Christian worldview and the churches' mission? In section *A Historical and Theological Approach* (1.3) it was deliberated on the historical and theological approach of the thesis. The *ETH141 ACT Appeal and Research Limitations* (1.4) described the historical case of the South Sudanese refugee response (the ETH141 ACT Appeal) which frames the research limitations of the thesis.

Chapter two, *The ETH141 ACT Appeal – Assisting Refugees*, contains the case of the ETH141 ACT Appeal to support South Sudanese refugees in Ethiopia for the sake of identifying the aims, methodologies, conditions, and challenges of the refugee assistance rendered by the ACT Ethiopia forum. It is a textual study and in the first section, *Sources to the Appeal* (2.1), the primary sources of the appeal, the appeal documents, and auxiliary primary documents are outlined. In the second section, *Emergency Preparedness* (2.2) the preparedness of the ACT Ethiopia Forum is discussed and the question of why churches engage with refugee assistance is brought up. *ACT Response to the Refugee Crisis* (2.3) analyses the response in terms of examining the alert, the preliminary appeal, and the full ETH141 ACT Appeal documents in light of the events in 2014. The next section *A Silent Crisis Is Rapidly Evolving* (2.4) discusses the challenges the ACT Ethiopia Forum faced in meeting the needs of the refugees once the appeal was launched. As the lack of funding was critical, the last section of the chapter, *Funding Tension: The Ideal and the Practical* (2.5) discusses the tension between the appeal mechanism for assistance and the practical challenges refugee assistance brings about.

Chapter three, *International Framework and Stakeholders,* identifies the main principles of the ETH141 ACT Appeal by a textual study of the international standards to which the ACT appeal adheres, for the sake of deepening the discussion on the fundamental goals and principles of the assistance. The first section, *A Commitment to High Standards* (3.1) describes and discusses the international standards referred to in the ETH141 ACT Appeal in chapter two. The aim is to map the contemporary institutional framework of humanitarian assistance and to identify the main principles outlined in the international standards referred to in the ETH141 appeal. This is the main section of the chapter which all the rest depends upon. In the second section, *The Humanitarian Moral Argument* (3.2), it is argued that the basis for humanitarian work is a moral argument from natural law, what I call the "humanitarian argument." The humanitarian imperative is framed as a categorical imperative and applied in international standards. Here basic morality is viewed as common among all peoples. In the next section, *Action Based on International Law* (3.3), it is argued that despite the differences between *International Humanitarian Law* (IHL), *International Refugee Law* (IRL), and *International Human Rights Law* (IHRL), these legal systems are based on the idea of the rule of law and natural law morality. This implies that the intent of law is to protect the weak against the strong, outlaw reckless political action, and to permit relief assistance. Thus, there is a law-based approach within humanitarian action in line with Christian teaching on morality as God-given to all. In *African Gate Keeper States and Stakeholders* (3.4) deals with the fact that *ACT Alliance* is not acting in a social and political vacuum but in a context that became more complex because of how modern African states mimic colonial policies of what is known as the gate keeper state. Finally, in *Morality, Principled Action, and the Church* (3.5), a plausible relation between morality, legality, and church tradition is argued for. This discussion grounds the discussion on the traditions of the Orthodox and the Mekane Yesus churches. It is the focus of the following chapter.

Chapter four, *Ethiopian Churches: Ecumenical Engagement*, sets the idea of ACT Alliance as action by churches together in relation to views of the Ethiopian Orthodox Tewahedo Church and the Ethiopian Evangelical Church Mekane Yesus for the sake of contributing to a discussion on ecclesial engagement, and the question of how the ecumenical engagement has been motivated, understood, and critiqued by Ethiopian churches. The first section, *A Letter from Mekane Yesus 1972* (4.1) is a textual analysis of one important text from the Ethiopian Evangelical Church Mekane Yesus, *On the Interrelation between the Proclamation of the Gospel and Human Development*, (also called *the ECMY Letter*). The church officers wrote the ECMY Letter to the Lutheran World Federation in 1972 as a critique of a donor-oriented aid model in favour of a church-led aid model. *Passover Message 1983 from the Ethiopian Orthodox* (4.2) analyses the texts of a booklet written to showcase the church and its commitment to ecumenical collaboration for Ecumenical donors in 1983. (4.3) *Gospel and Liturgy Form the Christian* uses insights from liturgical theology to discuss the role of the historical liturgy in forming Christians to those on the margin of the community. I also expand on the evangelical understanding of the gospel outlined in the ECMY Letter to clarify the importance of the gospel. The section *Voluntary Societies and Church Contributions* (4.4), takes up the question of the voluntary nature of the work. The last section, *Ethiopian Church Basis for Ecumenical Engagement* (4.5) brings the two Ethiopian views together in light of the present engagement in ACT Alliance and offers a concluding discussion on the voices from the Ethiopian churches.

Chapter five, *Ecumenical Models: For Acting Together,* sets the contemporary work of ACT Alliance into a larger historical context by naming some historical initiatives of ecumenical collaboration in Ethiopia and drawing attention to the fact that ecumenical bodies may be very different in nature. By using heuristic models based on different historical forms of ecumenical collaboration in Ethiopia the intent is to sketch ecumenical strategies from the mid-twentieth century (1944) to the beginning of the twenty-first (2014) and compare them with the contemporary ACT approach. The first section, *The Mission Model and the Integrated Church* (1944–1974) (5.1) summarises the post-Second World War approach of integrating a holistic sense of mission with the Ethiopian Evangelical Church Mekane Yesus. *The Inter-Church Aid Model* (1965–1984) (5.2) depicts the ecumenical approach of Western Churches showing practical solidarity with the Ethiopian Orthodox Tewahido Church in consequence of a sense of unity, *koinonia*, of the Christian Church. *The International Crisis Model* (1974–1991) (5.3) outlines some of the major collaborative schemes by ecumenical agencies bringing relief to Ethiopia during conflict and military regime. *ACT in Ethiopia* (1994–2014) (5.4) outlines the first years of ACT as an ecumenical enterprise in Ethiopia. The final section *Comparing Historical Models and ACT Alliance* (5.5) brings the different ecumenical approaches to a comparative discussion of the present ACT Alliance.

Chapter six, *Action by Churches Together,* discusses the findings of the study of ACT Alliance as an action by churches together, discusses the conclusions, and summarises the dissertation. It therefore discusses different senses of *action by churches together* by considering the case of refugee assistance, a principled approach, theological and ecclesial foundations, and models for common action. The first section, *The ACT Appeal and Its Standards* (6.1) discusses what the actual work, the refugee assistance, and the stated principles say about the meaning and extension of the action by churches together of ACT Alliance. *The Churches and Ecumenical Models* (6.2) brings the voices of the churches and the historical experiences into a discussion on ACT Alliance. *What "Action by Churches Together" Is and Is Not* (6.3) discusses the attributes of ACT Alliance in the ETH141 appeal and its principles and different senses of *action by churches together. Beyond ACT Alliance* (6.4) briefly discuss the matter of church ministry, *diakonia*, beyond the work of ACT Alliance. Last in the chapter, *Concluding Discussion* (6.5), will state the general conclusions of the dissertation in brief form.

2. The ETH141 ACT Appeal: Assisting Refugees

This chapter contains the case of the ETH141 ACT Appeal, ETH141 for short, for the sake of identifying the aims, methodologies, conditions, and challenges of the refugee assistance rendered by ACT Alliance members in Ethiopia, the so-called ACT Ethiopia Forum.[1] The chapter will describe the appeal (synchronic) and the historical process (diachronic) of the refugee assistance to South Sudanese asylum seekers.

The assistance took place in Gambella regional state, Ethiopia in 2014. The analysis is a textual study of primary sources with a focus on the ETH141 ACT Appeal documents, i.e. the alert, the preliminary appeal, and the full appeal.

Figure 2.1: *UNHCR Map locating the Gambella Region in Ethiopia which received asylum seekers from the civil war in South Sudan. The ETH141 ACT Appeal was launched by the ACT members in Ethiopia to serve the basic needs of these refugees of the conflict. Map: UNHCR Partners in Gambella Region, January 2023 by UNHCR SO Gambella Program Unit, 13 Jan. 2023.*

The focus of the whole chapter will thus be on the ACT members working in Ethiopia that are constituting the ACT Ethiopia Forum. It is their intervention

---

[1] Both ACT Alliance Ethiopia Forum and ACT Ethiopia Forum have been used in documents. The thesis will use the shorter form.

for the South Sudanese that will be studied. The refugees fled civil war and sought refuge in Gambella, a regional state in Western Ethiopia, bordering South Sudan. The appeal system is significant as a common plan for intervention, as a tool for resource mobilisation, and as the prescribed way for ACT relief coordination.

When violence broke out in Juba, the capital city of South Sudan, on December 15, 2013, and reports were spread about killings, relief organisations prepared themselves to meet the demands of an expected humanitarian crisis. The violence in Juba quickly spread and led to a refugee situation with internally displaced people in South Sudan and numerous asylum seekers leaving the country in search of refuge in Uganda, Kenya, and Ethiopia. The ACT Alliance office in Geneva coordinated a regional Skype meeting on December 20 with representatives from ACT members in South Sudan, its neighbouring countries, and Europe. An ACT Alert was issued the same day with "a brief description of the emergency and impact so far", a "rationale for an ACT response", a "summary of the humanitarian response so far", and an indication of planned activities that require financial support. The ACT Alert was the first document put in place of the humanitarian appeal system of the global ACT Alliance in response to the South Sudanese crisis.[2]

ACT Alliance globally has some 140 members, with a vast majority of them being faith-based agencies and churches from the global south. The ACT Ethiopia Forum in 2014 consisted of eleven members, with the Ethiopian Programme of the Lutheran World Federation World Service (here on LWF World Service), two church-based Ethiopian members, and nine Christian development and relief agencies from churches in Denmark, England, Germany, Netherlands, Norway, Sweden, Switzerland, and the USA. The ACT members, as agencies, each have differences in focus and aims of their work but come together in the loose form of cooperation as a forum with the authority of issuing ACT appeals in case of emergency.[3] The presence of both Ethiopian and northern-based organisations and the frequent appearances of emergencies make the ACT Ethiopia Forum an interesting showcase of the work of the global ACT Alliance.[4]

The first section of the chapter, *Sources to the Appeal* (2.1), will look at the primary sources available for researching the ETH141 appeal, and the second, *Emergency Preparedness* (2.2), the emergency preparedness of the ACT Ethiopia forum.

---

[2] 2013 12 20 Notes Skype Call South Sudan. 2013 12 20 Alert 48:2013 South Sudan Conflict.

[3] These differences are significant in themselves, and a proper study of the identity and history of each organisation would require several separate studies.

[4] 13 ACT members have signed the MoU of the ACT Ethiopia Forum from Oct 2012. In 2014, 11 members were active. See chapter one, s 46, n145.

The third, *ACT Response to the Refugee Crisis* (2.3), will examine the appeal documents with a regional ACT alert from December 20, 2013, a preliminary ACT appeal from December 30 of the same year, and the ACT Ethiopia Forum full appeal document from February 12, 2014. The initial focus will be on the aims, and methodology described in the appeal documents, and then the focus will shift to the historical process by viewing the main conditions and challenges faced by the forum when the appeal was launched. The fourth section, *A Silent Crisis Is Rapidly Evolving* (2.4), will sketch the challenges the ACT Ethiopia Forum encountered once the appeal was launched, and the fifth and final section, *Funding Tension: The Ideal and the Practical* (2.5), will analyse the implications that follow from the fact that the appeal was underfunded and discuss the tension between the appeal mechanism and the practical challenges the ACT members faced when bringing about the response to the refugee crisis.

2.1 Sources to the Appeal

How do ACT agencies respond to a crisis, and how does ACT Alliance raise the resources needed for the response? The primary instrument for responding to emergencies within ACT Alliance is *the ACT appeal system.*

Figure 2.2: *ACT Alliance steps in an emergency with the ACT Appeal System: an ACT Alert, Preliminary Appeal, and Full Appeal produced at the beginning of the appeal process. The planning and writing of the appeal is followed by a time of implementation of the plan laid out in the appeal and reported upon for accountability of the funding raised and the work performed. The end of the appeal is marked with the final reporting and evaluation of the assistance. The appeal documents (alert, preliminary appeal, and full appeal) are vital for an understanding of the refugee assistance and the requirements for each step of the process belong to the prescribed relief coordination of ACT Alliance. The ACT Appeal system stresses the importance of raising an alert within 24 hours of a crisis, followed up by a preliminary appeal within 7 days, and the full appeal within 30 days to intervene as soon as possible.*

Raising Relief Support to a Crisis Situation

ACT was initially created as an organisation for relief response, *ACT International*. It was an organ for collaborating and coordinating the relief response of an alliance of churches and faith-based aid organisations with links to the World Council of Churches (WCC) and the Lutheran World Federation (LWF). In 2007 *ACT Development* was founded as a separate organisation and in 2011 ACT International and ACT Development became *ACT Alliance* merging the relief and development efforts for a better continuity from relief to development. Still, relief response is at the heart of the alliance and the ACT appeal system is the main vehicle for a coordinated response.[5]

The appeal system was designed to be an instrument of coordination and cooperation between ACT members, and the appeal document is required for funding by those ACT members who are raising funds for emergencies. The ACT appeal appears in three stages: as an alert, as a preliminary appeal, and as the final, or full, appeal. The *ACT alert* document is intended to give a "heads-up" notice that external resources may be needed for an emergency. When there is an emergency, be it a natural disaster or a man-made crisis, the ACT forum in the country, after performing a quick assessment, may issue an ACT alert. The alert is followed up within a seven-day deadline by a *preliminary appeal* document with more details about the emergency and planned response. It is then followed by a *full ACT appeal* document, with additional narratives, a logical framework of the response plan, a budget, and statistics, sent by the forum within 30 days.[6]

ACT Members that are seeking financial support through the appeal system are called *requesting members*. These agencies are the ones doing the implementation – the actual work on the ground – of the emergency response activities based on the plan in the appeal. Funds come from *funding ACT members* allocating resources, and contributing to the appeal in other ways, such as communication, advocacy, monitoring, and evaluation. The *national ACT forum* is responsible for coordination of the emergency response while *the ACT secretariat* in Geneva is responsible for global coordination and the issuing of the appeal documents on its webpage.[7]

In this case, the full Ethiopian ACT appeal, named *ETH141 ACT Appeal*, was published on February 12, 2014, requesting 3,5 million USD for the emergency response of the Lutheran World Federation (LWF) and the Ethiopian Orthodox

---

[5] ACT Alliance presentation for ACT members, Powerpoint presentation, March 2010.

[6] ACT Alliance Response to and Emergency: Dec 2011.

[7] ACT Alliance Response to and Emergency: Dec 2011.

Church Development and Inter Church Aid Commission (EOC-DICAC) working in close collaboration with the International Orthodox Christian Charities (IOCC). Apart from the Ethiopian appeal, there was also a Kenyan (KEN141), a Ugandan (UGA141) and an ACT appeal issued from South Sudan (SSD141), all in all with planned budgets exceeding eight million USD.[8]

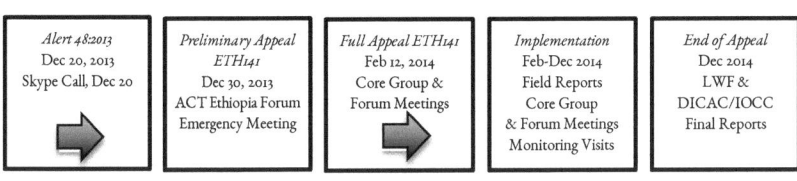

Figure 2.3: *The common regional ACT Alert 48:2013 (Dec 20, 2013) initiated a response through the work with the Ethiopian Preliminary (Dec 30, 2013) and the Final Appeal ETH141 (Feb 12, 2014). The illustrations show some of the components in the different stages of the appeal, such as Skype calls for coordination, emergency, core group and forum meetings, assessments, field reports, monitoring visits and final reports. The ETH141 emergency response led to revisions in the appeal itself and the setup of an alternative form of collaboration from that of the appeal system – that of a consortium, not shown in the figure. So the implementation did not actually end in Dec 2014.*

Documents are produced in aid work which may be used as primary sources in research. In this case, *the ETH141 ACT Appeal document* with its preceding forms, *the ACT Alert*, and *the Preliminary Appeal* documents, constitutes the plan which not only directs the actual work but also sets up requirements for reporting and evaluation which for the researcher gives a paper trail to follow in the investigation into the specific work of refugee assistance. Even when the humanitarian situation on the ground necessitates major changes, a revised appeal would be written based on the original appeal. The already mentioned ACT alert, through a preliminary appeal, resulted in the ETH141 ACT Appeal document published on February 12, 2014. These appeal documents will be used as primary sources supplemented by reports and minutes from meetings.[9]

---

[8] ACT Appeals: ETH141 ACT Appeal in Ethiopia, Kenya KEN141 Preliminary Appeal; Uganda UGA141 Preliminary Appeal; SSD141 Preliminary Appeal South Sudan.

[9] See unpublished sources in the bibliography for a list of the more important primary sources. See appendix A For ETH141 Primary Sources directly linked to the appeal.

The Study of the Primary Sources of the Appeal

How is it feasible to analyse these documents and answer the research questions? By using these documents as source documents and written records from historical developments, it is possible to analyse both the planned ACT response and its follow-up in terms of reports and meetings. The ETH141 document represents an ACT appeal. It is an appeal, i.e. a request for funding on behalf of people at risk. The appeal is based on a plan for intervention. The appeal also functions as a basic tool for accountability complete with an approach, goals set, and requirements for operation including a budget proposal. For a potential donor, the full ACT appeal document is intended to give a good overview of these three aspects. These documents were not written to be used as academic sources, but to be used for a specific purpose. This gives limitations to what kind of questions these documents will be able to answer. Therefore, for the study of the main documents of the ETH141 ACT Appeal, the main task will be to ask for the *intentio auctoris*, the original function and purpose of the authors, regarding the structure of the documents, and the main content therein. This way the documents will be able to communicate the main idea, objectives, and process of the appeal.[10]

An analysis of the documents will allow the authors of these texts to speak also to the research questions respecting the integrity of the sources and their purpose. The analysis of the main documents of the ETH141 ACT Appeal will be done in the light of context, both in terms of the historical process itself, and in the immediate textual context of auxiliary documents such as minutes of meetings, policy documents and agreements related to the appeal, the ACT forum, and ACT Alliance: see appendix A and below figure 2.4.

The "auxiliary documents" represent the collaborative work of the appeal, the internal communication between the ACT Ethiopia Forum members: This regarded the so-called "core group" of members during its first months. Minutes of meetings capture oral communication and events in a selected and partial way, designed to briefly capture the essence of what was said, the decisions made, and the next steps in terms of action. These auxiliary documents will give us a fair chance to describe the process and the arguments of the forum members making explicit what is implicit in the appeal documents. The main line of argument will follow the ACT appeal process and the historical events it sparked.

---

[10] See chapter one for a fuller account on the epistemology of the thesis as a whole.

A source critical approach has been used in relation to the documents.[11] It has been important to identify the source in terms of legitimacy, check for dependencies and tendencies, and make contextual checks with facts. A special case is the prevalence of operational "draft" documents in relief work. Ideally, documents used in relief work are properly dated, named, and signed, but that is not always the case. In some cases in aid work, a "draft" is not a draft in the sense of being a hypothetical document. It may function as an operational document, and people may act upon it, despite its draft status. It may be that the status is related to an ambition to publish the document at a later stage, complete with illustrations and case studies, while the content, (a policy, strategy, or guideline), of the document as such is a finished product.

Significance for Appeal	Type of Documents	Primary Material
Main primary documents	Appeal Documents	Alert
		Preliminary Appeal
		Full Appeal
		Reports
Auxiliary Documents	Coordination of Response	Core Group
		Communication material
		Consortium
	Forum Documents	Membership
		MoU
		Regular Meetings

Figure 2.4: The appeal documents are analysed in the context of auxiliary documents such as coordination of the appeal (minutes of core group meetings, communication material and consortium meetings) and forum documents in general (regular and emergency meetings as well as Memorandum of Understanding (MoU) and similar documents). See appendix A for a list of meetings and material, and unpublished sources for specific documents.

Relief work is finally not primarily about documents, but about practical work in concrete situations. Documents are tools produced for the sake of the work, not the other way around. It means that some staff members rather than polishing a document may put their energy into the actual work to assist people in need. Necessity forces people onto new tasks and a draft document may never officially be

---

[11] Bradley and Muller 1995. Marius and Page 2010. Hallencreutz 1981.

finalised. It may also happen that some documents are not finalised, stamped, and signed because of inherent disagreements. Documents are helpful in the work, but only to a point, and may lack a value of its own beyond its instrumentality.[12]

It is in head offices, and the offices of donors, that documents may take more of a symbolic value of its own. This is because the staff are trained to follow the trail of documents. They act like accountants for whom a missing link in the paper trail may indicate that funds have been diverted to other ends. In relief work that may be the case, but mistakes are also made because of other causes. These may be related to extreme working conditions as staff deal with practical issues such as electricity cuts, internet failure, or a physical computer breakdown. Staff under pressure to work simultaneously on several difficult tasks also may make mistakes.

In the work with the documents, carefully analysing various documents using source critical methods therefore is part of the methodology. The documents from the ACT agencies and the forum have been accessed by the researcher in printed and digital form. Digital files may contain metadata which may give indications as to when a document was created or modified. At times an author may be named. Comparing the date in the file name of the document with the metadata may help certify the date it was produced, or last edited.[13]

Relief work is evidence-based, which means there is data available on needs, resources, outputs, and impact. Project documents therefore often contain numbers and statistics. It may be the number of people in need of assistance, the proportion of women and men, age groups, and people with special needs. It may be resources, either stockpiled or a calculation of resources required. It may also be a quantitative measurement of achievements, such as counting the number of latrines, schools, or water systems produced and compared with the estimated need. These numbers are tools used to judge the best cause of action in the light of the best evidence available. There are, however, different kinds of statistical numbers. There is a difference between projected numbers used to produce possible future scenarios and actual numbers carefully counted and registered by field staff. Any

---

[12] As in all human interaction – people disagree about the most appropriate course of action. A rational discourse does not have to entail immediate agreement – quite the contrary. A document that stays in a draft status may therefore represent a dispute, but that is not always the case.

[13] One example was a file in which the file name was dated incorrectly. By contextual fact checking and consultation of the file meta data it was possible to determine that the file referring to "Jan 2014" actually came from "April 2014". The error was deemed to be a typo by one or another individual handling the file.

reading of these documents and usage of these numbers in research need to take into consideration what kind of numbers are specified in each case.[14]

2.2 Emergency Preparedness

The first aspect of intentionality and preparedness for refugee assistance regards the establishment of ACT Alliance itself and by extension the institution of the ACT Ethiopia Forum. According to the memorandum of understanding of the forum, the main objective "is to increase the effectiveness and impact of the ecumenical humanitarian emergency and development response to persons and communities in the country."[15] There is thus a dual focus – emergency and development response. As a forum for relief response – every emergency may be considered for response.

Why would the churches engage with refugee assistance and how would they prepare for an emergency response? It is difficult to find any deliberations on why the ACT Ethiopia Forum should respond to the emergency with South Sudanese asylum seekers pouring into the safety of the Ethiopian side of the border in the written sources for the ETH141 refugee appeal. The appeal documents ask: "Why is an ACT response needed?[16] And answers by stating the seriousness of the situation and citing protection issues, thus assuming rather than discussing the motives for the refugee response. The reasons are taken for granted. The authors call attention to the "humanitarian" needs of the people seeking refuge with the implicit argument that ACT should contribute to the support of refugees "in fulfilling their rights for dignified living"[17] through the instrument of the appeal.[18] There are, however, aspects of the question "why" which may be analysed from the

---

[14] A more comprehensive picture of the appeal, the actual work on the ground, the impact on and the reflections of the people involved would have been gained by an extensive field work in the refugee camps and nearby communities, in Gambella town in, and Addis Ababa. There would be much to gain from such a work. In an ideal scenario this would be included in the present work. This however was not feasible due to COVID-19. It would however be possible to follow up the present thesis with an ethnographical approach gathering more information and more views on the work. For now, however, it is outside of the limitations of the present thesis.

[15] 2009 12 18 ACT Alliance Ethiopia Forum MoU. The forum is at times referred to as ACT Ethiopia Forum (AEF) and at times as ACT Alliance Ethiopia Forum (AAEF), in this thesis the shorter form will be used. The MoU was first signed in 2009 and later updated in 2012.

[16] 2013 12 20 Alert 48:2013 South Sudan Conflict, "Why is an ACT response needed?

[17] 2013 12 30 ETH141 South Sudanese Refugees Preliminary Appeal: "Overall Goal"

[18] 2014 02 12 ETH141 Asylum Seekers South Sudan 12 Feb 2014. Requesting 3.5M USD.

appeal documents regarding preparation and planning, and we will now turn to those aspects.

At the beginning of 2012, when Sudanese asylum seekers sought protection in the Benishangul-Gumuz regional state, Ethiopia, LWF World Service had independently raised an ACT Alert (ETH121) to seek financial support for intervention in the Sherkole and Tongo refugee camps. The background was that the government refugee authority, ARRA, and the UNHCR had directly requested the LWF World Service to intervene in the refugee assistance of the camps.[19] The issue of the independent alert was raised during an ACT retreat the same month. A complaint was raised that no communication regarding the alert had reached the forum and that there is a "need for a long term plan and cross border perspectives." In response, another question was raised: "Can we [as a forum] act as a fire brigade to every emergency?"[20] For LWF World Service the issue was clear: "The entry point is emergency. The initial demand is only about the first year."[21] It means, LWF World Service as a relief agency focusing on refugee assistance did not want to wait for forum deliberations when there was an urgent need to respond. Other ACT members would be able to contribute to the work of LWF World Service – particularly in strengthening the long-term assistance to the refugees. If LWF was to respond, it had to be immediate, and by raising an alert, it showed ARRA and UNHCR that LWF World Service was serious by contributing with financial resources, through an ACT-appeal, to an operation mainly financed through the UN, through its back donors. LWF has the ability and preparedness to quickly draw up a proposal on their own, but if LWF World Service would have to wait for the forum, the question would be – would it be too late to act?[22]

The ACT Ethiopia Forum – and the member agencies – have been set up for emergency and development response. For relief agencies – the question then is not whether some people are worthy of a response and others not. Any human deserves support in a life-threatening situation. That is the moral answer that is part of the raison d'être of these agencies. The forum is intended as the main vehicle for emergency preparedness for ACT Alliance and by extension the churches – a joint venture to share information and jointly plan, prioritise, make strategic decisions, seek funding, and coordinate emergency response.[23] To make these

---

[19] 2012 02 02 Alert 04:2012 (ETH121) Emergency Assistance to Sudanese Refugees in Ethiopia.

[20] 2012 02 14–15 ACT Ethiopia Forum Retreat. # 8 of the regular ACT meeting.

[21] 2012 02 14–15 ACT Ethiopia Forum Retreat. # 8 of the regular ACT meeting.

[22] 2012 02 14–15 ACT Ethiopia Forum Retreat. # 8 of the regular ACT meeting.

[23] 2009 12 18 ACT Alliance Ethiopia Forum MoU "Objectives."

objectives feasible, all members agree to adhere to a code of conduct and follow proper procedures,[24] holding one another accountable to high standards, and collaborate in a spirit of a "participatory gathering of peers" in which each member participates "to the best of their ability."[25]

If every emergency may be considered for a relief response, how would the actors know whether to respond or not?[26] To begin with, there are deliberations regarding the tactical and strategic issue of whether to engage. These are not about the deeper motives behind the work, yet they are important because when an emergency crisis appears, ACT agencies act in very different ways as we shall see in this section. These deliberations primarily take the form of emergency preparedness and agency and forum deliberations of whether or not to engage and launch an appeal. Therefore, we turn to the question of to what extent the ACT Ethiopia Forum was prepared to respond.

How did the ACT members prepare for the intervention? There was a general preparedness before the outbreak of a crisis and a particular preparation after a crisis event. Here, a distinction needs to be kept in mind between the preparedness within a particular ACT member, and the preparedness in the form of the common effort of the forum. For the general preparation of the forum, before the outbreak of the crisis, several things were in place. The forum itself was well established, with regular forum meetings allowing its members to deliberate on and decide upon emergency issues.[27] The forum had its structure and procedures were in place for handling different matters.[28] An *emergency preparedness response plan* (EPRP) was in the stage of a late draft document, not yet decided upon, but progress had been made.[29] ACT Alliance has its own ACT appeal system with structures and requirements for how an emergency response is to be handled.[30] Unless committed to and acted upon, these steps of preparedness may remain on a policy level and not translate into practical action.

---

[24] 2009 12 18 ACT Alliance Ethiopia Forum MoU 1.1 "ACT Alliance Ethiopia Forum: Introduction." For the code of conduct and other international standards, see chapter three.

[25] 2009 12 18 ACT Alliance Ethiopia Forum MoU "Basic Operating Principles for AAEF."

[26] Anderson and Woodrow 1989, 27–35.

[27] A committee was set up in 1998 with the first ACT emergency appeal in Ethiopia in 1999. 2010 05 27 AFET81 Final Report. The ACT forum also deals with matters related to development work, advocacy, and the agencies' relatedness to the churches. See chapter five.

[28] 2009 12 18 ACT Alliance Ethiopia Forum MoU.

[29] 2013 04 12 ACT Ethiopia Forum draft EPRP. 2013 10 25 LWF input to EPRP.

[30] 2013 12 04 ACT Alliance Response to an Emergency: Policy, Guidelines and Tools draft.

The ACT Ethiopia Forum functions as a forum, a loose network of organisations that are all members of ACT Alliance and all committed through a *Memorandum of Understanding* (MoU) to collaborate the efforts of these otherwise autonomous organisations in particular ways.[31] As such, the forum is not registered, or legalised, as an entity separate from its member organisations. The issue of formalising the forum as a separate organisation has been there since an early stage,[32] and the intention has been to "investigate and consider a possible future legal registration",[33] but for now, the forum was unable to move forward on this issue.[34]

Hiring a coordinator is of importance for the institutionalisation of a coordination device. Hence the ACT Ethiopia Forum also had shared the financial responsibility of an ACT staff member acting as ACT Coordinator. The staff member would work on commonly decided issues such as appeal coordination, according to a term of reference decided upon by the forum, but with employment from one registered ACT member, the so-called host agency. Historically, the Norwegian Church Aid (NCA) had shouldered that responsibility as host agency since the formation of the forum, hence the ACT coordinator had been formally employed by the Norwegian Church Aid.[35]

In December 2013, however, no ACT Coordinator was employed.[36] Hence, no one could take on administrative tasks on behalf of the ACT Ethiopia Forum.[37]

---

[31] 2009 12 18 ACT Alliance Ethiopia Forum MoU.

[32] E.g. the discussion of legality was brought to the attention of ACT Development Geneva in 2008. 2008 02 13 ACT meeting "Minutes of ACT – D/Ethiopia Consultative meeting."

[33] ACT Alliance Ethiopia Forum MoU Dec 2009. The wording is not present in the MoU from Dec 2012.

[34] A new legislation was promulgated 2009 with stricter regulation making it unfeasible to register the forum.

[35] ACT Alliance Ethiopia Forum MoU Dec 2009. In the MoU from Dec 2012 the one "host agency" was changed into "facilitating agencies" to enable several ACT members to share different facilitating tasks of the forum.

[36] A salaried ACT Coordinator was hired until mid-2012. 2012 12 31 NCA-E ACT Ethiopia Forum Appeal Coordination Financial Statement Dec 31, 2012. 2012 12 31 NCA-E ACT Ethiopia Forum Financial Statement Dec 31, 2012. Instead, a coordination committee was established with the chair, vice chair, and two forum members. The commissionaires of EOC-DICAC and EECMY-DASSC would always be part of this committee. As the previous institution of a host agency had been replaced with the possibility of facilitation agencies according to agreement and need, the administrative strength of the forum was very limited by Nov 2013.

[37] 2012 06 04 ETH111 working group 4 June 2012. The Norwegian Church Aid was managing the budget and financial resources, including financial audit and reporting. For some tasks focusing on the forum meetings, a part-time administrative assistant would be hired on a contract and trial basis. A proposal was put forward in December 2013, before the South Sudanese crisis.

The agreement of the forum was therefore to hire staff according to need, as in case of an emergency when additional work would be needed, and the additional financial cost could be forwarded to the appeal for coordination.[38]

By the time of the beginning of the crisis, the forum – as a forum – was simultaneously understaffed as well as overwhelmed with other issues to deal with.[39] The forum also encountered the newly developing church schism between the Ethiopian Evangelical Church Mekane Yesus (EECMY) on the one hand and the Church of Sweden (CoS) and the Evangelical Lutheran Church in America (ELCA) on the other regarding the introduction of same-sex marriage (CoS) and ordination of openly gay ordained ministers (ELCA). The ACT forum is not the venue for such theological discussions, but the developments were disconcerting

---

[38] AEF Coordination Committee Agenda 13 Dec 2013. E.g. In Jan 2013 it was decided to hire a consultant to prepare the annual report of ETH111 according to a previously (Dec 2012) agreed upon ToR. ACT Ethiopia Forum AGM 17 Jan 2013. The salary of a coordinator used to be the single largest expense of the forum, whether there was an active emergency appeal or not. The forum had become hesitant regarding the value of a permanent salaried coordinator and the previous contract had been terminated. Part of the reason for the termination was the perception that the coordinator "was ACT". The reasoning was that if each ACT member would be taking on more responsibility, a common ownership of ACT would be fostered.

[39] AEF Coordination Committee Agenda 13 Dec 2013. There were issues of action, planning and administration such as finalising the emergency preparedness response plan (EPRP), an action plan for 2014, budget and membership issues, the issue of an administrative assistant), issues coming from "above" – from the ACT Secretariat in Geneva (an upcoming ACT regional consultation in Nairobi, policy discussions on the "changing development agenda" and "How disasters disrupt development", the issue of establishing regional offices, a draft proposal of a global ACT Strategic Plan for 2015–2018), and any other business (such as an upcoming WCC -ILO meeting, the need to update the forum contact list, the usage of a common Dropbox folder, and farewell and welcoming parties of member of the ACT Ethiopia Forum). These type of issues enables the forum – and therefore local ACT members to participate in policy issues decided at the global level of the alliance and, as such, are to be treated as opportunities to give voice from particular contexts. Few national organisations – including large ones such as EECMY-DASSC and EOC-DICAC have the equivalent of policy department like the Northern ACT members for whom such organisational capacity has long-standing traditions. Consultancies of this kind, therefore, are difficult to handle in the forum as previous internal discussions have not taken place in the national organisations. It is not an impossible task as many national staff members have long work experience, are well educated, and are rooted in their respective organisational cultures, but it takes time and resources to facilitate meaningful discussions. Of necessity, requests for input from the ACT Secretariat have fairly short deadlines in order to move issues forward. The issue of the "new development paradigm" was raised in the Nov 21 forum meeting, discussion was facilitated by DCA on Dec 2, and feedback was due Dec 31. 2013 11 21 ACT Ethiopia Forum AGM Minutes.

and made collaboration more difficult.[40] In addition to these issues, consideration also had to be made regarding other emergencies.[41]

When the ACT Ethiopia Forum was holding its last regular meeting for the year, Thursday December 19, 2013, South Sudan was not yet on the agenda. News about the crisis, from December 15, had not yet reached the forum coordination committee. Apart from normal agenda items such as budget endorsement and comments on the new strategic plan, the ACT members were discussing two other crisis situations, a hailstorm in Southern Wollo, and the sudden evacuation of some 150 000 Ethiopians being thrown out of Saudi Arabia and airlifted to Ethiopia.[42]

---

[40] The EECMY Sixth Council meeting in 2010 had critiqued the actions taken by CoS and ELCA. The EECMY General Assembly in January 2013 decided to break up its bilateral partnerships with CoS and ELCA. EECMY GA 2013 President Report. 2013 02 11 EECMY News Release 11 Feb 2013. How this would impact CoS - DASSC collaboration was still an open question. The church schism caused by ELCA and CoS would require its treatise. For EECMY the issue is first, a matter of fidelity to scripture and the evangelical faith and, as such, a prerequisite for partnership in the common mission of God, second, a matter of the importance of marriage as instituted by God, and third a matter of the church having the courage to stand up for truth in a context of cultural and political pressure. EECMY 2010. On evangelical churches' dogmatic teaching on marriage, CA XXIII and CAA XXIII, 9. On the two different views of what marriage is, Girgis, George, and Anderson 2010. In the "Conjugal View", marriage is the permanent and exclusive union of a man and a woman, naturally fulfilled by bearing and rearing children together, and in the "Revisionist View" marriage is the union of two "romantically loving and caring" people who share domestic life. As such, political, ideological, and philosophical factors are more relevant than theological. On the critical theory employed, Svartvik 2018. On the long-term cultural changes, Trueman 2020. On the problem of the sovereignty of state power behind, Cavanaugh 2011. On the ecclesiology of the *folk*-church, Eckerdal, Jan 2012, 67–108. On the harmful cultural and medical practices in the US that came as a result of the new view on identity, Shrier 2020. On the threats to academic and democratic liberties, Pluckrose and Lindsay 2020.

[41] AEF Coordination Committee Agenda 13 Dec 2013. One was an ACT alert issued by EECMY-DASSC to respond to a hailstorm in South Wollo Zone, another was the request for an evaluation, or internal review, of an on-going flood relief response (EECMY-DASSC), and a third emergency was the concern for more than 150 000 migrant workers from Ethiopia who were in the process of being expelled from Saudi Arabia and Yemen and were being flown back to Ethiopia. These people needed immediate assistance as many had been forced to leave without salaries or possessions.

[42] ACT Ethiopia Forum Dec 19, 2013.

2.3 ACT Response to the Refugee Crisis

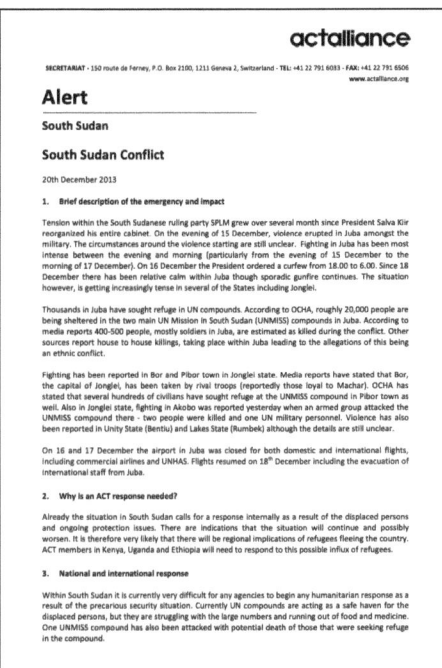

Figure 2.5: *The ACT Alert 48:2013 sets in motion the ACT response and gives potential donors an alert that their contribution may be needed. As the requirement is within 24 hours from emergency, a Skype call between the ACT forums in South Sudan, Ethiopia, Kenya, Uganda, and the ACT Secretariat in Geneva was held for initial information sharing and planning. The Alert is a two-page document. It was published Dec 20, 2013, the same day as the Skype call.*

An ACT Alert December 20, 2013

The day after the ACT Ethiopia Forum meeting (Dec 20th), the forum was contacted regarding the emerging crisis in South Sudan. In a matter of hours, the new issue was discussed, and it was immediately decided that the ACT members in Ethiopia also would respond if asylum seekers would come to Ethiopia. Emergencies may happen inconveniently. On that day several representatives of the European agencies had already started their Christmas vacation and left the country.[43]

---

[43] ACT Ethiopia Forum Emergency Meeting Regarding South Sudan Dec 23, 2013. ACT Alliance. (Dec 23, 2013) *South Sudan crisis: Brief notes of ACT Skype meeting of December, 2013.*

A regional ACT alert, the ACT Alert 48:2013, was launched on December 20, 2013, for the South Sudan crisis. It was a common alert for the ACT members in South Sudan, Ethiopia, Kenya, and Uganda. An alert document contains a "brief description of the emergency and its impact so far", a "rationale for an ACT response", a "summary of the humanitarian response so far", and an indication of planned humanitarian activities that require financial support. The indications of ACT Alert 48:2013 are very preliminary and vague, but they do present the difficulty of the moment to respond within South Sudan because of the precarious security situation leading to the evacuation of international aid workers rather than mobilisation and noting that preparations of LWF in Kenya, Kakuma refugee camp, and planning by ACT members in Ethiopia is taking place to prepare for the "possible influx of refugees in the Gambella region."[44]

The level of preparedness in Uganda was high, with LWF contingency plans in place, and activities already set in motion to allow for more housing, prepositioning of stock and staff on standby mode. The ACT Ethiopia Forum had by phone conversations confirmed that they would engage in the refugee assistance of asylum seekers in case they would come to Ethiopia. The first heads up on the emerging crisis had come from LWF World Service, which through its regional hub in Nairobi had been monitoring the situation in South Sudan, and whose Ethiopia programme also had contingency plans in place.[45]

In terms of response to the crisis in South Sudan – the initial focus of ACT Alliance was on peace resolution. Church leaders were already trying to bring the conflicting parties together. A contact had also been made with the South Sudanese president. The church leaders were concerned about the humanitarian situation – particularly in Bor and the Unity State where a lot of looting was going on.[46]

---

[44] 2013 12 20 ACT Skype Call South Sudan. 2013 12 20 South Sudan Forum. 2013 12 20 Alert 48:2013 South Sudan Conflict.

[45] 2013 12 20 ACT Skype Call South Sudan. 2013 12 20 South Sudan Forum. 2013 12 20 Alert 48:2013 South Sudan Conflict.

[46] 2013 12 20 ACT Skype Call South Sudan. 2013 12 20 South Sudan Forum. 2013 12 20 Alert 48:2013 South Sudan Conflict.

actalliance

SECRETARIAT - 150 route de Ferney, P.O. Box 2100, 1211 Geneva 2, Switzerland - TEL: +41 22 791 6033 - FAX: +41 22 791 6506
www.actalliance.org

Preliminary Appeal

Ethiopia

Assistance to asylum seekers and refugees from South Sudan – ETH141

Preliminary Appeal Target: US$2,364,264

Balance Requested: US$2,364,264

Geneva, 30 December 2013

Dear Colleagues,

There has been tension within the South Sudanese government since President Salva Kiir reorganized his entire cabinet in July 2013, including the dismissal of his vice president, Riek Machar. On the evening of 15 December, violence erupted in Juba. According to UNOCHA, a total of 58,000 people have sought refuge in UNMISS compounds in the country. Another 92,500 people have been internally displaced in five states and in Juba. These figures keep changing with new developments.

What started out as a political crisis has now mutated into an ethnic-based conflict. The three states closest to the Ethiopian border are mostly inhabited by people of Nuer ethnicity making the likelihood of an influx into Ethiopia low. However, if the government decides to attack Bor in Jonglei State, a stronghold of the ex-Vice President, the likelihood of a massive influx into Ethiopia is high. Ethiopia therefore is expecting close to 20,000 refugees to arrive in Ethiopia should the latter scenario prevail. The majority of the population is expected to be women and children.

As of 26 December 2013, Ethiopia has received 3,122 refugees from South Sudan. The new arrivals include 2,186 people from the Anuak tribe, 400 from the Dinka, 447 from the Nuer and 89 from the Murle tribe. The regional government in Gambella has reported that 414 ethnic Anuak Ethiopians have also returned from South Sudan. (ARRA/UNHCR) ACT Ethiopia Forum members are closely monitoring the situation and working on their respective contingency plan in the event that the situation in South Sudan escalates as expected.

Figure 2.6: *The ACT Preliminary Appeal lays out the basics of a response and ACT Alliance prescribes that it should be written within seven days of the emergency for donor agencies to mobilise resources on time. Here, the front page of the ETH141 preliminary appeal published Dec 30, 2013.*

Four Preliminary ACT Appeals

The initial timetable for a preliminary appeal had been set for the 25th of December as a deadline for submitting the documents from the ACT members in the three countries so that it could be published on December 26.[47] ACT Alliance stipulated for an alert to be released within 24 hours and for a preliminary appeal within seven days.[48] This would have been a challenge for the Ethiopian forum. The European ACT agencies were unable to contribute to the preliminary appeal as the heads of the agencies were out of the country for the Christmas holidays. Earlier the forum had had a technical committee in place to deal with such issues – now there was none – nor was there an ACT coordinator who could take charge

[47] 2013 12 20 South Sudan Forum Skype Meeting Notes 20 Dec 2013. 2013 12 23 ACT Skype Call South Sudan Crisis Notes 23 Dec 2013.

[48] ACT Alliance "Steps in an ACT emergency response."

of the coordination. In the ACT Skype meeting, on December 26th, only a preliminary ACT appeal from Uganda had been received by the ACT Secretariat, and the Ethiopian forum was requested to send their appeal by January 1st, 2014.[49]

On Monday 23 December, an emergency meeting scheduled for a discussion on the returnees from Saudi Arabia was turned into a planning meeting for the setting up of a response to the expected influx of asylum seekers from South Sudan. Whereas in Kenya, refugees had already started to come to the pre-existing *Kakuma* refugee camp in the northern part of the country, there was still less movement across the border into Ethiopia, and UNHCR did not at this moment expect the need to open new camps to receive newcomers in Ethiopia. A misjudgement that would bring challenges at a later point in time. In Ethiopia, five so-called reception centres where asylum seekers could get immediate assistance near the South Sudanese border were available in Akobo, Dimma, Lare, Pugnido, and Tongo. The refugee department (RRAD) of the Ethiopian Orthodox Church Development and Inter Church Aid Commission (EOC-DICAC) and another ACT member, the LWF World Service Ethiopia Office, had already attended a meeting with UNHCR and the refugee authority of the Ethiopian government (ARRA) since they were both working in various camps and the urban refugee programme in Addis Ababa with refugee assistance as partners of the UNHCR and ARRA.[50]

Christian Aid was tasked to continue to follow up on the issue of the returnees.[51] Christian Aid was working neither in the Gambella nor in the Benishangul regional state but was planning "to enter into those areas." Christian Aid was offering technical assistance in writing the appeal. Church of Sweden and Norwegian Church Aid participated in the meeting but did not at this point do anything more. The other forum members were not present since this was the holiday season and the country representatives were away, responding to emails, but not being physically present.[52]

---

[49] 2013 12 26 ACT Skype Call South Sudan Crisis Notes 26 Dec 2013.

[50] ACT Ethiopia Forum Emergency Meeting Regarding South Sudan Dec 23, 2013.

[51] 2013 12 23 ACT Skype Call South Sudan Crisis Notes 23 Dec 2013. ACT Ethiopia Forum Emergency Meeting Regarding South Sudan Dec 23, 2013. LWF, EOC-DICAC, EECMY-DASSC, IOCC, CA, NCA and CoS were present in the meeting. CCRDA, (former CRDA), were unable to continue in the same way as before because its structure did not fit into the new law concerning charities and societies. As a consortium (the additional C) however, it could register and function under the new regulations. These kinds of legal challenges made it more difficult also to register the ACT Ethiopia Forum. On CCRDA, see chapter five.

[52] ACT Ethiopia Forum Emergency Meeting Regarding South Sudan Dec 23, 2013.

EOC-DICAC was at the time already operating in the *Pugnido* refugee camp in the Gambella regional state in education, and vocational skill training sessions and was ready to scale up with a psychosocial programme in Gambella. That camp however was already at full capacity with 41 000 inhabitants, so if many asylum seekers would come, there would be a need to establish one or several new camps. The Orthodox Development Commission (EOC-DICAC) decided to work jointly with the International Orthodox Christian Charities (IOCC).[53]

LWF World Service had no established presence in the Gambella region but acted upon contingency plans made after the creation of the independent republic of South Sudan with a preparedness to receive South Sudanese asylum seekers in camps near Asosa, to the Northeast of Gambella where LWF was already working with water, sanitation, and hygiene (WASH), livelihoods, and psychosocial support (CBPS) since the ETH121 appeal in 2012. There was at this point no way of knowing which populations would move and which routes they would take. One scenario indicated an equal estimation of people arriving in the Bengishangul-Gumuz region and the Gambella region. Both the refugee department of EOC-DICAC and LWF World Service were at the time of the meeting working on their parts of a preliminary appeal.

The development commission of the *Ethiopian Evangelical Church Mekane Yesus* (EECMY-DASSC), one of the largest churches in the Gambella region, had yet to communicate with its regional offices but was interested in joining the appeal. The development commission, however, was more accustomed to working with the government of the regional state of Gambella and rendering support through local communities than within the UNHCR matrix, the accountability framework, of refugee camps.

After the Monday meeting, EOC-DICAC, IOCC, and LWF World Service worked hard on their respective project proposals. The central EECMY-DASSC office in Addis Ababa requested project proposals from the two synodal

---

[53] It is natural for the IOCC to work in close collaboration with DICAC. At this moment there were two outstanding issues between DICAC and ACT Geneva making the joint venture a necessity in order to avoid complications with the ACT Geneva Secretariat. DICAC had not paid membership fee for 2014 according to ACT Geneva. According to DICAC, the payment was made. DICAC had not been compliant during ETH111 and had used funds to buy/repair the generator with funds from the appeal without asking donors in advance. The funds were repaid.

development offices – East and West Gambella Synods.[54] Neither of those synods were able to produce proposals on such short notice and deliver them to the central office for further refinement. This meant that DASSC already at this stage dropped out of the formal process of the ACT Appeal. LWF made sure to be in direct contact with EOC-DICAC and IOCC and these three organisations worked jointly on the preliminary appeal document in several draft stages until it was sent to ACT Geneva on December 27 for finalisation and publication.[55]

In one of the comments on the document in a draft stage was the question of whether the forum should be the one requesting the funding with all its members, rather than specific implementing members (EOC-DICAC, IOCC and LWF World Service). This raises the issue of the relationship between the forum, the requesting (implementing) members, and the other forum members regarding the appeal.[56]

The published ETH141 preliminary appeal comes with a cover letter; I) an executive summary, II) a narrative summary, III) a financial summary, and IV) appendices. All in all, it is a fifteen pages long document complete with appendices.

---

[54] The synodal structure of the church was formed in such a way that the institutions built through mission societies could be handled by the synod offices, see Launhardt 2004. The old synods had bilateral agreements with the mission agencies that had contributed to the church in that synod. The church was founded with four synods according to where the missions were assigned places to work. As the church has grown, additional synods have been added. Generally, synodal development offices, DASSC branch offices, have been created along the new synods, but not necessarily with the kind of mission support the old synods had. Newer DASSC offices without a mission history, therefore, may not be as institutionally strong as the former ones. After the new legislation in 2009, the central DASSC office in Addis have expressed a need to strengthen the capacity of DASSC branch offices through four Area Capacity Building Offices, see DASSC Annual Report 2011. The split in the Gambella Synod into an Eastern and Western synod largely follows the Nuer – Anuak ethnical lines complicated by the large refugee influx of Nuer population. On Nuer culture, Evans-Pritchard 1969.

[55] 2013 12 27 "South Sudan Refugee Crisis ACT Ethiopia Forum Preliminary Appeal," as well as 1 "FIRST DRAFT," 2 "REVISED FIRST DRAFT," 3 "SGE Comments on REVISED FIRST DRAFT," 4 "SECOND DRAFT," 5 "SECOND DRAFT Draft 3" of "South Sudan Refugee Crisis ACT Ethiopia Forum Preliminary Appeal" all dated Dec 27, 2013. In Geneva, the document was scrutinised and amended by an ACT Senior Programme Manager. The final version of the document, which for all practical purposes remained the same as the one sent from Ethiopia was not published until December 30 as ACT Alliance "Preliminary Appeal: Ethiopia: Assistance to asylum seekers and refugees from South Sudan – ETH141" in which "ETH" stands from an appeal coming from the Ethiopian forum and "141" stands for appeal number one, 2014.

[56] 2013 12 27 "SGE Comments South Sudan Refugee Crisis ACT Ethiopia Forum Preliminary Appeal REVISED FIRST DRAFT."

As will be seen, there had been considerable work on planning what could be done given that the appeal would be approved, and finance provided for the work.[57]

The one-page cover letter contains a narrative description of the emergency. The tension within the South Sudanese government since July 2013, the outbreak of violence in Juba, on December 15, and some key figures of people seeking refuge are first provided as background. Then focus shifts towards "the likelihood of a massive influx in Ethiopia is high" with a possible scenario of some 20 000 refugees arriving in Ethiopia, out of which a majority is expected to be women and children. The situation and the assessment at this point were already different from a week earlier when the focus in the Alert was on peace resolution – the situation on the ground had changed. It would not be prudent to wait any further to raise humanitarian support. As the final data provided in terms of "new arrivals" in Ethiopia shows, people were already crossing the border, although not in massive numbers. The situation called for contingency plans in case the situation in South Sudan would escalate further.[58]

On this rationale, the "I Executive Summary" of two pages provided in tables the comprehensive "raw data." The appeal was requested in the name of the ACT Ethiopia Forum with three requesting members, LWF World Service and EOC-DICAC working jointly with IOCC. The project was planned to commence in January 2014 and end in December of the same year. Both LWF World Service and the joint EOC-DICAC and IOCC proposal were requesting a preliminary amount of circa one million USD each, to cover the costs of the intervention.[59] The purpose of the document is hence very clear – its intention is to appeal for contribution thus enabling the relief work detailed in the document as a response to the crisis.[60]

---

[57] 2013 12 30 ETH141 South Sudanese Refugees Preliminary Appeal 30 Dec.

[58] 2013 12 30 ETH141 South Sudanese Refugees Preliminary Appeal 30 Dec.

[59] There is also a reporting schedule included showing each organisation committing themselves to sending situation reports every two weeks in the beginning and then monthly report throughout the appeal period. In addition, interim reports were scheduled for in July, final reports in February 2015, and audit reports in March 2015. Contributors would be able to transfer funds and to ask for more information through the ACT secretariat. The second page provides information on bank account details and contact details for The ACT Secretariat in Geneva.

[60] 2013 12 30 ETH141 South Sudanese Refugees Preliminary Appeal 30 Dec. LWF is stated to respond in Lietchor refugee camp, Gambella regional state, and in Tongo refugee camp in Benishangul-Gumuz regional state, with water and sanitation (Lietchor), psychosocial support (Tongo) and livelihood activities (Lietchor and Tongo). EOC-DICAC and IOCC were

The second part of the document, "II. The narrative summary", contains the major share of the document. More information on the crisis had been fed into the planning process, as UNCHR and the Ethiopian government agencies were planning to open new camps in addition to the existing ones. In the preliminary appeal, the indications of camps were planning rather than factual figures.[61]

The starting point for LWF World Service was the Tongo refugee camp, close to the Bambasi refugee camp, where the organisation had an established office and was running various activities. If refugees would come to Tongo, it would neither be costly nor difficult to extend services to those newly arrived. In addition to this, LWF planned to work in the new camp to be opened, Lietchor. The main objective was to supply water for the refugees – if this service was granted then it would be possible, in an extension, past the emergency phase, to work on more long-term activities such as livelihoods.[62]

The refugee department of EOC-DICAC, working with IOCC, was already working in Pugnido and aimed at adding services in one more camp to assist the newcomers. For EOC-DICAC the long-term aim was to work with secondary education, so – covering urgent emergency needs such as water and sanitation – would grant the agency an entry ticket for rendering long-term support, if needed.[63]

As things were still uncertain, a contingency plan was planned. If however the situation would turn out differently and it would be possible to support the displaced people through a "humanitarian corridor" in South Sudan, the proposal was to render support using a corridor from Ethiopia instead of working through camps within Ethiopia.[64]

The financial summary shows a breakdown of expected costs counted both in local currency and USD.[65] The major share in the planned budget is the "direct

---

planning to respond in Okugo, Lietchor and Pugnido refugee camps, all in the Gambella regional state, with water and sanitation, psychosocial support, distribution of food and non-food items, health, and livelihoods.

[61] 2013 12 30 ETH141 South Sudanese Refugees Preliminary Appeal 30 Dec. It gives details on the emergency, actions to date and emergency needs, proposed emergency response, target population, arrangements for implementation, coordination and communication, principles and standards followed, specified implementation period, human resources, and administration procedures of funds, and finally systems of monitoring and evaluation.

[62] 2013 12 30 ETH141 South Sudanese Refugees Preliminary Appeal 30 Dec.

[63] 2013 12 30 ETH141 South Sudanese Refugees Preliminary Appeal 30 Dec.

[64] 2013 12 30 ETH141 South Sudanese Refugees Preliminary Appeal 30 Dec.

[65] "III. financial summary" in the preliminary appeal moved into "IV. Appendices."

costs", for LWF World Service mainly for water, sanitation, and hygiene and for the joint EOC-DICAC and IOCC operation, mainly for emergency food items, latrine construction and the construction of health posts. Salaries for project-level field staff constitute a significant portion of direct costs in the budget.[66]

Once the preliminary appeal is published on the webpage of ACT Alliance, it will provide a basis for churches to support the appeal. Potential donors would be able to contact the ACT Secretariat, or the ACT forum, directly to inquire about more information. Churches around the world may support an ACT appeal. For all practical purposes, as will be argued later, the members of the ACT Ethiopia Forum are also the main financers of Ethiopian ACT appeals.

By December 26th, the ACT Secretariat intended to launch one regional appeal for the South Sudan crisis.[67] By the 30th of December however, the Ugandan (LWF World Service), Kenyan (LWF World Service and the National Council of Churches of Kenya) and Ethiopian ACT Forums (LWF World Service, EOC-DICAC, and IOCC) had published their respective preliminary appeals on the ACT website. The security situation in South Sudan had occupied the ACT members in South Sudan to such an extent that the priority, at least for LWF World Service, was to safely evacuate all non-essential staff from South Sudan rather than planning relief operations.[68]

By Jan 6, 2014, the ACT South Sudan Forum released its preliminary appeal with three requesting members Norwegian Church Aid, Dan Church Aid and World Renew.[69] The preliminary appeal of the South Sudan ACT Forum downplays the movement across borders to Kenya, Uganda, and Ethiopia because at this point, people were on the move, but few had crossed national borders. It

---

[66] 2013 12 30 ETH141 South Sudanese Refugees Preliminary Appeal 30 Dec, "IV. Appendices." All projects put a strain on the central administration of an organisation. Emergency relief projects create administrative work to a larger extent than other projects because of the work needed to plan for projects, collaborate with UN and government bodies, negotiate with donors, recruit and induct new staff members, set up new offices, physically move items to the field, and establish monitoring and evaluation systems – all under stressful and eventful circumstances with many unknown parameters. This is reflected in the budget by a percentage of the salaries of key staff such as country, programme and finance directors expected to come from the appeal and its budget. Finally, the ACT Secretariat in Geneva is deducting three per cent of the funding as an "international coordination fee" to cover the expenses occurring directly due to the appeal.

[67] 2013 12 26 ACT Skype Call South Sudan Crisis Notes 26 Dec 2013.

[68] 2014 01 03 Eberhard Hitzler Email to Arie den Toom on Security Update 3 Jan, 2014.

[69] 2014 01 06 SSD141 South Sudan Conflict Preliminary Appeal. World Renew, is the relief and development arm of the Christian Reformed Church in North America (CRCNA).

highlights the humanitarian situation within South Sudan and the internal displacement of people, which was visible from numerous sources.[70] Norwegian
Church Aid intended to work with partner churches with relief and assess "possible advocacy actions" and Dan Church Aid intended to work through their local
partners. This represented a shift in strategy for Norwegian Church Aid and Dan
Church Aid as their head offices in Oslo and Copenhagen attempted to focus on
raising funding for direct intervention in South Sudan thus giving less room for
Norwegian Church Aid and Dan Church Aid in Ethiopia to support of the
ETH141 appeal financially.[71]

It is good to notice at this point that Dan Church Aid was chairing the South
Sudanese ACT forum and Norwegian Church Aid had a strong historical track
record in Sudan and South Sudan. During the Sudanese civil war, the Norwegian
Church Aid was engaged in *Operation Lifeline Sudan* working with, the civilian
aid organisation (the SRRA) of the liberation army (SPLA). It was also from Sudan, thanks to the initiative of Norwegian Church Aid, and through the Sudan
Christian Council, that relief had reached Ethiopia in the famine-struck northern
territories of Ethiopia held by rebel forces in the 1980s.[72]

In Ethiopia, Norwegian Church Aid, LWF World Service, EOC-DICAC and
IOCC planned to have a joint assessment report for sanitation – for the Lietchor
camp. As will be seen below in the full appeal document, this was due to a stronger
collaborative approach than first conceptualised in the initial planning of the preliminary appeal. The full appeal was delayed since UN security assessments had
delayed the UN-led joint assessment team of the situation (15–19 Jan).[73]

Meanwhile, Bread for the World, Norwegian Church Aid, EOC-DICAC and
EECMY-DASSC were working on a proposal to reach out to host communities
beginning with activities of water and sanitation. The local population are the first
ones to respond in an overwhelming situation like this when people *en masse* are
crossing the borders and supporting services are not up and running. People share
whatever they have at hand with people in need in true solidarity. It means, however, that the local communities themselves, in an overwhelming situation, are

---

[70] 2013 12 30 UGA141 South Sudanese Refugees Preliminary Appeal; 2013 12 30 KEN141 South
Sudanese Refugees Preliminary Appeal.

[71] 2014 01 06 SSD141 South Sudan Conflict Preliminary Appeal.

[72] See chapter five.

[73] 2013 12 30 ACT Skype meeting on South Sudan 30 Dec 2013. 2014 01 22 ACT Webex Call
on South Sudan.

soon drained of their resources and risk being impoverished. That is why this second initiative came to be conceptualised, strengthening those local communities.[74]

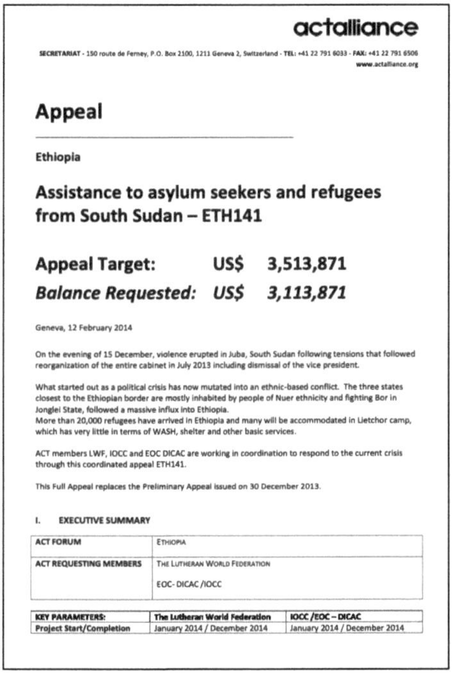
actalliance

SECRETARIAT - 150 route de Ferney, P.O. Box 2100, 1211 Geneva 2, Switzerland - TEL: +41 22 791 6033 - FAX: +41 22 791 6506
www.actalliance.org

Appeal

Ethiopia

Assistance to asylum seekers and refugees from South Sudan – ETH141

Appeal Target: US$ 3,513,871
Balance Requested: US$ 3,113,871

Geneva, 12 February 2014

On the evening of 15 December, violence erupted in Juba, South Sudan following tensions that followed reorganization of the entire cabinet in July 2013 including dismissal of the vice president.

What started out as a political crisis has now mutated into an ethnic-based conflict. The three states closest to the Ethiopian border are mostly inhabited by people of Nuer ethnicity and fighting Bor in Jonglei State, followed a massive influx into Ethiopia.
More than 20,000 refugees have arrived in Ethiopia and many will be accommodated in Lietchor camp, which has very little in terms of WASH, shelter and other basic services.

ACT members LWF, IOCC and EOC DICAC are working in coordination to respond to the current crisis through this coordinated appeal ETH141.

This Full Appeal replaces the Preliminary Appeal issued on 30 December 2013.

I. EXECUTIVE SUMMARY

ACT FORUM	ETHIOPIA
ACT REQUESTING MEMBERS	THE LUTHERAN WORLD FEDERATION EOC- DICAC /IOCC

KEY PARAMETERS:	The Lutheran World Federation	IOCC /EOC – DICAC
Project Start/Completion	January 2014 / December 2014	January 2014 / December 2014

Figure 2.7: *cover page of the ETH141 ACT Appeal published Feb 12, 2014, by the ACT Secretariat in Geneva on the website of ACT Alliance. The first page covers the essentials and includes a narrative summary of the crisis and the intended response. It is followed by an executive summary with the names of the organisations involved in the appeal.*

ETH141 ACT Appeal February 12, 2014

The *ETH141 ACT Appeal* is a fairly bulky document of 44 pages.[75] To a large extent the reader of the preliminary appeal would recognise much in the full appeal document. There are differences, however, and the most important ones will be

[74] 2013 12 30 ACT Skype meeting on South Sudan 30 Dec 2013.

[75] 2014 02 12 ETH141 Asylum Seekers South Sudan. The appeal consists of a cover page, an executive summary (I p.2–3), a narrative of the operational context (II p.4–7), proposed emergency response (III p.7–20), and appendices with maps, budget breakdowns and logical frameworks by requesting ACT members (IV p.21–44).

mentioned, and the significance of the changes explored. In this way, the historical progression of the appeal process will be shown. The appeal document serves as a call for donor support based on the activities, objectives, and methods specified. *Requesting ACT members* petition other ACT members and affiliated churches for a financial contribution. The document follows a format prescribed by ACT Alliance from the end of 2011.[76]

Once the appeal has been funded, the requesting members are held accountable towards the donors based on what has been specified in the document. The appeal document therefore is a request for funding, a plan of action, and a foundational document to look back upon when evaluating the impact of the appeal. It is a rather technical document, and it needs to be. It is the basis upon which presumptive contributors determine whether to support the appeal. The appeal for funding itself is assessed by potential donors based on the document, and a poorly written document would not generate the trust needed for funding.

The final appeal requests about one million USD more funding than the preliminary appeal. Almost all the increase is asked for by the LWF World Service. At this point, however, 400 000 USD is noted as either being pledged or contributed to LWF World Service. The money pledged is therefore reduced in the balance of requirements. That specific amount is no longer needed to be raised. LWF World Service is, therefore, in real terms asking for 600 000 USD more than in the preliminary appeal from ACT Alliance. For EOC-DICAC and IOCC nothing is noted as pledged.[77] The last comment is important as no operation can go ahead without funding. More than one month into operations, if there is no funding pledged, emergency services cannot be put in place.

In the final appeal document, LWF World Service, EOC-DICAC and IOCC agreed to work in the same camp – Lietchor – as a means of coordinating the work of ACT. The efforts of ACT Alliance would thus make a larger impact for that refugee population. Intervention in Tongo camp, previously planned in the preliminary appeal by LWF, had now been dropped, simply because the South Sudanese asylum seekers to Ethiopia are coming almost entirely to the Gambella region, and not to the Benishangul-Gumuz. EOC-DICAC and IOCC in the full appeal dropped emergency food items – the major item on their budget in the preliminary appeal. In the so-called WASH sector, of water and sanitation, the EOC-DICAC and IOCC focus now is on sanitation – for the building of latrines. For long-term involvement, secondary education and vocational training were added, as the

---

[76] 2011 11 23 ACT Alliance Response to Emergencies and Annexes.
[77] 2014 02 12 ETH141 Asylum Seekers South Sudan, 1–2.

refugee department (RRAD) of EOC-DICAC provides secondary education in many camps all over Ethiopia. This means that in the final appeal, the work planned by LWF World Service, EOC-DICAC and IOCC was better coordinated, and the impact of the ACT response to such an appeal would be easier to follow up and measure.[78]

In the full appeal, there are more "details of the emergency", a whole page narrating what has happened compared to half a page in the preliminary.[79] This added narrative gives the reader more information on what has happened, along with an analysis of why things developed in that way, what the consequences are, and an analysis of probable future developments. One example from the introductory paragraph of "details of the emergency":[80]

> Since the dismissal of the cabinet along with the former Vice President Riek Machar by the President Salva Kiir in July 2013, South Sudan has gradually descended from political instability into all-out civil crisis. With violence erupting in Juba on the 15th of December 2013, what started as political struggle has now spiralled into all-out conflict with alarming prospect of civil war.

The writer aims at a careful balance between giving as accurate a picture as possible to inform donors and entice interest in support for the appeal, and at the same time not giving in to speculations on things. There is a careful wording of the political events leading to the humanitarian situation. There is tension between the explicit words of insurance and professed will for peace by the South Sudanese government and the actual violence taking place. The ACT prognosis is that there will be "a long-term humanitarian crisis" rather than a return to peace. Relief workers were planning for the worst.[81]

> Despite the on-going peace negotiations and cessation of hostilities agreed, hostilities are expected to persist. President Kiir has stated that strategic areas previously governed by the rival forces have been reclaimed by the government army and that refugee[s] can return to their homes. However, with livelihoods and infrastructure destroyed in

---

[78] 2014 02 12 ETH141 Asylum Seekers South Sudan, 1–2; 6. ETH141 section 1.

[79] The preliminary appeal was written December 27 (published Dec 30) with much of its data gathered from before that date. The full appeal was published February 12th with editing going on right up until the publishing. That leaves almost six weeks for the situation on the ground to change between the preliminary and full appeal. The full appeal document reflects the development of the conflict, its humanitarian consequences, and the relief response in South Sudan and neighbouring countries since the end of 2013 when the preliminary appeal was published until the writing of the full appeal.

[80] 2014 02 12 ETH141 Asylum Seekers South Sudan, 4.

[81] 2014 02 12 ETH141 Asylum Seekers South Sudan, 4.

addition to fears of reprisals, it does not seem likely that stability can be established any time soon.[82]

The situation report gives a brief overview of what has happened in South Sudan. This includes the humanitarian situation which describes the vulnerability of ordinary people and their basic needs. The report uses information from the UN agency for humanitarian disasters (UN-OCHA)[83] to show that what began in South Sudan as an internal conflict with "thousands of casualties" had led to people seeking refuge in Uganda, Kenya, and Ethiopia with a particular emphasis on women and children.[84]

The account moves on to describe events in Ethiopia as asylum seekers have begun to reach the border. The South Sudanese have arrived at three different "entry points" with most people reaching the border town of Akobo after "walking for days and swimming across the river" separating the two countries. This is the most western point of Ethiopia. Neither the Ethiopian authorities (ARRA) nor the UNHCR would like the refugees to stay at that place for long. Security cannot be assured so close to the fighting and the logistical situation of reaching these people with emergency supplies is difficult, requiring the reloading of the goods from the road network onto boats and using the river to reach the people. Smaller groups of asylum seekers had already been relocated to the pre-existing camps of Pugnido and Okugo, but most were being transported to a new camp, Lietchor, north-east and closer to the regional capital town of Gambella. A plot of land for the camp was allocated, but basic infrastructure needed to be developed in the new the camp site to serve the basic needs of the refugees. Lietchor camp was planned to be able to serve 20 000 people.[85]

When numbers and specific facts are available on the people seeking refuge, these are stated to provide for an understanding of the scale of the situation. The Ethiopian refugee authority (ARRA) had a planning figure which by that time was 40 000 people.[86] Most of the text material under "details of the emergency" is coming from external sources such as UN agencies and is compiled to give a quick overview of the situation, a sense of what is going on, an understanding of what

---

[82] 2014 02 12 ETH141 Asylum Seekers South Sudan, 4.

[83] The United Nations Office for the Coordination of Humanitarian Affairs (UN-OCHA).

[84] 2014 02 12 ETH141 Asylum Seekers South Sudan, 4–5.

[85] 2014 02 12 ETH141 Asylum Seekers South Sudan, 4–5.

[86] A planning figure is a tool to prepare for events that have not yet occurred, but if they occur, the readiness has to be there. Preparations hence need to be in place for the reception of more people than those already arriving.

the primary needs are, and what could be done to fulfil those needs. This is how the descriptive text of the crisis, along with estimates of future scenarios, moves towards becoming actionable information for relief operations.[87]

In the second part of the appeal document, "actions to date", provides a comprehensive summary report of two pages showing how the resources and capacity available would be able to meet the most basic needs of the people given a good coordination of efforts both on behalf of ACT Alliance and external coordination offered by the UN (UNHCR) and the Ethiopian government (ARRA).[88] The aim is to show how the effort of the requesting ACT members (LWF World Service, EOC-DICAC and IOCC) with their organisational capacity fits into the overall effort of other organisations to assist the refugees. The plead is to immediately mobilise the resources necessary to assist refugees in the Lietchor camp.

---

[87] 2014 02 12 ETH141 Asylum Seekers South Sudan, 4–5.

[88] 2014 02 12 ETH141 Asylum Seekers South Sudan, 5–6, "Action to date." It begins with a "needs and resources assessment" (ETH 141 2.1), moves on to describe "capacity to respond" (ETH 141 2.2), and ends with "activities of forum and coordinator".

Description	Total in USD
Fair protection processes and documentation	140 000
Security/protection	67 000
Public health	530 000
Reproductive health and HIV	30 000
Nutritional well-being improved	590 000
Potable water	300 000
Sanitation and hygiene	470 000
Shelter and infrastructure	1 976 000
Access to energy (cooking fuel etc.)	900 000
Core relief items	1 112 470
Services for persons with specific needs	50 000
Population has optimal access to education	370 000
Community empowerment and self-reliance	86 000
Leadership, coordination and partnerships	3 000
Logistic and operations support	2 179 000
Operations management, coordination and support	650 000
Total immediate needs	*9 453 470*

Figure 2.8: *Table from the ETH141 ACT Appeal, 5: "Estimated immediate needs (30 000 persons of concern) as per UNHCR update 23rd January 2014." The table represents generic funding needs in categories of intervention according to UNHCR in a camp setting.*[89]

"Needs and Resources Assessment" (ETH141 2.1) The needs, see figure 2.8 above, are stated in terms of funding needs for each area of intervention according to UN-HCR categories. It is not a representation of assessed needs on the ground, or people's expressed and prioritised needs, but rather a standard calculation of what it would take, in broad terms of funding, to cover the expected basic needs of the refugee population of Lietchor based on the planning figure of 30 000. This represents the overall planning approach by UNHCR and creates a general framework under which partners to UNHCR may take their part in the work. It will also give prospective donors, such as government funding agencies, a rough estimate of the overall funding needs. In this sense, the table in Figure 2.8 represents

---

[89] 2014 02 12 ETH141 Asylum Seekers South Sudan, 5.

the funding requirements of UNHCR for the agency to fulfil its mandate of refugee protection. It is thus a plea to prospective donors for funding[90]

Once the ACT members are working in the camp, these rough estimates of needs and resources would be complemented by various specific assessments of needs and resources. In addition to this general estimate of needs provided by UNHCR, it is stressed that there are immediate needs in the area of "WASH, food, shelter and health services". The ACT appeal also gives reference to an "inter-agency assessment mission report from Akobo." The report speaks of incidences of sexual and gender-based violence (SGBV) which have occurred in South Sudan and the presence of "unaccompanied minors and separated children" among the asylum seekers. For the planners of the ACT Appeal, the report highlights the urgent need for psychosocial services.[91]

Assessments are important tools in an evidenced-based approach to relief work. The constant need for renewed assessments, however, puts pressure on each agency that may be required to put activities on hold to create yet another assessment. It also puts pressure on the people who must participate in yet another survey. Joint assessments are examples of a collaborative approach reducing the workload and resources spent on measuring, minimising redundancy and overlap, and granting the refugee population a sense of normalcy.

The thrust of the ETH141 appeal is the work with water and sanitation. ACT members in Ethiopia have vast experience in water projects.[92] LWF World Service had been assigned by UNHCR and ARRA to construct the permanent water system in Lietchor camp based on the earlier provision of providing both emergency water supply and constructing permanent water systems in refugee camps in Dollo Ado, Jijiga and Asosa, in this case. Both LWF World Service and EOC-DICAC had made initial plans to provide water. Under the UNCHR system of

---

[90] 2014 02 12 ETH141 Asylum Seekers South Sudan, 5. UNHCR and other UN agencies are developing from a limited legal "protection mandate" towards more of service providing.

[91] 2014 02 12 ETH141 Asylum Seekers South Sudan, 5.

[92] There is however a difference between working on long term development projects to improve the provision of water and to do the same in an emergency context. A person may survive for extended periods with smaller amounts of food, but only a few days without water. The aggregation of many people in one place, a refugee camp, makes it possible to centralise and render effective services but also puts pressure on service delivery. Failure to deliver water in time, lack of water quality or obstacles to access to services may become life-threatening for the people whose lives are entrusted in the hands of a relief operation.

coordination, implementing agencies may request areas of responsibility.[93] In this case, as LWF World Service was assigned the permanent water system and no other camps were planned to be established for the moment, the initial plan of the preliminary appeal of the ACT Ethiopia Forum that both LWF World Service and EOC-DICAC would engage in the construction of water system in separate camps failed. LWF World Service and EOC-DICAC together with IOCC after several meetings with different stakeholders had finally decided to work together in the sense that LWF would construct the permanent water system while EOC-DICAC would contribute to sanitation activities such as constructing latrines and promoting good hygiene practices. The Orthodox commission would also work with psychosocial support, vocational training, livelihood assistance and secondary education.[94]

This unexpected turn of events presented an opportunity for three ACT members to work closer together in the field than previously planned. The former experience in earlier appeals such as the ETH111 coordination had primarily meant that each ACT agency would be working in a specific area, thus covering more areas and complementing each other's work.[95] Now there would be more opportunities for collaboration, and it would even be possible for the ACT agencies to construct a common office.[96]

At this time, as stated earlier, the planning figure for asylum seekers coming to the Benishangul-Gumuz regional state, northwest of the Gambella region, was 20 000. As current camps in the region were full, the plan was to refurnish the site of a previous refugee camp, *Tsore*. Since LWF World Service was already working in the Asosa area nearby, the agency had indicated to UNHCR and ARRA that it would be ready to scale up operations regarding psychosocial support if funding would become available.

---

[93] If several agencies show interest within the same sector of intervention such as food and nutrition, shelter or water and sanitation (WASH), this will lead to a discussion in which UNCHR has the final say on which organisation ends up on the accountability matrix for that sector in a specific camp. It may also be the case that several agencies share responsibilities in the same sector and the same camp which creates a further demand for good coordination and collaboration between those agencies.

[94] 2014 02 12 ETH141 Asylum Seekers South Sudan, 5–7. 2011 07 14 ETH111 Ethiopia Drought Response.

[95] See chapter five. Also ETH111.

[96] 2014 02 12 ETH141 Asylum Seekers South Sudan, 6.

"The capacity to respond"[97] is a crucial characteristic of relief agencies. It contains different aspects. LWF World Service highlights their experience of working with Somali refugees in Dolo Ado on the southern tip of Ethiopia, bordering Kenya and Somalia (ETH111), in Jijiga in the East, on the border to Somaliland, and with Sudanese refugees in the Asosa area (ETH121). In those previous appeals, LWF World Service had been working with water supply, environmental protection, the strengthening of livelihood status and psychosocial support. LWF deliberates on their present staff capacity and the availability of experienced WASH staff both at the head office in Addis Ababa and in field offices. It means that LWF World Service would be able to use existing staff from the beginning of the project and recruit additional staff along the way. This brings up the issue of the general need for relief agencies to recruit new competent staff each time there is a new emergency. Using available staff speeds up the starting up process of a project and ensures the quality of staff at a time when experience and competency are mostly needed.[98] EOC-DICAC and IOCC focused in the text on the strong partnership of the two organisations and their long experience of working together in "large scale, multispectral and complex programs"[99] such as the ACT Appeal ETH111 which in 2011 focused on drought response.[100]

It was also brought to attention that EOC-DICAC already was working in various refugee centres in Gambella. Thus, partnerships with UNHCR, ARRA, regional government and host communities were already established.[101] This brings up the next issue – about the ACT Ethiopia Forum's involvement and external coordination of UNHCR and ARRA. The forum is "monitoring the situation" and it has a mandate to ensure "effective coordination" among members. In order to prepare for the preliminary appeal, the LWF World Service, EOC-DICAC and IOCC "conducted a joint rapid assessment."[102] EOC-DICAC and LWF World Service were also attending task force meetings in Addis Ababa and Gambella as well as group meetings with donors, both chaired by UNHCR and ARRA. This shows several levels of coordination: (1) between LWF World Service, DICAC and IOCC, (2) the ACT forum, (3) with implementing agencies,

---

[97] 2014 02 12 ETH141 Asylum Seekers South Sudan, 6–7: "The capacity to respond."

[98] 2014 02 12 ETH141 Asylum Seekers South Sudan, 6.

[99] 2014 02 12 ETH141 Asylum Seekers South Sudan, 7.

[100] 2011 07 14 ETH111 Ethiopia Drought Response.

[101] 2014 02 12 ETH141 Asylum Seekers South Sudan, 7.

[102] It took place in Gambella Jan 20–24, 2014. The plan was to follow up with "[m]ore detailed planning, designing and implementation in close cooperation with the representatives of both refugees and host communities." 2014 02 12 ETH141 Asylum Seekers South Sudan.

UNHCR, and ARRA in Addis Ababa, (4) with implementing agencies, UN-HCR and ARRA in Gambella, (5) with donors, UNHCR, ARRA, and implementing agencies. Later, (6) there would also be additional camp-level coordination meetings with refugees and host communities.[103]

UNHCR and ARRA are more inclined to work with established partners who have proved their reliability in the field. It takes a longer time for an organisation which has not been in the "intervention matrix" of UNHCR to show that it is sincere, has the capacity, and is willing to commit to refugee assistance. This was one of the main reasons why it was difficult for EECMY-DASSC to enter into the ETH141 appeal on the same terms as LWF World Service and EOC-DICAC. Both LWF and the refugee department of the Orthodox Church were long-standing partners of UNHCR and ARRA, but EECMY-DASSC was not. EECMY-DASSC had a strong organisational presence in the Gambella region, but it had partnerships only with the regional government, not with the UN refugee agency and the Ethiopian government refugee authorities. LWF World Service and EOC-DICAC both regularly sent representatives to UNCHR coordination meetings in Addis Ababa, thus they were informed of what was going on, they were visible, and they were able to discuss and collaborate with UNHCR and ARRA officers. The central EECMY–DASSC office coordinated with the ACT members but did not send representatives to the coordination meetings of UNHCR. It shows that coordination within the ACT Ethiopia Forum is not enough when the main forum for coordination is elsewhere.

---

[103] 2014 02 12 ETH141 Asylum Seekers South Sudan, 7.

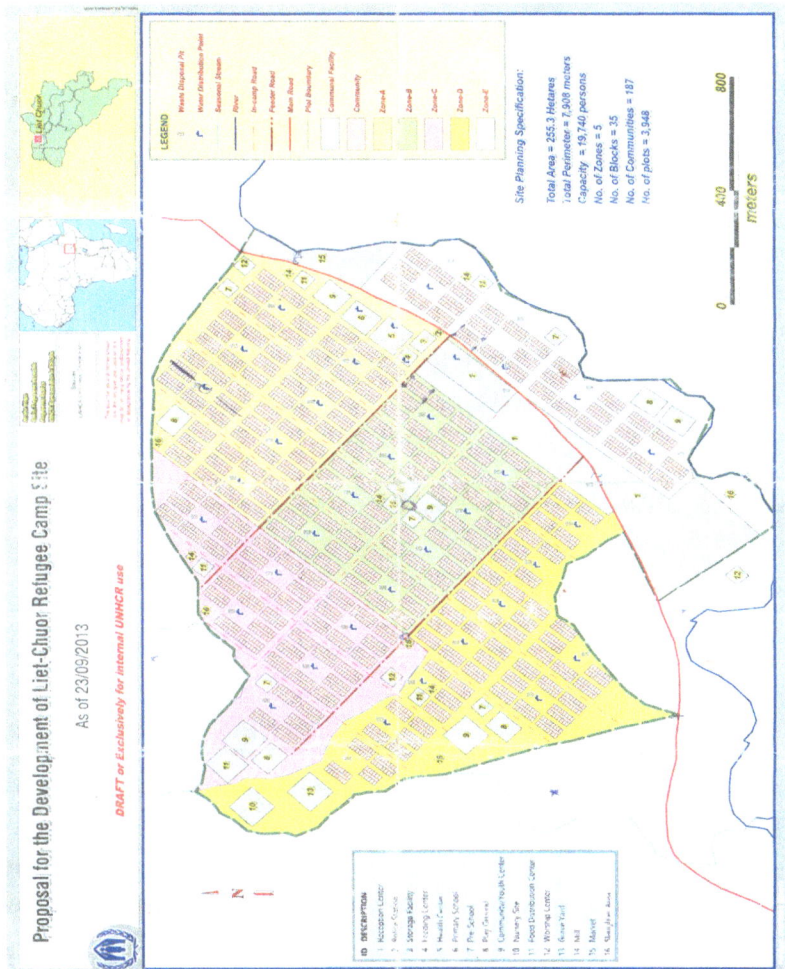

Figure 2.9: *UNHCR Draft site planning of Lietchor (or Liet-Chuor) Refugee camp 23rd Sep 2013 from appendix IV of ETH141. This map gives condensed information, such as the geographical location, the planned number of refugees, and a division of the camp into administrative units such as zones and blocks.*

The third part of the appeal, "Proposed Emergency Response" (ETH141 III 1.–4.) is a major section of the document (pages 7–20) and contains 1. A description of "target populations, areas and sectors of response", 2. "overall goal of emergency response", 3. "expected outcomes" of the response, and 4. "the proposed implementation plan." The last part is divided up in four categories (4.1–4.4).[104] "Target populations, areas and sectors of response", (ETH141 III 1.) fleshes out what has already been stated – that LWF World Service and EOC-DICAC will work in Lietchor camp. As this is a new camp – the demographic data of the population had not yet been established, but a basic outline of the camp with its five zones was provided as an appendix.[105]

An important aspect of service provision is beneficiary selection. When it comes to water and sanitation – these are stated as "basic needs for all." That means that all refugees have a right to access, and the intervention will aim to reach everyone. Selection is needed for activities in which not everyone will directly benefit such as vocational training, livelihood training and secondary education. LWF World Service states that they will use the "UNHCR Standard Operation Procedure" (SOP) to determine who will benefit from these services. This is a way to make sure that subjectivity on behalf of the staff will be checked by a procedural selection based on an external standard. The role of standards will be discussed in the next chapter on the humanitarian framework.[106]

The overall goal of emergency response is stated:

> To contribute to the all-rounded support of refugees from South Sudan in fulfilling their basic rights for dignified living in Lietchor camp in Gambela and Tsore camp in Benishangul-Gumuz.[107]

The work of ACT is part of – not itself constituting the whole – support system of these refugees aimed at fulfilling their basic rights with reference to their life in Lietchor camp. It is not enough for the people to survive – but the goal is "dignified living." It does not take away the fundamental responsibility of the people themselves but aims to assist them, as the words "contribute" and "support" indicate. The "fulfilling their basic rights" shows that it is a rights-based approach in which these agencies take part in the overall support. The overall goal sets the tone, but in itself, it is not enough to explain what the main objectives are or how the agencies plan to achieve those objectives.[108]

---

[104] 2014 02 12 ETH141 Asylum Seekers South Sudan, 7–20 "III Proposed Emergency Response."

[105] 2014 02 12 ETH141 Asylum Seekers South Sudan, 7-8 "1. Target populations, areas and sectors of response."

[106] 2014 02 12 ETH141 Asylum Seekers South Sudan, 8 "1. Target populations, areas and sectors of response."

[107] 2014 02 12 ETH141 Asylum Seekers South Sudan, 8.

[108] 2014 02 12 ETH141 Asylum Seekers South Sudan, 8.

In the next section on "expected outcomes", the main objectives of each organisation are stated followed by the "proposed implementation plan" narrating how these objectives are to be operationalised. What are the main objectives stated by the requesting ACT members? LWF World Service have four main objectives, three for the initial "crisis phase" of the intervention and one for the "post-crisis phase." EOC-DICAC and IOCC have three objectives, two for the crisis phase and one for the post-crisis phase: [109]

Crisis Phase LWF Ethiopia Response: [110]

Objective 1: Access to adequate quantities of potable water for drinking, cooking and hygiene purposes for refugees from South Sudan in the Lietchor refugee camp.

Objective 2: The South Sudanese refugees in the Lietchor refugee camp live in healthier, sanitary conditions with improved awareness and practice in hygiene and sanitation.

Objective 3: South Sudanese refugees in the Tsore camp live in less stressful situation

Post-Crisis Phase LWF Ethiopia Response:

Objective 4: The livelihoods status of the South Sudanese refugees in the Lietchor camp is improved.

Crisis Phase IOCC/EOC-DICAC Response:

Objective 1: Hygiene and Sanitation: Sustained and expanded use of sanitation services ensured for the target communities.

Objective 2: Psychosocial Support: Psychosocial wellbeing of the most affected refugees improved.

Post-Crisis Phase IOCC/EOC-DICAC Response:

Objective 3: Secondary Education and Vocational Education: Refugees become middle level workers after completion of secondary education or are enabled to join higher education.

Figure 2.10: *Table from ETH141 "Expected Outcome" with the stated outcome of the intervention by LWF Ethiopian Response and the combined IOCC and EOC-DICAC response stated as objectives in two phases.*

---

[109] 2014 02 12 ETH141 Asylum Seekers South Sudan, 8 "Expected Outcomes."
[110] 2014 02 12 ETH141 Asylum Seekers South Sudan, 8 "Expected Outcomes."

The crisis phase objective regards water, sanitation, hygiene, and psychosocial support and the post-crisis phase regards vocational training, secondary education, and livelihoods. In the first phase, the priority is to make sure that there is a provision of basic needs in a way that does not harm but improves the wellbeing of the refugees. Once the main objective has been stated the appeal document moves to show how these objectives are to be achieved. The same information is provided as a narrative in this part of the appeal and also in the form of a logical framework (log frame). Here we may refer to appendix five and six of the appeal which shows the logical frameworks of the interventions planned by LWF World Service and EOC-DICAC.[111]

Information may be presented in different ways, as logical framework:

---

[111] 2014 02 12 ETH141 Asylum Seekers South Sudan, 25–30 "Appendix five" and 31–33 "Appendix six."

Project structure	Indicators	Means of Verification	Assumptions
Goal			
To contribute to the all-rounded support of refugees from South Sudan in fulfilling their basic rights for dignified living in Lietchor camp in Gambela and Tsore camp in Benishangul-Gumuz.	20 000 refugee men, women and children find protection in Ethiopia The basic needs of the refugees relocated to Lietchor and Tsore camp are fulfilled Targeted 20 000 refugees are enabled to lodge complaints about the project easily and safely through transparent and timely procedures for response and remedial action	Data from UNHCR, ARRA, implementing partners and coordination meetings Complaints and response mechanism (CRM)	The targeted number of refugees materializes Sufficient funding is available
Outcomes			
1: Access to adequate quantities of potable water for drinking, cooking and hygiene purposes for refugees from South Sudan in the Lietchor refugee camp.	Potable water is provided as per the minimum Sphere/UNHCR standards of 15 litres/person/day and after the immediate emergency phase, 20 litres/person/day. No of functional water points No of people living within 500 meters from water points	Field monitoring reports	Availability of ground water in the camp area No excessive additional influx of refugees Security situation remains suitable for the interventions to be carried out

Figure 2.11: *Extract from Appendix 5: Log frame by Lutheran World Federation (LWF)*

The first example is from the LWF World Service log frame showing the overall goal and the first outcome regarding access to potable water.[112] For each goal, outcome, or output (first column), there is at least one indicator (second column) showing whether the objective has been met, or indicating that is the case. These indicators may be quantitative, for example showing the number of litres of water provided per day, or the number of people who have participated in a training. They may also be qualitative showing for example a change in behaviour.[113]

The third column shows the "means of verification", evidence in terms of reports or other means by which the agency may establish whether indicators have been met. A monitoring team from within the organisation, or from donors, or an UN-agency, may ask to see the documental evidence showing that activities have taken place, items have been delivered, services have been rendered, or improvement of conditions have actualised as a result of the efforts of the organisation.[114]

The fourth column outlines if particular "assumptions" have been made as a basis for the planning. The three basic assumptions for LWF World Service outcome 1: access to potable water are, the availability of ground water in the camp area, a stable security situation, and that the number of refugees do not suddenly grow in such a way that LWF would be unable to provide water according to established standards. Note that the availability of sufficient funding is a requirement for the work.[115]

Second, another example, this time rendered in narrative form:

> This initiative is inclusive and addresses the needs of all vulnerable women, children, adults, and elders who are affected by the current crisis. The methodology is purely community-based psychosocial supports that give more emphasis on the resources the community has to combat individual and social problems. To this end, awareness raising workshops on community-based psychosocial supports will be provided to elders, women, and religious leaders who are equipped with the appropriate tools to involve in community mobilization to the benefit of the entire camp community.[116]

An attempt is also made to mainstream psychosocial support to other program activities in the refugee camp. This intervention will also ensure the active involvement of the refugee community since the commencement of the project and will continue during the implementation, monitoring, and evaluation phases.[117]

---

[112] 2014 02 12 ETH141 Asylum Seekers South Sudan, "Appendix 5": Log frame by LWF.
[113] 2014 02 12 ETH141 Asylum Seekers South Sudan, "Appendix 5."
[114] 2014 02 12 ETH141 Asylum Seekers South Sudan, "Appendix 5."
[115] 2014 02 12 ETH141 Asylum Seekers South Sudan, "Appendix 5."
[116] 2014 02 12 ETH141 Asylum Seekers South Sudan, 14, IOCC/DICAC Response.
[117] 2014 02 12 ETH141 Asylum Seekers South Sudan, 15, IOCC/DICAC Response.

This second example is a quote from the narrative description of how the psychosocial support provided by EOC-DICAC and IOCC is planned to be "inclusive", "community-based", and "mainstreamed." The purpose is to reach all vulnerable individuals of the population (inclusivity), mobilise the community through elders, women, and religious leaders (community-based), and bring a psychosocial approach to all activities (mainstreaming). Furthermore, the active participation of the refugees will be encouraged from the start to the end of the project. As it will be shown in the next chapter, the approach thus narrated follows from an international standard of providing community based psychosocial support.[118]

The starting point for the narrative of the proposed implementation plan is the expected outcomes – what the agency would like to see as the end result of the work – and then moving to show the reader the logic of how it would be achieved. The methodology therefore does not explicitly begin with a need and then propose activities to fulfil that need. As we have seen, the needs are important, but the end goal is to reach a state beyond needs-fulfilling.[119]

There are still more questions related to the how: how to achieve those objectives stated. More answers are found under "Implementation methodology" on pages 15–20, which deals with several issues.[120] The agencies are showing that they adhere to core humanitarian standards such as *the HAP Standard, the SPHERE Minimum Standard, IASC Mental Health and Psychosocial Support guidelines (MHPSS), ACT principles and guidelines, the Code of Conduct for LWF World Service, for ACT Alliance, and for the International Red Crescent Movement and NGOs in Disaster Relief and Humanitarian Charter.* This would among other things entail the setting up of a formal *Complaints Response Mechanism* (CRM) by which the refugees would be able to give feedback and file complaints both regarding quality matters and abuse. These standards will be discussed in the next chapter.[121]

---

[118] 2014 02 12 ETH141 Asylum Seekers South Sudan, 14–15, IOCC/DICAC Response.

[119] 2014 02 12 ETH141 Asylum Seekers South Sudan, 9–13 "proposed implementation plan" LWF, and 13–15 DICAC.

[120] There is a need to set up field level offices which relates to the head offices in Addis Ababa. Therefore, the main staff such as project coordinator, water engineers and psychosocial officers are spelt out and their responsibilities and relationship to the head office. This regards issues such as quality control, financial management and control, and accountability.

[121] 2014 02 12 ETH141 Asylum Seekers South Sudan, 15–20 "implementation methodology." See chapter 3 for the significance of these international standards, principles and guidelines.

The methodology also regards the way the refugees are involved as "active participants and stakeholders" of the assistance. If the site plan, roads, and water infrastructure represent the "hardware" of refugee assistance, the "software" is represented by the setting up of refugee community structures, such as *the Refugee Council Committee* (RCC) with its sectoral sub-committees, women and youth associations, and arrangement for "elders and religious leaders." This is related to how the agencies bring up cross-cutting issues. [122] Cross-cutting means that whether the response is concerned with water and sanitation, livelihoods or psychosocial support, considerations will be taken based on these issues. This will affect what will be done, but more importantly, how things are done. [123]

LWF World Service Ethiopia, EOC-DICAC, and IOCC are given brief descriptions. It is stated that UNHCR and the government of Ethiopia will provide for the main coordination. National as well as international organisations all work under the UN cluster system to respond to a humanitarian crisis. Second, the ACT Ethiopia Forum would follow the appeal during its monthly meeting. There was also a core group of ACT members created to follow and support the ETH141 more closely. [124]

Among the appendices of the appeal, there are maps, charts, and the tables with log frames already mentioned. [125] What we need to bring to attention here however are the budgets of the requesting agencies. Compared with the budgets in the preliminary appeal there are changes. First, the budget of the full appeal is more specific outlining in more detail how the cost of water, sanitation and hygiene is distributed. Whereas the preliminary appeal gave more of an overview, by scanning through the full budget, it is possible to get a better idea of what is more costly, such as the "hardware" of drilling boreholes, constructing a reservoir and the water distribution system, and constructing a secondary school, and what is less costly such as the "software" of establishing and training WASH committees, working on community mobilisation, cultural and sports events and small-scale gardening. [126]

---

[122] Cross-cutting issues such as gender, capacity building, empowerment, disabilities, and HIV & AIDS.

[123] 2014 02 12 ETH141 Asylum Seekers South Sudan, 16–18 "cross-cutting issues."

[124] 2014 02 12 ETH141 Asylum Seekers South Sudan, 19–20 "Human resources and administration of funds" and 18 "Coordination."

[125] 2014 02 12 ETH141 Asylum Seekers South Sudan, 1–8 "Appendix."

[126] 2014 02 12 ETH141 Asylum Seekers South Sudan "Appendix 7 Budget LWF" and "Appendix 8 Budget IOCC / EOC-DICAC."

Second, the changes in the permanent water system caused an addition to the budget from the preliminary to the full appeal. During the preliminary appeal, the site was not determined, either Okugo or Lietchor. By the time of the full appeal, the site was known, and the number of expected refugees had risen. LWF World Service also had made a feasibility assessment in Lietchor showing that there were no spring sources available, leaving ground water as the only option, thus bringing up the cost. By dropping the construction of latrines, funding could be reallocated to items related to water and sanitation to be distributed to all households, such as jerry cans, buckets, baby potties, sanitary packs for women, and soap. While the total budget for EOC-DICAC and IOCC remained almost the same as in the preliminary, there were changes in budget items. Water provision and food provision were dropped, and sanitation services such as the construction of latrines and water basins were added. In the post-crisis phase, the construction of a secondary school was added. The EOC-DICAC changes represented a shift from relief and development to the refugee department (RRAD), which focuses on setting up and providing for secondary education for the youth.[127]

2.4 A Silent Crisis Is Rapidly Evolving

The appeal to support refugees from South Sudan encountered challenges, in recruiting new staff, in mobilising the support of all ACT Ethiopia Forum members, and in attracting the funds needed. In addition to such internal challenges, the Baro river flooded the area of the newly established refugee camp. As the appeal document with its aims and methodologies have been described, (in 2.3), this section will outline the main challenges and discuss what the ACT members did to overcome challenges when the plan to assist was put into practice.

Challenges to the Refugee Response

One of the challenges of implementing the appeal concerned the recruitment of qualified staff. The refugee operation took place in Gambella, one of the smallest federal regions in Ethiopia, considered a remote area. Its population is rather small, with 300 000 inhabitants, compared with an almost equal number of refugees. Hiring local staff with technical expertise proved to be difficult in competition from other aid agencies. Also, national technical staff sent from other parts of

---

[127] 2014 02 12 ETH141 Asylum Seekers South Sudan "Appendix 7 Budget LWF" and "Appendix 8 Budget IOCC / EOC-DICAC." 2014 02 12 ETH141 Asylum Seekers South Sudan, 9–15.

Ethiopia by the organisations were objects of active recruitment from other humanitarian organisations willing to pay more for the staff.[128]

The urgency and the need for coordination among the appeals in South Sudan, Kenya, Uganda, and Ethiopia meant that not only the Mekane Yesus but also other interested ACT members were not part of the original appeal as was seen in the previous section.

Without an ACT coordinator to do the actual coordination and to actively seek funding, the appeal itself did not attract the needed funds for the objectives set out in the appeal document. In June, Dan Church Aid took the initiative to create a consortium. In this form of cooperation, it would be possible to apply for funding from the humanitarian funding organisation of the European Union (ECHO). A lot of work and effort was put into creating a consortium with terms which all partners could agree upon.

In August the *Lietchor* refugee camp was flooded twice. First by heavy rain and a second time when the Baro River six kilometres away overflowed its banks. The refugees were initially moved to a host community in the village of *Nyine Nyang* which created tensions between the host and the refugee communities. The Ethiopian refugee authority (ARRA) ordered the camp to be closed, but no other feasible options were presented for a long time. Meanwhile, all work on permanent structures, such as the permanent water system, was put on hold. For the LWF World Service, this created a dilemma – they had all the staff and materials, such as water pipes, ready to finalise the water systems, and the refugees were still there – but without permission, work could not continue. So, they were stuck in Lietchor.[129]

---

[128] The problem becomes more acute as ACT members make use of few expatriate staff compared with international relief agencies. An advantage of expatriate recruitment is the ability to have a surge capacity of highly qualified staff who may be employed at short notice thus reducing the strain on present staff members and other projects. ACT Alliance has lists of people who may be recruited for an emergency at short notice.

[129] 2014 10 21 ETH141 Revision 1 Ethiopia Refugees from South Sudan. 2015 04 27 LWF Request for Extension and Revision ETH141. Where would the refugees go? It was difficult for UNHCR to acquire land in a suitable – flood secure – location. The refugees were offered to go south to *Okugo*. A site with an existing camp with opportunities for extension. The refugees, though, had several reasons not to be inclined to go. Their present location was close to the border to South Sudan and their relatives. Okugo was several days of journey away, so both considering the hardship of transportation and the dislocation was not favourable. One reason was fear of violence. Some of the refugees had experienced violence in Okugo before. That was however

In general, relief agencies are expected to act, but more specifically, there are situations which demand from a particular agent to respond. The EECMY-DASSC did not respond quickly to the emergent refugee influx, but in a way, the church did. Many people from the local communities where the refugees first arrived, before refugee camps were established, were members of Mekane Yesus. Once the scope of the emergency was clear, the regional government also expected EECMY-DASSC to assist since the development agency of Mekane Yesus was already one of the larger stakeholders in development work in the region. As EECMY-DASSC did not have a history of being a partner of ARRA and UN-HCR, however, the question then arises – how could the church act upon such expectation? This is why, in the revised appeal, the proposal came about working in the host communities to raise their local capacity.

As we saw above, for LWF World Service the expectancy to act, in the form of a direct request from ARRA and UNHCR was a clear case in point of the same principle. These agencies are called to serve in times of need, and when called upon to act, it is hard to say no. The humanitarian moral obligation to act in these situations has been called upon. The question is how to act upon such an obligation. If ought implies can, some of the relevant factors regarding whether there is a presence in the locality, whether an agency is known as a stakeholder, or known for a specific task, and whether there is a previous working relationship with relevant UN and government authorities.

EECMY-DASSC has a strong presence and is one of the most active development agents in the Gambella region. The name refers back to the church, Mekane Yesus, as people may say "DASSC" or "Mekane Yesus" interchangeably when referring to the development commission and the church also has a significant constituency. Such an identification of an ACT member with a church gives substance to the idea of calling the aid work of ACT Alliance *action by churches together.*

It was thus very well known by the regional government counterparts. It was however not well known either by ARRA or by UNHCR. LWF World Service did not previously have a presence in Gambella, but it is well known for its refugee

---

a long time ago before the present Ethiopian government had firmly achieved control over border areas after the fall of the Derg regime in 1991. For the refugees this created a difficult dilemma which was not resolved until months later with opening of new refugee camps near Gambella town. LWF World Service stayed with the refugees until the camp was finally closed.

assistance.[130] Globally, it is one of the largest partners of UNHCR. In Ethiopia, as mentioned in the appeal, its staff has rendered service to Somali refugees in Dolo Ado and Jijiga (ETH111) before the establishment of service to Sudanese refugees (ETH121) and South Sudanese refugees (ETH141). [131] Water and sanitation, (WASH), is one of the areas of refugee intervention, but being development-minded in approach, LWF has sought to act in areas such as environmental protection, livelihoods, and vocational training.[132] These are not lifesaving activities but areas of intervention which improve sustainability, and quality of life, and give people a sense of meaning and responsibility in life.

Historically, it had been LWF World Service that acted in terms of refugee assistance in the country on behalf of Mekane Yesus. We need to remember here the strong ties between Mekane Yesus and LWF World Service. The Lutheran World Federation – not World Service but the communion of churches – had been instrumental in supporting the building up of Mekane Yesus as a church. The Mekane Yesus, on their part, had been heavily involved in the federation from 1957 onwards. It was the church that invited the LWF World Service office into Ethiopia in the first place to counter the famine in 1974.[133] The LWF World Service Ethiopia Programme shares the same office building as EECMY-DASSC, the former head office building of the church next to the congregation that gave its name to the national church, "Mekane Yesus", the place of Jesus.[134] The Mekane Yesus vice church president is the chair of the local board of LWF World Service Ethiopia Programme. When LWF World Service operates, it is customary for it to utilise church property when it sets up an office. This was also the case in Lietchor camp, where LWF World Service began with setting up two tents as staff accommodation within the Mekane Yesus church compound. Such collaboration between the church and the aid agency reduces time and costs and fosters a sense of belonging to the church.[135]

The Refugee and Returnee Affairs Department (RRAD) of the Orthodox development commission (EOC-DICAC) has an even longer history than the commission which was established in 1972. It is currently a special department within

---

[130] The refugee engagement for LWF begun in 1947. LWF, as a mission, had taken over a German mission hospital and naturally responded to assist people fleeing the conflict.

[131] The ETH111 ACT Appeal took place in 2011, ETH121 in 2012, and ETH141 in 2014.

[132] 2011 07 14 ETH111 Ethiopia Drought Response, 2013 06 20 ETH121 Final Narrative Report.

[133] Emmanuel Abraham 1995.

[134] The name is adopted from the Orthodox practice of naming churches, Toll 2014.

[135] 2012 06 04 Brief Profile AEF Members 4 June 2012.

the commission with its own structure and budget. For many years it has been one of the chief partners of UNHCR within the urban refugee programme in Addis Ababa. During the years 2009–2017, the number of people seeking refuge in Ethiopia from neighbouring countries rose from less than one hundred thousand to eight hundred thousand. RRAD expanded during those years specialising in education setting up secondary schools in almost all locations of refugee assistance. Within that field, RRAD was a trusted partner of ARRA and UNHCR. The whole development commission, EOC-DICAC, has a much larger scope with a long history of water provision and food aid when it comes to relief work and diverse development activities for long-term development as will be seen in chapter four and five.

There are however two other considerations at stake as well. One is the issue of mutual accountability within the ACT Ethiopia Forum. There is a general commitment in the forum to coordinate and to share information which raises the question of what information to share and when.[136] This commitment is even stronger in emergencies where information sharing is seen as mandatory.[137] The forum has the authority to oversee ACT Appeals on behalf of churches and ACT members who contribute financially to an appeal but are not able to send teams for monitoring and evaluation. This raises the principal question of who owns the appeal – the requesting member(s), or the forum? The other and more contentious issue regards which organisations may implement on behalf of ACT Alliance. In the earlier case of ETH121, and LWF World Service moving ahead without giving a heads-up to other ACT members, no other member could enter into the ACT Appeal as a requesting member, as mentioned earlier.[138]

During the ETH141 there were both frequent reporting and items of raising interest and request for funding. When the appeal was released there was very little interest – even from the ACT Ethiopia Forum international members to raise awareness, but one of the non-relief members of the forum – Bread for the World – which is a development organisation – drafted "an open letter" describing what was seen as a "silent crisis" evolving without much attention from the world as the crisis in South Sudan was not at that time in the focus of international media. It was signed by all members of the forum. It seems that the letter helped raise the

---

[136] ACT Alliance Ethiopia Forum MoU Dec 2009 (6.2 and 6.3).

[137] 2013 09 19 ACT Ethiopia Forum Meeting.

[138] The forum attempted to bring IOCC and EOC-DICAC into the appeal at a later stage, through a revised appeal. It became a matter brought to the attention of ACT Geneva. 2012 06 04 ETH111 working group 4 June 2012.

matter to the home offices of the international agencies of the forum. It thus became an instrument for those working in Ethiopia to advocate for prioritising the crisis within their organisations.[139]

Despite efforts to raise attention to the crisis, funding was slow and insufficient. As a result, implementation was also delayed and partial rather than comprehensive. The lack of funding impacted the coordination and fundraising ability of the forum as no relief coordinator was hired due to lack of funding. Why would the implementing partners prioritise a coordinator when funding for activities was unavailable? The refugee crisis grew, however, and intervention was critically needed. As can be seen from the ACT joint Skype call on April 30, 2014, almost 100 000 refugees had crossed the border into Ethiopia and the Gambella region. The newly opened camp, Lietchor, to which the ACT members had committed itself in the preliminary appeal and in conversations with UNCHR, was bursting its limits with 47 000 people arriving. The camp was planned for 20 000 people – now there was a need for space, infrastructure, and resources for more than the double amount, at least temporarily.[140]

As the funding of the appeal was sorely insufficient, members sought to find other mechanism for fundraising and collaboration – apart from the appeal system. Several members created a consortium as an alternative model to the appeal to jointly raise funds. Established on July 28, the consortium, *Partnership for South Sudanese Refugee Response* (PSSRR), managed to raise funds in its own name and took control of the coordination of the relief efforts.[141]

2.5 Funding Tension: The Ideal and the Practical

This chapter has followed the developments of the South Sudanese crisis with its subsequent refugee crisis and an influx of asylum seekers in Gambella regional state, Ethiopia. The thesis has been able to utilise the primary sources to describe the ETH141 ACT Appeal. The churches had set up ACT Alliance and its national forum, the ACT Ethiopia Forum, as vehicles of emergency preparedness. This

---

[139] 2014 04 09 ACT Ethiopia Forum, "A Silent Crisis is Rapidly Evolving": an open letter from the ACT Ethiopia Forum, April 9, 2014.

[140] *ACT Skype meeting on South Sudan 30 Dec 2013*. It happens that refugee camps for a short while have to make do with a population larger than the one planned for. This allows the aid workers to look for places to establish yet new camps. At this stage in the conflict, there were talks among ACT Alliance of seeking to involve South Sudanese church representatives in peace negotiations in Addis.

[141] 2014 07 29 PSSRR MoU DCA, EOC DICAC, IOCC, LWF DWS, NCA.

included the ACT appeal system as the main instrument for common planning, fundraising, action, and accountability. The ETH141 ACT Appeal, in its three stages, the alert, the preliminary appeal, and the full appeal, therefore, represents the prescribed way the *action by churches together* ought to be pursued according to ACT regulations. As the implementation of the plan of action laid out in the appeal was encountering challenges, it shows tension between the ideal prescribed in ACT policies and the practical reality on the ground. The most significant challenge of the ETH141 appeal was the delay of the work and the lack of funding. This in itself is an important finding. This section will discuss the problem of funding and the tension between the ideal and the practical in ACT Alliance.

The Problem of Funding

Why was the ETH141 underfunded? And what does it have to do with the appeal mechanism and the idea of ACT Alliance as action by churches together? How significant is this question? Primarily, unless there is funding, it is not possible to work towards the objectives in the appeal. Hence the refugee community would be let down by ACT Alliance.[142] If promises were made, or hopes raised, the promises would not be honoured, and the hope turned out to be false. The needs which were stated in the appeal as crucial might not be fulfilled, unless met in some other way, or by other actors. There is, hence, a risk of a failing mission. Secondarily, individual ACT members might be able to raise funding in other ways, but the rationale for ACT Alliance in the first place was for the coordination and cooperation of ACT members in relief, development, and advocacy. Unless there is common funding, there is little use in talking about coordination or working together. Thus, the whole idea of ACT Alliance may be in jeopardy, unless it sorts out a way for common funding. As such, it touches on an important aspect of the ecumenical movement: that of working together, as churches, for peaceful and just societies. It also carries a risk of losing identity as an *action by churches together* for the common good in society. The ACT Alliance document on responses to emergencies says:

> *The commitment of all members to work together and help each other*
> A primary reason for the formation of the ACT Alliance is the firm belief that together ACT members can accomplish more than any one member can do alone, and that by doing so the response will be more effective. Along with this commitment is the recognition that by working together it will be possible to address and overcome inherent issues of justice and equality among and between members. For these reasons, the ACT

---

[142] See chapter three on accountability frameworks on this point of delivering on promises.

Appeal continues to be the primary mechanism within the ACT family for emergency response.[143]

Third, by finding out the reason why the appeal mechanism is not functioning, there may be ways to amend it or abandon it for a better way of common resource pooling. This third reason is not part of the aims of this thesis, but by pointing at the issue, others may deal with this practical matter.

The problem related to funding shows a tension between the ideal and the practical in ACT Alliance. The problem of funding consists of distinct but related issues all pointing to a tension beyond funding itself: a) Funding is the *sine qua non* of refugee assistance, a necessary but not sufficient prerequisite. b) Inadequate, or insecure funding is detrimental to the work. c) Funding works differently for different ACT members. d) Funding refugee assistance is difficult. e) Funding is predicated upon government assistance. f) Government funding threatens operational independence and integrity as well as potentially ecclesial identity. g) Also voluntary funding has its issues. h) Focus on funding may shift from problems to symptoms. Based on the ETH141 appeal a discussion will follow on why issues regarding funding point towards a tension between the ideal and the practical.

Funding is the *sine qua non* of refugee assistance. Without funding the appeal and all the planned interventions for the refugees will fail. Funding – from one source or another – is a necessary but not sufficient requirement for refugee assistance.[144] Inadequate, late, or insecure funding is detrimental to the work. An appeal will not be implemented according to plan if the funding is inadequate, late, or insecure.[145] The practical matters of hiring staff, procuring materials, setting up

---

[143] 2011 11 23 ACT Alliance Response to Emergencies and Annexes, 4.

[144] South Sudanese asylum seekers begun to cross the border to Ethiopia in December 2013. As seen in the stages of the appeal, alert, preliminary, full and revision, no one knew how many there would be, but estimates projected large numbers of people. These people would be allowed by the Ethiopian government to cross the border and enter Ethiopian territory, but where would they go and how would they support themselves? As asylum seekers, the Ethiopian refugee authority (ARRA) seeks to find space for one or several refugee camps. A camp setting entails that means for providing for their own sustenance are scarce and it becomes necessary to provide for the means for their livelihood. The Ethiopian government, as subscriber to the UN-convention on refugees, allows the UN family, northern humanitarian agencies, and national and local humanitarian agencies to assist the government in providing for the asylum seekers. For ACT members to provide services and provisions for the South Sudanese asylum seekers, funding is necessary. A humanitarian response means hiring people, acquiring resources, setting up operation, and planning, managing, and reporting on the whole process.

[145] 2017 01 23 ACT Ethiopia Forum Annual Report to ACT Geneva.

offices, and beginning to assist, it all depends on funding. The importance of this will be clarified in chapter three when going through the accountability standards.

The ACT Ethiopia Forum members are not equal concerning funding schemes. This is a fact that also needs to be clear. It is not a matter of organisational size or strength. It is a matter of funding opportunities. The ACT Ethiopia Forum members, in terms of funding, can generally be classified into three groups: 1) agencies (the E8 group and IOCC) that raise voluntary funding from churches and church constituencies (including the general public), 2) multilateral agencies (LWF World Service and ACT Alliance) that do not raise funding directly from churches but need agencies from group one to support their budgets, and 3) agencies that, though they are church agencies (EOC-DICAC and EECMY-DASSC), do not seek voluntary funding from their churches and church constituencies. Besides voluntary funding, all agencies depend on bilateral government and multilateral intergovernmental funding from funding bodies, such as UN agencies and the humanitarian agency of the European Union (ECHO). Also, in this case, the agencies are not equal regarding access to governmental and intergovernmental funding, but that is a more complicated picture.[146] This means that the northern-based

---

[146] Churches are able to raise voluntary funds from their members attending church. Churches need to raise funds for their expenses. Whatever funds are raised for relief is in addition to those funds. Lower participation by members entails lower income and low fundraising for other causes. The exceptional case is churches that are able to use tax funding based on the historical appropriation of church property by the state. Very rarely are churches allowed to use funds from their own budgets. Funds raised by the agencies may come from fund raising among the general public, from regular supporters, and from government sources. Voluntary fund raising from the general public is significant when it comes to (sudden) natural disasters with significant media coverage where human suffering is apparent. Church attendees are more prone to sharing their resources than the general public, but their attention is divided between different valuable causes. In cases of relief work, they may give to the Red Cross or Doctors without Borders, as likely as to their church relief agencies, particularly if the church agencies are operating with little attention to participatory forms of engagement in the life of the churches. This leaves the final source of income – stat-financed funds. The most significant northern based ACT agencies match about half of the most significant government donors in humanitarian relief, the OECD's Development Assistance Committee (DAC). These DAC members are also among the most significant providers of aid overall, as defined as Overseas Development Assistance (ODA) by the OECD. Foreign aid article on Britannica written by Victoria Williams, https://www.britannica.com/topic/foreign-aid, The vast majority of ODA comes from the countries of the Organisation for Economic Co-operation and Development (OECD), specifically the nearly two dozen countries that make up the OECD's Development Assistance Committee (DAC). The DAC includes western European countries, the United States, Canada, Japan, Australia, and

ACT agencies have potential access to some of the most important donors of the humanitarian sector. So, what is the issue? Solidarity in funding between ACT members is essential for ACT Alliance. If the ACT Ethiopia Forum members are unable to assist one another with funding, the collaboration is endangered, and the idea of ACT, as agencies working together, is jeopardised. It is not enough to put the responsibility on requesting agencies to themselves raise funding. That would be a separatist approach of every agency fending for themselves, not the ACT approach of acting together. This point is valid regardless of which agency (for example LWF World Service in ETH121) or agencies (EOC-DICAC, IOCC, and LWF in ETH141) are involved in the appeal, or whether Ethiopian church agencies are involved or not. One of the main reasons why this is a valid point is that there are always more requests than funding available within the network of ACT Alliance.[147]

New Zealand. Other providers of significant assistance include Brazil, China, Iceland, India, Kuwait, Poland, Qatar, Saudi Arabia, South Korea, Taiwan, Turkey, and the United Arab Emirates.

[147] The main vehicle of ACT Alliance in raising funds for humanitarian relief is through its emergency appeal mechanism in which the local ACT forum, the members working in the country, come together, assess the needs, plan for relief work, and appeal for funding to ACT Alliance. ACT Alliance consists of ca 140 member organisations, mostly southern based churches, church-based or faith-based organisations and a smaller number of northern-based agencies. The southern-based organisations do not contribute as donors to the budget of ACT appeals, except to their own work and indirectly through ACT Alliance fee system. It means that the funding of ACT Appeals comes from, or through, the northern based agencies and the sources from which they can acquire funds. ACT Alliance 2009 "Procedure for Funding the Unified ACT Alliance."

A common complaint with ACT Alliance regards the member fees because the perception is that the alliance would bring income, not costs. The agencies of the churches all seek funding, but few are the churches that contribute to the common pool of resources. Many agencies have a constituency of individuals who contribute regularly, but those funds are distributed across the globe according to set priorities in the head offices. In the case of the ACT members in Ethiopia – most of them are fundraisers – but they are also acting themselves, on their own accord or through one or more partner organisations. Among six European ACT members, there were 64 partner organisations in Ethiopia. The issue of the mechanism of channelling humanitarian ACT resources either through only members or through other non-ACT members was raised and discussed. For the European ACT members, the question was whether ACT funding should go to ACT partners or also to "non-ACT outlets," i.e. partners that are not ACT members. It was identified as an important issue to solve for a "strengthened ACT fellowship". This was a discussion on relief and did not touch on issues of development collaboration. 2008 08 05 Minutes of August 5 E8 Meeting.

This shows that unrealistic hopes are raised by the ACT appeal system. Is funding raised through the system? Yes, globally it is a notable number, but the number of emergencies and the amount of funding required for adequate responses are greater still. In Ethiopia, if all the ACT members would have contributed with funding, perhaps a core funding could have been raised to help the appeal to start with. In the actual case, the European agencies spread their attention in the South Sudanese crisis, into four different appeals, and for good reasons. It makes sense to respond within South Sudan if feasible. Several ACT agencies with years of experience and offices and staff in place would be able to offer services close to home. The LWF World Service in Kenya and Uganda[148] had been serving South Sudanese refugees for years, and so were able to quickly increase their operations to accommodate recent arrivals, in Kenya in collaboration with the National Council of Churches of Kenya (NCCK).[149] However, it had the effect of leaving the requesting members in Ethiopia, at first, on their own to raise funding. In the end, all ACT members contributed to the refugee response in one way or another, but few contributed to the funding of the appeal.[150]

If all the ACT members did not plan to contribute their share of the funding, how did ACT Ethiopia Forum expect to raise the funds? The only reasonable answer would be through government funding. As I will show in chapter five, the ACT members – before ACT was founded – had worked through several crises before by appealing both to voluntary contributions and the good will of governments for funding. There are no reasons to believe that the dual strategy of voluntary contribution and government contributions had changed in this case. It did not work well in the ETH141 appeal.

A survey on the work of the ACT members in Ethiopia, when considered as a whole, showed 300 projects all across Ethiopia with a total budget of above one billion Ethiopian Birr. 2011 ACT Alliance Ethiopia "2011 Mapping." The survey was done in 2011 as part of setting up ACT Alliance. It showed that the 9 ACT members together had 300 projects in Ethiopia with a 1.35 B ETB total budget. Oromia region had the largest budget at 429M ETB and 108 projects, and Livelihood and food security was the largest thematic area with 353M ETB. In comparison, the Gambella had 18 projects. The EECMY-DASSC funding from ACT partners had been excluded to avoid double counting. Of the ACT members, the EECMY-DASSC had the largest budget in 2011, EED second, EOC-DICAC third, and LWF fourth. Relief funding was ca 13% of the total.

[148] LWF was operational 1986–2007 serving Sudanese refugees in the Adjumani district, Uganda. 2015 07 LWF Uganda Situation Report. 2013 12 30 ACT UGA141 Preliminary appeal South Sudanese refugees.

[149] 2013 12 30 KEN141 ACT Preliminary Appeal South Sudanese Refugees.

[150] ACT Alliance 2009 "Procedure for Funding the Unified ACT Alliance." 2014 11 17 ACT Ethiopia Forum Annual Report 2014 Nov 17.

The LWF World Service and the refugee department of the Ethiopian Orthodox agency regularly serve refugees with funding from UNHCR. The UN agency in its case receives its funding from governments, mainly from OECD nations. LWF World Service is able to receive funding through the member churches of the Lutheran World Federation as well as from ACT Alliance. These LWF and ACT contributions help LWF World Service to get started while negotiating with UNHCR according to the cluster system.[151] As such, LWF World Service does not count on being able to receive full funding through donations through ACT Alliance, but early core funding still makes a difference.

Funding refugee assistance is difficult. It is hard for several reasons, among them, as the case study has highlighted, is the suddenness of a major humanitarian crisis, the uncertainty of how many people are in need and for how long they may stay. All basic needs have to be covered because refugees leave their assets behind and have lost their livelihoods. Hence, the level of assistance needed is high. A crisis caused by conflict generates less empathy than a natural disaster, so less voluntary funding may be raised. Voluntary funding also requires media attention, and media tend to focus on one crisis at a time. This was the time of the Syrian crisis. Secure funding is for all these reasons predicated upon government assistance. Since it is beyond voluntary funding to cover great needs during an extended time, refugee assistance will be based on government assistance. Significant changes to humanitarian governance were made during the second half of the twentieth century to accommodate the regular funding of a large refugee population. The previous approach was to fundraise by voluntary contributions on a case-to-case basis. Also government contributions were set up on a case-to-case basis.[152]

The contemporary international framework of relief is built on the assumption that substantial relief funding will be part of the standing budget of some nations. This dependence on government funding may threaten the operational independence and integrity of relief agencies and, potentially, the ecclesial identity of church agencies. For church agencies receiving government funding, this raises questions. One aspect regards operational independence and integrity, see humanitarian principles in chapter three. Another aspect concerns the identity of church assistance when the funding is not coming from churches with the risk that donor

---

[151] The UNHCR uses a system of thematic sectors – clusters – in which one or several aid agencies receives a responsibility for the sector. The system makes the agencies accountable for the services of that sector.

[152] 2018 07 25 UNHCR "2017 Year-End Report GR2017-Ethiopia-eng-2." UNHCR 2019 "UNHCR in 2019: Overview Mission." UN 2016 02 02 Ban Ki-Moon 2016.

compliance may lead to loss of ecclesial identity for the agencies and inner secular-isation for churches.

Also voluntary funding has its issues. It is not simply a matter of government funding being problematic while voluntary funding is not. Plenty could also be queried about agencies raising funds from ordinary people. Since the focus of the research project is on Ethiopia, this aspect is outside of the scope of the thesis. At least one of the questions that could be asked has theological bearing with regard to the old question of penance. Since relief agencies continuously stress the ur-gency of the needs, which may be true in each case, consciously or not, there is a risk of spiritually coercing people into paying, lest they become guilty of injustice towards people in need. The worst form of this is the projection of a colonisation complex, see chapter four. In this scheme of thought, people in the West owe it to people in Africa to atone for the sins of colonialism and imperialism by repeatedly paying retroactively back. This resembles the system of indulgences of the medie-val Latin church. In the modern world, it is sometimes thought of as social justice.

Shifting Focus from Problems to Symptoms

Focus on funding may shift attention from problems to symptoms. Since funding is needed, and humanitarian needs are urgent, the dual focus on funding and alle-viation raises the issue of treating the symptoms rather than dealing with the prob-lems. Refugee assistance may become a generation-long engagement of rendering relief without the political issues causing the crisis being solved.[153] The UN was created to help resolve these kinds of political issues and the World Council of Churches had a similar obligation to seek peace and sustainable political solutions on behalf of the churches. To what extent these institutions can be blamed for not solving the political issues is another question, but the fact is that "the interna-tional community" of nations and institutions have prioritised relief assistance over political problem-solving.[154]

---

[153] The case in point is the Palestinian communities that LWF World Service have catered since 1947-1948. It is a special case. Still people are growing up in refugee camps as if camps were the solution, not a temporary alleviation of suffering. Cf. 2014 07 22 UNHCR Policy on Alter-natives to Camps.

[154] Cf. the stress on political solutions and not only humanitarian relief in UN 2016 02 02 Ban Ki-Moon 2016. See research in this area. Hovil 2016, 12 on misdiagnosis of conflict.

Tension between the Ideal and the Practical

What is common among these issues is that they show a tension between the ideal and the practical. What do I mean by this? The ideal denotes an idea that given the progress of modern civilisation, there is no good reason for people to suffer and die in vain. Given enough resources, human suffering in terms of a humanitarian crisis or hunger can be dealt with as yet another problem to solve. Since modern civilisation has managed to create an excess of resources – a positive balance between needs and resources – there is a moral imperative to assist all those in need and alleviate their suffering. We can and therefore we ought, to refer to Immanuel Kant. This is the ideal driving the humanitarian sector. In practice, it is not that easy. Theoretically, it may sound possible, and many near-impossible feats have been done to interact with disasters and conflicts in such a way that the ideal seems feasible.[155] And yet there is a gap between what people want to accomplish, *the ideal*, and that which is achieved, *the practical*. This is what I would call the tension between the ideal and the practical.

End of Appeal – End of Engagement?

It is good to be reminded that the thesis is limited in its extent to the ETH141 full appeal period which extended from January to December 2014. The political crisis in South Sudan whose humanitarian consequences the ETH141 appeal was to alleviate did not follow the schedule of a standard relief project of six to twelve months. In 2018, UNHCR reported that more than 400 000 refugees from South Sudan were staying in Ethiopia throughout 2017.[156] By the beginning of 2018, the conflict in South Sudan had generated some 2.4 Million refugees placing South Sudan at the top five list of countries from whom people were fleeing political violence.[157] The extension of the ETH141 appeal ended in December 2015 with final

---

[155] Cf. de Waal, Alex. 2018, 5 "The near-eclipse of famine in the last three decades is the result partly of the positive efforts of humanitarians and others concerned with human welfare and development, but much more so of the decline of megalomania and of political attitudes that regard people as dispensable. To overcome famine in the modern era, our main adversary has been political leaders, not the weather or the poor state of the roads."

[156] UNHCR reported circa 900 000 refugees in Ethiopia and more than one million displaced people due to conflict in 2017. 2018 07 25 UNHCR "2017 Year-End Report GR2017-Ethiopia-eng-2."

[157] UNHCR reported that by the beginning of 2018, South Sudan was the third on the top five list of countries with the Syrian Arab Republic (6.3M) and Afghanistan (2.6M) being the top two, and Myanmar (1.2M) and Somalia (almost 1M) being number four and five. UNHCR 2019 "UNHCR in 2019: Overview Mission."

reporting in 2016.[158] In the forum annual report for 2016 to the ACT Secretariat the author had this to say about the ETH141 appeal:

> The forum has successfully accomplished one of the most complex ACT appeals, ETH141 in response to the overwhelming influx of refugees from South Sudan. The appeal has been implemented from January 2014 to December 2015. The appeal has been revised and extended twice during this course of implementation. Even though only 25% of the appeal has been funded, members were able to mobilize other bilateral funding from UNHCR, EU and other major donors to respond to high priority needs.[159]

Such a positive self-evaluation of the longer historical scheme should remind us that challenges were partially overcome, and assistance rendered. The appeal was not in vain. It does not entail that the kind of challenges mentioned above were a one-time event, as the next statement in the report clarifies:

> The ETH161 appeal funding response was slow and late so it was difficult to pursue timely response to height priorities. Requesting members have to ask an extension and revision of the appeal as the targeted six months response ends. Additional six months extension and revision of the budget to meet the current needs has been approved by the secretariat.[160]

By 2017 unrest was part of the situation in Ethiopia complicating the work.[161]

---

[158] 2016 02 LWF ETH141 Final Narrative Report Feb 2016.
[159] 2017 01 23 ACT Ethiopia Forum Annual Report to ACT Geneva.
[160] 2017 01 23 ACT Ethiopia Forum Annual Report to ACT Geneva.
[161] 2017 01 23 ACT Ethiopia Forum Annual Report to ACT Geneva.

3. International Framework and Stakeholders

In this third chapter, the institutional framework of international standards will be analysed to identify the main principles of the ETH141 ACT Appeal by a textual analysis of the standards referred to in the appeal, for the sake of deepening the discussion on the fundamental goals and principles of the assistance. These standards are part of an international framework of humanitarian governance. Considered as a whole, the standards also express a principled approach to the relief work of ACT Alliance. An ethical and theological discussion of the principles on which the standards are built will held.

This thesis focuses on the engagement of the churches, via church-based and faith-based humanitarian agencies, ACT Alliance and its members, in refugee assistance. It needs to be considered that the churches are not the only actors in the humanitarian arena. In relief assistance, there are several major stakeholders such as the parties in the conflict, the national states involved, the UN, the donor states, various relief organisations, the refugee population, the local host communities, and the local churches.[1] All of these stakeholders interact in the same space, and the collaborative approach of ACT Alliance ought to be seen also with this in mind. The policies analysed in this chapter exist because of this complex interaction of many people from various organisations and communities. ACT adheres to standard policies to work with multiple stakeholders, not just churches.

The international relief apparatus system has been developed step by step through a historical process. Experiences, such as the Israel-Arab War 1948,[2] the

---

[1] In the case of both South Sudan and Ethiopia this include federal as well as national states.

[2] The war 1948 led to a protracted refugee crisis which is still not solved. LWF World Service have been serving the Palestinian refugees and communities during these seventy years.

Rwandan genocide in 1994,[3] and the earthquake in Tahiti 2010,[4] and the chaos resulting from the numerous and uncoordinated humanitarian agencies. Different crisis events in the Horn of Africa, and not the least the famine across the Sahel in 1984, have contributed to the learning and fine-tuning of the system. This insight from Walker and Maxwell shows the importance of the study of the historical events in which the humanitarian system was developed.[5]

The chapter consists of five sections. *A Commitment to High Standards* (3.1) describes and discusses the international standards referred to in the ETH141 ACT Appeal. The aim is to map the contemporary institutional framework of humanitarian assistance in 2014, as a synchronic study, and to identify the main principles outlined in the international standards referred to in the ETH141 appeal. This is the main section of the chapter which the rest of the chapter depends upon.

The Humanitarian Moral Argument (3.2) argues that the basis for humanitarian work is based on a moral argument from natural law, what I call the "humanitarian argument." The humanitarian imperative as the first principle of humanitarian relief work is framed as a categorical imperative, in the manner of Immanuel Kant, modified and applied in the international standards. Here I discuss the nature of morality, and I argue that the default Christian view is that basic morality is common among all peoples, part of common sense, and the "ought dimension" of the moral law.

In *Action Based on International Law* (3.3), I argue that despite the differences between *International Humanitarian Law* (IHL), *International Refugee Law* (IRL), and *International Human Rights Law* (IHRL), these legal systems are based on the idea of the rule of law and natural law morality. This implies that the intent of law is to protect the weak against the strong, outlaw reckless political action, and to permit relief assistance. Thus, there is a law-based approach within humanitarian action in line with Christian teaching on morality as God-given to all.

African Gate Keeper States and Stakeholders (3.4) deals with the fact that *ACT Alliance* is not acting in a social and political vacuum, but in a context that became

---

[3] The international community failed to prevent or mitigate the Rwandan genocide in 1994. In the ensuing refugee crisis, the people who fled the Rwandan Patriotic Front were practically hostages by the Interahamwe, the instigators of the genocide. Humanitarian agencies were unable to separate combatants from civilians, a prerequisite in humanitarian aid.

[4] After the earthquake in Tahiti 2010, chaos resulted from the lack of coordination among the numerous humanitarian agencies, many of which had not been working in Tahiti before.

[5] Walker and Maxwell 2009.

more complex because of how modern African states mimic colonial policies of what is known as the gate keeper state.

In *Morality, Principled Action, and The Christian Church* (3.5) I argue for a relationship between morality, legality, and church tradition. This discussion grounds the discussion on the traditions of the Orthodox and the Mekane Yesus churches, which is the focus of the next chapter.

3.1 A Commitment to High Standards

In the ACT Appeal ETH141, agencies are declaring that, besides ACT principles and guidelines, they also adhere to international standards such as *the Sphere Standard, the HAP Standard, the IASC Mental Health and Psychosocial Support guidelines* (MHPSS), and *The Code of Conduct for the International Red Cross and Red Crescent Movement and NGOs in Disaster Relief.*[6] In this thesis, these international standards and guidelines will be understood as constituting an institutional framework as part of an effort to distinguish the humanitarian relief sector – in this case engaged in refugee assistance – from other social and political engagements. As the standards are considered the principles upon which the appeal – and therefore the refugee assistance – is based, the policies and guidelines as these are referred to in the ACT ETH141 final appeal document are important for an analysis of the refugee assistance of the churches through their aid agencies.[7]

A commitment to high standards is part of the idea of ACT Alliance and the ecumenical movement at large. On behalf of its member churches and related agencies, ACT Alliance and the Lutheran World Federation are part of a network of relief agencies that are setting humanitarian policies, creating a framework of principles for the work, and furthering the institutionalisation of a humanitarian sector. In this case study of refugee assistance, this is particularly clear from *the Humanitarian Charter and Minimum Standards in Humanitarian Response* from *the Sphere Handbook* of 2011, and the accountability standard of *the Humanitarian Accountability Partnership* (HAP) – the so-called "HAP-standard" of 2010 – promoted by ACT Alliance.[8]

---

[6] 2014 02 12 ETH141 Asylum Seekers South Sudan, 15–20 "implementation methodology."

[7] Sphere Project 2011. HAP 2010. IASC 2007. These documents are updated regularly.

[8] ACT Alliance is not only a signatory to the highest humanitarian codes and standards, including ICRC 1994 *the Code of Conduct for the International Red Cross and Red Crescent Movement and NGOs in Disaster Relief.* Before the formation of ACT Alliance, WCC was part of the

ACT Alliance. 2011a. *ACT Alliance Code of Conduct: For the prevention of sexual exploitation and abuse, fraud and corruption and abuse of power*.

HAP. 2010. *The 2010 HAP Standard in Accountability and Quality Management*. 2nd ed.

ICRC. 1994. *The Code of Conduct for the International Red Cross and Red Crescent Movement and NGOs in Disaster Relief*.

Inter-Agency Standing Committee. 2007. *IASC Guidelines on Mental Health and Psychosocial Support in Emergency Settings*.

Sphere Project. 2011. *Humanitarian Charter and Minimum Standards in Humanitarian Response*. 3rd ed.

Figure 3.1: *The International Standards Cited in the ETH141 ACT Appeal, the primary documents in this chapter. Later developments of the standards will not be dealt with.*

Sphere, Quality Standards and Principled Humanitarian Action

The Sphere Project was set up in 1997 to improve the quality of disaster response and to enable accountability towards populations at risk. The initiative was taken by a group of relief agencies in collaboration with the International Red Cross and Red Crescent Movement. The ETH141 Refugee Appeal refers to the 2011 edition of *the Sphere Handbook*. This handbook has four major parts: the humanitarian charter, the protection principles, the core principles, and the minimum standards. *The humanitarian charter* draws on the development of international standards as provided by organisations such as the International Federation of the Red Cross (IFRC), the Sphere Association, the Inter Agency Standard Committee (IASC), and the Core Humanitarian Standards Alliance and it provides the ethical and legal framework, or "shared belief" for the rest of the handbook.[9]

The order of priority in the handbook is to work from core principles towards standardised humanitarian action of high quality. The principles give the impetus for the quality standards. Therefore, the main structure of the handbook is based and contingent upon a principled approach from which it provides practical

---

group of organisations behind the "Code" 1996. ACT Alliance is a member of the International Council for Voluntary Agencies (ICVA), and the Steering Committee for Humanitarian Response (SCHR). The Lutheran World Federation and ACT Alliance are both members of the Sphere Project and were two of the 14 organisations behind the Humanitarian Accountability Partnership (HAP) in January 2003. ACT Alliance is also a member of Reuters' AlertNet.

[9] Sphere Project 2011, 4, 20.

guidelines in terms of objectives and quality measurements. What are those principles? The main principles outlined in the Sphere handbook are based on two core beliefs: first, that those affected by disaster or conflict have a right to life with dignity and, therefore, a right to assistance; and second, that all possible steps should be taken to alleviate human suffering arising out of disaster or conflict.[10]

The handbook's structure reflects Sphere's aim to firmly anchor relief response in both a rights-based and a participatory approach. It is a statement of established legal rights and obligations, and of shared beliefs and commitments of humanitarian agencies, all collected in a set of common principles, rights, and duties.[11]

Founded on *the principle of humanity* and *the humanitarian imperative*, the rights of those affected by disaster or conflict include the right to a life with dignity, the right to receive humanitarian assistance, and the right to protection and security. Besides the principle of humanity, the principles of impartiality, neutrality, and independence are mentioned – particularly as part of the Code of Conduct that will be explained below.[12]

Protection is a core part of relief assistance and "the Protection Principles"[13] point to the responsibility of all relief agencies to ensure that their activities are concerned with the more severe threats that affected people commonly face in times of conflict or disaster in terms of external threats to physical and psychological harm, the issue of limited access to assistance, and even harm from humanitarian actors and people involved in the relief work. In the context of humanitarian action, then, protection has a broader meaning than legal protection.[14]

The minimum standards are based on a utilitarian structure for the sake of the moral good of human life and dignity. The standards focus on attaining concrete results, and a level of achievement necessary for a dignified sustenance of human life – a measurement of decent living standards, or at least acceptable minimum

---

[10] Sphere Project 2011, 4.

[11] Sphere Project 2011, 4.

[12] Sphere Project 2011, 6.

[13] "All humanitarian agencies should ensure that their actions do not bring further harm to affected people (Protection Principle 1), that their activities benefit in particular those who are most affected and vulnerable (Protection Principle 2), that they contribute to protecting affected people from violence and other human rights abuses (Protection Principle 3), and that they help affected people recover from abuses (Protection Principle 4). The roles and responsibilities of humanitarian agencies in protection are, generally, secondary to the legal responsibility of the state or other relevant authorities. Protection often involves reminding these authorities of their responsibilities." Sphere Project 2011, 6.

[14] Sphere Project 2011, 6; 25–47. Cf. Hovil 2006, 61; O'Sullivan and Stevens 2017, 6.

standards of living in a short-term crisis. These concrete results to be achieved by relief agencies are in the handbook structured into four main categories, so-called sectors, regarding: (1) water, sanitation, and hygiene,[15] (2) food and nutrition,[16] (3) shelter, settlement and "non-food items",[17] and (4) health.[18] These categories help coordinate relief response into sectors in which one or several agencies assume responsibility either for a whole sector or for a specified part of that sector. The achievements and shortcomings of one agency may be measured against the needs of the population according to standard assessments.

The Sphere Handbook is highly regarded among relief staff and used precisely for its concrete detailing on the number of litres of water needed per person each day to stay clean and healthy, or the number of calories necessary for daily consumption to prevent undernourishment and malnutrition. However, the authors of the handbook point to the importance of the fundamental principles of the so-called "Humanitarian Charter" to be able to use the utility-based minimum standards correctly. In this way, the different parts of the handbook should be evaluated in the light of the whole. One example of this is the importance of the so-called core standards regarding the minimum standards of the sectors mentioned above.

The core standards describe processes and approaches within a humanitarian response which show that the skills of a water engineer need to be complemented with other skill sets which have more to do with people skills, humanitarian know-how of various vulnerabilities, and the ability to encourage, foster and facilitate participation among the people the agencies aim to assist. These "humanitarian concerns", which the core standards are injecting into the rather technocratic work of the sectors, also include "cross-cutting themes" such as children, elderly people, people with disabilities, gender, psychosocial issues, HIV and AIDS, and environment, climate change and disaster risk reduction. In this way, the core standards complement the "hard issues" of building an infrastructure of the sectors with "soft issues" of building a community of sorts and bridging the gap between agencies and the population.[19]

Each chapter of the sectors contains a sector-specific introduction to how the humanitarian charter, international law, protection principle and core standards are linked to the issues of water, food, shelter, and health. These include

---

[15] Sphere 2011, 79–137.
[16] Sphere 2011, 139–238.
[17] Sphere 2011, 239–86.
[18] Sphere 2011, 288–354.
[19] Sphere 2011, 50–75.

descriptions of how specific vulnerabilities may reinforce one another for an individual and highlight the need for relief workers to facilitate people's participation, using disaggregated statistical data for analysis of vulnerabilities, and to ensure that aid is "accessible to all members of the community."[20]

The Sphere Handbook is designed to facilitate the work of staff members of aid agencies by explaining "*what* needs to be in place in order to ensure a life with dignity for the affected population" [emphasis added] by providing key actions, but not by specifying *how* to achieve the standards. Therefore the Sphere Handbook 2011 leaves considerable freedom to each agency to work according to internal policies and to customise a response with respect to the cultural context. The handbook was written as "a voluntary code and self-regulatory tool for quality and accountability" and as oriented towards compliance towards a process of accreditation. The purpose was to encourage various actors to engage with the handbook without prescribing one specified form of action. The authors recognise that "[t]he degree to which agencies can meet the standards depend on a range of factors, some of which are outside of their control", for example, the lack of access to the community, the lack of cooperation from authorities, or an uncertain security situation. In those types of situations, the handbook prescribes reporting the gap between standard and outcome, explaining the reasons for the shortage, indicating what needs to be changed, assessing the negative impact of not meeting the standards, and acting in such a way as to mitigate the harm.[21]

Although the Sphere Handbook provides an overview of short-term humanitarian relief work, one guideline may not be sufficient or comprehensive in scope or depth. Therefore, the handbook gives plenty of references both to areas not covered – such as education, and livelihoods activities[22] – and to further readings in the areas covered. For example, Sphere dedicated five pages to mental health thus showing the importance of mental health for the overall response and outlining the minimum response in any crisis. Those pages in Sphere link up with the Inter-Agency Standing Committee *IASC Guidelines on Mental Health and Psychosocial Support in Emergency Settings* (MHPSS) from 2007 with its almost two hundred pages including further references to indicate how actors may improve the relief response.[23]

---

[20] Sphere 2011, 50–75, 248.

[21] Sphere 2011, 8–9.

[22] Sphere 2011, 12.

[23] Sphere 2011, 333–37.

Besides the Sphere standard which gives a general overview and introduces the main humanitarian principles, it is of importance to further examine *the IASC Mental Health and Psychosocial Support guidelines* (MHPSS) in order to understand the principles behind the ACT ETH141 appeal. It is one example of a standard of a more specific kind. Other standards often focus on sectors, such as water and sanitation, food security, shelter and necessary "non-food items." As mentioned above, mental health and psychosocial support may refer a) to specific operations and activities in mental health and psychosocial support, b) or to psychosocial issues as a cross-cutting concern, or c) to an overall approach which does not neglect that man needs more than bread to survive.[24]

LWF World Service as well as the refugee department of the Orthodox commission were using an integrated approach to mental health and social issues. As such, mental health and psychosocial support are of special interest to this thesis. These are also areas of overlapping between the teaching of churches and the thinking in this field because it pertains to the human person as something with more than a body with bodily needs, as will be shown in chapter four.[25]

Rwanda and Do No Harm

The 1994 Rwanda genocide constituted a crisis for the humanitarian sector. The international community were unable to prevent the genocide. In addition to the lack of international peacekeepers at the beginning of the crisis, humanitarian agencies were unable to uphold the civilian nature of the subsequent refugee camps when people fled the rebels who put an end to the genocide. Unintentionally, relief workers ended up helping the perpetrators of the genocide to hold the population "hostage" and to misuse the camps, using them to raid Rwanda.[26] The issue was not the relief assistance to participants in the genocide. It was that the principles of humanitarian action had not been upheld, with disastrous consequences for both sides of the conflict. The 1996 "Joint Evaluation of Emergency Assistance to Rwanda", with John Borton as lead author, gave rise to several

---

[24] Horn, Besselink, and Tankink 2016; IASC 2007. See Sphere Project 2011 for minimum standards in these sectors as well as protection principles and cross cutting issues.

[25] 2014 02 12 ETH141 Asylum Seekers South Sudan, 14–15 "IOCC/DICAC Response." See chapter two for the plans of working within this field. See chapter four for churches' stress that man needs more than material goods for life. On the concept of person, Zizioulas 1985.

[26] Terry 2002, 2.

different initiatives to improve the accountability of humanitarian agencies towards the populations they serve. The Sphere project represents one of these initiatives.[27]

The standards, the setting of principles, and the rise of organisations that hold humanitarian agencies accountable should be understood as a twenty-year process of aid agencies creating a framework for dealing with the complex political dynamics of the post-Cold-War era of intra-state conflicts, as well as demands from donor agencies for transparency and compliance in line with the ideas of New Public Management.[28]

One of the most significant contributions was given by Mary Anderson, whose *Do No Harm: How Aid Can Support Peace – or War* from 1999 described the problems of the humanitarian sector, and outlined practical ways to deal with the dynamics of conflict.[29] Despite attempts to deal with the issues, Anderson, Brown, and Jean's research shows that the major actors still envisage an inability to listen to the communities they aimed to serve.[30]

Humanitarian agencies operate in complex conflict situations – as in the example above from Rwanda, where distinguishing perpetrators and victims becomes as crucial as it may be difficult. In addition, the agencies may come under pressure from both donor and host governments.[31] By holding themselves accountable primarily towards the populations they aim to serve, but also towards governments and donors, the aid agencies attempt to create a humanitarian space outside of political ambitions and armed conflicts while operating close to or even within conflict zones. Orobator has stated it as "the moral priority of crisis-affected people":

> One important ethical consideration that should inform the behavior of humanitarian organizations is *the moral priority of crisis-affected people*. This means that the primary goal of humanitarian action should be always to serve the interest of the beneficiaries. In other words, NGOs are morally accountable to the crisis-affected populations that they serve and on whose account they solicit donations. No initiative, no matter how laudable, can compensate for the subversion of this principle. This does not undermine the validity of humanitarian organizations' accountability to a variety of donors and to themselves as goal-oriented and objective-driven institutions.[32]

---

[27] Terry 2002. HAP 2011. Walker 2009, 129.

[28] HAP 2011. Walker 2009, 129. For a critique of bureaucratic compliance, Bornemark 2018.

[29] Anderson 1999.

[30] Anderson, Brown, and Jean 2012.

[31] SCHR 2013 09 10 SCHR Proposed Certification Model: "Humanitarian organisations are facing increasing demands from donors, host governments and affected populations to demonstrate that they are professional, capable and accountable for achieving quality results."

[32] Hollenbach 2008, 236. Orobator in Hollenbach 2008, 236. Stress added.

Thus there are two demands to be distinguished: the requirement of responsibility towards donors and host governments to show effectiveness and efficiency, and the moral demand of serving "crisis-affected people" with a bottom-up accountability.[33]

An NGO Code of Conduct

The first instrument aid agencies put to use in the endeavour to safeguard a humanitarian space and give attention to populations at risk was a normative, but voluntary, code of conduct. *The Code of Conduct for the International Red Cross and the Red Crescent Movement and NGOs in Disaster Relief* was published in 1996. It states ten principles for humanitarian agencies. The four principles of humanity, impartiality, neutrality, and independence are followed by four principles aimed at giving space to the communities by respecting local culture and building on local capacity, participation, and resilience. There is one principle of dual accountability towards both "donor and beneficiaries." Finally, there is one principle of seeking media attention without competing for funds through the humiliation of the population by portraying them as helpless victims. The NGO Code of Conduct has been widely spread among humanitarian agencies, and its principles are generally held in high regard.[34]

Humane, Impartial, Neutral, and Independent Agencies

Four principles have become basic to humanitarian action: humanity, impartiality, neutrality, and independence. By bringing these principles into the code of conduct of an organisation – such as when the ETH141 appeal refers to *the Code of Conduct for the International Red Cross and the Red Crescent Movement and NGOs in Disaster Relief* – brings a particular principled mindset into the fore: that of "a humanitarian." These four principles are debated, and at times contested, and there are traces of this debate also within the Sphere handbook.[35]

The right to receive humanitarian assistance is a necessary element of the right to life with dignity. This encompasses the right to an adequate standard of living, including adequate food, water, clothing, shelter and the requirements for good health, which are expressly guaranteed in international law.[36]

---

[33] Hollenbach 2008, 236. Orobator in Hollenbach 2008, 236.

[34] Sphere 2011, 368–72, annex 2: "The Code of Conduct."

[35] Sphere 2011, 368–72, annex 2: "The Code of Conduct."

[36] Sphere 2011, 22. The principle of impartiality is affirmed both in the Humanitarian Charter of Sphere (p.19) and in the Code of Conduct (annex 2, p. 368 of Sphere).

To save lives and alleviate suffering according to the principle of humanity, other principles are needed as well. Two of these were already stamped out in the early days of the International Committee of the Red Cross: impartiality and neutrality. These two principles are derived from the context of disaster or conflict. *Impartiality*[37] means that relief should be rendered to the population on both sides of the conflict. In the present extended usage of the term, it entails that assistance should "be provided solely on the basis of need and in proportion to need", and also that no one should be discriminated against in such a way that their personal status would impinge on the principle that assistance would be rendered to all in need.[38]

In the practice of the ETH141 appeal, the principle of impartiality leads to the attempt to include the host community as well as the refugees in the response. The host community were also affected by the refugee influx. First as they acted as first responders – sharing what they had when the refugees arrived – they were in danger of becoming impoverished, and hence at risk, because of their solidarity with the refugees. For this reason, and for the sake of justice, some of the services rendered to the refugee community were also extended to the host community. For example, the water system planned by the LWF World Service in the refugee camp was calculated to be able to cater for the needs of the community as well. The UNHCR strives towards sharing 30 per cent of the resources with the host community.[39] Second as the Lietchor camp area was flooded, the refugees sought safety "in higher drier grounds and in host community settlement areas in Jikawo, Makuey and Wanthowa woredas. Assistance provided to the refugees should thus be

---

[37] "6. The right to receive humanitarian assistance is a necessary element of the right to life with dignity. This encompasses the right to an adequate standard of living, including adequate food, water, clothing, shelter and the requirements for good health, which are expressly guaranteed in international law. The Sphere Core Standards and minimum standards reflect these rights and give practical expression to them, specifically in relation to the provision of assistance to those affected by disaster or conflict. Where the state or non-state actors are not providing such assistance themselves, we believe they must allow others to help do so. Any such assistance must be provided according to the principle of impartiality, which requires that it be provided solely on the basis of need and in proportion to need. This reflects the wider principle of non-discrimination: that no one should be discriminated against on any grounds of status, including age, gender, race, colour, ethnicity, sexual orientation, language, religion, disability, health status, political or other opinion, national or social origin." Sphere 2011, 22.

[38] Sphere 2011, 22, 37. This principle was upheld in the early church as witnessed in Acts 2. The second principle of non-discrimination against anyone in need corresponds to the Jesus' admonition to "love your enemies".

[39] 2014 02 12 ETH141 Asylum Seekers South Sudan 12 Feb 2014.

extended to the host community." As the development commission of the Mekane Yesus was not a known partner of UNHCR, this task suited the commission since it could work with local authorities on it.[40]

As Henri Dunant – the founder of the Red Cross – describes in the classical *A Memory of Solferino* about his experience and thoughts about the battle in the north-Italian Solferino 1859, he was horrified with moral outrage over the wasteful exploitation of human lives and wanted to aid to the best of his abilities. Accustomed as he was, as a Pietist Christian, to set up a free society for the aid of others, this led him to ask himself: "Would it not be possible, in time of peace and quiet, to form relief societies for the purpose of having care given to the wounded in wartime by zealous, devoted and thoroughly qualified volunteers?"[41]

The account inspired many to the cause of the Red Cross movement. Regarding the possibility of giving impartial aid to both sides of a conflict and for a relief society to gain neutral status, he then had the idea to formulate an international principle as a basis "for societies for the relief of the wounded in the different European countries." This means that the principle of neutrality at its root is the idea to consider relief aid – also to the enemy – not as an act of war or hostility, but as a neutral act on the basis of common humanity. That this was a transferable idea from Christian Western Europe to other cultures was shown in the introduction of the Red Crescent Societies in the Ottoman Empire.[42]

The Swiss International Committee of the Red Cross (ICRC) notion of neutrality was "inextricably linked with the neutrality of the Swiss state." Herbert Hoover's, Woodrow Wilson's, and Henry Davison's actions to promote the American Red Cross Society as a "real International Red Cross" challenged both the leadership of the International Committee of the Red Cross within the Red Cross and the Red Crescent Movement, and the principle of neutrality towards a "US-led active and global relief body." The International Federation of the Red Cross and Red Crescent Societies (IFRC) with support from Britain, France, Italy, Japan, and the United States soon grew from this American ambition.[43]

Many relief societies – including many Christian-based and church-based agencies – began as agencies of solidarity. The Norwegian Church Aid and the DanChurchAid for example were formed to rebuild their own societies after the

---

[40] 2014 10 21 ETH141 Revision 1 Ethiopia Refugees from South Sudan, 4–5.

[41] Walker 2009, 22–24; Bugnion 2012, 1305.

[42] Walker 2009, 22–24.

[43] Walker 2009, 27–28.

Second World War[44] aided by Church of Sweden Aid and American Church agencies in acts of solidarity as an effort to rebuild the trust and social cohesion which had broken down during the war – also within the churches. Lutheran churches in America aided Lutheran churches in Germany and thus were crucial in healing the wounds of the war-torn Europe. When the Marshall Plan made some of the church mobilisation of voluntary effort superfluous in Europe – some of these solidarity efforts were channelised into other geographical areas. The Lutheran World Federation acted in Palestine after the first Israeli-Arab war of 1947, due to its prior engagements in mission work in the area. This led to a long-standing engagement with refugees as such – regardless of nationality, creed, or political ideologies. So, the initial relief works based on principles of solidarity were soon extended to other groups and societies. Some aid-agencies have followed a course of political solidarity, not the least with various liberation fronts around the world.[45] This was not the original path of the World Council of Churches. The Council was instrumental in the building up of the original Declaration of Human Rights. It saw itself as a peace organisation. Later though, the focus on justice and solidarity, particularly regarding issues of racism, created pressure within the movement to take sides, leaving neutrality behind.[46]

In the code of conduct from 1995, the principles of neutrality and independence were worded as, "[a]id will not be used to further a particular political or religious standpoint" and "[w]e shall endeavour not to act as instruments of government foreign policy."[47] The way the code was formulated shows that the authors were primarily concerned that a) good intention may be combined with incompetence, b) relief agencies may be used as a front for government policies, and c) aid may be used as a means of proselytizing beneficiaries for political or religious standpoints.[48] The principle of independence as interpreted by the Red Cross and Red Crescent movement entails that humanitarian agencies "must resist any interference, whether political, ideological or economic, capable of diverting it from the

---

[44] Taylor 1995, 2.

[45] Walker 2009, 22–23. For a critical discussion on how solidarity movements with support from SIDA by supporting various socialist liberation movements in Africa may have contributed to wars and terror in Africa, at times in the name of humanitarian assistance, see Nilsson 2008 *Sveriges Afrikanska Krig* and 2017 *I tyst samförstånd: Sverige och Sovjet i kalla krigets Afrika*.

[46] Tergel 1998. WCC 1982.

[47] Walker 2009, 130.

[48] Walker 2009, 129.

course of action laid down by the requirements of humanity, impartiality and neutrality."[49]

When *the International Committee for the Red Cross* was conceptualised, despite the closeness between the work of Red Cross volunteers and the military units with which they collaborated and served, self-rule – autonomy – was the aim, and the principle of independence stated that goal. "The Red Cross, although started outside of governments, relied upon government recognition, funding, and law."[50] This shows that there is an ambiguity here and that there are many challenges in maintaining operational and principled independence, particularly in relief work with many stakeholders and representatives of different states involved. The concern is clearly stated in the Sphere standard:

> an increased involvement of the military in humanitarian response, a set of actors not primarily driven by the humanitarian imperative, requiring the development of specific guidelines and coordination strategies for humanitarian civil–military dialogue – an increased involvement of the private sector in humanitarian response requiring similar guidelines and strategies as the civil–military dialogue.[51]

This brings in a historical example with relevance to the ACT members in Ethiopia. ACT agencies brought in aid across the border from Sudan to Ethiopia during the civil war in the 1980s. As the Derg regime only allowed aid to be distributed within government-controlled areas, the aid organisations were only able to serve those within government provinces including internal refugees who had crossed the frontline and surrendered to the Derg military regime. In addition, the Derg was combining relief support with the politically motivated development plan of moving drought victims to new settlements in other areas, such as Gambella. Most aid agencies were not willing to accompany the efforts of the Derg to move substantial portions of the population, but some did.[52]

In order to reach those suffering from drought within rebel-held territories, a plan was devised to cross the Sudanese border with aid supplies. This meant not respecting the sovereignty of Ethiopian borders in order to pursue the humanitarian imperative also for that part of the population. The operation necessitated

---

[49] IFRC "The Movement is independent. The National Societies, while auxiliaries in the humanitarian services of their governments and subject to the laws of their respective countries, must always maintain their autonomy so that they may be able at all times to act in accordance with the principles of the Movement." https://www.ifrc.org/en/who-we-are/vision-and-mission/the-seven-fundamental-principles/independence/ accessed 10 Dec 2020.

[50] Walker 2009, 25

[51] Sphere 2011, page 11.

[52] Bennett 2013, 35.

close collaboration with the liberation fronts, and aid agencies were formed and trained in delivering aid. A few Christian agencies, led by the Norwegian Church Aid (NCA), therefore set up a consortium, formally in the name of the Sudan Council of Churches (SCC), and collaborated with the secular relief agencies of the liberation fronts: the Eritrean Relief Agency (ERA), the Relief Society of Tigray (REST), and the Oromo Relief Agency (ORA).[53]

This was a controversial cross-border operation against the thinking and policies of that time. It challenged the United Nation's notions of sovereignty and the humanitarian principle of neutrality by operating in areas not controlled by the government and through community-based organisations and collaboration with the liberation fronts.[54] This was in stark contrast to the opinion held by the UN General Assembly which has "emphasised the respect for sovereignty and noted that humanitarian assistance should be provided with the consent of the affected country and in principle on the basis of an appeal by the affected country."[55]

Among the humanitarian principles – the independence of aid agencies vis-à-vis government agencies has since the 1990s been the one most debated.[56] By the end of the Cold War, the UN envisioned a larger role – not hindered by veto in the Security Council – in which the initial vision of the UN could be realised. The *Responsibility to Protect* and *Humanitarian Intervention* forwarded the good intention of the international community being able to intervene in situations such as in the former Yugoslavia, or Rwanda, in which people are not protected against hostile political parties who have no scruples about ethnic cleansing, or even attempted genocide.[57] The long-held principle of respecting state sovereignty would no longer be a guarantee for state actors who act in violence against their own population. Thus, there have been attempts to converge all "good efforts", military, UN agencies, state agencies, and humanitarian agencies towards a common goal –

---

[53] ERD provided some 685 000 tonnes of food to ERA, REST and a small amount to the ORA 1981–1992, Bennett 2013, 30. After the fall of the Derg, May 1991, REST and ORA became associate members of CRDA. Bennett 2013, 35.

[54] See chapter (5:3) on ERD and KdK. Bennett 2013; Henrich, Laban and Willemse 2015.

[55] Luopajärvi 2003, 682; see 682n 17: "UN GA res 46/182, 19 Dec. 1991, para.3. See also Declaration on the Inadmissibility of Intervention in the Domestic Affairs of States, UNGA res 2131 (XX), 21 Dec. 1965; and Declaration on principles of international law concerning friendly relations and co-operation among states in accordance with the Charter of the United Nations 1970, UNGA res 2625 (XXV), 24 Oct. 1970. Both declarations were regarded as customary international law by the ICJ in Nicaragua v. United States, n. 15 above, para. 203."

[56] Walker and Maxwell 2009, 137.

[57] Walker and Maxwell 2009, 144–45.

the establishment of stable democratic regimes, with law and order, and respect for human rights. This would involve, however, for humanitarian agencies to work together in closer collaboration and dependency upon military force for the safety and security of their staff.[58]

Security for the staff is a major concern in humanitarian action.[59] This is partly because contemporary relief work may be performed close to and even within conflict zones and not only from a safe distance. Humanitarian agencies are attempting to render aid directly into war zones.[60] The ACT members in Ethiopia were instrumental in setting precedence of crossing boundaries of sovereignty and bringing aid into areas controlled by rebel groups already in the 1980s.[61]

During the post-Cold War era, there were also examples of government attempts, outside of the UN framework, to integrate humanitarian efforts with military, political and economic aims into a comprehensive political response to a crisis. This kind of comprehensive approach might be rational from the perspective of a foreign government. There is also justification for seeking long-term political solutions. Nevertheless, it also makes humanitarian agencies part of a political rather than a humanitarian response to a crisis.[62]

During the twentieth century, one enduring trend has been the strive towards a totalisation of the political, that is all human life conceived of as being political. The humanitarian principle of independence counters such an attitude by attempting to safeguard an area outside of political control and the grasp of a government.[63] The concept of civil society[64] is one way of expressing the idea that not everything social is political, in the modern sense of the term, not all power is state power, and hence not all power belongs to the state government.

The case study showed that the ACT appeal was dependent on state financing, which negatively impacted the ability to act in response to the refugee crisis. Such

---

[58] Walker and Maxwell 2009, 76–81.

[59] Korff *et al* 2015. On *Contemporary Security Studies*, Collins, Allan 2013.

[60] ACT Security Course Addis Ababa 15–17 July, 2014 James Davies. 2014 06 19 James Davies ACT Security Course Overview.

[61] Bennett 2013.

[62] Walker 2009. One of the major themes dealt with is "the rise in humanitarian action as a political tool." Barnett 2011, 4, 39. Barnett's distinction between what he calls "emergency humanitarianism", and "alchemical humanitarianism" belongs to this historical context. See (3.3.)

[63] Walker and Maxwell 2009, 137. Cf. UN 2016 02 02 Ban Ki-Moon 2016 "One humanity: shared responsibility English Report of the Secretary-General for the World Humanitarian Summit" which stresses the need for political solutions.

[64] Hillbom 2010. See below on the concept of civil society.

a dependence, in terms of financing, on government authorities may lead humanitarian actors into compromising their principles. Likewise, humanitarians may be tempted to bargain in order to have access to people in need.

In the field of refugee assistance – until the beginning of World War I, voluntary organisations dominated relief activity, whereas the next hundred years would see the successive involvement of states and international organisations.[65] "With the end of the Cold War, the UN system and regional organizations became more deeply involved in all aspects of humanitarianism."[66]

The challenge of independence for civil society organisations mimics the struggle of the Christian Church to stay independent of political powers. It has been and remains a perennial issue. The call for separation of state and church is at times conceptualised as freedom of the state from the church, but the opposite may be the case – that the church needs independence – autonomy – from political authorities and those in power. When the Ethiopian Orthodox Church became autocephalous in 1959, the result was even closer ties to the emperor with a subsequent "Amhara" nationalism to serve the interest of the imperial state. When the military regime took over through the revolution of 1974, the military government strove to control the Orthodox Church in order to pacify the population.[67]

In the case of the ETH141 appeal, the work was done in Gambella, Ethiopia, outside of the civil war in South Sudan, and with the border protected by Ethiopian military forces. The power of the Ethiopian state in this case protects the refugees and humanitarian workers from harm. In the ACT Security Course provided by ACT Alliance in connection with the ETH141 appeal for the ACT Ethiopia Forum members, it was stressed that humanitarian security for ACT members primarily requires dependence on the local community they serve for

---

[65] Barnett 2011, 168.

[66] Barnett 2011, 169. This is contra to the earlier assessment that: "the United Nations system is not geared for action of this kind, nor is it realistic to suppose that given its structure, it could become so." Barnett 2011, 169.

[67] Atiya 1968, 166. Prunier 2015, 83. From a theological viewpoint, the difference between the church and state is derived from its origin in Christ who answered Pontius Pilate, "My kingdom is not of this world. If my kingdom were of this world, my servants would have been fighting, that I might not be delivered over to the Jews. But my kingdom is not from the world." John 19:36 ESV. Hovorun 2017, 89: An autocephalous church elects its own primate and consecrates bishops "without being accountable to any external ecclesial authority." The idea is derived from the Council of Ephesus (431) canon 8 which differentiated the civil *dioecesis Oriens* of Antioch to which the church of Cyprus belonged from the ecclesiastical governmental structure of episcopal authority.

protection. This attitude of community-based safety as distinct from government protection strengthens the neutrality of a humanitarian actor and may improve the way different actors perceive the agency and its staff.[68]

ACT and Principled Humanitarian Action

The ETH141, by referring to international standards, shows the commitment of ACT forum members to principled humanitarian action regardless of differences in organisational identity, culture, and history. A claim to adhere to standards is not enough though. If the actual intervention cannot be shown to be based on the standards, the professed "commitment" becomes empty and void of meaning. One of the main challenges of organisational leadership therefore becomes the setting up of an organisational framework to ensure that a principled approach is used throughout all the work of the organisation and that accountability is built into the organisational mode of action. In this way, the appeal to accountability carries the cost of revising the operational mode of the organisation.

The Humanitarian Accountability Partnership (HAP) was a Geneva-based organisation set up in 2003 to create an international standard for accountability, to enable organisations to set up their own systems of accountability, and to enforce the standard through a system of accreditation. The idea was to foster a sense of accountability towards crisis-affected populations and to improve quality programming.[69]

Most European ACT agencies in the forum, by the time of the appeal, were HAP members in different stages of the accreditation process and they were promoting the HAP standard by giving training sessions to its local partner organisations, and by creating a separate HAP working group in 2009 for mutual learning and accountability together with other northern aid agencies.[70]

---

[68] ACT Security Course Addis Ababa 15–17 July, 2014 James Davies. 2014 06 19 James Davies ACT Security Course Overview. Still, there are major risks to staff members such as vehicle accidents, flooding, violence in camp areas or in local communities, health hazards such as tropical diseases and long-term mental stress, and robbery or other crimes. The staff who put themselves at risk, in the case of ACT agencies is mainly national and local staff, with only a few expatriates.

[69] HAP 2013, 5 "[The sector] needed to guarantee improved accountability to crisis-affected populations, not only for ethical reasons but also because it would result in better programme quality management."

[70] 2012 08 30 HAP Working Group of Member Agencies in Ethiopia ToR, Oct 2012. Members agencies in 2012: CAFOD/Trócaire/SCIAF (CST), CARE, Childfund, Christian Aid (CA), Church of Sweden, Concern, Danish Church Aid (DCA), International Medical Corps

The core of the HAP standard consisted of six benchmarks in the areas of 1. establishing and delivering on commitments, 2. staff competency, 3. sharing information, 4. participation, 5. handling complaints, and 6. learning and continual improvement. In addition to the four humanitarian principles of the earlier mentioned code of conduct, the HAP standard listed the following principles: participation and informed consent, duty of care, witness, offer redress (regarding complaints), transparency and complementarity. The standard took into consideration that some organisations were "multi-mandated", i.e. in addition to relief work these were also engaged in other activities such as development work and advocacy. It also had found a way to deal with the fact that many HAP-certified organisations did not implement the work themselves but worked through other organisations, so-called local partners. These latter features applied to northern ACT members in Ethiopia that engaged in relief and development activities, preferring to work with local partners.[71]

The HAP Standard promoted the use of a staff code of conduct. This latter code was personal and hence fosters a personal responsibility, including everyone from head office management staff to volunteers, one example from the ACT Secretariat:

> The ACT Code of Conduct applies to all staff of ACT member organisations, local, national and international, and the staff of the ACT Secretariat. It also applies to temporary personnel such as consultants and volunteers who work in ACT member development and humanitarian programmes.[72]

ACT Alliance thus had written their own code of conduct and expected member agencies to follow suit:

> The main purpose of the ACT Code of Conduct is to promote greater accountability among and between members of the alliance and the people with whom we work in our humanitarian and development programmes. It seeks to protect staff as well as every woman, man, girl and boy with whom we work from abuse by individuals or groups from within our ACT member organisations. The Code is intended to serve as a guide

---

(IMC), Islamic Relief (IR), Lutheran World Federation (LWF), Merlin, Norwegian Church Aid (NCA), Oxfam America, Oxfam GB (OGB), Plan Ethiopia, Save the Children UK, and Tearfund.

[71] HAP 2013.

[72] ACT Alliance 2011a, 2, ACT Alliance "Code of Conduct," approved 05 February 2011.

for ACT staff to make ethical decisions in their professional lives and at times in their private lives.[73]

The idea was that the staff code of conduct would make ACT Alliance "responsible for upholding and promoting the highest ethical and professional standards in their work" and to have a common commitment to "prevent sexual exploitation and abuse, fraud and corruption and abuse of power." This gives the management of each ACT member responsibility "to ensure that all staff are aware of this Code of Conduct, that they understand what it means in concrete behavioural terms and how it applies to their programme context." So, the responsibility runs from the management all the way to the beneficiaries, with the major weight on the management, even for the behaviour of temporary employed staff members and volunteers. This is the reason why there were references to the Code of Conduct for LWF World Service, for ACT Alliance, as well as for the International Red Crescent Movement and NGOs in Disaster Relief and Humanitarian Charter in the ACT appeal.[74]

HAP International was not the only accountability initiative, however, but one of many. These system approaches towards accountability each required organisational resources and high learning curves, and thus for agencies to deal with multiple accountability protocols became cumbersome and confusing. Besides the explicit accountability agenda of HAP and the Core Humanitarian Standards, other standards, such as Sphere, had their separate way of framing quality standards and accountability. Each standard was also regularly updated making compliance a continuous effort rather than an application of a fixed and stable standard.[75]

Behind the various initiatives from the major international players among humanitarian agencies, there was a perceived threat of donor agencies setting separate standards focusing on donor compliance. "However, when demanding that states

---

[73] ACT Alliance 2011a, 2. ACT Alliance Code of Conducts also refers to ACT Alliance Guidelines for the Prevention of Sexual Exploitation and Abuse (revised 2011) and ACT Alliance Guidelines for Complaints Handling and Investigations (2010).

[74] ACT Alliance 2011a, 2. 2014 02 12 ETH141 Asylum Seekers South Sudan, 15–20 "implementation methodology."

[75] HAP 2013, 9. The guide to the 2010 HAP standard counts several contemporary initiatives: HAP, ALNAP, People In Aid, the Sphere Project, Coordination SUD, Groupe URD (*Urgence, Réhabilitation, Développement*), the Emergency Capacity Building Project, CDA Listening Project and Communicating with Disaster Affected Communities (CDAC), Red R, Keystone Accountability, CBHA, Bioforce, the Accountability Charter, DEC, Keeping Children Safe, and ELRHA, among others. To this list, one might also add PHAP – professionals in humanitarian assistance and protection – an association of humanitarian workers.

act responsibly internally, towards its own citizens and externally, towards the international community, we must also ask the international community to act responsibly when stepping in to provide surrogate assistance and protection."[76] Unless the humanitarian agencies were able to agree – the main donor countries would impose separate regulations to follow.[77]

Therefore, ACT Alliance and other actors settled upon a common joint venture – *the Joint Standards Initiative* – with the aim of following one common standard, one certification model, and one organisation with a mandate to certify according to the standard. *The Core Humanitarian Standard* (CHS) as the new standard was named was intended to replace other standards including the HAP standard which was concurrently familiar to most ACT members.[78]

By the time of ETH141, the work on the Core Humanitarian Standard was ongoing simultaneously with the implementation of the HAP standard, and high-level international discussions on which standard (or standards) and which overseeing organisation (or organisations) would be for the future. Sphere withdrew from the joint venture for a while when negotiations stranded.[79]

The overall intent of the Core Humanitarian Standard and the *Sphere Core Standards* were largely the same: communities and people affected by crisis are placed at the centre of humanitarian action and if the standards are applied in practice, the sense was that it would improve the quality and effectiveness of the assistance provided and facilitate greater accountability to communities and people. That at least was the idea. After the ETH appeal was completed, the Core Humanitarian Standard was integrated into the Sphere Handbook, which now with the Humanitarian Charter, the Core Humanitarian Standard (replacing the Sphere Core Standards), its Protection Principles, and its sectoral quality Minimum Standards show a greater clarity, convergence and comprehensiveness than earlier versions. This is due to the combined work of the International Federation of the Red Cross (IFRC), the Sphere Association, the Inter Agency Standard Committee (IASC) and the CHS Alliance.[80]

---

[76] Luopajärvi 2003, 678 and 685.

[77] 2013 09 10 SCHR 2013 Proposed Certification Model "Professionalising the Sector."

[78] HAP 2013, 1. 2013 09 10 SCHR Proposed Certification Model.

[79] 2013 09 10 SCHR Proposed Certification Model. 2013 11 06 ACT Ethiopia Forum "SCHR certification model feedback."

[80] Sphere Association 2018.

Standards and Subsidiarity

A letter from the ACT Ethiopia Forum to the ACT Secretariat regarding the new certification model, however, shows some concern that the consultative process "may not be equitable" given the short time given, and the fact that the forum, as a forum, had not been asked to give feedback, but only individual ACT organisations. The main concern with the model as such was the focus on compliance of "technical and administrative nature", which would favour large international agencies, and disfavour local and voluntary organisations that depend on community mobilisation.[81]

The question was asked: "Will this take focus away from real results i.e. that compliance becomes more important than making significant changes in people's lives?" The request in the forum letter was therefore for a peer-review system fostering "mutual learning and development" rather than "control, supervision and regulation" used as tools to limit access to funding. As such "accountability" may imply relief agencies seeking to be auditor-friendly and conform to donor requirements rather than *do no harm* to the people who are assisted which was the rationale of the accountability agenda from its inception.[82]

ACT Alliance is not only committed to setting up a system of principles and guidelines for the members of the Alliance, but also to actively participate in and contribute to the development and enforcement of international standards of humanitarian aid through active membership coordinating bodies such as HAP and the Steering Committee for Humanitarian Response (SCHR), and engagement in other standards such as Sphere and diverse IASC standards.[83]

This should be seen in historical continuity with ecumenical ambitions to strive for common ethical and legal standards. As the World Council of Churches and its member churches were working for the introduction of and compliance with International Human Rights Law, ACT Alliance continues to advocate for an increasing space for humanitarian action. This advocacy which used to be driven by northern churches (WCC), is now forwarded by northern agencies (ACT). The work is not limited to ACT members – even though the scope of this research is – but it is important to mention the local participation of Catholic and Evangelical agencies in the accountability working group in Ethiopia, and beyond Christian churches, Islamic Relief.[84]

---

[81] 2013 11 06 ACT Ethiopia Forum "SCHR certification model feedback."

[82] 2013 11 06 ACT Ethiopia Forum "SCHR certification model feedback."

[83] SCHR has eight members, CARE, Caritas, IFRC, ICRC, LWF, Oxfam, Save the Children, and ACT Alliance, Walker 2009, 126–27.

[84] Tergel 1998. See footnote on HAP Working Group of Member Agencies in Ethiopia.

One of the challenges for ACT Alliance, when acting on behalf of its members, is that the northern agencies, in their pursuit of both public funding and advocacy – mainly towards their national states and respective societies, can dedicate both time and resources for research, policy creation, and advocacy work, whereas southern ACT agencies and their churches do not have such resources at disposal.[85] This is briefly seen in the forum plea to the ACT Secretariat for more time and the use of the national ACT forum as the place for deliberation of such issues to give southern agencies and their churches reasonable opportunity to participate in consultation processes such as the one in question.[86]

The kind of certification processes that were decided upon will in the future dictate how southern organisations will function. This is an example of the imbalance of power that characterises aid. This recognition lies behind the principle of subsidiarity as promoted in Roman Catholic social teaching: that decisions ought not to be taken by a higher authority than necessary. Applied to the refugee assistance it would entail an actual localisation of humanitarian response and thus to move decisions from New York and Geneva down to refugees, host community, and local church and civil authorities, unless absolutely necessary.[87]

Donor agencies have a legitimate demand for accountability of granted resources for humanitarian relief. Resources should be used for the designated purpose and not diverted for other ends. This is a good reason for separating relief funds from general church funds. Donated funds should be used well so that resources may efficiently and effectively aid the people in need. This is a good reason for transparent financial accounting systems and clear planning, reporting, and evaluation as exemplified in the ETH141 ACT Appeal and the standards in chapters two and three.

When accountability frameworks and international standards primarily serve the interest of donor agencies, however, the basic sense of accountability from below, to the people who are served, may be lost. This was seen in the critique from the ACT Ethiopia Forum on some of the developments from the bottom-up and community-friendly approach of the HAP Accountability Standards in comparison to more donor-related standards that replaced HAP.

---

[85] Northern ACT agencies are set up with policy departments, there is no such equivalent for "implementing" ACT agencies in the global south. The European ACT members run an advocacy agency, Aprodev, in order to be able to speak towards the important European Union and influence EU-policies directly; Aprodev 2008.

[86] [86] 2013 11 06 ACT Ethiopia Forum "SCHR certification model feedback."

[87] A localisation of humanitarian response was discussed and promoted in Istanbul 2016.

For the churches and their aid agencies, there are two distinct senses of accountability "from below": accountability towards the people who are served, in this case, the refugees from South Sudan, and accountability towards the church constituency, as seen in the constitutional set up of the Mekane Yesus Church and the parish movement of the Orthodox Church in chapters four and five. When accountability "from above", as in the dual sense of responsibility towards government or UN controlling agencies, and donor agencies becomes the primary, rather than the secondary concern, considerations are skewed from humanitarian and people-oriented concerns towards the political interests of national and donor governments.

This is the rationale behind the operating humanitarian principles of neutrality and independence. These principles will remain at risk as long as relief is financed by state donors. It follows from the ideological belief in sovereign state power, and from the natural power and influence of a donor. As humanitarian organisations are described as humane, impartial, neutral, and independent, state authority is, in modern thought, for some, envisioned as the sovereign ruler and arbitrator of civil society.[88]

Accountability and Moral Responsibility

There is yet another sense of accountability and sovereignty "from above" than responsibility towards donors and governments. If God is the creator of everything and the author of the moral law, all mankind is accountable to God for all their actions. This is moral responsibility and the root of all kinds of accountability. If there is no ontological ground for accountability, i.e. if accountability is not grounded in reality, then there is no objective standard from which accountability is derived. In the Christian view, this is the objective moral standard, all stakeholders and all actions are ultimately judged by and may fail to live up to. God is also seen ultimately as the sovereign ruler of the universe, not in the sense of a dictator whose subjects obey every arbitrary whim, but as Christ, the suffering servant who died to redeem humanity from sin and bring new life also from suffering.

As the churches will bring up in the next chapter, this is brought about in the redemption and forgiveness of sin in baptism and absolution, in the liturgical turning from a world of sin towards the celebration of and participation in Christ's death, and resurrection – his Passover from death to life – and the living out of the Christian faith in service to neighbours, including asylum seekers from South

---

[88] See discussions on Cavanaugh 2011, Insole 2006b, and Hopgood 2013 in the literature review (1.1). Cf. Cavanaugh 2009 and Insole 2019. Also Deleskamp-Hayes 2009.

Sudan. This may be in the form of church-based aid, or in other forms, such as neighbourly assistance of the host communities, and the sacrifices people are willing to make for the sake of other's wellbeing and safety. Christians are called to integrate their faith in action. The work of ACT Alliance is one such example.

These kinds of meta-ethical questions on what morality is, where it comes from, and what obligations Christians have towards people in need are seldom discussed in the literature on relief aid. Morality and its foundation are taken for granted and applied rather than argued for in the context-bound ethics of humanitarian aid. Such discussions, however, have been held, and are being held in the academic fields of ethics and theology. As these discussions have a particular significance for the study of Christian aid organisations, the next section will make explicit what is often implicit in aid.[89]

3.2 The Humanitarian Moral Argument

Why do people engage in refugee assistance? Why not rather follow a laissez-faire approach – particularly in the light of critique from post-colonial theorists for whom everything is a play of power?[90] There is a need to clarify the main motives which motivate stakeholders into humanitarian action. The ETH141 appeal – as I have shown in chapter two – does not as such produce an argument. That being said, the appeal document itself is an argument for the support of asylum seekers from South Sudanese, but the motive is implicit, not explicit: one ought to assist people seeking refuge. In this section, I would like to discuss the question of why and present what I would call *the humanitarian moral argument*, or the humanitarian argument for short.

---

[89] Bainton 1960; Barnett 2011; Bexell and Grenholm 2003; Biggar 2020; Cunningham 2008; Goulet 2006; Haakonssen 1996; Hildebrand 2019 and 2020; Hollenbach 2008; Insole 2019; Koterski 2002; Kreeft 2003; Liederbach 2008; McGrath 2017; Milevsky 2017; Nordquist 1998; Novak 1999; and Slim 2015.

[90] Compare the approaches of Baaz 2005, Ers 2006, and Nolan 2012 with regard to ethnography and aid in a post-colonial academic context. One of the tools of ethnography is the suspension of judgement. The purpose is to move beyond personal and cultural prejudice and seek to understand a foreign culture through the eyes of the community the researcher studies. Whereas Baaz and Ers uses that technique for one group they study, the other, the aid-workers, are not given the benefit of a doubt. Nolan, on the other hand, knowledgeable both of the resources and gaps in ethnographical studies, and the resources and gaps in aid, seeks to give a fair account of both. (Nolan uses the term anthropology.)

The Question of Why and an Evolutionary Explanation

What is the humanitarian argument? The answer to this question is directly related to the question of why. Why would people go out of their way, encounter many challenges, and persist in their endeavour to assist refugees who are neither friends nor family? I will present that the case for refugee assistance is rooted – in a moral argument – the humanitarian argument. This position is contrary to the evolutionary global ethics of Peter Walker and Daniel Maxwell. They ask why Jean Henri Dunant organised relief for the wounded on the battlefield of Solferino in Italy in 1859. In their *Shaping the Humanitarian World* they write that "[m]any look to moral philosophy or religious beliefs to justify such seemingly selfless behavior, but this reasoning is self-evidently flawed."[91]

The reason that they hold this position is that they are searching for a general scientific explanation, and they believe that recourse to moral philosophy (ethics) and religion is not general. They write that this is self-evident, and so they do not argue for their case. Their readers are to take their word for it – to believe it on authority. Either their position is the claim that there are no objective values and no ultimate truth, which is a philosophical view regarding ontology, what is real. Or they argue that since there are different philosophical and religious positions, therefore one position may not stand as a general ground for humanitarian action in a context where people hold to different worldviews. Instead, they turn to Charles Darwin, Peter Kropotkin (1842–1941), and Robert Wright, to argue that Dunant's actions were determined by a cultural evolution of altruism.[92]

Peter Walker and Daniel Maxwell begin with biological evolution, which in their view, explains that "[t]he urge to assist others", is "an innate part of being human" in the context of the family. This they claim, is confirmed by mathematical theorems. The next step in their argument is to claim that "*Homo sapiens* go further and appears to apply the evolutionary mechanism of altruism to the larger family of mankind, choosing, as it were, to conceive of mankind as the family." Then they cite support from the theory of cultural evolution by Robert Wright, who, as an axiom, claims that mankind has a tendency "to drive social and cultural evolution in one direction – towards greater complexity of relationships and towards greater 'win-win' situations wherever larger and more diverse groups... mutually benefit from their relationships."[93]

---

[91] Walker 2009, 12.

[92] Walker 2009, 11–12.

[93] Walker 2009, 11–12. Cf. Adler 1963 on the importance of rationality in human nature.

In "humanitarianism", Walker and Maxwell therefore argue that altruism is a result of "15 000 years of human cultural evolution", and is no longer limited to the family, but may be applied to humankind, within participatory systems, for the sake of humanitarian action. This was, Walker and Maxwell write, foreseen by Darwin who argued that the move from man extending "his social instinct and sympathies to all the members of the same nation, though personally unknown to him" to additionally cross the "artificial barrier" between "men of all nations and races."[94]

The explanation that they offer runs into several problems. An important objection is that they set out to answer the question why? "Why bother?" So, when they ask why Jean Henri Dunant organised relief to the wounded on the battlefield of Solferino in Italy in 1859, they answer these questions with an elaboration of altruism, conceived as biological and cultural evolution. By seeing the development of nation-states as a natural process, the nation-state becomes the last barrier and the global society becomes the final stage in a 15 000-year process of natural forces of evolution. That is one way to naturalise a political vision.[95]

Explanations run at different levels. It is important to distinguish between a natural cause explanation and an agent explanation.[96] Scientific explanations, in general, tend towards natural causes, whereas answers from the studies of humanities may be more directed towards human ends and purposes, looking for an agent explanation, or reasons for action.[97] A scientific theory of evolution seeks to answer questions of what is, and what naturally caused that which is. It does not,

---

[94] Walker 2009, 11–12.

[95] Walker 2009, 11–12. Critique by the theologian Cavanaugh 2011, 37 "The nation-state is not a genuine community, a functioning rational collectivity."

[96] Take as an example two different ways of answering the question: why did the women assisting Dunant use cloth to bind the wounded soldiers? 1. *The women used cloth because the fibres stop the bleeding by hindering the blood from exiting the body and it keeps the wound clean.* The fibres, as a natural explanation, become the efficient cause of stopping the bleeding. 2. *The women used cloth to stop the wounded soldiers from dying because it was the morally right thing to do in that situation.* The women were not driven by natural causes but acted on their free will to act morally. Their deliberate actions were the final cause to explain what happened. These answers respond to different types of questions, in which the first answer does not invalidate the second. Both are relevant and important for a comprehensive analysis of the same situation. If only natural causes are referred to as answers to historical questions, the reasons why people act in one way remain unanswered. It also removes the moral agency of the women and Dunant.

[97] For a discussion and critique of moral empiricism, see Nordquist 1998, 97, 100. Nordquist argues for a position in which moral statements are neither expressions of feelings or ordinary statements of fact, but that "moral statements constitute a specific category of statements."

however, and cannot, from natural science answer the question of "ought": why should anyone bother?[98] David Hume clarified that you cannot have an imperative in the conclusion if all premises are stated in the indicative. In other words, one cannot get an "ought" from "is." It is an example of invalid reasoning; the conclusion does not follow from the premises.[99] Why did Dunant engage in the practical relief of the wounded soldiers? Why should anyone engage in humanitarian assistance? The human question of Dunant's motivation and intention remains unanswered in a scientific account.

The Walker and Maxwell account starts from a premise that misconstrues moral philosophy and religious beliefs. The objective of moral philosophy is to state the truth about all of morality, not just personal truth. Therefore, moral philosophy cannot be assessed by the number of followers it has, the particularity of a view. The true standard of philosophy – as in science – is truth, i.e. correspondence to reality. Since something may be true without being fully known, people may follow the precept of a particular moral philosophy without subscribing to it. Similarly, with religious beliefs, it is important to note that religious claims are truth claims whose ultimate validity depends on the truth they assert. This is the reason that people may recognise truth in other people's belief systems. Philosophical arguments are assessed on the strength of their premises and the validity of their reasoning. This includes the philosophical argument Walker and Maxwell made that Darwinian and cultural evolution explains the actions of Dunant and, more generally, humanitarian action as such. Their evolutionary argument is philosophical, not scientific, and it can be evaluated on those grounds.[100]

---

[98] Walker 2009, 10.

[99] David Hume (1711–1776) in *A Treatise of Human Nature* (1739–1740). See Ward 2021, 157–58.

[100] The scientific theory of Darwin needs to be clearly distinguished from Darwinism as a metaphysical philosophy in which "evolution" takes on divine qualities. Some critique of Darwinism is premised on the metaphysical and even religious claims by some followers of Charles Darwin. Church historian Alf Tergel mentions Ernst Haeckel (1834–1919) as "the biologist who gave Darwinism a metaphysical foundation as a monist religion". It led Haeckel to abandon belief in creation and immortality for a pantheistic religion with Nature as an object of worship. Tergel 1994, 477. Herbert Spencer (1820–1903) gave evolution theory a philosophical foundation. For Spencer, the world moved from chaos to a climax of cosmos, followed by dissolution. Tergel 1994, 477. Richard Dawkins assumes that evolution requires ontological naturalism, and hence atheism. In *Where the Conflict Really Lies* on science and religion, philosopher Alvin Plantinga argues: "Turning to naturalism, clearly there is superficial concord between science and naturalism—if only because so many naturalists trumpet the claim that science as a pillar in the temple of naturalism. As I argue in this

Likewise, the term religion should be used with care in the context of global humanitarian action. To use it, as if all "religions" are the same, is false, because religions are not the same. Religions are different and have opposing truth claims, contain varied worldviews, and substantiate their claims differently. "Lived religions" also differ in all kinds of ways.[101] Philosophically stated, there is not one abstract nature of religion. For the sake of being able to compare "religions" as common phenomena in religious studies, scholars treat "religions" as abstract entities, but that is a theoretical construct, not to be confused with concrete reality.[102]

If what Walker and Maxwell aim to say is that all "religions" are wrong, it may entail one of two things: a) All religions indicate a divinity of some kind, as opposed to the atheist position that there is no such "thing" as divinity. b) All cultural worldviews are wrong, except their own, which is right because it is "scientific." Since they mention Richard Dawkins, it might indicate that they have adopted his philosophical scientism, even as they also attempt to refute Dawkins' evolutionary argument of the "selfish gene." A combination of scientific theories and atheism may lead to the epistemological stance of scientism, in which empirical science is used to validate a particular worldview; that of naturalism. This leaves them open to the critique of Einstein that you cannot get morality from science, and the insight from Nietzsche that without God, there are no objective values.[103]

---

chapter, they are mistaken: one can't rationally accept both naturalism and current evolutionary theory; that combination of beliefs is self-defeating. But then there is a deep conflict between naturalism and one of the most important claims of current science. My conclusion, therefore, is that there is superficial conflict but deep concord between science and theistic belief, but superficial concord and deep conflict between science and naturalism. Given that naturalism is at least a quasi-religion, there is indeed a science/religion conflict, all right, but it is not between science and theistic religion: it is between science and naturalism. That's where the conflict really lies." Plantinga 2011, 349–50.

[101] Benedict 2023, 15–16 "Many today, indeed, have the notion that the world religions should respect one another and, in the dialogue between them, become a common force for peace. In this way of thinking, most often the presupposition is that the different religions are variants of one and the same reality; that 'religion' is the common genus that takes on different forms depending on the different cultures, but expresses the same reality anyway. The question of truth, the one that originally motivated Christians more than anything else, is bracketed off here. It is presupposed that the authentic truth about God, in the final analysis, is unattainable and that at most we can make present the ineffable only with a variety of symbols. This renunciation of the truth seems realistic and useful for peace among the religions in the world."

[102] Against a common abstract nature of religion, see "What is Religion" in Benedict 2023, 21. For a critical discussion on the problem of defining religion, Cavanaugh 2009, 57–122.

[103] Walker 2009, 11. Kreeft 2003, 26.

The Humanitarian Moral Argument

What is the humanitarian argument? In section 3.1 of this chapter, the ethical foundation in the Sphere Handbook was spelt out as *the principle of humanity* and *the humanitarian imperative*, which together implied a right to life with dignity, a right to receive humanitarian assistance, and a right to protection and security. Humanitarian action, therefore, in ethical theory, gets its moral force from the principle of humanity:

> that all human beings are born free and equal in dignity and rights[104]

and the humanitarian imperative:

> that action should be taken to prevent or alleviate human suffering arising out of disaster or conflict, and that nothing should override this principle.[105]

The abstract adjective humanity signifies sharing in the same human nature as beings of the same species.

The principle of humanity and the importance of alleviation of suffering belong to a discussion regarding Enlightenment philosophy with reference to the works of Immanuel Kant and the utilitarian philosophers Jeremy Bentham and John Stuart Mill.[106] When discussing the eighteenth- and nineteenth-century Enlightenment intellectual movement, there is a need to recognise both the plurality of ideas and the eighteenth-century historical context.

Kant's categorical imperative has several formulations, two of which are relevant in the context of humanitarian action, first the general principle: "act only according to that maxim through which you can at the same time will that it become a universal law."[107] Then another version of Kant's formulation, which constitutes the concept of humanity:

> So act that you use the humanity, in your own person as well as in the person of any other, always at the same time as an end, never merely as a means.[108]

---

[104] Sphere 2011, 6, 20.

[105] Sphere 2011, 6, 20.

[106] The second founder of the International Committee of the Red Cross, Gustave Moynier, a Calvinist, was inspired by utilitarian philanthropy. Hutchinson 1996, 12.

[107] Nyholm 2015, 280. Quote Kant 2011, 70–1 (GW 4:421).

[108] Kant 2011, 87 (GW 4:429).

This means that people never should be treated as mere objects – instruments to people's goals – but always as ends in themselves. This is an insight into the onto-logical nature of man with ethical implications. This is what appears to have in-spired the thinking in the Sphere Handbook. The formulation of the humanitar-ian imperative in the Sphere Handbook, as quoted above, may then be seen as a development from the general principle of Kant applied to human suffering in general.

There is however a significant difference between Kant's formulations of the categorical imperative and the humanitarian imperative in the Sphere Handbook. In order for a rule of conduct to be raised to the level of a categorical imperative in Kantian thought, it has to be universal, that is, it has to be valid in all cases and regardless of context. That is not the case with the humanitarian imperative.

Suffering is a universal experience of human life, and it is not true that in all cases suffering should be suppressed at all costs. One example is when a person is dying, and the doctor knows that if the patient receives medicine to relieve the pain, it will shorten his or her life. In that context, it is not necessarily true that the right action is to deliver the painkiller. For a categorical imperative, if the principle is demonstrably wrong in one case, it should no longer be considered categorical. Hence, the humanitarian imperative, as rendered in the Sphere Handbook, is not fulfilling the basic requirement of Immanuel Kant's categorical imperative.

If the humanitarian imperative is not following the rules of Kant's categorical imperative, what is it? How should it be evaluated? In the Sphere formulation, alleviation of human suffering is either raised to the level of the highest good, or as a matter of the highest importance. Perhaps, it is related to a particular view of the highest good? Is the alleviation of suffering important because of its relationship with intrinsic goodness – with happiness? The humanitarian imperative of the al-leviation of suffering can relate to the utilitarian idea of suffering and pleasure as the two poles of human moral experience in which suffering in itself is always bad and pleasure good, as in the thinking of Jeremy Bentham.

Both "humanitarian Kantians", and utilitarians, though from radically differ-ent standpoints – the duty approach or the consequentialist approach – may agree that humanitarian action to alleviate suffering is agreeable from their different eth-ical standpoints. Kantians from the concept of humanity, as distinct from the principle of humanity in the Sphere Handbook, and utilitarians from their desire to minimise suffering and maximise happiness. Humanitarian agencies may thus get much popular support since these are two of the most influential ethical frame-works of the era of modernity.

Humanitarian action and the imperative to alleviate suffering, historically considered however, is a way of framing relief work in the language of humanity favoured by the International Committee of the Red Cross (ICRC)[109] resulting from a long historical process in which Dunant plays one part. Growing up as a Swiss Reformed Christian with the rationalistic approach of that time, Dunant was touched by the Pietistic revival. It was the same type of revival that inspired social reforms during the era of industrialisation, the abolition movements, the global mission movement, and – its later offspring – the ecumenical movement. Barnett writes, "Dunant hoped that Christians who joined voluntary medical teams would become more religious as a consequence of tending to soldiers."[110] This is one of the many connectors between secular humanitarian action and its roots in Christian thought and practices.

In times of conflict, and short-term emergencies, it is of high value to reduce tensions, to "humanise" antagonists, to save lives in the short-run and alleviate suffering coming as a direct consequence of conflict (or disaster), and to limit collateral damage. Humanitarian action, therefore, primarily targets these limited aims, and not the seeking of long-term social and political solutions. When political agents are actively using conflict and aiming to destroy people's lives and livelihoods, "humanising" the opponents, whilst not a solution, is rather the beginning of an argument from common sense aimed at calling antagonists back to negotiable solutions rather than making use of excessive violence.

The root of the argument is the value ascribed to human life and the dignity of the human person with corresponding consequences for human action. The humanitarian argument is institutionalised in *International Humanitarian Law* inscribed in the Geneva Conventions and protected by the International Committee of the Red Cross (ICRC).[111]

It creates challenges regarding refugee assistance however, because when considered as relief work in humanitarian terms – in which suffering becomes the defining factor – the assistance promotes short-term thinking driven by the need of the humanitarians to act according to the principles, thus avoiding long-term solutions. This can be seen in the ACT Appeal system which is geared towards six to twelve months relief work, with the possibility of a six-month extension. The South Sudanese political conflict and its adjunct refugee crisis did not end after

---

[109] Barnett 2011, 168.

[110] Barnett 2011, 168, 227.

[111] On human dignity, Bischofberger 2012; Bischofberger, and Brattgård 2012.

twelve, or even eighteen months, as the relief project corresponding to the ACT appeal did.

Here is the dilemma of humanitarian action: although the action itself may temporarily save and sustain the lives of hundreds of thousands of people – it will not solve the main issues, and yet it forces people to survive in conditions – the camp setting – which when it becomes long-term may become detrimental to people's sense of purpose in life.[112]

The second part of the dilemma is that while it is possible to handle the humanitarian crisis with humanitarian action with the help of outside support, solving the political crisis is fraught with difficulties. Any attempt by outsiders to engage in the civil conflict risks making the conflict worse. In the final analysis, it is the people in conflict themselves who have to call off the conflict and seek solutions, not the people who aim to assist them.[113]

The humanitarian argument then, I would argue, is based on the major premise that the life of the human person is invaluable, and the minor premise that people have a duty to respond to persons in dire need. It is a moral argument based on the dignity of each human person.

It is of high value to respond to a person in crisis and for that person to be able to receive aid when needed. The challenge with humanitarian responses however is that they will not solve the underlying political crisis that caused it, and, in the meantime, the assistance may do harm as well as good, for example by pacifying people to be recipients of foreign aid rather than tending to their own basic needs.

The principled approach of ACT as exemplified in the international standards aims to mitigate those challenges. What is demonstrated here is that morality cannot be reduced to one of its aspects, the imperative to assist a person in need. Moral responsibility is more complex than what evolutionary, Kantian, or utilitarian accounts give it credit for.

From a realist, and common sense, perspective of morality, everything counts; the act itself, its consequences, the situation, the intent and attitude, and the moral

---

[112] See Abebe Feyissa and Horn 2008. Also, Joint Commission for Refugees of the Burundi and Tanzania Episcopal Conferences 2008. See page 55, "In theory, under international law the right to asylum is intended to augment the existing rights that a refugee possesses under other international conventions, such as the United Nations Universal Declaration of Human Rights. In practice, however, when refugees are granted asylum, particularly in prima facie cases where refugee status is granted *en masse*, significant restrictions are placed on their other rights and freedoms." Both in Hollenbach 2008.

[113] Sadako Ogata, former UN High Commissioner for Refugees, she wrote: "There are no humanitarian solutions to humanitarian problems." As quoted in Walker 2009, xi.

person with his and her ontological dignity, the direction in life, habits, character, and ultimate end (τέλος). To investigate human morality, one may study habits with reference to virtues and vices, the formation of character,[114] the *telos* of human action, and the human actor, precepts and principles, the order and disorder of passions and loves, and the specific character of the moral law – "the ought" or duty to do the right thing and refrain from doing that which morally bad.[115]

Thus, we may see that although morality is a common aspect of human life and common sense shows that it entails many features, a "scientific" morality may fail to offer a full account of it. The same goes with the evolutionary account offered by Walker and Maxwell – as an account of what is (and has been) it fails to account for the "ought" in the universal experience of morality.[116]

Providing for clean water, latrines, and other basic human goods, are good things. Action that aims to provide these goods is morally relevant simply because men and women need water, latrines, and other basic human goods. This is true in a normal context – outside of a crisis– and it takes on a higher significance in crisis because lives are at risk when people are unable to provide for themselves. This can be universally recognised, as in the countless examples of local inhabitants providing for the urgent needs of refugees to the extent of their ability.

In Christian thought and practice, the goodness of kindness, mercy, and compassion are taught and emulated after the model of Jesus Christ, and the saints. However, the uniqueness of Christianity in comparison with other religious traditions does not lie in the teaching of a higher standard of morality. Commonly, value opinions are derived psychologically from cultural and religious upbringing which allows people to recognise and act upon values when encountered in life.

In a philosophical study of comparative ethics and religion, Catholic philosopher Peter Kreeft described three levels of morality. The lowest level would be "enlightened self-interest or calculated egotism" based on an agreement between people. If the agreement is failing, public shame would be the result. The second level

---

[114] In the ethics and ecclesiology consultations of WCC, the moral formation of churches was an object of particular interest in Johannesburg 1996. Best and Robra 1997.

[115] Aristotle (384–322 BC), Thomas Reid (1710–1796), and Dietrich von Hildebrand (1889–1977) are three examples of philosophers from different periods who approached morality from a realist perspective. Kreeft 2003, 35–39, 71–72; Pakaluk 2002, 564–581; Hildebrand 2019 and 2020.

[116] Biggar 2020, 5 states that if an evolutionary drive to survive is called in as explanation of morality, "such a Hobbesian, materialist, naturalist reading of evolution in fact denies that humans have evolved morally at all, for it tells us that, at base, we are still driven by the primordial fear of pain and death." Such an explanation cannot account for the willingness to risk pain and death for values such as truth and justice.

morality concerns justice. One ought to do the right thing because it is the right thing to do. The one who fails to be just carries personal guilt. The third level morality goes beyond justice to "mercy, charity, unselfishness, self-sacrifice, and even martyrdom." A most interesting aspect of the study of comparative religion is that "every major world religion teaches this third level of morality. In fact, this third level of morality is specific to these religions and rarely seen outside of them." This connection between the major religious traditions and a high sense of morality can be considered subjective or psychological, just as the vehicles of learning morality in life are subjective, in the sense of parents, communities, and cultures. The objective relation of morality and religion, Kreeft writes, comes up when people justify morality. If people say that all people should be loved because we are all God's children, then religion is the justification for ethics. This brings the philosophical question of whether, ultimately, religion can be the only ground for ethics.[117]

At the heart of the matter refugee assistance is a moral issue. To analyse the refugee assistance within a theological framework, it is useful to grapple with ethical issues and morality itself. The first level of response is targeted towards assisting people in such a way that their lives are no longer at risk, that the worst form of suffering is alleviated, and people's dignity as human beings is upheld. This is the heart of the humanitarian argument. Philosophically, this raises questions of suffering, anthropology, moral responsibility, duty, and solidarity.[118]

In the study of morality, "[o]ne basic assumption is that there is such a thing as a 'natural morality'." This means that there are ethical principles that are objective and that the goods of human flourishing stem from human nature. Such a moral realism was denied by logical positivism, leading to an emotivism of subjective feelings. From a positivist perspective, what the Nazi regime did, duly under Nazi law could not rationally be objected to without invoking some "trans-cultural moral authority." Even from a practical point of view, positivism fails.[119]

A humanitarian appeal is launched to aid people who are in such a dire situation that their lives are at risk, unable to cope with the situation on their own. That is at least the assumption. The main reason people should be assisted is that every man and woman has an inherent dignity. People are more valuable than things and (other) animals. Protecting people's lives, therefore, is a morally good thing to do.

This applies even when there is a conflict of interest, such as in a state of war, or civil conflict. Such a moral action of relief assistance is part of natural law, and

---

[117] Kreeft 2003, 3. Cf. Bexell and Grenholm 2003: 28–68.
[118] For a critical analysis, Deleskamp-Hayes 2009.
[119] Biggar 2020, 4.

therefore universally applicable regardless of culture or political structures. It ought not be prohibited by law or government actions. It is a given, *donatum*, outside of the competency of any government to take away. Rather, humanitarian action should be protected and promoted by international law. It has consequently become protected and encouraged in International Humanitarian Law.

There have been attempts at setting up ethical systems and frameworks – to describe or to prescribe a systematic approach to morality – often by emphasising one aspect at the cost of another. The utilitarian attempts to show the utility of the outcome of actions but may end up disregarding the whole moral dimension that man ought to do good and ought not to do evil.[120] This easily results in an economic view of man which reduces the story of humanity into economic history – useful but reductive and when this dimension of human life is stressed too much – it ends up thinking that man is more useful to economy than economy to man.

In the Marxist version which combines economy with a sense of solidarity – the underlying economic view of man necessarily leads to oppressive political systems despite its communal ethos. The liberal version which combines economy with a sense of individuality – when not reinforced by other views – ends up reducing morality to individual pursuit of happiness.

Immanuel Kant wanted to create a rational moral philosophy. He ended up with the "ought" of the moral law thus succeeding to move beyond the impasse of David Hume whose empiricism threatened both rational thought and morality.[121]

One challenge with Kant's ethics – which as I have shown lies behind the modern principle of humanity – is that it is all form and no content;[122] thus, it gives very little in terms of practical guidance in social life.[123]

---

[120] Kreeft 2003, 72.

[121] Kreeft 2003, 63. Hume's empiricism eliminates moral knowledge because it is not empirical. Ethics, in Hume's thought, becomes an emotive theory of values. As such morality is emotional and subjective. C.S. Lewis *The Abolition of Man* from 1943, Lewis 2001, was written to counter its dehumanising influence on society through the logical positivism of A.J. Ayer and I.A. Richards. See Lewis scholar Michael Ward 2021.

[122] Kreeft 2003, 71. Cf. Bexell and Grenholm 2003, 107–11.

[123] "Morality, for Kant, depends upon pure reason being 'in itself' practical, which means, providing for itself, and from itself, the unconditioned good that it seeks. Kant puts this by explaining that the will can have no 'external object', whereby 'object' Kant means any dimension of reality, created or uncreated. For example, the 'essence of poetry' can be the object of our thought, without itself being an empirical, or quasi-empirical, 'object'. If the will can have no principle or reality that is *heteros*, or *ab alio*, 'from another', then, it follows, it must have a sheerly

It shows that morality as such is rational but leaves it to all – as human beings endowed with reason – to use our rationality to figure out what to do and what not to do. Since modern philosophy often has been sceptical of tradition – the universal guiding tool of mankind, each generation has to reinvent the wheel and learn from its mistakes rather than from culture.

A second challenge with Kant is that it seems that the end point of morality moves from God to the moral law as ascribed by the human subject. Man becomes the lawgiver, and God is no longer the ultimate end for human beings, man is his own end.[124]

The formal logic of Kant was successfully able to reach morality, but compared to common experience – or common sense, morality was reduced to a formula with only one pure motive – duty, and one formal concept of humanity.[125] As Barnett argues:

> Humanity can be lonely and alienating. The discourse of humanity, once it spreads to cover all human beings, can reduce individuals to superficial qualities, stripping them of the very cultural, historical, and social processes that make them human and confer genuine dignity on them.[126]

Together with Kant, the historical common view is that there is an innate human ability to distinguish right from wrong. In common experience, however, in what can be called "common sense morality", not only the motive but "everything" counts as mentioned above. Humanitarians – together with Kant – arguably, are correct to argue that morality is essential and the "ought" of the moral law to be objective. But if it is also true that morality is part of the common human experience, then all may participate – not only certified humanitarians – but also

---

intrinsic object, or, in other words, it must make itself its own object. And this is precisely what Kant says. In one of the most electric and illuminating lines in the Groundwork of the Metaphysics of Morals, Kant writes that the will 'has as its object', 'itself as giving universal law' (GW 4, 432)." Insole 2019, 473.

[124] "In making this move, Kant departs from the central claim of the Christian tradition, which is that God, and not just the moral law which God necessarily commands, is the all-satiating end-point and final object of our loving and knowing, and where God is, in the technical terms employed here, an external object (and so not co-extensive with our own moral law-giving), who nonetheless, and uniquely, acts interiorly within creatures, in all they do, in a way that does not violate, but constitutes, their freedom. In relation to this claim, for the traditional theologian, Kant's God seems awkwardly on the outskirts of the ideal moral community, or to disappear entirely within it." Insole 2019, 473.

[125] Kreeft 2003, 71–72.

[126] Barnett 2011, 228.

volunteers, refugees, and the host community, in the alleviation of suffering, as well as searching for solutions to the issues caused by the conflict. Natural law grants the communities the responsibility for their own lives. This is the fundamental truth and meaning inherent in the right to the pursuit of happiness with a corresponding duty to take care of one's own life. In modern realities, this responsibility may be taken away, by paternalism.[127] This is the risk involved in the extended use of "protection" in relief work. It may justify paternalism.

An important aspect of morality regards the relationship between the moral law and the law of men. Christian thought, i.e. Christian thinking informed by a biblical worldview, has traditionally favoured a natural law approach to the connection between law and morality. Natural law jurisprudence respects the differences between morality and legality while setting the basic common norms for legality as the rule of law. Positivist jurisprudence posits a radical freedom of the legal system from morality and establishes rule by law by will.[128] The problem is, as ethicist Nigel Biggar puts it:

> if there is no objective moral reality, then rights lack moral justification and have only the same amoral, conventional status, as say, racist law that denies rights to Jews or blacks.[129]

In the case of supporting refugees through the aid system, legality refers both to the national legal system of the hosting nation – the Ethiopian Federal Democratic State – and applicable areas of international law, as will be looked into in the next section. So far, the international standards have appealed to a principled ethical approach to aid which, for good reasons, is grounded in international law. Hence, the standards presuppose the need for moral and legal principles grounded in morality.

In one important sense, morality is no different for a Christian than for any other person. If it is true that morality is objective, true to reality, then as Catholic philosopher Dietrich von Hildebrand stated, Christian ethics is common morality.[130] Morality is a common feature for all humanity. If Christianity is true, this can be explained by Christian doctrine, inherited from Judaism. If God is the creator of all things, including every person, it follows that there is a basic structure

---

[127] Cf. Singer 1972 argues that it is always right for people in richer nations to give to charity.

[128] Cunningham, Davi 2008.

[129] Biggar 2020, 5.

[130] Hildebrand 2020, 479 is clear that there is only one ethics to which differing moral systems relate, but that there are still reasons to speak of a Christian ethics.

in life, a *donatum*, a given,[131] which includes a common morality and a *telos* of the human life, which gives objective meaning to life.

Theism – as a philosophical worldview – structures a basic anthropology which may be experientially and intellectually discovered in life. The theistic worldview – which Christians share with Jews and Muslims – explains why it must be the case that morality is common, whereas opinions about morality – value opinions – differ. An atheistic or agnostic worldview does not explain why it has to be the case – because of inherent materialistic and naturalistic assumptions.[132]

This view of a common "basic" morality for all humanity brings vast implications for aid work as it shows that there is a common foundation – a given – which may serve as a starting point. Without this view, one approaches philosophies, such as that of Friedrich Nietzsche, in which all is reduced to a play of power since there is no standard for truth and morality. If this were true, there could be no progress since development has to be measured against a standard. Likewise, there would be no room for critique of abuse since there would be no objective standard to assess conduct against. The existence of a common morality explains that, as Barnett argues, even though "humanitarianism" originated with the Enlightenment and was sparked by Christianity, since: "[a]ll the major religions have traditions of compassion and charity", the idea and practice of humanitarian aid "belongs to everyone and no one."[133]

The importance of a common moral foundation, as a necessary presupposition of such a difficult task as international humanitarian aid work, has to be stressed. A theistic worldview, which is a given for Christians, is positioned to make sense of why there is such a thing as a common moral law. Theism enables people to argue for and defend human dignity – and therefore basic human rights. A theist can stress the importance of human solidarity against those who are unwilling or unable to do so. In the context of refugee assistance, some are unwilling because of other motives, or unable because of other ontological and epistemological presuppositions, rendering them blind to a common humanity. A defence, therefore, is not an academic issue, but a "live issue"[134] of immense import for working together in humanitarian action. It could be further argued that the weight given to

---

[131] Olofsson 2015, 133–50 on *Humanum* as a given on human nature and condition.

[132] Kreeft 2003.

[133] Barnett 2011, 228.

[134] For William James' view on a "live issue", see Williams and Saunders 2018 "Practical Grounds for Belief: Kant and James on Religion."

human rights as well as a just legal system depends on strong philosophical arguments.[135]

The materialistic worldview – which Kant struggled with because he inherited the epistemological problem from David Hume – is one view within Western Civilisation which may be traced through Thomas Hobbes, back to Machiavelli,[136] and from him back to some of the Greek Philosophers, such as Democritus.[137]

The issue that the Enlightenment philosophers struggled with was how to account for the mind-body problem – with some leaning towards idealism and others toward materialism. When taken to its extreme, the tendency of Hume to reduce morality to pure feelings,[138] may give rise to a purely materialistic worldview, while others may follow a neo-Platonic path towards an idealistic worldview. The question is whether any one of these options can give a full account of human life or have the explanatory power of a theistic worldview, in which mind and body are distinct but correlating to the same person.

When the ideas of Immanuel Kant are taken out of their theistic context, his main point – that rationality shows the obligation for each person to follow the moral law – is lost. Kant followed the tradition back to Plato and Socrates for whom rationality implied morality in opposition to rhetoricians who were able to convince people, not based on truth and morality, but simply by the power of persuasion. Kant followed the main tradition from Plato through the important additions and corrections of a theistic tradition. Jewish thinkers like Philo of Alexandria, followed by Eastern and Western Church fathers, took up this line of thought. It was then brought into renewed discussion throughout the Middle Ages by Jewish, Christian, and Muslim thinkers, simply continuing the "Great Conversation." Kant had to work with the presuppositions of his interlocutors – such as David Hume and Jeremy Bentham – and with the "Enlightenment project" of bringing greater clarity to all things including morality.[139]

---

[135] Though natural law and human rights historically derived from Theism, once there, it is possible to find and defend such ideas also on the basis of other traditions beyond Judaism, Christianity, and Islam and indeed such defences are being made.

[136] Kreeft 2003, 49.

[137] Koterski 2002, 24.

[138] When ethical statements are seen as non-cognitive, "such statements only reflect a feeling, or a wish", Nordquist 1998, 97 n122.

[139] What Kant seems to have been unable to do was to defend the philosophical method from the empiricism of David Hume to the detriment of Western humanistic, philosophical, and theological traditions. Hence the strong reaction in the Romanticism that followed in the wake of the Enlightenment.

This thesis focuses on the "Christian" and "church-based" aspects of ACT member organisations. Hence there is a need to give an account of what the "Christian" and "church-based" might be. This is a more difficult task than showing the common moral foundation and arguing for how a theistic worldview may account for why there is such a common foundation. Chapter four will engage with this task using texts – one Orthodox and one Evangelical – to bring resources from the Christian tradition into the discussion.

If Christians believe that there is a basic morality and if this is, at least to a large extent, shared among all human beings as a common given, there to be discovered, where does Church tradition come in? This is a difficult area to explore particularly due to the debates during the Reformation Era about Scripture and Tradition and their relationship. Despite the entrenchment of confessional traditions, this discussion has continued during the twentieth century, however, not the least due to Russian Orthodox theologians who, as emigrants from Russia – after the Russian Revolution 1917 – ended up in Europe and the USA and needed to grapple with the way philosophy and theology were pursued in the West.

If one would follow the main thought in Kant, which reduces the Christian faith to morality – a morality as stated by the philosopher, in which the Christian faith would become nothing but morality. This string of thought has had a great impact on intellectuals in Western Europe, and it still captures the imagination of many, Christians and atheists alike. This would, however, deny basic facts and cannot be said to be based on historical knowledge but on philosophical speculation – from a thinker who denied theologians the right to speculate about metaphysics – this sounds like a rather arbitrary judgement coming from such a great thinker. By Kant's critiques, this amounts to the establishment of a new religion: a religion of humanity.[140] The Polish philosopher Leszek Kolakowski (1927–2009) argued that the functional religion of the Enlightenment attempted to replace God with something else, but that the attempt, ultimately, was a failure.[141]

3.3 Action Based on International Law

In this part of the chapter, the principles and standards outlined in the chapter are seen as grounded in a law-based approach which seeks to ground the assistance of relief agencies in public international law. There are three ways in which international law is connected with refugee assistance; through *International*

---

[140] See Mahoney 2018.
[141] McGrath 2017, 142.

Humanitarian Law (IHL), *International Refugee Law* (IRL) and *International Human Rights Law* (IHRL) which are made up of treaties, customary international law, and general principles of law. What is common is the attempt to seek legal redress and to find a law-based approach to the plight of the refugees and the underlying conflict.

Legal protection is of primary concern in human society. A primary obligation of any state is to protect human life. It is when there is a violation of this responsibility, when a government no longer extends protection to all people within its borders, that a humanitarian crisis may begin. As this is to its nature a legal, as well as a moral issue, legal instruments have been a way to address it. A legal redress means that the protection of refugees – including humanitarian assistance – ought to be beyond political discussions, and hence humanitarian, in the sense of common concern for all. That is the argument made in the standards. International law is built upon the idea that the world ought to be governed according to the same basic standard of the rule of law, at times identified as human rights, and that states are accountable not only to their citizens but also to the international community, embodied by the United Nations.

A particular problem in modern society is the danger of people being defined as outside the legal protection of the law. Hanna Arendt when dealing with the rise of the totalitarian states of Nazi Germany and Communist Russia pointed to the move from area-bound law in which the law is applied to all to law concerned primarily with people: the citizens. Despite efforts to deal with the issue, statelessness, which began as a modern issue, remains.[142]

The term "stateless" acknowledged the fact that persons had lost the protection of their government and required international agreements for safeguarding their legal status. The postwar term "displaced persons" was invented during the war for the express purpose of liquidating statelessness by ignoring its existence. Nonrecognition of statelessness always means repatriation, i.e., deportation to a country of origin, which either refuses to recognize the prospective repatriate as a citizen, or, on the contrary, urgently wants him back for punishment.[143]

---

[142] Arendt 1967, 279. Cf. Hovil 2006, 56–62.

[143] Arendt 1967, 279. "It would seem that the very undeportability of the stateless person should have prevented a government's expelling him; but since the man without a state was 'an anomaly for whom there is no appropriate niche in the framework of the general law'— an outlaw by definition — he was completely at the mercy of the police", Arendt 1967, 283.

Law tends to focus on the negative – what people ought not to do – and less towards the positive – the common good of the community.[144] Setting limits of what is lawful, rather than encouraging and setting directions towards that which is good, beautiful, and just. So also, human rights, and its related kinds of international law, set limits – also to what is legitimate politics – to protect that which is valuable such as life, freedom, and the pursuit of happiness. The positive aspects – the will towards good – are nurtured in human communities as culture and religion, as that which is cultivated (La. *cultura* and *culturare*) and binding (La. *religio*) in the life of the community and its people. The negative tendency is strengthened by the negative definition of freedom inherent in liberalism – as freedom from restraint – rather than liberty to do good.[145]

International Humanitarian Law

As a crisis overwhelms local resources and capabilities, a humanitarian crisis calls for external assistance. This is rooted in the tradition of *International Humanitarian Law* (IHL)[146] with its focus on limiting the consequences of warfare by protecting non-participants of the conflict and imposing limits on the means and methods of war. By using a law-based method of holding the parties of war accountable for the use of limited means of warfare (*ius in bello*) and regulating whether a state may lawfully resort to armed force (*ius ad bellum*) through the Charter of the United Nations,[147] international law attempts to limit the collateral damage of a military conflict. This seeks the good of political peace without which human flourishing is difficult.[148] The World Council of Churches was founded on the idea that churches too, and not only states, should contribute to peace in the world in an organised manner.

The laws of warfare were followed up by the Red Cross and Red Crescent civil society mobilisation to heal the wounds and tend to humanitarian needs with both

---

[144] Cunningham, Davi 2008, 10, "the law (at least, the positive law with which we are primarily concerned here) tends to be focused primarily on preventing bad behavior, rather than encouraging good behavior. We can't enact a law that will require all human beings to be people of good will."

[145] See discussion in Deneen 2018 on negative freedom as distinct from liberty.

[146] Also called Law of Armed Conflict (LOAC).

[147] The charter only allows force against another state in cased of self-defence against an armed attack, or when authorised by the United Nations Security Council.

[148] Biggar 2020, 2.

parties in a conflict being accountable for their treatment of prisoners of war.[149] This second aspect of organisations capable of healing wounds has been useful not only in times of conflict but also in connection to accidents and natural disasters. As the humanitarian sector has grown and developed through the years – humanitarian – is more associated with the mitigation of suffering than with dealing with political conflicts turned violent. As such "humanitarianism" can be abused by political actors who may "agree" to the usefulness of humanitarian mitigation of suffering of their people, without holding themselves accountable to the rules of engagement in conflict and allow humanitarian access to political opponents.

Some relief agencies came about, or developed, as a moral outcry, in concrete situations in which the total war concept, which included economic warfare, was utilised as a method of war. During the Second World War, Oxfam was created to advocate against and mitigate the starvation of the Greek population resulting from the naval blockade of Allied forces.[150] During the Nigerian Civil War, Médecins Sans Frontier (MSF) was created, and the organisation split on the issue of the conscious starvation in Biafra. The Lutheran World Federation, during the same conflict, as part of the Joint Church Aid, created an air bridge for provisions to the starving population. As the issues are of high relevance to stances taken by the northern ACT members of ACT Ethiopia Forum, I will quote a longer statement from Walker and Maxwell on what was at stake in the Nigerian civil war:[151]

> The contentious issues faced by humanitarian workers in Biafra still echo in contemporary debates: questions over national sovereignty versus regional self-determination; the instrumentalization of humanitarian assistance for political purposes; the physical security of humanitarian workers; maintaining political neutrality vis-à-vis belligerent while expressing solidarity with humans caught in conflict; objectively measuring the evidence versus being forced to act in an extremely information-scarce (and in retrospect, propaganda-rich) environment; and the imperative to assist acutely disaster-affected people, but without prolonging the source of suffering or contributing to its impact. As in later conflict emergencies, many humanitarian workers saw the Biafran people as an

---

[149] The first Geneva Convention was held in 1864 for *the Amelioration of the Condition of the Wounded in Armies in the Field*. In 1868, the Declaration of Saint Petersburg prohibited the use of certain projectiles in war. According to Abass 2012, 195, the ICRC is a Swiss private international organisation, (international NGO), founded by an individual, Henry Dunant in 1863, which implements international law mandates, such as the international humanitarian law.

[150] Walker 2009, 42–44. The early Oxfam stance was that of 'a radical independence' against its government in sharp contrast to the policy of the ICRC.

[151] Walker 2009, 46–49. The airlift operation in Biafra is estimated to have prolonged the war with its consequent suffering.

oppressed minority, and identified as much with their political cause as with their human suffering.[152]

Beginning with the French Revolution, the successive Napoleonic wars, and the democratisation of armies, warfare began to change from one in the premodern era (1648–1789) in which smaller professional armies fought on behalf of rulers against other smaller armies into one with large armies of citizens with a view that the whole of society was involved in war.[153] This would, in stages, develop into the modern concept of total war, beginning with the American Civil War and further developed in the Spanish Civil War, and the First and Second World Wars. In this economic conception of war – the total surrender of the enemy is the goal, by any means necessary. The notion of war – following *ius in bello* principles in the Geneva Conventions is different. Recognising that war may be fought for a just cause, the conventions seek to argue for limited means and considerations of the civil population.[154]

The issue here is not war as such, but the action of external actors with regard to conflict and aid. Humanitarian aid, rendered in a context of conflict, is a practical moral argument that it is not right to starve or military harm a civilian population. On the contrary, there is a right to assistance with humanitarian aid.[155]

Barnett in *Empire of Humanity* evaluates "humanitarians" as falling into two categories, those who want to reserve "humanitarian" as only relief work in situations of dire need, and those who see emergency relief work as an entry point for engagement which then could be expanded into "postconflict reconstruction, human rights, development, democracy promotion, and peacebuilding." The first category Barnett labels "emergency humanitarianism", and the latter "alchemical humanitarianism." The International Committee of the Red Cross would belong to the first category, while many others, though labelled "humanitarian", would belong to the latter. Barnett's distinction should be seen in the light of the discussions on humanitarian intervention, "responsibility to protect", and US post-Cold war foreign policy. The main humanitarian principle in question is *the principle of independence*, i.e. that relief agencies may act on moral principles and not on policy decisions from those who finance or allow the relief operations.[156]

---

[152] Walker 2009, 48.

[153] Walker 2009, 42.

[154] For *ius ad bellum* and *ius in bello* discussion, see Nordquist 1998.

[155] Walker 2009, 46–49.

[156] Barnett 2011, 4, 39.

This leads to two principled issues on which the humanitarian sector is divided. One between the Red Cross and Red Crescent Movement which uses its position as a privileged organisation to combine the legal mandate of International Humanitarian Law with relief work without openly confronting the combating actors and their external supporting states and vocal agencies, such as Oxfam[157] and Médecins Sans Frontier, who uses advocacy and media to call attention to the conflict and demand cessation of hostilities and abuse of human rights.[158] ACT Alliance, in this regard, was set up with advocacy as one of its main aims with an advocacy bureau towards the European Union, and another toward the United Nations. Individual ACT members, however, may be divided on this issue.

A second divide is between agencies aiming toward temporary relief with a view of pulling out once the immediate crisis is over and agencies who aim at supporting the population at risk for a longer period through development projects or social services. ACT agencies in general belong to the latter category on account of the connection to local churches as the constituency of ACT agencies. Local churches do not move away, so why should their agencies?

When framed as a common international humanitarian framework, however – the dividing issues are less important than the common ones. The Sphere Project and the Core Humanitarian Standards both aimed at creating a consensus of the different voices within the humanitarian sector.

The call for accountability among humanitarian actors as represented by Core Humanitarian Standards and the importance of minimum standards in humanitarian response did not contradict one another but rather represented different aspects and emphases according to differing organisational setups and cultures of the same core principles. In 2018, the Core Humanitarian Standards were integrated into the Sphere Project showing their inherent compatibility and mutual strengthening of a principled humanitarian approach. The enforcing of international standards is a step towards further institutionalisation of the aid sector in the context of the dramatically increased budgets granted by Western governments.[159]

International Refugee Law

The reason why the refugee crisis is framed primarily as a humanitarian issue, as I have discussed above, is two-fold, the connection with conflict and the alleviation

---

[157] Walker 2009, 42–44.

[158] Walker 2009, 48, 73 for this side of MSF and the "new humanitarianism" of the late 1990s.

[159] Walker 2009, 73.

of suffering based on the idea of humanity. But what about refugee conventions? Would it not be more natural to deal with the issue in terms of International Refugee Law?

The idea and practice of asylum has a long-standing tradition in Europe, the birthplace of political liberalism, and in other places too. The challenge is that the modern right to seek asylum is thought of in terms of legal rights to be applied for in court. The law is written for individuals, not considered for a large population of asylum seekers.[160] The African Refugee Convention shows an understanding of massive influx of refugees, written as it was with European colonisation in mind. The early political leaders of a freed African continent could not imagine that they themselves would become the main cause of refugees in Africa. When African countries did not see themselves fit to assimilate newcomers into their nations, refugee camps became the temporary resolution with "voluntary repatriation as the ideal solution."[161]

It means that even though there is a body of international refugee law and an international organisation dedicated to the legal protection of asylum seekers and refugees (UNHCR), the system is unable to solve a large refugee crisis by assimilating the asylum seekers into the host nation. It manages the crisis rather by setting up camps, conceptualised as temporary shelters, but often remaining for years at length. This leads to an ethical dilemma – is it ethical to confine people to camps for years with no clear way out – creating both a need for constant funding and the denial of a normal life?

The purpose of the Nazi concentration camp was to degrade human beings into less than human, to show proof of their ideology of superiority. Indeed, they succeeded in bringing about a human condition so terrible that many people perished. But some survived. The common feature of those who survived was a sense of meaning, of purpose. People are not material machines predetermined by biochemical reactions, but human beings with desires beyond the biological instinct of self-preservation – and these motives – their will for meaning, kept them alive in the camps.[162]

---

[160] Arendt 1967, 280 "The first great damage done to the nation-states as a result of the arrival of hundreds of thousands of stateless people was that the right of asylum, the only right that had ever figured as a symbol of the Rights of Man in the sphere of international relationships, was being abolished. Its long and sacred history dates back to the very beginnings of regulated political life. Since ancient times it has protected both the refugee and the land of refuge."

[161] Murray 2004, 201–11. Salomon 1991 on *Refugees in the Cold War*.

[162] Frankl 1986.

A framework of International Humanitarian Law, even though it is set up to deal with military conflict, has severe limits when dealing with a refugee crisis. Conceptualised during the modern wars of Europe – the idea was to limit the collateral damage of these political conflicts while diplomacy would sort out the issue at hand. When the conflict is not solved, the crisis is handled by confining the asylum seekers to semi-permanent camps. This dilemma of the inadequacy of International Humanitarian Law and International Refugee Law leads humanitarian agencies to seek solutions within a human rights framework.

International Human Rights Law

As seen in the Sphere Handbook, among the basic principles outlined was a human rights approach to the humanitarian crisis. This is not self-evident and not without complications, however, but it creates the possibility of positing a limited human rights framework even within a conflict context and within the setting of a refugee camp. The literature on rights is vast and covers a range of academic disciplines, and the ethical and theological issues involved are debated.[163]

Hence, we see the ACT Agencies – particularly LWF World Service and DICAC-RRAD with years of experience of working with refugees in Ethiopia – through the appeal, arguing for activities such as vocational training, community based psychosocial support (CBPS) and secondary education. The community based approach is thought to be a bridge from relief support towards self-sustainment by involving the refugee community – and the host community – in activities, both in terms of seeing the local resources and capabilities – as contrasted to only seeing needs – and in terms of a participatory approach to let the people work themselves through the crisis. This kind of work is easier done within a human rights framework – to argue towards donor states and the host state that it belongs to mandatory rights to serve the refugees with education and development projects.[164]

While scholars argue about the compatibility of International Refugee Law, International Humanitarian Law and International Human Rights Law, and the extent of application of International Humanitarian Law or Human Rights Law

---

[163] Biggar 2020, 3. Hoffmann 2011. Hollenbach 2008. Hopgood 2013. Hovorun 2017. Mertus 2009. Murray 2004. Novak 1999. Also FDRE 1995 Constitution art. 10, "1. Human rights and freedoms, emanating from the nature of mankind, are inviolable and inalienable. 2. Human and democratic rights of citizens and peoples shall be respected."

[164] See Murray 2004, 216–19.

for refugees[165] practitioners bring the three fields together – using their interpretations – and argue for support among donor states. The same goes with regard to bringing the issues of peace and reconciliation into the picture. Is anything lost on the way from the narrow "humanitarian" argument – that it is always important to consider one human life as valuable even in a context of conflict – towards bringing these frameworks into a common nexus with the view of a future merger of humanitarian – refugee – human right – peace and reconciliation together?

There is a practical as well as a principled aspect involved in this issue. The practical issue has to do with the representatives of humanitarian aid organisations' ability to negotiate and deal with commanders, generals, politicians, and other stakeholders about the dignity of human life and the moral obligation for care in each case. Once the humanitarian argument has taken hold of the conscious, or pragmatic sense, of the counterpart at hand, expanding the argument to involve more and more can take place. Barnett warns of what he calls "alchemical humanitarianism", as seen in this section.[166]

The principled issue regards the danger of compromise, for the sake of the greater good, and the history of humanitarian action is filled with such examples. How do humanitarian actors determine the right course of action in a "minefield" of actors whose interests are contrary to the mission of the aid agency? It is in this context, that humanitarian principles are tested.

3.4 African Gate Keeper States and Stakeholders

There are aspects of thematic importance for our study of the present refugee crisis and its response: the development of independent African Gate Keeper States, the crossing of African borders, the promotion of civil society with subsequent tension between African civil society and the state, and stakeholder in refugee assistance. Let us briefly look at these interrelated issues to set the general context.

The Gate Keeper States

The modern states of Africa were born from the process beginning with *the Scramble for Africa*. During a short period of time the map of Africa was carved

---

[165] Cantor and Durieux *Refugee from Inhumanity?* contributes to the "debate about whether persons fleeing war to seek asylum in another country – 'war refugees' – are protected by international law" and "the extent to which the application of international humanitarian law (IHL) may usefully advance the legal protection of such persons." Cantor and Durieux 2014.

[166] Barnett 2011, 4, 39.

up and designated for separate spheres of interest. At times, "African societies were rent apart", as people groups were separated or brought together regardless of geographical or cultural differentiations or similarities.[167] The newly drawn borders created colonial states with little or no historical justifications. By the 1930s, however, these borders and states had acquired a sense of legitimacy. By that time though, Europe had less interest in colonies and kept the administration to a bare minimum. It meant that a few administrators with a high degree of authority often relied on newly installed African "chiefs" to exercise control over their areas.[168] Colonialism, as well as a political system, also created new economic patterns. In the so-called *gate keeper states,*[169] a new development from the 1920s, the colonial administrations moved away from flexible market-oriented development into a regulated production of raw materials for the global market. This hampered agricultural development in African rural areas.[170]

The Second World War brought several changes, in terms of infrastructure, and in terms of recruitment of thousands of African troops for the war efforts. The end of the war meant a shift of power from European countries to the United States and the Soviet Union. The rebuilding of African countries devastated by the war, like Ethiopia, was not supported in the same way as European countries, but the principle of self-determination as signed in the Atlantic Charter in 1941 also included colonial people. Colonial powers like Britain and France introduced reforms in the post-war era including political reforms, unlike Belgium and Portugal. The war experience of many soldiers fighting in the war was one of the factors speeding up the efforts to create independent African states.[171]

As the Cold War followed the Second World War, it impacted both the road to independence and the initial path as sovereign countries for many an African nation. As the East and the West fought for the attention of other nations, the struggle for liberation often got caught up in "socialist trappings", even though the prime aim was the removal of foreign domination. As both sides of the Cold War got engaged, it encouraged violent resolutions and did nothing to keep authoritarian tendencies at bay. The ideal was often the creation of a welfare state,

---

[167] Meredith, Martin 1998, 1–8.

[168] For Biggar 2023, part of the issue with the colonial system was the lack of actual control.

[169] The concept of Gate Keeper State was developed by the historian Frederick Cooper to characterise a state primarily geared toward controlling goods entering and leaving its ports; educational opportunities; and regulations and licenses for trade and commerce. Cooper 2002, 5.

[170] Meredith 1998, 1–8. Hillbom 2010, 20.

[171] Meredith 1998, 8–12. The Marshall Plan was generally not applied to Ethiopia.

but the local African elites kept much of the colonial state and its economic and social systems intact and consolidated the gate keeper state. Development efforts were caught in these macro-economic dynamics and the expected "big-push" never took place. Independence was not enough to foster a prosperous Africa.[172]

Beginning with the oil crisis and the following world economic crisis in the 1970s, the economics of most Sub-Saharan African states were struggling, as debts were increasing, and the Cold War factor lessened as a motivating factor for aid from the East as well as the West. Economic politics aimed at increasing exports did not stimulate local food production. Existing production could not keep up with population growth and urbanization. Food imports based on aid – loans – contributed to the debt crisis. The gate keeper state was in crisis, the belief in social and economic development in Africa in general was in doubt and the confidence in African leaders was low. The economic and political power had ended up in very few hands, excluding most of the population from making rational decisions regarding their economic development. The societies were thus not flexible enough to develop and change to the extent needed, and conflict and power struggles arose in the wake of the socio-economic crisis.[173]

The crisis in Sub-Saharan Africa during the 1980s was severe with almost a doubling of the number of people ending up in poverty, a stagnation in the agricultural sector, and the disastrous impact of HIV and Aids. The crisis gave impetus to a deregulation of the economy and decentralisation of politics in a spirit of new liberalism. The end of the Cold War with the fall of the Berlin Wall in 1989 and the Soviet Union led African states to seek aid in the West regardless of ideological viewpoints. With aid came demands from donors for structural changes aimed at stimulating the private sector, strengthening the so-called civil society and local communities, and advancing democratisation. The World Bank and IMF introduced *Structural Adjustment Plans* (SAP) to finance comprehensive reforms. The result, particularly in former Communist states, was negative growth and high inflation. "Paradoxically, the West tried to *plan* how to achieve a *market*."[174] This was an underestimation of how difficult it is to get a market to work in a socially beneficial way. The plans were replaced in 2000 by *the Millennium Development Goals* (MDG) and then by *the Sustainable Development Goals* (SDG) in 2016 as

---

[172] Meredith 1998, 13. Prunier 2015, 209. Hillbom and Green 2010, 11, 204–23. Easterly 2006.

[173] Hillbom and Green 2010, 11; 20–21, 204–26.

[174] Easterly 2006, 54.

the overall framework for financing development aid with social indicators com-plementing the financial targets of the previous plans.[175]

Crossing African Borders

A major issue in Africa during the second half of the twentieth century was the crossing of African borders by refugees and migrants. Most of the present borders on the African continent follow the former borders set during the time of coloni-sation. Initially many assumed that the borders would be changed in a liberated Africa. There were however internal reasons to keep the set borders. One of those reasons was for the African states to protect natural resources available within the current borders of the nations. Modern African states have been set up as modern nation-states controlling the natural resources within the area, i.e. the gate keeper state. Governments have depended on these resources for their economic survival. Thus, it became of importance to the newly formed African independent states to reinforce the validity of the borders formed during the Scramble for Africa.

In the early times of *the Organisation of African Unity* (OAU) in the 1960s, the factors leading to a refugee crisis were mainly seen in the light of colonialism and the struggle for liberation. Hence, generous policies were in place for neigh-bouring nations to receive and integrate refugees as a sign of solidarity. As African states began to acknowledge that refugee situations were caused not by external forces or colonial powers but by African states, this led to a preference for tempo-rary solutions. A prima facie status as refugees may thus be granted temporary pro-tection living in camps. This status however does not grant the full benefits granted to refugees under the UN and OAU Conventions.[176]

The Organisation of African Union, since 1994, has advocated for voluntary repatriation as the preferred solution. African states have thus been focusing on the principle of non-refoulment such that:

> no person shall be subjected by a member state to measures such as rejection at the fron-tier, return or expulsion, which would compel him to return or remain in the territory where his life, physical integrity or liberty would be threatened.[177]

This was combined with a recommendation to seek opportunities for voluntary repatriation of refugees. This recommendation was given in the Addis Ababa Conference in 1994 despite constraints due to the prevailing security situation of

---

[175] Hillbom 2010, 235–37. Easterly 2006, 53–62.

[176] Murray 2004, 209.

[177] Murray 2004, 211–12. Murray quoting Article 2(3) of the OAU convention.

some African countries. There was, however, also the consideration that in some cases an "inter-African resettlement" in some cases may be the only solution. Therefore, the conference added a recommendation for African states to offer resettlement and for the UNHCR to facilitate the process.[178]

Since the Organisation of African Unity was replaced in 2001 by the Charter of the African Union, there have been several initiatives to promote regional trade in the continent of Africa and its regions. African nations have had tendencies to produce the same kind of agricultural products, to lack the capacity for processing industry, and to have undeveloped home markets. Regional trade however has been growing yearly and several regional organisations, such as the *Southern African Development Co-ordination Conference* (SADCC), promote regional interaction across national borders.

As trade and interaction between African Union members develop, it will probably be easier for people to migrate and work in different member states. That in itself may not benefit refugees though as they are not part of bilateral agreements between two states, but rather come out of internal conflicts of particular states.[179] The idea of trade and interaction as a means to solve African issues may in the long run be one of the factors in moving Africa forward in prosperity and peace.

Promotion of Civil Society and Tensions with the State

The failure of the states to bring prosperity led to an upgrading of the idea of civil society as a promoter of development. This idea is of particular interest to this thesis as the churches and their organisations often appear under the rubric of civil society. The concept of civil society was introduced to a field, by then, dominated by state actors. "Civil society" was intended not to act as a radical force but as a collaborative partner with the state and foreign donors. The background was both the positive role played by civil society organisations in the development of Western nations and the importance attributed to civil society in African societies. The modern state, in its initial developments in Africa however, had tried to centralise power and limit the role of other actors to the detriments of societal development. From the 1980s, there was a tendency to focus less on state-led development and more on civil society-led development. Part of the intention of donor agencies was

---

[178] Murray 2004, 211–12.

[179] Citizens of Kenya and Ethiopia have ample opportunities to move between the two countries without a visa for example. Kenya and Ethiopia have been among the more stable countries in the Horn of Africa.

to facilitate democratic development and encourage political opposition to ruling parties.[180]

It is difficult however to determine what the generic term "civil society" means in each case. Behind the positive attribution, lies the assumption that the organisation of civil society would promote equal opportunities and give voice to different groups in society. It was also assumed that the arena of civil society would be less concerned with politics and the interests of groups. These ideas came from Western societies which had positive experiences of abolitionist, temperance and mission societies, and the social movements spearheaded by them. As this view of civil society was instrumentalised, as a donor-initiated tool for the implementation of state development policy, the immediate recipients of the aid channelled to the civil society were development, humanitarian, and other agencies – so-called non-government organisations (NGO). As with "civil society", the meaning of the acronym "NGO" as a generic term is very fluid and ambiguous. Since the 1980s, the number of registered non-government organisations involved in social service, development, humanitarian assistance, advocacy, and peace and reconciliation has exploded. These organisations may range in scope from a loose local network to multilateral professional humanitarian agencies with a budget rivalling that of small states. The idea is that non-government organisations may increase the participation of local communities. When local communities define their issues and solutions, development is possible.[181]

Representatives of African states have been ambiguous in their view of the civil society sector and the involvement of large multilateral humanitarian, development, and advocacy organisations. These organisations attract donor funding from areas where governments used to be privileged. Civil servants are often attracted by the salaries, the benefits, and the freedom offered at a time when governments have not been able to offer decent wages.[182] There is also the claim that these organisations are run by larger budgets and with more resources than public funding can provide. Several organisations are also led by foreign professionals

---

[180] Hillbom 2010, 248–49.

[181] Hillbom 2010, 250–51. On civil society in an ecclesial context, see also Axelson 2006.

[182] Civil servants and church employees tend to move to these organisations. This type of labour movement includes an internal hierarchy among relief agencies with local and church-based organisations at the lower end and Western, UN, and donor agencies at the top. As such, it constitutes an internal brain drain from primary institutions in society to extraordinary structures. Cf. chapter two and the challenge to hire staff, and the fact that educated people are often drawn from civil offices or church administrations.

with a scope exceeding that of government colleagues. These factors increase a sense of competition.[183]

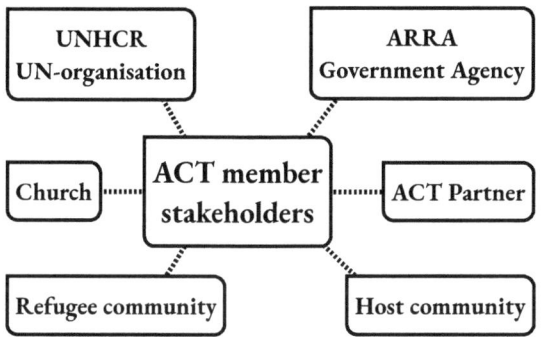

Figure 3.2: *A stakeholder analysis seen from the perspective of an ACT member engaged in refugee assistance. The ACT member relates to UNCHR as the coordinating UN agency mandated with refugee assistance, ARRA[184] the Federal government agency responsible for refugee protection, ACT Partners who contribute with finances, capacity building and analysis, the refugee population it aims to assist, the host community who lives in and around the refugee camp, and the church on whose authority the ACT member operates.*

Stakeholders

Refugee assistance is not a solo act. Church-based and faith-based actors work using the UN framework, under the authority of the specialised refugee authority of the Ethiopian federal government (ARRA), and in collaboration with other agencies – some transnational and others national.[185] Important aspects of the concrete work in the field are done by local companies, local host community members and members of the refugee communities themselves. There is also at times collaboration with local churches, for example, the LWF World Service asks local churches for permission to use their premises and the locality of their offices and storage facilities.

The refugee assistance is being performed by different agents together in a complex set of relationships. Rather than one actor planning, raising funds, implementing the plans and evaluating its results, the work is divided among the agents

---

[183] Hillbom 2010, 252–53.

[184] Ethiopian Administration for Refugee and Returnee's Affairs (ARRA).

[185] Milner 2014 for a discussion of refugee policy in an arena with different "actors".

and different roles are distributed to ease the collaboration of the different parties. This thesis examines some of those factors which may hinder and facilitate collaboration between different stakeholders with a focus on the common work of ACT Alliance in Ethiopia.

Humanitarian work guided by humanitarian principles entails a critical and even cautious engagement with local authorities to promote the values of humanity – the value of life, dignity, and respect for other human beings, even for an enemy. That is promoting certain main values by working for the welfare of a particular group of people in need. Indirectly, it is advocacy for those people, and the dignity of all men and women. It does not entail either a total acceptance or rejection of government authorities at hand but rather asking them to accept the charge of acting morally towards that group of people.

In the case of the South Sudanese crisis, it was the asylum seekers themselves who took the first initiative – in the light of indiscriminate violence by their compatriots – to seek refuge in a foreign country. They took a great risk and went through trouble at great cost to reach safety. The relationship between these asylum seekers and the conflict may vary, but the reason why it was almost only women and children crossing the border was that the men stayed either to fight or to tend to their farms and animals. So whereas some would indirectly be involved in the political strife, others would not. International Humanitarian Law therefore grants people who are not actively taking part in a conflict the status of civilian, which may also be granted to soldiers.

The internal relationships between asylum seekers themselves may differ. The refugee population may not, in the strict sense, be a community at all, but instead, it may consist of individuals, families, and groups who by coincidence have travelled the same route but may have little else in common. To become a recognisable community, therefore, these people need to act positively. The way asylum seekers act – once they have arrived in safety inside – the borders of Ethiopia – carries importance. Systems of assistance that do not recognise this fact risk making matters worse. The community-based psychosocial approach of the ACT agencies recognises this fact and consciously strives to minimise the negative impact of the relief assistance.

The host communities are the first responders. In the case of ETH141, the locals were receiving the asylum seekers and sharing their resources long before any organised aid reached them. In the case of a large refugee influx, such as the South Sudanese crossing the border to Ethiopia in 2014, the situation quickly overwhelms the local population, their resources are strained, and relationships may become tense.[186]

This is the starting point when ACT agencies move in. There are differing state interests and organisational setups as regulated by laws, policies, and procedures. Host and refugee communities may become doubly overwhelmed and constrained as stated above. It is in this type of complex situation that the international standards attempt to foster a disciplined approach following humanitarian principles. Once the humanitarian apparatus is being put in place, there is a great shift from these community actions – both by refugees and by hosts – to the "machinery" of the aid system and the differing stakeholders of state (federal and regional), donors, aid agencies, and the private companies who see business opportunities in the wake of the humanitarians.

There is an assumption of responsibilities by agencies coordinated by the UN-HCR. This may cause a second type of overwhelming situation in which community responsibilities may dissolve as the mandated agencies take over the control.[187] Such a dynamic – that encourages NGO action – is contrary to the idea of ACT as actual churches working together enabled by facilitating ACT agencies. It is also contrary to the idea of building local resilience and local capacities as represented in the ETH141 appeal both by the community-based psychosocial approach of building on available resources and capacities and the revised appeal with its project of empowering the local communities through EECMY-DASSC. These two initiatives were born because ACT Alliance is not simply another humanitarian entity, but a comprehensive alliance that may bring both a developmental viewpoint and a church perspective. That is a step towards recognising refugee populations and local host communities.

---

[186] 2011 11 23 ACT Alliance Response to Emergencies and Annexes: ACTs definition of an emergency is directly connected to the inability of a community to cope with an emergency: "An emergency is a disruption of the functioning of a community, population or society, causing human (including social and psychosocial), material, economic and/or environmental losses and destruction, which generally exceed the capacity of the affected persons and community to cope using its own resources. Emergencies may be categorized by scale (small, medium, large or mega) or by type (natural, complex, protracted or forgotten)."

[187] Government funding is always limited as only a small portion of government budget may be used for various forms of aid – hence there is always the need for rationing available funds. As the South Sudanese crisis began at the end of a budget year, in December, the funds available for 2013 were depleted. The specific rationing decisions and the basis for those deliberations in government bureaucracies are generally not transparent and made public. This is true not only about international aid, but also public health care. See discussion in Shapiro 2007, 36–42.

It is precisely when people – the refugee population and the host communities – have been affected both by the emergency and by "humanitarian-induced social problems"[188] that principles of building on local capacities, participation, and resilience matter for the relief assistance not to do further harm. The idea is to affirm "the importance of including the affected population and local and national authorities at all stages of the response" with a view towards "agency accountability to affected communities."[189] Such principles aim to return responsibility as soon as possible back to communities themselves by allowing participation and responsibility, to the extent possible. This begins with a principled approach in addition to agency principles of humanity, neutrality, impartiality, and independence. It is in this situation with many and differing stakeholders, of state agencies, international organisations, diverse communities, and large and small aid agencies that this thesis asks questions about Christian and church-based agencies engaging in refugee assistance.

3.5 Morality, Principled Action, and the Church

The purpose of the thesis is to highlight the problem of the identity of ACT Alliance as an *action by churches together* by rendering an account of the "Christian" and "church-based" of the refugee assistance of ACT Ethiopia Forum to South Sudanese refugees in 2014. As such the thesis is a contribution to the discussions on *faith and development* and *religion and development*. As I have shown in chapters two and three – there are very few references to the Christian faith in the ETH141 appeal with appending reports, and even though ACT Alliance have some specific guidelines for the work of the member organisations, the ETH141 appeal explicitly refers to international guidelines – rather than customary ACT guidelines. When analysing these guidelines in chapter three – there are no references to God, the Christian faith, or the Christian Church. There seems to be a tension between ACT Alliance as *action by churches together* and this seemingly "secular" account. Is it possible to give an account of what "Christian" and "church-based" means in the context of the refugee assistance of ACT Alliance?

---

[188] IASC 2007, 2 lists significant social problems including pre-existing factors (such as poverty, social marginalisation and political oppression), emergency-induced factors (such as family separation, and destruction of communities), and humanitarian aid factors (such as the undermining of family and community structures).

[189] Sphere 2011, 6 on the Humanitarian Charter, Protection Principles and Core Standards.

In this section, I will make six points, moving from refugee assistance to the life of the churches. First, the main reason for people to engage in refugee assistance is that it is a morally good thing to do. Second, morality is objective. Third, a principled approach is better than a pragmatic approach to avoid doing harm. Fourth, this is the main reason for the principles outlined in chapter three. Fifth, there is an affinity between a principled moral approach and the teaching of the Christian churches. Sixth, the refugee assistance of ACT Alliance, though a moral good, does not exhaust the meaning of either ACT Alliance or church ministry, and taken in itself reveals only partially the theological meaning of the church.

A Moral Argument for Refugee Assistance

First, the ecumenical refugee assistance of ACT Alliance, as exemplified in the case study of the ETH141 ACT Appeal to support refugees from South Sudan, is a moral response to a humanitarian crisis: the situation of the refugees. This is implicit in the appeal as a plea for help for people in desperate need. It is also indicated by references to international standards in the form of rights: the right to assistance by people in need and the right to assist by aid agencies. No other motivation to the work is given. There is, in this, no principled difference between the ACT approach and other actors who act on moral grounds.[190]

An Objective Moral Law

Second, morality, as such, is assumed in the refugee response, neither argued for nor proven, but taken for granted as a given. This is in line with pre-modern thinking in which people took for granted the existence of a moral law together with the realisation that men do break this law with the consequent tension between ought and is: the moral demand and the behaviour of people. Therefore "the ought" is not derived from what men and women actually do "empirically", or from their emotions. The moral law is assumed from the outset as pointing men towards a greater reality of objective values. There is, at this point, no difference between Christians and others. In this customary view of morality, all are under the obligation to follow the same law, and all fail to fulfil it to its fullness.[191]

---

[190] See the argument for universality in Bello 1980 on *African Customary International Law*.

[191] Lewis 1943. Lewis outlines how this pre-modern basic assumption of the existence of objective values and a universal moral law clashes with modern attempts to either prove or replace traditional morality with aspects of the old morality. This attempt, Lewis argues, is as futile as branches attempting to saw themselves off from the tree and will and with some men, the

A Principled Approach

Third, by setting up organisations through which men and women may collaborate and coordinate the assistance, i.e. the moral response, the principled matter has not changed, *de iure*, but the practical matter has become complex, *de facto*, with rising complexity considering various stakeholders and their respective agencies. Each man and woman still acts, *de iure*, according to their ability and judgement, *de facto*. Each person is accountable, *de iure*, for their actions and failure to act, as seen in the personal Code of Conduct.[192] This is one of the reasons why *the principle of subsidiarity*, in which decisions are pushed down to the lowest possible level, has been argued for. This includes the imperative of local participation of refugees and local inhabitants alike, and the call for a downward accountability.[193]

In the principled approach of ACT Alliance, this is stressed, in continuation with the long term social engagement within the ecumenical movement. This matter is made more difficult by the use of public rather than ecclesial funding, and the trend towards donor compliance and the fact that donors are not in any real sense accountable to the people they serve, or to the aid organisations they support. The risk is that accountability is perceived as a one-way street of donors demanding accountability from implementing organisations, rather than a two-way street of mutual accountability. In principle, donor-centred aid frames ability as capital. The important aspect of aid is financial means. That is the ability that counts.[194]

"innovators" and the "conditioners", controlling the lives of all other men to the destruction of civilization. These men are no longer true men, but "men without chests", since they have put themselves outside of the "Tao", the tradition to which all belong, and outside of which no man can live. This position, that morality is innate or natural to humanity has practical import in relief work since aid workers may then presuppose that the people they work with already know the moral law. Lewis' position is fundamentally different from the position of the Russian Patriarch Kirill's "traditional values", that are specifically Russian and anti-Western. See Hovorun 2023.

[192] The principled example is the Nürnberg trials after the fall of the Nazi regime in Germany. Three matters are of principal importance here: 1) Each individual was held accountable according to their actions and could not hide behind references to duty or the carrying out of orders. 2) The American judges made their cases by reference to natural law, i.e. the existing German law as posited by German authorities was assessed in the light of a higher standard, a universal law according to which all mankind were judged. 3) For the Universal Declaration of Human Rights, natural law language was not used explicitly, but the intent was there.

[193] See quote from Orobator in p. 131.

[194] Here is a conundrum of state aid agencies. One agency cannot both be a seat of accountability and an active agency at the same time. ARRA falls under this problem of being a regulatory agency, a coordinating device, and an implementing organisation. For foreign donor

Do No Harm

Therefore fourth, the operational principles of humanity, impartiality, neutrality, and independence are essential for agencies to be able to operate ethically within a conflicted context of many stakeholders, including funding agencies. A stress on accountability as donor compliance risks doing more harm than good by prioritising economic factors such as effectiveness and efficiency and neglecting the importance of prudential judgements thus threatening the moral integrity of the staff. By pointing towards the rights of asylum seekers, emphasis is put on the objectivity of the moral law under which all stakeholders ultimately are accountable for their actions and inaction.

The *Do No Harm* approach is a reminder that all stakeholders – including the refugee population themselves may make things better or worse. Moral and political judgements have to be made considering the best course of action in the context of conflict. This is the reason why the four principles mentioned above are important but not enough but have been complemented by others such as participation and building on available capacities and resources.[195]

Ethics and Ecclesiology

Fifth, the fact that moral values need to be recognised as such does not mean that teaching is not involved, by parents, teachers, and communities. The moral and social teaching of the Christian churches come into this context by validating moral experience by moral teaching and by providing a moral framework based on the main Christian doctrines of the faith.[196]

---

agencies, it is even more intricate. As agencies under their foreign ministries, they are accountable to the ministry, and the ministry to their respective government and parliament. That system of accountability, however, is only in a moral sense and highly indirect sense, connected to the people who are served, and the organisations who serve with governmental support. Upward accountability systems are a one-way-street. A government is accountable to their people, but not in any real sense, to other populations. Stress on donor compliance therefore shifts the focus away from people towards the donors. See Easterly 2006.

[195] The dilemma of appealing to rights in a refugee crisis is that the people responsible for upholding the rights of the refugees have already failed in that task. That is why there are refugees in the first place. The secondary (hosting government) and tertiary (assisting agencies and donor agencies) responsibilities regarding rights should not be confused with the primary responsibility of any government to uphold the rights of its citizens. See Cantor and Durieux 2014.

[196] Historically, one can argue that contemporary international relief systems are derived from Christianity. Since the international community of the United Nations is comprised of

Many a Christian – from a variety of churches – have been inspired to do more for their fellow man because of the Christian gospel. This was the turning point in the ecumenical discussion on *Ethics and Ecclesiology*. The recognition that churches are moral communities that form their members gave a rationale for no longer ignoring the churches but instead working for an *action by churches together*, as seen in the literature review. Christian teaching, however, cannot be instrumentalised only for aid work. If the moral law is real and true – it applies to all life – and the moral law demands justice as well as mercy, as the next chapter on the churches will show.[197]

Narrow Agencies and Broader Mission of the Church

Sixth, practically speaking, the work of ACT Alliance is not exhausted by refugee assistance. The 140 ACT members are involved in various forms of relief, development and advocacy works as well as rendering social services beyond the limits of aid collaboration. The work of ACT Alliance – taken here in the most comprehensive sense of the total acts of its members – does not exhaust the ecumenical movement.[198]

The ecumenical movement in all its variety is only one expression of the life of the churches. In the sense of communal ecclesial life, the church ministers serve the church communities, and the members serve others. In the sense of Christian life,[199] Christians serve their fellow man through private and professional life as

---

peoples of all faiths and diverse cultures, they are unable to agree on first principles. The Enlightenment project, historically situated in Western Christianity as divided into national churches and nation-states, pushed for unity as there was essential agreement, though not doctrinal, on first principles. This was in continuity with the natural law tradition. Cf. Tergel 1998.

[197] Relief workers are torn between the will to serve people by providing for the most basic needs as an expression of mercy and rendering long-term justice. Cf. Abebe Feyissa and Horn 2008.

[198] WCC have been striving to keep different strands of the ecumenical movement together under one umbrella organisation. The council has been supporting relief assistance as well as peace negotiations, missions as well as political activism, the unity of the church as well as the unity of the world, all under one roof. The council has been able to impact world politics while world politics has impacted the council. Cf. Howell 1982 and Visser't Hooft 1982.

[199] The term Christian most fundamentally refers to Christ and through him to his Church. The church was instituted to enable human beings back into relationship with God, thus fulfilling their ultimate purpose, complete happiness in communion with the eternal life of God. How does the ultimate purpose of human life (*summon bonum*) relate to other good purposes in life? This is where theology is bound up with ethics as will be seen in the next chapter.

well as other forms of communal life, including political engagements and public commitments.

If the essential Christian dogma is true, it cannot be limited to service in any sense of the word. The Christian faith is, as will be seen in chapter four, rooted in the historical event of the resurrection of Jesus Christ. Christ's loving service and his overcoming of death, sin, and the devil. This is the heart of the Christian gospel. It cannot be reduced to any sense of human services or social or political engagements. Neither can it be reduced to "religious activities" apart from social life.

The main mission of the Christian church is to be a faithful servant of the gospel. This is what makes the church unique. Therefore, ACT Alliance cannot be a substitute for the church. An organisation is set up for a specific human purpose. The Christian church claims that it is different. ACT Alliance may however be a legitimate agency for common social concerns of the churches. What this means and does not mean in practice is what this thesis has been asking about in the case study.

4. Ethiopian Churches: Ecumenical Engagement

This chapter sets the idea of ACT Alliance as *action by churches together* in relation to the views of the two Ethiopian ACT members for the sake of contributing to a discussion on ecclesial engagement, and to pose the question of how the ecumenical engagement has been motivated, understood, and critiqued by Ethiopian churches. This chapter makes use of primary sources from the two Ethiopian churches of ACT Ethiopia Forum to allow them to speak about their self-understanding, engagement in ecumenical diakonia, and mission in the world. These two ACT members are *the Ethiopian Orthodox Tewahido Church* and *the Ethiopian Evangelical Church Mekane Yesus*.

Within the framework of Christian life, there are different ways in which service to others may be motivated, understood, and carried out. A comprehensive study of the historical and current life of the churches and their sources is beyond the limits of this research as there has never been a century for the last two thousand years without Christianity in Africa.[1] This becomes evident in any study of the churches in Egypt, Sudan, South Sudan, Eritrea, and Ethiopia where Christianity has apostolic roots.[2] The Ethiopian Orthodox Church[3] and the Mekane Yesus Church[4] have both joined ACT Alliance and contributed to its work.

---

[1] Bauer 1994, 17. Atiya 1968, Harmless 2004, Swanson 2010 *et al* have renewed the study of Orthodox churches, the desert fathers and early monasticism, and pre-Chalcedonian churches.

[2] Atiya 1968; Bauer 1994; Isichei 1995; Sundkler 2000; Swanson 2010; Tadesse Tamrat 1972.

[3] Among studies on EOC: Abate Gobena 2023; An 2015; Atiya 1968; Bahru Zewde 2008; Binns 2017; Chaillot 2002; Fritsch 1999; Getnet Tamene 1998; Mebratu Kiros Gebru 2012; Melketsedek 1997; Mengistu Gobezie Worku 2018; Negussie 2010; Nigussu Legesse 2014; Paulos Yohannes 1998; Seblewengel Daniel 2019; Tadesse Tamrat 1972 and 1998.

[4] Among studies on EECMY: Arén 1978, 1999; Bakke 1986; Balisky 2009; Dawit Olika 2017; Debela Birri 1995; Eide 1996; Ezra Gebremedhin 1988; Forslund 1993; Grenstedt 2000 and 2024; Jonsson 1998; Launhardt 2004; Misgana Mathewos 2010; Sæverås 1974; Tolo 1998.

Omitting their voices altogether would distort the overall picture of ecumenical diakonia in Ethiopia. It would be reduced to an international affair outside of the study of the church. Since omitting the ecclesial dimension of the work from the thesis would be detrimental to the purpose of investigating the ecclesiological claims of ACT Alliance, the choice here was to limit the material studied. The primary texts of the two Ethiopian churches function as a bridge between the life of the Ethiopian churches and the aid-based assistance of refugees within a global framework of relief work. Thereby, this chapter serves to render a contextual character to the ecumenical diakonia of ACT Alliance by investigating the ecclesial foundations for ecumenical engagements in Ethiopia.

To explore the Ethiopian church perspective, I will analyse two important primary sources: *On the Interrelation between the Proclamation of the Gospel and Human Development* (*the ECMY Letter*) from the Mekane Yesus and the first issue of *Maedot* from the Orthodox Church. Both these texts are written in the context of aid and present the views of their respective Ethiopian churches. These texts are historical, the former written just before the 1974 Ethiopian revolution and the latter in 1983 during the transitional time of the Derg military regime of 1974–1991. The changes that took place in the life of the churches during the Derg period make these texts relevant for a discussion on the current self-understanding of the churches. Relevant sources should be able to speak with some authority on topics of significance regarding the life of the churches and its relation to aid work.

Several criteria have been used for the selection of texts: They should be primary texts, 1) expressing the self-understanding of a church, 2) addressing the topic of church-based aid in the life of the churches, 3) be written near or during the formative period of the Derg, and 4) being part of the ecumenical dialogue. These selected sources are relevant to the broader theme of ecumenical diakonia but are not limited, as with chapter two, to issues of refugee assistance.

Chapter four, therefore, sets the idea of ACT Alliance as *action by churches together* in relation to views of *the Ethiopian Orthodox Tewahedo Church* and *the Ethiopian Evangelical Church Mekane Yesus* for the sake of contributing to a discussion on ecclesial engagement, and the question of how the ecumenical engagement has been motivated, understood, and critiqued by Ethiopian churches.

The first section *A Letter from Mekane Yesus 1972* (4.1) is a textual analysis of one important text from the Ethiopian Evangelical Church Mekane Yesus, *On the Interrelation between the Proclamation of the Gospel and Human Development*, (also called *the ECMY Letter*). The church officers wrote *the ECMY Letter* to the

Lutheran World Federation in 1972 as a critique of a donor-oriented aid model in favour of a church-led mission model of human development.

Passover Message from the Ethiopian Orthodox in 1983 (4.2) analyses the texts of a booklet written to Ecumenical donors to showcase the church and its commitment to ecumenical collaboration in 1983.

Gospel and Liturgy Form the Christian (4.3) expand on the evangelical understanding of the gospel, outlined in the *ECMY Letter*, to clarify the importance of the gospel. I also use insights from liturgical theology to discuss the role of the historical liturgy in forming Christians to care for those on the margin.

Voluntary Societies and Church Contributions (4.4) discusses the relationship between civil society, i.e. voluntary societies in the Ethiopian churches as well as the ability of the churches to contribute to work such as refugee assistance.

The last section, *Ethiopian Church Basis for Ecumenical Engagement* (4.5) brings the two Ethiopian views together in light of the present engagement in ACT Alliance and offers a concluding discussion on the self-understanding of the Ethiopian churches.

4.1 A Letter from Mekane Yesus 1972

From the Ethiopian Evangelical Church Mekane Yesus, there is one important document with which to open the discussion on church and aid, namely, *On the Interrelation between the Proclamation of the Gospel and Human Development* (*the ECMY Letter*). It was written two years before the revolution. This text is a letter sent from the Mekane Yesus church officers to the Lutheran World Federation, advocating for a more balanced funding of evangelism and development based on the church's service to the whole man.[5]

Earlier Research on the ECMY Letter

The ECMY Letter introduces the theme of *holistic ministry*. After it was published, Mekane Yesus (EECMY), with its development wing (EECMY-DASSC), took up "serving the whole person" as its motto. This is still important for Ethiopian theological students and faculty at the *Mekane Yesus Seminary* (MYS) and at *the Ethiopian Graduate School of Theology* (EGST) in Addis Ababa, aiming for a

---

[5] Bakke 1987, 225–27. Emmanuel Abraham 1995, 273–77. Eide 2000, 54. *On the interrelation between Proclamation of the Gospel and Humans development* is named *the ECMY Letter* in Eide 2000. I will follow that designation. Also printed in ECMY 2007, 85–98 in *The Essential Writings of Gudina Tumsa*.

holistic understanding of theology. The concept of holistic ministry is vital in the academic discourse. The Master thesis of Temesgen Shibru Galla's "The Mission Thinking of the Ethiopian Evangelical Church Mekane Yesus" is one example of how the theme of holistic ministry is theologically central in Mekane Yesus.[6] Temesgen Shibru Galla gives several reasons to study the church document. It is an official statement of the Mekane Yesus of that time. It represents the EECMY framework for addressing socio-economic concerns. It also has influenced the ecumenical thinking of the Lutheran World Federation. Finally, it represents an attempt "to show the theological fallacy that undergirds the donor criteria."[7] These reasons make the ECMY Letter relevant to discussions on church-based and Christian faith-based aid.

The ECMY Letter and similar documents produced by Mekane Yesus have been part of scholarly discussion, beginning with Øyvind Eide's dissertation from 1996 on Revolution and Religion in Ethiopia: A Study of Church and Politics with Special References to the Ethiopian Evangelical Church Mekane Yesus 1974–1985.[8] Eskil Jonsson's critical organisational study of the development work of Mekane Yesus, Narrow Management, on how church leadership following the requirements from donor partners can lead to an inner secularisation of churches, is part of this discussion.[9] Following the ECMY letter, the issue of holistic ministry and the underlying holistic anthropology became part of the ecumenical discussions on inter-church aid and ecumenical collaboration. Therefore, the analysis and discussion that follows, which will deal with the ECMY Letter, is a revisiting of old themes within the ecumenical movement.

---

[6] MTh-thesis from the MF Norwegian School of Theology. Temesgen does not explicitly deal with all four texts but moves from the first texts into a discussion with interviewees from EECMY. For examples of Holistic Ministry within EECMY, Temesgen 2011, 48–64.

[7] Temesgen 2011, 48–49.

[8] Øyvind Eide 1996, also as a monograph in 2000, dealt with the era of the Marxist regime in Ethiopia 1974–1991. Four texts are available in appendices to the dissertation: "On the Interrelation Between Proclamation of the Gospel and Human Development" (1972) (the ECMY Letter), "Pastoral Letter: The Evangelical Church Mekane Yesus in the Ethiopian Revolution" (1975) (the Pastoral Letter), "Memorandum to the Church President Regarding Some Issues" (1975) (the Memorandum), and "The Role of a Christian in a Given Society" (1978) (the Role of a Christian). The Gudina Tumsa Foundation has since 2001 arranged missiological seminars and published three books. These seminars have had a more narrow focus on the person of Gudina Tumsa, but the themes of holistic ministry and a holistic view of mission are very relevant to the EECMY.

[9] Gudina Tumsa Foundation 2007a, 2007b, and 2010. Jonsson 1998, 201. Dawit Olika 2017.

Proclamation of the Gospel and Human Development

The ECMY Letter will now be analysed and discussed bearing in min the ETH141 appeal (chapter two) and its framework of standards and principles (chapter three). *On the interrelation between Proclamation of the Gospel and Humans Development,* signed May 9, 1972, was sent from the Mekane Yesus church officers to the Lutheran World Federation and its churches, advocating for a more balanced funding of evangelism and development based on the church's service to the whole man.[10] This was a follow-up measure of the church officers from the Mekane Yesus general assembly to ask donor agencies to "include direct support for congregational work, leadership training and Church buildings."[11]

> At the same time, [as ECMY is engaging in development projects] the Church in faithfulness to her Lord, realized her obligation to proclaim the Gospel to the ever-growing crowds expecting more than bread. The Church cannot possible remain silent where a genuine spiritual need is prevailing and people in the thousands are flocking to newly established churches and in places where there are no churches to the GOOD NEWS. Finding that her own resources are insufficient both in personnel and funds, the Church has called on a number of Churches and Mission Organizations in the West to come and help. In spite of the encouraging response received, the Church is not able to cope with the situation.

> [...] In turning to her Overseas partners and sister Churches in the West for assistance in the work which has been regarded as the prime responsibility of the Church both in the field of development and proclamation of the Faith, it has become evident over the last few years that the Churches and Agencies in the West are readily prepared to assist in material development while there seems to be little interest in helping the Church meet her primary obligation to proclaim the Gospel. From the African point of view, it is hard to understand the division and the dichotomy created in the West and reflected in the criteria for assistance laid down by the Donor Agencies.[12]

In *the ECMY Letter*, the Mekane Yesus officers first state that the Evangelical Church Mekane Yesus (ECMY)[13] both has a social obligation to serve the communities and "to proclaim the Gospel." The church officers claimed that in view of

---

[10] Bakke 1987, 225–27. Emmanuel Abraham 1995, 273–77. Eide 2000, 68–70. The full letter is published as appendix II: The EMCY letter, *On the Interrelation between Proclamation and Development.*

[11] *The EMCY letter,* referring to Jan. 1971, ECMY Seventh G.A.

[12] *The ECMY Letter.*

[13] "Ethiopian" in the Ethiopian Evangelical Church Mekane Yesus (**E**ECMY), had been dropped by demand from some, who protested against the description of the Mekane Yesus Church as "Ethiopian". It was by them considered to be *mete,* meaning *coming* from outside, representing the idea that the Mekane Yesus was foreign and not local, national, or indigenous.

the dual obligation to witness and to serve, there was an imbalance in the assistance given to the ECMY by its partners. Therefore, they argued that the criteria for aid should include direct support for church work. While churches and agencies were readily "prepared to assist in material development", they showed "little interest in helping the Church to meet her primary obligation to proclaim the Gospel." From an "African point of view", this was seen as a division between proclamation and service.[14]

The expressions "crowds expecting more than bread" and "remain silent where a genuine spiritual need is prevailing" are directed as a critique of a mindset in which "bread for the world" and "humanitarian needs" appear as self-evident arguments for a mobilisation of resources and action.[15] In Temesgen's analysis of the ECMY Letter, the argument then turns to the other side "where social service is seen as the 'means to an end'" and the church officers critique such and approach as false piety. These two approaches are in stark contrast to the obligation of churches to care for and nourish souls as well as bodies.[16]

It should be noted that the primary addressees of the letter are the churches of the Lutheran World Federation. Mekane Yesus had been supported by Lutheran and Presbyterian mission agencies. These mission organisations were running clinics and schools according to the 1944 Ethiopian government regulations of mission work,[17] thus contributing to national development, but their main desire was to share the gospel of Jesus Christ. Mekane Yesus had come about as a fruit of the common work of missionaries and local evangelists, and its structures were being built jointly. However at this point in time, the Mekane Yesus had been able to integrate the work of the missions into the national structure of the church. Thus, the resources, personnel, and institutions of the missions were formally under the national leadership of the church officers of the Mekane Yesus. This was the chosen path of Mekane Yesus. Some had vouched for mission agencies to work in parallel to the mission church. Others, in the wake of the African independence movement, called for a moratorium of support from mission agencies.[18]

At the time of the letter, besides the mission agencies, the Lutheran World Federation encouraged development works separate from church structures. These projects were not set up with the same basic ideas as the mission organisations.

---

[14] *The ECMY Letter.*
[15] *The ECMY Letter.*
[16] Temesgen 2011, 53.
[17] Cf. Grenstedt 2000, 76–80; Grenstedt 2024, 103–4 on the 1944 Decree on Missions.
[18] Sæverås 1974.

Their mission – their main objectives – did not include the support of local churches. The focus was the development of the nations, not the development of churches. The aid of these agencies to the church may be understood in terms of development cooperation between the global north and south, but not as a striving for a common witness and service. Local churches were instruments of the Lutheran World Federation, but neither the recipients of aid nor the owners of the work. The collaboration was not set with the same premise as the holistic approach of the mission societies, and the letter of the Mekane Yesus as a vocal member of the federation aimed at changing that premise. At an earlier point in time, the Lutheran World Federation had been instrumental in forming national churches out of the mission efforts in different countries. The Mekane Yesus had been engaging in the Lutheran World Federation even before becoming a national church and a formal member. In the letter, it used its good offices to argue for a change in the development policies of the federation and its member churches.

Material versus Holistic Anthropology

The second part of the letter analyses the reasons why the policies had changed. The ECMY Letter depicts the efforts of development in an unjust world, in which economic and material growth becomes the standard according to which societies are evaluated. Contrary to this "materialistic Western concept of development", the authors claim that there are other important values in life[19] and a one-sided material development may become a threat to those values that make life meaningful.

In the following passage, the Mekane Yesus officers show that they were actively engaging in the development discussion of that time:

> *Our understanding of man and his needs*
> It is generally known and admitted that we live in a divided and terribly unjust world, where some people have more than enough and others do not have enough even to survive. We talk today about "rich" and "poor" nations, about "developed" and "underdeveloped" or "developing" societies and even of the "Third World." In doing this we are using only generally adopted socio-economic measurements to determine which society is rich or poor, developed or underdeveloped. *The standard of human life and that of society is normally evaluated in terms of economic growth and material wealth or in*

---

[19] Cf. EOC-DICAC commissioner, Nigussu Legesse: "Ethiopia has a culture, which values above all things, solidarity and community values. It is our tradition that not only the rich give to the poor, but also those with limited means share what they have with the less fortunate." EOC-DICAC 2009, 2.

technology and production.[20] Based on this materialistic Western concept of development and in an effort to find a remedy at least two things seem to have been largely over-
looked, namely: a) that there are values in life beyond those of modern technology and
economic betterment without which man's development will never be meaningful And
lasting. b) that man is not only the suffering creature who needs help but that he is also
the most important development agent.[21]

The letter offers a critique of a utilitarian framework of development and its materialistic assumptions for two reasons. First, there are "values in life beyond" tech-
nological and economic development, which means that material development is
not itself the source of meaning and end-goal, *telos*, in life.[22] That is not to say that
economic development is not important. It is a task which the church was itself
heavily engaged in. Second, there is an issue of philosophical anthropology. Man,
according to Mekane Yesus, is not only a suffering creature in need of outside assistance but an agent who ought to be "the most important development agent."[23]

The issue of anthropology links back to the case study in chapters two and
three. There is a risk that a focus on basic needs may slip into a view of human
beings as *patients*, that is people who are in pain. Humanitarians, out of respect
for human dignity, engage to relieve people of their suffering, attempting to fill the
most basic needs for people to survive. If they don't, people will die. As human life
is precious, saving a person's life is a moral act of great worth. Mobilising support
for humanitarian assistance requires someone to point out the needs of people at
risk. Such a depiction of human conditions risks both blotting out human dignity
by depicting people as "suffering creatures" and creating passive people who need
aid and yet, according to Mekane Yesus, should be "the most important development agents."[24]

In chapters two and three, dealing with the ETH141 refugee appeal and the
international standards the appeal was built upon, we saw how contemporary relief work attempts to integrate this lesson. This was done by the ACT agencies
using community-based approaches and encouraging the participation of people
in need of humanitarian assistance.

---

[20] The underlining is part of the original text.

[21] *The ECMY Letter.*

[22] Cf. the classical fact-value distinction of David Hume. In Hume's worldview facts are facts
and there is a sharp contrast between facts and values. Values are in this variant of a worldview
not real in the same sense that facts are. Therefore his empiricism may lead to a world of facts and
unsettled values.

[23] *The ECMY Letter.*

[24] *The ECMY Letter.*

In the case study, the Lutheran World Federation and the Orthodox refugee department both adopted a community-based psychosocial approach. It combines a communal approach with a holistic view of human needs and capabilities, bridging the gap between a need-based approach and a family and community approach. Within a community approach to relief assistance, people are not isolated and helpless individuals in need of external support but rather are embedded in families and communities with their own capabilities and resources. People have a willingness and ability to mobilise a community response to the crisis.[25]

Integral Human Development

The ECMY Letter continues to develop its central argument:

> We therefore see the development of the inner man as a pre-requisite for a healthy and lasting development of our society. Unless our people are helped to the spiritual freedom and maturity which enables them responsibly to handle material development, we are afraid that what was intended to be a means of enhancing the well being of man can have the opposite effect and create new forms of evil to destroy him.

Here is the centrepiece of the argument in which the foundation for development is seen as a transformation "of the inner man."[26] Without an inner transformation the good intention of improving the "well being of man" may backfire and the assistance may "create new forms of evil to destroy him." The argument thus critiques the rationality of a utilitarian approach of means and ends. In the short term, those who aim to assist will be able to fulfil basic needs, but if people are treated as objects, the assistance will fail in the long run. One reason is that by focusing on specific problems, and methods to solve them, only those problems will be considered, rather than focusing on the growth and development of people and communities. A second reason for the failure of a utilitarian approach is that for the effect to be sustainable it must come from within man, not from outside.[27]

> We believe that an integral human development, where the spiritual and material needs are seen together, is the only right approach to the development question in our society. The WCC Central Committee also pointed to this when it was stated in the Meeting in Addis Ababa in January 1971, that from the Christian point of view development should be understood as a process of liberation by which individuals and societies realized their

---

[25] Church of Sweden *Community Based Psychosocial Support Training Manual* 37–38. See 3.1 on CBPS.

[26] Cf. Luther *The Freedom of a Christian*. Luther 1999 *LW* vol. 31.

[27] Cf. Johnson 2016 on the oil resources found in South Sudan. Instead of being a source for the well being and development of two prospering nations, the oil has become a major cause of conflict both between South Sudan and Sudan and internally in those nations.

human possibilities in accordance with God's purposes. Charles Elliott, in his book, The Development Debate, goes as far as to say that "humanism closed in on itself and not open to the values of the spirit and to God Who is their source could achieve apparent success. True, man can organize the world apart from God, but without God he can organize it, in the end, only against man. An exclusive humanism is an inhuman humanism. There is no true humanism but that which is open to the Absolute and is conscious of a vocation which gives human life its true meaning. Far from being the ultimate measure of all things man can only realize himself by reaching beyond himself. As Pascal has said so well, 'Man infinitely surpasses man.'[28] The spiritual is thus easily linked to the secular vision; indeed the two merge."[29]

The main argument is here developed further. Man, in the view of the letter, is "the most important development agent" and development should be seen as an "integral human development", where the spiritual and material needs are seen together. Development should therefore "be understood as a process of liberation by which individuals and societies realise their human possibilities in accordance with God's purpose." The Mekane Yesus church officers argued that there is "no true humanism but that which is open to the Absolute and is conscious of a vocation which gives human life its true meaning." This argument is against a reductive anthropology of exclusive humanism, and towards an anthropology in which man is called to a life beyond flourishing.[30]

The concept of *integral human development* is derived from the *Populorum Progressio* promulgated by Pope Paul VI.[31] By including this concept, the church

---

[28] *Populorum Progressio* §42 Conclusion: "What must be aimed at is complete humanism. And what is that if not the fully-rounded development of the whole person and of all people? A humanism closed in on itself, and not open to the values of the spirit and to God Who is their source could achieve apparent success. True, people can organise the world apart from God, but 'without God people can organise it in the end only to their detriment. An isolated humanism is an inhuman humanism.' There is no true humanism but that which is open to the Absolute and is conscious of a vocation which gives human life its true meaning. Far from being the ultimate measure of all things, one can only realise oneself by reaching beyond himself. As Pascal has said so well, 'Man infinitely surpasses man.'" See Jacobs 2018 for examples of Christian humanism in line with the original establishment of WCC and its work for peace.

[29] *The ECMY Letter*.

[30] *The ECMY Letter*.

[31] The social teaching of the Roman Catholic Church was a response to both the societal developments of the modern world in which old protective social structures such the guild system broke down and the philosophical and ideological developments of the modern West. During the twentieth century, as *Nouvelle Théologie* opened new ways for Roman Catholics to look at ecumenism and to appreciate positive aspects of the modern society, Catholic Social Teaching begun to influence theologians from the churches descending from the Reformation. The

officers of Mekane Yesus show that they take part in the current development debate from an established Christian perspective. The church officers quote the argument for "true humanism" against "exclusive humanism." By linking the humane to the "vocation which gives human life its true meaning", there is no secular sphere in the sense of a life separated from the spiritual dimensions and relationship with "the Absolute." In this way, the "exclusive humanism" is critiqued as not being humanism at all.

The papal social teaching on the issue of the development of nations takes its vantage point from the human person. It was Jacque Maritain who laid the philosophical foundation of the papal document. Maritain was also one of the philosophers behind the Universal Declaration of Human Rights. In this regard, it is possible to follow two strands of Christian thought into the Universal Declaration of Human Rights: the importance of the human person and natural law. Thus, the authors of the ECMY letter stand in the tradition of Christian humanism against the teaching of "exclusive humanism."[32] As in Boersma' research on De Lubac, a natural longing for God is here seen as included in the way natural law is understood.[33]

> We also maintain very strongly that it is the need that should determine where assistance should be given and not criteria laid down by the Donor Agencies which reflects trends in the Western societies and Churches. It is the need in a given situation that should be the guiding principle for assistance and therefore there ought to be more flexibility in order to meet extraordinary opportunities an African Church which does not necessarily share all the views of Western Churches and Agencies.[34]

The next part of the argument is important to understand the position of Mekane Yesus. It begins from the common premise that "the need should determine where assistance should be given." The relief assistance of ACT Alliance as we have seen in chapters two and three is need-based, while they also aim to be rights-based.

---

invitation of the Roman Church to Evangelical and Orthodox Churches to send observers to Second Vatican Council opened for sharing thoughts on social issues. The World Council of Churches and the Lutheran World Federation took part in this exchange of ideas and influence from the Roman Catholic Church.

[32] Gudina Tumsa is explicitly referring to the Greek philosophers of Democritus, Epicurus, and Lucretius as the ancient Greek roots of atheistic humanism in his lecture on "Unbelief from Historical Perspective" delivered at the ECMY General Assembly in Nedjo 1976 in opposition to the state ideology presented by his brother Baaroo Tumsa, Eide 2000, 109–10, GTF 2007, 25–33.

[33] Boersma 2009, see 1.1.

[34] *The ECMY Letter.*

There are three points in the argument: needs are holistic, assessments need to be based on a given situation, and African Churches are more capable of determining priorities than donor agencies. "Needs" in *the ECMY letter* – referring primarily to basic needs – include spiritual needs and the need for personal and community development. It goes together with a view of man – true of all people and all circumstances as it refers to man's nature – as active as well as passive.

Second, needs must be assessed "in a given situation" as the situation changes, needs change. Man does not change essentially so basic needs such as food and water are constant, but the historical context is relative and ever changing.

This is the reason why third, "an African Church" is more able to assess the needs, set priorities, and adjust to changes in situation than "the Donor Agencies", whose criteria more "reflects trends in the Western societies and Churches" rather than actual needs on the ground. This is a more controversial idea than the previous ones as it challenges the policies set by donor governments and would allow African churches and nations to set their own priorities. Part of the controversy was that African church authorities held other views than those circulating in the West. Demanding compliance with criteria set by donor agencies would imply that the donors knew better.

The Mekane Yesus argument is that service should not be seen as a means to another end, such as evangelisation. That would be "false piety." Neither should service be seen as an end-in-itself. That – for the authors – would be the other extreme exemplified by some voices in the Uppsala 1968 meeting of the World Council of Churches. Such a view of mission as humanisation was, the Mekane Yesus argued, carried out with post-colonial guilt as the motif. Christian mission – or ministry – for the authors of *the ECMY Letter* entails both to witness and to serve, for the sake of human beings and their eternal ends; the true end-in-itself.

The Mekane Yesus position is argued from the standpoint of Christian anthropology, in contrast to utilitarian (materialist) or deontological (idealist) alternatives. The Christian humanism favoured by the authors understands human nature as holistic and the human person as naturally directed to God. God is the origin (creation) and destiny (salvation) of human persons.

The explicit anthropological position is based on the personalism of Jacque Maritain. His philosophy is rooted in the theological research that led to an ecumenical opening of the Roman Catholic Church. Maritain's work is grounded in the historical works of de Lubac, who in dialogue with exiled Russian Orthodox theologians in Paris uncovered significant philosophical changes in the medieval Latin Church with direct implications for anthropology and theology.[35]

What are the implications of the view in *the ECMY Letter*? Based on Christian anthropology, human persons need to be served both bread and gospel, because they have a "hunger for God" and for bread. This step of the argument is important. If this "hunger" is innate, then it is grounded in human nature, relating to how the world really is, and in line with the objective *telos* of humankind and the world. On this basis, the claim is not subjective but objective, grounded in how things are and should be. A Christian anthropology and worldview point towards an objective meaning in life. As such, if true, this view is neither subjective nor sectarian. It is also not merely Western, in the sense of representing only the Western Latin Church, but rather represents Florovsky's sense of an ecclesial "catholicity [that] requires both lunges of Christendom, Western and Eastern."[36] That is why the authors may claim that the holistic view is authentically African and may be appropriated by an African church.

"Needs" in *the ECMY letter* – referring primarily to basic needs – include spiritual needs and the need for personal and community development, which, the community-based psychosocial approach in the case study also affirms.

Second, needs must be assessed "in a given situation" as the situation changes, needs change. Even though basic needs such as food and water are constant, the context determines which need is more pressing. This relates to the principle of impartiality which states that assistance would "be provided solely on the basis of need and in proportion to need", as discussed above in chapter three.[37] This is the reason why local assessment in relief work – in the camp – takes precedence over decisions made in Addis Ababa or Geneva.

A treatment of human beings which only considers material needs, based on a material conception of man, would be false. The donors, the Mekane Yesus church officers argue, are unwilling to aid the church in its full ministry because they do not see the people and their true needs since they are too far away to see

---

[35] Boersma 2009, 93–98.

[36] Kalaitzidis *et al* eds. 2014, 149. The quote is a citation of Kalaitzidis, not a direct quote from Florovsky. Cf. Schmemann 1973, 14 "Man is a hungry being. But he is hungry for God. Behind all the hunger of our life is God. All desire is finally a desire for Him." [Underlining in original.] See reference to Boersma 2009 in earlier research *re* the *ressourcement* movement.

[37] The principle of impartiality was initially founded on a triage situation. When people in a crisis have different medical needs that needs attention, the most pressing needs such as breathing and heavy bleeding have to take priority. To stop the bleeding and assist with breathing is more important than other considerations.

the realities on the ground. Criteria for service should be set on actual needs. According to the ECMY, the assessment of the needs must be done locally, rather than remotely. Therefore, the church appeals to the Lutheran World Federation to reconsider the criteria on which aid is based. This is the practical reason for *the ECMY Letter* in the first place.

If the arguments of *the ECMY Letter* are not adhered to, development efforts will necessarily fail. This is because people are treated as *patients*, suffering creatures, and not as agents in their own lives. Development, it is indirectly argued in the text, needs to be an enabling rather than a spoon-feeding process. Material development may succeed in raising economic standards while failing at becoming sustainable due to a lack of simultaneous development of the "inner man." If human beings are an ontological whole, development efforts must be holistic to be sustainable. Actions need to correspond to reality.

The authors argued, to the churches and agencies of the Lutheran World Federation, that an African church is best placed to work on holistic ministry, in this case, the Mekane Yesus. This is first, because it is local: the congregations share the life of the people and understand their needs. Second, the African churches have a holistic view of man, corresponding to a Christian anthropology. Finally, local Christians live to witness and serve not only their community but the communities beyond the constituency of the local church.

4.2 Passover Message 1983 from the Ethiopian Orthodox

In this section, the ecclesial foundations for ecumenical engagements will be analysed based on an analysis of primary texts and Orthodox theology. I will be investigating the following questions: What do the articles in the *Maedot* journal say about the self-understanding of the Ethiopian Orthodox church, its social works, and ecumenical commitments in the 1980s? And what can the *Maedot* articles tell us about the present engagement of the Orthodox Church in ACT Alliance?

During the Derg regime (1974–1991), the Ethiopian Orthodox Church published the *Maedot* journals (1983–1990). These journals are rich sources, containing different voices from the church during a period of political controversy. Once per year, these journals were published in English to an international audience. The development wing of the church (EOC-DICAC) has, in addition to project documents, been writing publications geared towards donor agencies. These publications are still active today and are in continuity with the *Maedot* journals of the

1980s. As these texts are primary sources, they help set the work of ACT Alliance in the context of the Ethiopian Orthodox Tewahido Church.[38]

The *Maedot* journals were published yearly from 1983 to 1990. The name *Maedot* (ማዕዶት) means Passover and refers to the liturgical theme of Easter Monday, wherein Christ descends to Hell releasing souls and leading them to paradise. The Orthodox celebration is reminiscent of the Jewish *Pascha* celebrating the release from slavery in Egypt and conveying the transfer, *adawa,* from death to eternal life. The name reflects the self-understanding of the Orthodox Church as the vehicle of salvation. *The Maedot journals* and subsequent publications of the development wing of the Ethiopian Orthodox Church cover many topics. They are good sources for providing insight into the concurrent perspectives in the Orthodox Church and how it relates to social issues.

The *Maedot* #1, 1983, deals with matters such as the history and self-understanding of the church, the relation between church and society, the life of the patriarch, the Sunday School of the church, evangelical outreach, and the role of the church in the ecumenical movement and development programmes. Therefore, it is useful for the current research on ecumenical diakonia in this chapter to go through the first issue. I will analyse the *Maedot* articles in relation to the case study of refugee assistance with a focus on articles dealing with the topic of social and ecumenical engagement.[39]

The Derg period, as a transitional time between Imperial Abyssinia and Federal Democratic Ethiopia, was a formative time period for the church and its social engagements. The *Maedot journals* give insight into the views of the church on these developments. The Christian churches had been under ideological and political attack since the revolution in 1974, particularly by the Socialist military regime of the Derg. From the stance of the Marxist ideologues, churches were seen as something of a bygone era and the *l'ancient regime,* to be surpassed by a superior

---

[38] There are several relevant publications by the EOTC and EOC-DICAC: the EOC 1984–1990 *Maedot Journals*, as well as publications and reports by EOC-DICAC such as EOC-DICAC (May 1992) *Ethiopian Orthodox Church Development and Inter-Church AID Department (*EOC-DICAC*)*; EOC-DICAC (Aug 10, 2005) *EOC DICAC Final Brochure*; EOC DICAC (2005) "Ethiopian Orthodox Church Development and Inter Church Aid Commission (EOC-DICAC)" in *Gender and Development Division Ladder Newsletter* Sep 2005 Vol 1:1; EOC DICAC (2008) *The Ethiopian Orthodox Church in Development/ 36 years in Action. Development and Inter-Church Aid Commission Millennium Committee*; EOC-DICAC (Jan 2009) *EOC-DICAC: Success Stories, Round Table and Bilateral Partners*; and the EOC DICAC (2013) *Developmental Bible.*

[39] *Maedot* 1983–1990.

"scientific socialism." Mekane Yesus and other Evangelicals suffered when their churches were closed, leaders imprisoned, and property confiscated. The Orthodox Church was politically needed, however, by the regime to mobilize people, and the regime attempted to control and subdue rather than eradicate it, as it attempted with other less politically significant church bodies. The *Maedot* sheds light on this time period and on Orthodox believers who wanted to advocate for the Christian Church during a time when the church and its Christian beliefs was put into question by political groups including the Derg regime itself.[40]

The English annual edition of the *Maedot* was intended for an interested international audience of potential donors. The purpose was to introduce and describe the Orthodox Church in such a way that potential donors, such as the aid agencies related to the World Council of Churches, would support its relief and development work. As such, the *Maedot* embodies a unique self-representation of the Ethiopian Orthodox Church and the church's willingness to participate in ecumenical endeavours.

The authors of the articles primarily represented groups of the Orthodox Church who were able to work within the framework of the socialist system. The Derg regime – despite its atheistic character and formal policy of separation of church and state – continued to appoint government representatives as head administrators of the church.[41] Therefore, the reading needs to be critical to features that belong to the socio-political context of the 1980s and therefore do not necessarily represent the views of the church. The journal has here been analysed both with *benevolentia*, i.e. a readiness to listen to the Orthodox voices and their messages, and a critical eye to be able to see the content in its historical context and discuss its contemporary significance.[42]

---

[40] Eide 2000, Haustein 2009, Seblewengel 2019, and Tibebe 2009: all deal with issues of church and state during 1974–1991.

[41] Tibebe 2009 and Seblewengel 2019. Haustein 2009 states that the transitional government of 1991 also replaced the general manager of the church despite its policy of non-interference in religious affairs.

[42] Bradley and Muller 1995, 25 "The ecclesiastical and social contexts in which we work demand an emphatic, sensitive study of other traditions, and presumably, this may be accomplished without compromising one's own confessional distinctives."

The *Maedot* Journal of 1983

What is the theological foundation for the *Maedot* journal of 1983?[43] The Easter Address of *Abuna* Tekle Haimanot gives emphasis to the Christian gospel of Jesus Christ: "His incarnation, services, suffering, death and resurrection" and with an understanding of life as "the most sacred gift of God both in the visible and invisible world", the world as being in need of the blessing of peace that comes "not only from below but also from above."[44] The peace that Christ made between God and man is therefore extended "among the people in the world."[45]

> The Risen Christ is indeed the resurrection and the life of all human being. Thus, life is the most sacred gift of God both in the visible and invisible world, which needs the blessing of peace forever. Jesus Christ came into the world to reveal the everlasting love of God to men through His incarnation, services, suffering, death and resurrection. Because He lived in the world for us, suffered and was crucified for us. Our Lord did this in order to make peace between God and man and also among the people in the world.[46]

---

[43] The *Maedot* 1983 Issue One: [1] *Maedot* no. 1 1983, 6–9. The editorial "Knowing the Ethiopian Orthodox Church." The editor of the publication was Teshoma Zerihun from the Ethiopian Orthodox Church Foreign Relation Department.[2] *Maedot* 1983, 13–14 "Address of His Holiness Abuna Tekle Haimanot Patriarch of Ethiopia Delivered on the Occasion of Easter." [3] *Maedot* 1983, 15–17, "The History of the Ethiopian Orthodox Church in Brief." [4] *Maedot* 1983, 18–21, "Actual Life of His Holiness Abuna Tekla Haimanot." [5] *Maedot* 1983, 21–23 Getaneh Bogale, "The Church and Society: Helping the Poor – The Role of the Church." [6] *Maedot* 1983, 23–26. Abera Bekele, "A Glimpse into EOC Parish Council Structure." [7] *Maedot* 1983, 26–28 Haddis Terefe, "Accomplishment of the Apostolic Diakonia in the Church Today." [8] *Maedot* 1983, 29–30 Yemane Birhan Teshome, "Sunday School Activities in the Ethiopian Orthodox Church." [9] *Maedot* 1983, 30–33 Belay Tegegne, "Evangelical Out-Reach Across the World." [10] *Maedot* 1983, 33–34 Teshoma Zerihun, "The Role of the Church in Ecumenical Movement." [11] *Maedot* 1983, 34–36 Berhe Beyene of the Ethiopian Orthodox Commission for Development (EOCD), "The Role of the Church in Development Programmes." [12] *Maedot* 1983, 36–37 Zemedhun Bezuwork, "The Publishing and Printing Work in the Ethiopian Orthodox Church." [13] *Maedot* 1983, 37–39 Teshoma Zerihun, "The Ethiopian Orthodox Church Historical Possession of the Holy Places in the Holy Land Jerusalem." [14] *Maedot* 1983, 39–40 Mekonen Zewdie, "Jerusalem Memorial of Ethiopian Believers." [15] *Maedot* 1983, 40–42 *Like Seltanat* Habte Mariam Workineh, Dean of the Seminary, "Re-Establishment of the New Theological Seminary." [16] *Maedot* 1983, 43–44 Eshetu Mehretu, "Ethiopian Orthodox Tewahedo Church Council for Child Care."

[44] *Maedot* 1983, 13. The text is in English, but the original address was probably in Amharic.

[45] *Maedot* 1983, 13.

[46] *Maedot* 1983, 13. Extract from *Maedot* 1983, 13–14 "Address of His Holiness Abuna Tekle Haimanot Patriarch of Ethiopia Delivered on the Occasion of Easter."

According to the patriarch, Christ's church is commanded to work for peace on earth and good will towards men. Therefore, Christians are called upon to contribute to world peace and to fulfil this mission in the unity of the church.[47] The united witness of all Christians is an instrument of the proclamation of the gospel contributing to "brotherhood among peoples" and the "peace of the world."[48] Enduring peace requires Christians to stand for justice as a precondition for peace and societal structural changes.[49] The patriarch therefore calls on Christians all over the world to fulfil their social duty, give voice to common sense, and seek the blessing of peace from God as well as men.[50]

What does it say about the church, its social works, and its ecumenical commitments in the 1980s? The unity of the Christian Church in the *Maedot* #1, 1983, is described as something inherent in its very nature. Since the one "church of God" is divinely instituted by Jesus Christ, the Christian faith has created an ecumenical family made up of different languages and cultures across the world.[51]

> Naturally, the church of God is one. Our Lord has instituted on earth but one Holy and Apostolic Church – made of all ecumenical family of different races, tongues and varying backgrounds. And so far as the church is one, millions of Christians all over the world are meant to be one or as one, and lead the same life in the same family under the roof of this very one Apostolic Church, because faith is strong enough to bring all the faithful (born a new not the will of flesh-but of God) into one family under the care of the one Heavenly Father of all, they vividly acknowledge the existence of the one, Holy Apostolic Church in the World.[52]

It is on this ecclesiological basis of "the one, Holy Apostolic Church" that the Ethiopian Orthodox Church has joined institutions, such as the World Council of Churches, for collaboration of relief work and the restoration of the historical unity of the church.[53]

As the church is holy and apostolic, Christians need to guard against teachings not in line with church doctrine as represented by the early ecumenical councils.[54]

---

[47] *Maedot* 1983, 14.

[48] *Maedot* 1983, 14.

[49] *Maedot* 1983, 14.

[50] *Maedot* 1983, 14.

[51] *Maedot* 1983, 6–9, "Knowing the Ethiopian Orthodox Church."

[52] *Maedot* 1983, 6. Extract from the editorial of *Maedot* no 1, 1983, 6–9 "Knowing the Ethiopian Orthodox Church." The biblical references in the first paragraphs of the text refer to Eph 1:4–10, Rom 8:29, John 1:12–14 and Rom 1:21. The editor of the publication was Rev. Teshoma Zerihun from the Ethiopian Orthodox Church Foreign Relation Department.

[53] *Maedot* 1983, 6.

[54] *Maedot* 1983, 8.

The texts of the *Maedot* are an expression of a self-aware attitude of the importance of the Ethiopian Orthodox Tewahido Church as an ancient and significant church with its apostolic roots delineated from the episcopal See of Alexandria.[55] This importance extends to the present practice of "helping the poor",[56] serving their needs,[57] educating the young,[58] reaching out with the gospel across the world,[59] engaging in the ecumenical movement,[60] and ecumenical development programmes,[61] as well as strengthening pilgrimages[62] and theological education.[63] Contemporary "diakonia" is grounded in the sacramental and spiritual life of the church with its never ceasing prayers for "the sick, the oppressed, the prisoners, the refugees, the orphans, the hungry, and all the helpless."[64]

---

[55] *Maedot* 1983, 17. There is interest in the culturally integration of EOC in the African soil. The Sunday School Movement, public celebrations of church festivals in urban centres, and a revival of traditional means of healing are also examples of how the church positions itself in a new context and attracts new believers. Chaillot 2002, 51–63.

[56] *Maedot* 1983, 22.

[57] *Maedot* 1983, 26–28, 43–44.

[58] *Maedot* 1983, 29–30, 36–37, 43–44.

[59] *Maedot* 1983, 30–33. EOC has grown through the advance of the Christian gospel: through monasteries and church services. In Ethiopian history, from remote monasteries, monks brought the faith to an area. Iyäsus-Moʾa (d1292) from Däbrä Damo, travelled south and founded a school by Lake Hayq. Graduates, e.g. Täklä-Haymanot of Shoa, left Hayq and established monastic centres in other areas. Filipos and Anoréwos, disciples of Täklä-Haymanot, went South to Lake Ziway, preached and brought the church into Sidama country. Tamrat 1972, 156f. For the use of hagiographies as historical sources, Rubenson 2013. For Sidama, Tamrat 1972, 189; Balisky 2009, 84–85. The church also grew as the borders of the kingdom grew. When a new town was founded, a church was built, and sacraments were administered to the local administrator and his host. The celebration of the eucharist itself, the procession, and the reading from the Scripture and other church books, became a visible witness to the area. Thus the church was linked with the state such that if the local administrators were oppressive, the church could be seen as part of that oppression. The church has reached out to people outside of Ethiopia, to the Ethiopian diaspora as well as populations of African descent in Africa, the Caribbean, USA, and Europe. For many of African descent, in or outside of Africa, Ethiopia is a symbol of African freedom and pride. Ethiopianism in West and Southern Africa is one example of this. See Baur 1994, 125–33, Grenstedt 2000, 23–24; Sundkler and Steed 2000, 423f.; and Getnet Tamene 1998, 70.

[60] *Maedot* 1983, 33–34.

[61] *Maedot* 1983, 34–36.

[62] *Maedot* 1983, 37–39, 39–40.

[63] *Maedot* 1983, 40–42.

[64] *Maedot* 1983, 26–28.

The "Apostolic Diakonia" of the *Maedot* signifies church ministry and is not limited to charitable works.[65] This can be seen in the way the Eucharist forms "the focal point of all religious services rendered in the EOC", in which "service" is interchangeable with "diakonia."[66] The charitable works are derived from the Eucharistic liturgy and not the other way around.

Despite the ideological and political pressure of a modern age and an atheistic regime, the Orthodox writers in the *Maedot* found ways of expressing the faith and pointing towards its importance. This was not done in open opposition to the regime and its ideology, but in sophistication and carefully worded stories on the significance of the Christian Church and its faith. The tone in the *Maedot* Journal of 1983 is generally not apologetic, and there is pride communicated in the writing regarding the traditional ways of the church. This is particularly clear in the Easter Address of the Patriarch, who by focusing on the gospel contradicts the atheistic beliefs proclaimed by the military regime without going into polemics.[67] The tone is more open in the article "Church and Society" by Getanhe Bogale, but the rhetoric edge challenges the ideas of the donor agencies of the ecumenical partners of DICAC, rather than the regime.[68]

The social commitments of the church is stated to be rooted in the theological foundations of the church[69] and the spirituality of the faithful[70] because a "[d]eep conc[ern] for the poor springs forth" from this stance.[71] What others may see as an "otherworldliness" and a foreign ascetic spirituality,[72] Getanhe suggests, if

---

[65] *Maedot* 1983, 26–28 "Accomplishment of the Apostolic Diakonia in the Church Today."

[66] *Maedot* 1983, 28.

[67] *Maedot* 1983, 14.

[68] *Maedot* 1983, 21–23.

[69] Particularly in the Easter Address of the Patriarch, *Maedot* 1983, 13–14.

[70] *Maedot* 1983, 21–23.

[71] *Maedot* 1983, 22.

[72] Fagerberg 2018, 140 on asceticism as a third aspect of Orthodox culture alongside truth and beauty. Schmemann 1979, 49: "Man's sin and alienation from God, the radical illness of 'this world,' the narrow way of salvation" is an experience shaping the culture such that an Orthodox society is "a 'monastic' society in the sense that it accepts the monastic ideal as the self-evident norm and criterion of all Christian life." This is not driven by pessimism but by θέωσις (*theosis*), "the deification of man by the grace of the Holy Spirit", in Eastern spirituality and soteriology. Schmemann 1979, 50. This may be applied to the society: "It is often hard to separate the ecclesiastical from the secular events in that country", Atiya (1968, 147) writes in his seminal study on the Eastern Orthodox Christianity outside of the "Greek" Byzantine tradition. The "nine saints", who in opposition to the Council of Chalcedon travelled south across the Egyptian and Nubian

accepted by the ecumenical partner agencies, could become the basis for an "appreciated common ground from which donor-recipient cooperative ventures could start and grow to desirable heights." In contrast, a materialistic basis would place "the majority of people in the developing world [in the category of the poor] and [thus] dramatically alter the magnitude of the problem as well as the meaning and the strategy of helping the poor." This would make "the state the epi-center of action brushing churches aside to a marginal role."[73]

Many aspects of a social diakonia were touched upon in the first issue of the *Maedot*, such as how the Orthodox Church and its agencies have engaged in society. The ways are manyfold with everything from famine relief, refugee assistance, care for children and orphans, and various development works.[74] As the texts are giving witness to, however, these aspects of aid works have not exhausted the ways in which the Orthodox Church has engaged in Ethiopian society. Spiritual and cultural aspects should not be forgotten. As Getanhe warned the ecumenical donors, a materialistic basis for development brushes aside church life and therefore also the life of actual communities.[75]

Dawit Wolde Giorgis, the head of the Relief and Rehabilitation Commission of the Derg Government, in the end, realised the importance of these aspects. When writing on the failure to forward a materialistic development in the Marxist settlements, he wrote: "There are no churches or mosques on settlements sites. The whole idea of these settlements was to create the New Society without the 'opium of the masses', religion." The leadership proclaims mankind's domination over the God of nature; but in a country where faith is so much a part of the people's lives, they feel demoralized without it. The peasants will never be productive in the settlements. They are lost souls. They miss their communities, their land and

---

desert (c. 480) laid a foundation for a strong ascetic tradition in Ethiopia. The monasteries founded by these "Syrian" monks became centres of learning and the spreading of the Christian faith. Literature in Coptic, Arabic and Syriac was translated into Ge'ez along with a translation of the Bible and the liturgy of St Cyril the Great. Atiya 1968, 151–53; Bakke 1986, 87–103.

[73] *Maedot* 1983, 22. The position is not one of merely alleviating the worst of poverty without contribution to change. Cf. EOC-DICAC Commissioner Nigussu Legesse that the conviction that "the church could and should contribute to improving the lives" led to the establishment of EOC-DICAC, EOC-DICAC 2009, 2.

[74] *Maedot* 1983, 21–23 Getaneh Bogale, "The Church and Society: Helping the Poor – The Role of the Church." Getaneh Bogale was the commissioner of the Development Commission and had acted upon news of the famine already in March 1973 with support from the World Council of Churches.

[75] *Maedot* 1983, 22.

tools, their churches and mosques, their family members. They will never view the settlement sites as anything more than concentration camps."[76] The life of the churches – as communities – has its significance apart from any instrumental value to aid efforts.

In the *Maedot* Journal articles, there are several references to Orthodox church life and tradition that have relevance to Orthodox engagement in aid works. The texts deliberate on Orthodox foundations for engaging in issues like peace, development, and relief assistance. Taking a commitment to peace as an example, the then patriarch pointed to the resurrection of Jesus Christ as the historical event which grounds the value of life.[77] Not only the resurrection, but indeed the birth, ministry, and death of Christ are seen as essential events, not only for basic beliefs about reality but as foundations for the moral life.[78] As these events of Christ are celebrated as the great feast of the year, Orthodox Christians participating in the liturgy come to know the foundational truths that inform a moral character. We may ask, however, whether it is possible to move from the liturgical life of the church to issues of morality and Orthodox Christian engagement in the common life.[79]

Going back to the *Maedot*, education needs to be mentioned, particularly since a major part of the Orthodox contribution to refugee assistance is in the line of secondary education. Three concrete examples came up in the texts from the *Maedot* 1983 – that of the Sunday School Movement,[80] traditional training centres for clergy, and higher theological education.[81] The authors stress that education has always been important for the Orthodox Church. These new forms of education – the Sunday Schools and higher theological education – both build upon

---

[76] Dawit Wolde Giorgis 1989, 305.

[77] *Maedot* 1983, 13–14.

[78] *Maedot* 1983, 13–14.

[79] Schmemann, in *Church World Mission*, 1979, 210, ask the question: "Can a church whose life is centered almost exclusively on the liturgy and the sacraments, whose spirituality is primarily mystical and ascetical, be truly missionary?" This is the essence of a critique that a church dedicated to the liturgy is selfish and self-absorbed and not concerned about the world. For Schmemann, the question reveals a complete misunderstanding of the church, the world, and the mission of the church. Schmemann works out a liturgical theology, not about the liturgy as such, but as an Orthodox theology out of the eucharistic life of the church. See also Hjälm 2011.

[80] *Maedot* 1983, 29–30 Yemane Birhan Teshome, "Sunday School Activities in the Ethiopian Orthodox Church."

[81] *Maedot* 1983, 40–42 *Like Seltanat* Habte Mariam Workineh, Dean of the Seminary, "Re-Establishment of the New Theological Seminary."

that commitment to education and develop new aspects, such as the participation of the laity – including women – the conscious teaching of the Orthodox faith, and the need for academic excellence.

Church in Context

In the context in which the *Maedot* journals were written, the Derg regime attempted to clamp down on theological education.[82] The Marxist military regime saw no use for theological teaching and simply closed the college in Addis and confiscated the property.[83] The patriarch, *Abuna* Tekle Haimanot who himself had a traditional rather than modern theological education, would still see the value in theological training according to an academic mindset, albeit "well-grounded" in the Pre-Chalcedonian Orthodox Christian tradition.[84]

It could simply be that the military government saw no use in such a theological education in its pursuit of economic development, viewing religion as the opium of the people. It could also have been part of the attempt to control the Orthodox Church by making sure that an independent leadership of the church would not be developed. Either way, by hindering theological education, it became more difficult for Orthodox Christians to challenge the policies and practices of the Derg on intellectual grounds.[85]

The last point is of significance for the ecumenical relations within Ethiopia during the time of the Derg (1974–1991). Despite the theological grounds for peace, the ecclesiological grounds for Christian unity, a church ministry rooted in a Christian worldview, and an Orthodox *phronema* rooted in the liturgy,[86] the *Maedot* is silent about relations to other Christians within Ethiopia as a nation. As it was difficult for the Orthodox Church to critique the military junta on theological and moral grounds, the population of Orthodox Christians and Muslims could at the same time be manipulated by the dialectics of Marxism for political reasons.

---

[82] The Holy Trinity College, est. 1943, was closed in 1974 for 20 years and its premises confiscated.

[83] The Derg followed a pragmatic approach to education still guided by its materialist philosophy. It also closed for example the School of Social Work since there would be no need for such in a socialist society.

[84] The first dean of the Holy Trinity College was an Armenian. This was followed by a trend in which other seminary deans have been Copts and Indians – all from within the Oriental Pre-Chalcedonian family of Orthodox churches.

[85] The Mekane Yesus Seminary held seminars on socialism to educate people on the ideological ideas of Marxism, materialism, and atheism.

[86] Φρόνημα Gk. *way of thinking, mind*. See next section (4.3).

The Derg instrumentalised the suspicious attitudes of the majority constituencies of Orthodox and Muslims into persecuting minority groups such as Evangelical and Pentecostal Christians. This was done through ostracization, playing on pre-existing cautious attitudes, and fostering xenophobia by calling them *Mete,* outsiders,[87] and *Pente,* those who rebel against the religion of the fathers.[88] By turning majority groups against minorities, the Derg attempted to foster a nationalism of a combined Orthodox and Muslim nation under strict control of the military regime. The long-standing cautious attitudes against major political powers such as England, France, and the USA, could thus be further harnessed against part of the population.[89]

Prejudice in Christian communities became a political tool in the hands of the *cadres* of the regime. An autonomous church leadership could have counteracted these tendencies in Orthodox constituencies, but independent bishops were the first to be targeted by the revolutionary forces.[90] The Orthodox Patriarch *Abuna* Theophilos had been imprisoned in 1976, later to be executed without trial by the regime. Hence, it took time for Orthodox Christians to turn against the revolutionary forces of the time.[91]

It was the very same patriarch who had also founded EOC-DICAC in 1972 and entered into an agreement with the Commission for the Churches Participation in Development of the World Council of Churches (WCC-CCPD), regarding the development of an Ethiopian Orthodox Church Parish Council in 1976. Only two years later, nine of the fourteen bishops of the Holy Synod had been dismissed from their offices and several of them were arrested. These facts put the professed "freedom" of the church in a different historical light.[92] The election process of a Patriarch is indeed participatory and democratic in intention and setup, but the democratic processes may be interfered with by non-democratic

---

[87] Grenstedt 2024, 175. *Mete,* those who have come, i.e. foreigners not belonging to the nation.

[88] Grenstedt 2024, 174. Pentecostals, i.e. those of non-traditional religiosity.

[89] The backstory of Halldin Norberg 1977 was the fear that a world power would dominate the development in Ethiopia. The Emperor asked the SEM to bring Sweden as a development partner as Sweden was a small and neutral nation and missionaries had given a good impression.

[90] *Abuna* Theophilos had appointed some bishops who were also arrested. Among them *Abuna* Paulos, who remained in Derg prison for seven years (1976–1983). Haustein 2009a

[91] Theophilos remains were uncovered after the Fall of the Derg 1991. This was significant as according to Canon Law the validity of a new Patriarch cannot be established without the confirmation of the death of the former. Haustein 2009, 123.

[92] Cf. *Maedot* 1983, 18.

political forces representing not the Christian church but secular political parties with their own agendas.[93]

By controlling "the head", the Derg attempted to control the church in a similar fashion as other Communist regimes had done. *Abuna* Tekla Haimanot himself, however, collaborated less and less to the extent of going on a hunger strike in protest against the regime, to be replaced after his subsequent death by *Abuna* Merkorios.[94]

Attitudes fostered by a religious sensitivity to promote the common good were in this case abused by political forces. This is in stark contrast to the work of the Development Commission of the Orthodox Church. When the Orthodox Development Commission serves communities other than their own – exemplified by the refugees from South Sudan – they follow a principled approach with an emphasis being placed on the mutual respect of other people, and their language, culture, and religion. The attitudes fostered by the commission may in this sense also be an inspiration for other Orthodox communities who have not set the wellbeing of others in the forefront.

4.3 Gospel and Liturgy Form the Christian

The documents from the Orthodox Church and the Mekane Yesus Church presuppose that the Christian is formed in the life of the church to be able to love and to serve God and neighbour. These arguments that were mentioned in the texts of *the ECMY letter* and the *Maedot* will be outlined below starting with the argument from the gospel.

The Voice of the Gospel

The ECMY Letter addresses the dilemma that man through civilized history "may know what is good and right and even want to do the right things yet he fails to

---

[93] *Maedot* 1983, 18–21 "Actual Life of His Holiness *Abuna* Tekla Haimanot." Seblewengel, in 2019 writes that the patriarch was "deposed and replaced with a lesser educated monk from the South", later arrested (1976), and murdered. Seblewengel 2019, 77. Eide 2000, 111.

[94] Haustein 2009. *Abuna* Merkorios abdicated Aug 1991, and later claimed that he had not abdicated freely, but was forced out of office. In Oct. 1992, he declared the "Ethiopian Orthodox Church in the Western Hemisphere" and formed a synod in exile. Even though WCC recognised *Abuna* Paulos, unclarities regarding his election would lead the Coptic Church to be reluctant to do so which caused a strain in the relationship between the two churches. After the death of *Abuna* Paulos (r. 1992–2012) attempts to reconcile the Ethiopian Orthodox Church began. *Abuna* Merkorios (d. –2022) would later return to Ethiopia at an initiative of PM Abiy Ahmed.

achieve it."[95] The problem is not first of all knowing what is good, but the need for something to "make man do good."[96] The authors of the letter, turn to St. Paul in Romans 7:15–20 in which St. Paul outlines this dilemma of wanting to do what is good but being unable to do so because he is in bondage to sin. The authors comment that few would accept such a bleak picture, "a depraved view of man." Instead, many say that "Man is capable of reasoned response. If he knows what is right, he will do it."[97] This brings up the classical problem first raised by Socrates on which his disciple Aristotle disagreed with Socrates who said that knowing what is good will enable a man to do what is good. For Aristotle, man needs to acquire virtues to do what is just in each situation. Rather than agreeing with Aristotle, the church officers asked whether such anthropology can be supported by historical evidence.

To them, it was apparently not the case. Though certain flagrant abuses of justice have been removed from the affairs of man, unjust practices like racism, oppression and corruption continue wherever man is found. Thus man's basic need is not simply to be informed of what is good and right. Man's primary need is to be set free from his own self-centred greed. Here is where the Gospel of the Lord Jesus Christ comes in as the liberating power, in their thinking.[98]

Here Mekane Yesus forwards the notion of sin, "the idea that all human beings are predisposed to love the wrong things or to love the right things wrongly, and as a result to do both themselves harm and others injustice."[99] There are different kinds of freedom depending on what one is free from. Mekane Yesus, along with the Christian tradition, give precedence to freedom from sin. The gospel is that which can liberate man from sin and enable him to love God and his neighbour. This is clearly described in Martin Luther's *The Freedom of a Christian* from 1520, which *the ECMY Letter* possibly alludes to when speaking of the "inner man" and "spiritual freedom and maturity. Luther lays down two seemingly contradictory principles concerning the freedom and bondage of the spirit: "A Christian is a perfectly free Lord of all, subject to none." "A Christian is a perfectly dutiful servant of all, subject to all."[100]

---

[95] *The ECMY Letter.*
[96] *The ECMY Letter* with quote from Alvin Rogness in *Lutheran Standard,* Feb 1, 1972.
[97] *The ECMY Letter.*
[98] *The ECMY Letter.*
[99] Biggar 2020, 6.
[100] Luther 1999 *LW* vol. 31.

These two notions come from St Paul, in 1 Cor 9:19 (RSV) "For though I am free from all men, I have made myself a slave to all", and in Rom 13:8 (RSV) "Owe no one anything, except to love one another; for he who loves his neighbor has fulfilled the law." Luther then adds a third notion which explains the reason why these two propositions are not contradictory: "Love by its very nature is ready to serve and be subject to him who is loved."[101] So it is love that explains the paradox. This was modelled in Christ who was "born of woman, born under the law" (Gal 4:4 RSV), and at the same time being free, with reference to Phil 2:6–7 (RSV) "in the form of God did not count equality with God a thing to be grasped, but emptied himself, taking the form of a servant".[102]

The *Freedom of a Christian* was written to Pope Leo X in 1520 in response to his opponents who held that Luther was advocating a life without Christian ethics. Luther teaches that a "Christian is free from sin through faith in God, yet bound by love to serve his neighbour."[103] Here is the origin of the concept of *Diakonie,* the service, that any Christian may bring to his neighbour. This sense of practical service of Christians has brought about ACT Alliance as a common concern in the ecumenical movement. Real freedom is freedom from sin, that liberates man to love and therefore to serve his fellow man. The prerequisite, as in *the ECMY Letter,* is the inner freedom of man, which does not consist in external things of the body but in the freedom of the soul.[104] What then brings about this freedom and love to serve the neighbour, according to Luther? It is only the gospel of Christ which is read in the word of God.[105]

---

[101] Luther 1999 *LW* vol. 31.

[102] Luther 1999 *LW* vol. 31.

[103] Luther 1999 *LW* vol. 31. Quote from the editor's introduction.

[104] Luther 1999 *LW* vol. 31. "What can it profit the soul if the body is well, free, and active, and eats, drinks, and does as it pleases? For in these respects even the most godless slaves of vice may prosper. On the other hand, how will poor health or imprisonment or hunger or thirst or any other external misfortune harm the soul? Even the most godly men, and those who are free because of clear consciences, are afflicted with these things. None of these things touch either the freedom or the servitude of the soul."

[105] Luther 1999 *LW* vol. 31. "One thing, and only one thing, is necessary for Christian life, righteousness, and freedom. That one thing is the most holy Word of God, the gospel of Christ, as Christ says, John 11[:25], 'I am the resurrection and the life; he who believes in me, though he die, yet shall he live'; and John 8[:36], 'So if the Son makes you free, you will be free indeed'; and Matt. 4[:4], 'Man shall not live by bread alone, but by every word that proceeds from the mouth of God.' Let us then consider it certain and firmly established that the soul can do without anything except the Word of God and that where the Word of God is missing there is no help at all

When the church officers of Mekane Yesus are writing to the Lutheran World Federation asking them to reconsider their approach to service to the world, is it not probable that they do so with the teaching of the reformer in mind – and arguably St Paul's apostolic teaching as a foundation? The logic of change in the church officers' experience mirrors that of the reformer. The evangelical movement swept through Ethiopia – and through Africa – because people were longing for something more than physical bread to eat – and paradoxically the bread from heaven also brought about change in society. The change seemed to have followed the biblical principle of seeking first the kingdom of God. The opposite position was taken by African politicians who, rightly frustrated with colonial governments, argued to seek first the political kingdom, and all the rest shall follow. For, a Mekane Yesus mindset, that would entail setting secondary things first, with the risk of losing both primary and secondary things.

Secularity and Exclusive Humanism

This kind of thinking does not apply to a humanitarian sector that is based on state funding. It will fall on deaf ears as states do not integrate the gospel into their legal and governmental systems. Modern states are secular in the sense of being concerned with the things of this age. This Mekane Yesus-text shows that when churches engage in society, they are not secular in the same sense. The task of the church, according to Mekane Yesus, is set by the gospel of Jesus Christ and its apostolic commission. There is therefore a tension between the secularity of the state and the secular concerns, the secularity, of the church.[106]

The question is, however, whether this is a real conflict or a superficial conflict. During the time of the Derg military regime, there was a substantial conflict between the secular state and the churches and their Christian faith. The exclusive humanism, that guided the military leaders of the state, was in real conflict with the Christian worldview. There was no belief in the dignity of the human person because there was no belief in God. The exclusive humanism of naturalism – as critiqued by the church officers of Mekane Yesus – had become a religious substitute: religious secularism. When the Derg fell, and a new constitution was written, however, religious freedom was guaranteed by the state, not as something granted

---

for the soul. If it has the Word of God it is rich and lacks nothing since it is the Word of life, truth, light, peace, righteousness, salvation, joy, liberty, wisdom, power, grace, glory, and of every incalculable blessing."

[106] Temesgen 2011. On secularism/secularity distinction, Bretherton 2019, 227–56.

by the state, but as a given, *donatum*, recognised by it.[107] This shows that in principle, a modern secular state does not have to oppose the Christian gospel and its freedom.[108]

The Liturgy Forms the Christian

To address the concern of moving from liturgical matters into aid works, the first question to ask regards Christian formation: what is the process of people becoming "Christian" beyond baptism? Second, there is an epistemological question: how do Christians apply their faith in daily life? Eugenia Constantinou introduces the concept of *phronema*, an acquired Orthodox mindset, as a practical way for Orthodox believers to know the faith and discern what is and is not "Orthodox." For Constantinou, an Orthodox *phronema* is then understood as "the mind of the fathers"; for thinking and practice to be in line with the Tradition of the Christian Church.[109]

Unfortunately, there are not many theological works readily available to aid students of the Ethiopian Orthodox tradition in translating the Orthodox Christian faith to the moral life of Christians.[110] Mebratu Kiros Gebru's dissertation is an exception. His work takes advantage of the twentieth-century meeting between Eastern and Western traditions in Orthodox academic theology.[111]

By referring to contemporary scholarship in liturgical theology, I want to show that church celebrations matter to issues of morality. For the scholar, the primary sources to the liturgical life of the church are the written sources of the Christian

---

[107] FDRE 1995, Constitution art. 27: "Everyone has the right to freedom of thought, conscience and religion."

[108] See Desta Heliso 2021.

[109] Constantinou 2020, 33 ff. The Greek concept of *phronema*, Constantinou would translate into mindset, to acquire an Orthodox mindset and so be able to discern spiritual matters according to the Christian faith and the teaching of the early Church Fathers. Cf. Collins 2014, 136–37 "Christian order is not the result of 'an imperious call to obedience' but of discerning 'the mind of Christ' (1 Cor 2:16)", with further reference to Martin, Ralph. 1984. *The Spirit and the Congregation: Studies in 1 Corinthians 12–15*. Grand Rapids: MI: Eerdmans, 80, 60–68.

[110] There are several works on the Ethiopic liturgy, e.g. Fritsch 1999, Ethiopian Orthodox Church 1996, Getnet Tamene 1998, Melketsedek 1997, and Paulos Yohannes 1998.

[111] Paris became an ecumenical meeting point after the 1917 Russian Revolution.

faith; the liturgical books of the church,[112] the Scripture[113] and its commentaries, the doctrinal books and writings of the fathers, the writings of recognised church councils,[114] and hagiographies. Liturgical theology, however, is less an academic study of the liturgical celebration than it is an approach to theology. The liturgical worship of the church is not theology in the secondary sense as a science of God, making sense of God, but in the primary sense of *ortho-doxa* – a rightful praise.

Mebratu Kiros Gebru opens his dissertation on the liturgical cosmology in the Ethiopian Liturgy with a reflection on *lex orandi – lex credendi,* that "the prayers (worship) of the church ground its beliefs."[115] The living liturgical life of the church, with its divine Liturgy, *Qəddase* (ቅዳሴ),[116] its periods of fasting and feasting and ascetic and liturgical practices,[117] including its public festivals such as the Exaltation of the Holy Cross, or *Dämära* (ደመራ), and the Epiphany, *Ṭəmqät* (ጥምቀት),[118] and the contemplation of icons, form people to live life as Christians in terms of the virtuous life in livelihood, culture, statecraft, and warfare.[119]

There is thus a movement from the fundamental truth about God, the world, and morality, via the liturgical participation in the life of Christ in the sacramental community of the church, towards the believers' spiritual and moral formation and consequent motivation for seeking peace, life, and wellbeing of other people. The liturgical celebration of the resurrection of Christ as the sacramental centre of Orthodox Church life, with its fasting and feasting, is thereby essential for fostering a common life. Orthodoxy in this way strives to hold together the right beliefs,

---

[112] Mebratu Kiros Gebru 2012, 6, 8, 9, 20, 25–26, 28, 72, 76, 176–85. The liturgical writings of the church are books such as the Ethiopian Missal with its anaphoras, the Horologium (*Sä'atat* – ሰዓታት) with the liturgy of the hours, the lectionaries with the prescribed texts for each season of the liturgical calendar, and the hymnaries with its variety of hymns.

[113] Mebratu Kiros Gebru 2012, 20. The EOTC accepts 81 books as canonical.

[114] Mebratu Kiros Gebru 2012, 20.

[115] Mebratu Kiros Gebru 2012, 1–12. Wainwright 2002, 679–84 on Prosper of Aquitaine.

[116] Mebratu Kiros Gebru 2012, 6. Mebratu asserts, 2012, 14, that "The Ethiopian liturgy, despite its Alexandrian origin, has developed to be an independent rite as a result of the work of the *Mäməhran* – መምህራን (doctors) of the EOTC." The Ethiopian liturgical tradition was also influenced by the West Syrian, Antiochian, liturgical rite. Both these sources of the liturgical life were adapted to the Ethiopian context. Mebratu Kiros Gebru 2012, 22–23. It implies that attention needs to be given to the Ethiopian liturgical tradition as a direct source of Ethiopian Orthodox formation.

[117] Mebratu Kiros Gebru 2012, 25–26.

[118] Mebratu Kiros Gebru 2012, 9–10. The term Epiphany, *Epifanya* (ኤጲፋንያ) can be used.

[119] Mebratu Kiros Gebru 2012, 1–3.

worship, and practice.[120] The liturgical practices of the Orthodox Church thus should be understood as intimately connected with the moral life of the Orthodox believers.

Refugee assistance, as exemplified in the case study of chapter two, with its principles in chapter three, is not just an application of Christian faith in personal life. It is a sophisticated web of organisations, institutions, and principles mixed with the personal views and wills of different stakeholders. The work is not personal but operates at high levels of human organisation, and yet people are always involved. When we talk about organisations acting, it is, in fact, people acting through institutions. This means that people are morally responsible for their actions in an organisation. Whenever an Orthodox Christian is involved, the liturgical life of the church may be operative in that person's moral life. This is valid regardless of whether the Christian is attached to the development commission of the church, or working for another organisation, for example, a UN or government agency.

Then we could ask, are the liturgical sources mentioned above relevant to the study of the ecumenical diakonia of ACT Alliance? If these sources, as a living liturgical heritage and as literary sources to the life of the faith, are primary, that is to say, fundamental in forming Orthodox beliefs and practices, then as part of a living tradition they are operating in forming Orthodox Christians. Orthodox liturgy creates and sustains Orthodox Christians. People formed by liturgical practices will practice theology in the primary sense of speaking rightfully to God in the liturgy. They will also be formed as persons and their lives will be impacted by the liturgy in what, in Orthodox ecumenical theology, has been called "the liturgy after the liturgy": the service to the fellow man.[121]

There are also other means by which Orthodox spirituality and formation take place. The *Maedot* points to the *Nefs Abbat,* the spiritual father who shares the life of the community and counsels the Orthodox in daily life. There is the possibility of pilgrimages – the *Maedot* focuses on Jerusalem, but most spiritual journeys are directed to places like Axum, Lalibela and Debre Libanos within Ethiopia.[122] The

---

[120] See the works on liturgical theology by Alexander Schmemann. Fagerberg 2018a, 2018b.

[121] Bria 1978, 87. I am indebted to Timothy Quill for the significance of how a particular liturgical tradition forms people. Abate Gobena 2023 on liturgical use of hagiographies and the sanctity of church forests preserving indigenous forests when utilitarian ethics and state policies cause deforestation across the country. On church architecture, Mengistu Gobezie Worku 2018.

[122] *Maedot* 1983, 39–40 "Jerusalem Memorial of Ethiopian Believers."

life of the saints in stories and iconography is also part of this spirituality.[123] These features may seem otherworldly and remote, particularly for a modern liberal mindset, but the argument of one of the authors was that the "otherworldliness" of the Orthodox worldview, far from isolating the believers, forms a standpoint from which Orthodox believers may engage in social issues.[124]

At this point, it is important to note that "otherworldliness" is not a self-de-scription, but a classification given by others. Alexander Schmemann, in his en-gagement in the Ecumenical movement of his days, often made fun of this descrip-tion of the Orthodox Church, writing that "Orthodoxy is presented usually as spe-cializing in 'mysticism' and 'spirituality'."[125] Vladimir Lossky, in his classical "Mys-tical Theology of the Eastern Church" therefore sought to distinguish the Mystical Theology of the Christian Church, as rooted in the teaching of the church, in which the ultimate end of life is union with God, the θέωσις of the Greek Fathers, from a "mysticism" found in Bergson, Harnack, or in Gnosticism as "the personal experiences of different masters of the spiritual life."[126]

The sacramental dimension of the Christian life here makes its appearance. Schmemann, again, is clarifying that the life of which Christians speak is not a "*re-ligious life*" in a world of "spirituality" that would "*help*" man in his "secular life."

---

[123] The Ethiopian church, via St Yared and the Nine saints, followed St Ephraim and elabo-rated even further the symbolic representations of St Mary, Christ, and the cross. This way of talking, like the Pauline idea of the body of Christ, builds in the Semitic notion of *corporative personality* in which the many may be included in the one. In addition, the Enochian literature also spread and gave rise to further speculations on heavenly realities such as angels. The higher levels of the church educational system were dedicated to this fine art of theological exposition of symbolic representations of the celestial realities. The symbolism mentioned above has brought forth a theology, rich in meaning and depth. Binns 2002, 39–54; Bakke 1986, 87–103. For an introduction to the symbolic thinking of St Ephraim, Brock *The Luminous Eye*. The point of a symbolic interpretation of the liturgy is not to explain the meaning of the liturgy, but to medi-tate on the words and practices and to discover layers of meaning thus drawing the believer into the mystery. The Ethiopian Church, besides St Ephraim and St Yared, draws upon the teaching of Cyril of Alexandria. Ezra Gebremedhin 1977. In the Chalcedonian tradition, Maximus the Con-fessor continue this line of thought. For "corporate personality", Ratzinger 1996, 35 (1997, 30).

[124] *Maedot* 1983, 22.

[125] Schmemann 1973, 21. For missiological debates about worldliness, Bosch 2011, 391–92.

[126] Lossky 1976, 7–9. Ethiopian Orthodox tradition is not to be read as a gnostic tradition. Bishop Frumentius was ordained by Athanasius, patriarch of Alexandria (c. 340) and the rela-tionship to the Coptic Church has been strong. Athanasius introduced episcopacy in Ethiopia. Athanasius was important: in the trinitarian debates with Arius, in closing the NT canon, and in promoting the ascetic movement of the desert fathers. Athanasius' argument for the incarnation of Christ shows how deeply the Alexandrian tradition values the humanity and deity of Christ.

Nor is the activist vision "for the *better* life of the world" of the "Social Gospel" in which Christians are called to repent for spending time in "silence and liturgy" without having "dealt sufficiently with the social, political, economic, racial and all other issues of real life." The point is that "by itself action has no meaning" without knowing what life in its fullness is, "one cannot really act." "Man is a hungry being", Schmemann confirms, "[b]ut he is hungry for God. Behind all the hunger of our life is God. All desire is finally a desire for Him." God gave man food to eat, "given as *communion with God.*"[127]

What Schmemann seeks to outline is a Christian worldview, distinct from both Gnosticism and secularism, which affirms "both the *goodness* of the world for whose life God has given his only-begotten Son, and the *wickedness* in which the world lies." The real question for Schmemann therefore is: "how can we 'hold together'– in faith, in life, in action – these seemingly contradictory affirmations of the Church"? His answer is to point to the Eucharist in which the church becomes "that which she is: the sacrament of the world, the sacrament of the Kingdom." To interpret Christianity as a religion is to miss the point that it "is in a profound sense the *end of all religion*" and at the same time the "end of all natural joy." The latter does not entail "that this world cannot be improved", and Christians do "work for peace, justice, [and] freedom", but it does mean that the world "can never become the place God intended it to be" and that life can no longer be seen as a "reasonably organized 'pursuit of happiness'."[128]

So, the Orthodox argument is that the Christian liturgy fosters Christians, and formed Christians act in the world, not as instruments of activism, but for the true good of mankind in a sacramental understanding of reality.

4.4 Voluntary Societies and Church Contributions

The classical church aid organisations of the mid-twentieth century were voluntary societies set up for particular causes. This is the reason why civil society is advocated for in development aid. What about the Ethiopian churches and their ACT agencies? Is there any tradition of voluntarism in this specific sense?

---

[127] Schmemann 1973, 11–24. A classical account of *theosis*, Lossky 1976. *Theosis* is known in the West, in the writings of Martin Luther, as argued by the Finnish Luther scholars beginning with Tuomo Mannermaa *In ipsa fide Christus adest* (In this faith Christ is present). Jocic 2012. See discussion in Cooper 2014. On the Exegesis of 2 Peter 1:4 in its Hellenistic context, Starr 2000.

[128] Schmemann 1973, 11–24.

Voluntary Societies

Part of the Ethiopian Orthodox culture is the tradition of a voluntary society. *Mahaber*, associations, are formed for particular purposes as part of traditional Orthodox church life. The *Maedot* journal takes as an example *the Jerusalem Foundation*.[129] People join and contribute their time, talents, and resources for the sake of a common cause. This is what development literature refers to as civil society, a voluntary sphere outside of family and economic life. Despite direct attacks on Orthodox associations by the former Derg regime, new associations were formed. Free associations would, however, not have the economic strength to financially support the basic needs of a refugee population according to the standards of humanitarian aid.

The Mekane Yesus carries the mission heritage of the nineteenth- and twentieth-century Modern Missionary Movement.[130] As such, the church is no stranger to voluntary associations. A case in point is the way both congregations and synods were organised with volunteers in leadership and in all areas of life in the church.[131]

Church Contributions

What about the Ethiopian Orthodox Church? Would it have the financial strength to do the work on its own? The Orthodox Church moved away from an agrarian land-based economy when all land became nationalised after the revolution. According to the church administrator, the church became less dependent on the nobility and more on "direct contributions" to the local church communities and "subsidies" from the government. This, for Abera Bekele, meant that "the clergies and the laity" were no longer separated by a "tragic wall", but could "meet together as one body working together for the well-being of the church", and that "church-men" were "responsible to those people on the ground." The World Council of Churches participated in the new structure of the parish councils through financial assistance.[132]

---

[129] *Maedot* 1983, 37–39 "The Ethiopian Orthodox Church Historical Possession of the Holy Places in the Holy Land Jerusalem."

[130] Brodd 2005, 253.

[131] On the development of church synods, Launhardt 2004. On congregational organization, Toll 2014.

[132] The World Council of Churches were involved in this process as a financier. An "inter church aid" agreement was reached November 1976 with the Commission for the Churches Participation in Development (WCC-CCPD). For the World Council, once these parish councils

Would a church with such a large constituency be able to finance the humanitarian assistance of refugees? By going back to the time of the Derg, I want to show that neither the ecumenical agencies of ACT Alliance, nor the church, as an institution, have the economic means of supporting large-scale aid operations such as the ETH141 appeal and its operations. Given that the Derg had nationalised much of the property and capital assets of the Orthodox Church, remuneration from such assets could not support the work.

The church, as a constituency, is directly dependent on the wealth of its members for its economic capabilities. The members may form any number of associations for self-support, for the support of different causes, and to support the church. Those associations are, however, always dependent on the contributions of their members and therefore on the combined wealth of all members. The economic policies of consecutive governments since the revolution in 1974 have failed to lift the population at large out of poverty even though strides towards economic development have been made.[133] Therefore, even though there are wealthy members among the Orthodox, and parishioners are directly supporting their churches, taken as a whole, the Ethiopian Orthodox Church is not such a wealthy institution that it would have the capability of financing the support of refugee populations.

The Mekane Yesus Church experienced two major changes: first the handing over of the educational and health institutions of the mission agencies to the church. It brought about a new level of professionalisation and institutionalisation of the common life in the church. Second, there was a change from relating to mission agencies to development agencies and hence a shift in strategy from running institutions to organising development projects. It entailed a move from the possibility of financial self-sustainability to a new dependency concerning

---

became operational, local development projects could be financed and run by the church communities themselves. On a local level, the churches thus became strengthened and could serve their constituencies through small-scale community development projects. *Maedot* 1983, 24–26. The *Maedot* no 9, 1987 contains a report on the later years of the parish council movement (1983–1987). With the parish councils, the newly established synodal structure was complemented by the "idea of laymen participation in the affairs of parish churches." The church thus introduced a new parallel modern structure to its sacramental structure of deacons, priests and bishops, its monastic institutions, its regional structures such clerics of superior rank appointed by churches of rank, its council of scholars, and its influential rank of hermits, the *bahatawi*. *Maedot* 1983, 24. EOC-DICAC 2009, 3, the commissioner commented that the church's ability was "limited in post communist era" and therefore the founders of the commission extended a hand of friendship to ecumenical partners and bilateral organisations.

[133] Every year millions are dependent on aid regardless of whether it is a good harvest or not.

financing the social engagement of the church. The ECMY Letter was written during this transitional time, from what in the next chapter will be called *the mission model* to *the international crisis model*.

The Problem of Voluntary Funding

The way that refugee assistance has been set up – in principle by the external support of a large population for an indeterminate time – makes voluntary contributions, even of large constituencies such as the Ethiopian Orthodox, seem far from adequate to cater for the basic needs of the refugees. National resources are not enough, neither voluntary nor mandatory. The only way that contemporary refugee assistance is financially sustainable is with contributions from donor nations, i.e., citizens of other nations pay through their taxes to sustain people's lives. Voluntarism is not enough, so mandatory contributions of some – the nations of the north – are injected to compensate.

There are several reasons why these aspects are of interest. One regards the voluntary character of aid agencies. Regarding the Orthodox Development Commission (DICAC), the level of voluntarism is rather low. It was not set up with voluntary contributions of the faithful as the ideal but as a vehicle for the inter-church aid of the World Council of Churches. If the successor of the inter-church aid of the past, ACT Alliance, does not contribute to the work of the commission, voluntary contributions cannot compensate. Fortunately, the commission has shown its ability to raise resources outside of its ecumenical partners. The work of the commission has been supported by UN organisations and the US in historic continuity with the famine relief of the Joint Relief Programme.

These aspects are also relevant to the Mekane Yesus Church. Despite the fact that voluntarism was part and parcel with the initial setup of the church, as still guides much of its daily life, the Development and Social Service Commission is wholly dependent on external donors.[134]

There is, however, no good reason for the Mekane Yesus and Orthodox faithful not to contribute financially to the work of the church development commissions. The only way for these commissions, and by extension the churches, to be less dependent on donors is for the members to voluntarily contribute to the work. Aid agencies are beggars, asking for funds for the sake of their work. Some are international beggars, asking funds for work in another country than their own. The sustainability of ACT Alliance depends in the long run on a move away from the

---

[134] Cf. Aklilu Dalelu 2003; Aklilu Dalelo and Stellmacher 2012 on the Ethiopian Kale Heywet Church.

contributions of a few member churches and their "NGOs" – the international beggars – to the voluntary contributions of all, national and international. Such a long-term aim would need time: to change attitudes and organisational structures from White Man's Burden to an ecclesial sharing of burdens.[135]

4.5 Ethiopian Church Basis for Ecumenical Engagement

Chapter four has centred on giving a contextual perspective on the ecumenical diakonia of ACT Alliance by investigating the ecclesial foundations for the ecumenical engagements of the Ethiopian Orthodox Tewahido Church and the Ethiopian Evangelical Church Mekane Yesus. The case study of chapter two and the principles of humanitarian aid in chapter three has thus been linked with the teachings and self-understandings of these churches through two primary sources, *the ECMY letter* and the English issue of *Maedot* of 1983.

On the Interrelation Between Proclamation of the Gospel and Human Development (the ECMY letter) of 1972 was analysed as an official document of Mekane Yesus. *The ECMY letter* presented a framework for addressing socio-economic concerns that has influenced the ecumenical thinking of the Lutheran World Federation. It represents a theological attempt "to show the theological fallacy that undergirds the donor criteria" for aid.[136] *The ECMY letter* introduces the theme of holistic ministry which is significant in the Ethiopian church context and is of academic interest. It also raises the theological issue that compliance with donor requirements may lead to an inner secularisation of churches.[137] Finally, the anthropology explicit in *the ECMY letter* has been of importance for ecumenical discussions on inter-church aid and ecumenical collaboration.

The English issue of *Maedot* of 1983 was analysed as a rich source from the Orthodox Church with regard to its self-understanding as a church, social works, and ecumenical commitments in the 1980s which also may say something about its present engagement in ACT Alliance. The word *Maedot* means Passover conveying the meaning of transfer from death to eternal life, a name indicative of the self-understanding of the Orthodox Church.

---

[135] Cf. Easterly 2006 on the inherent problems of conventional systems of aid. On aid agencies as international beggars, I am indebted to Jember Teferra *in memoriam* at IHA-UDP. Her Orthodox faith, and dedication to ecumenical collaboration for the marginalised inspired many.

[136] Temesgen 2011, 48–49.

[137] Jonsson 1998, 201.

The ECMY letter was written just before the revolution, whereas the *Maedot* was published during the high time of the revolutionary regime. The period of the Derg military regime (1974–1991) as a transitional time was formative for the churches and their social engagements. While many Evangelical Churches were closed, leaders imprisoned, and property confiscated, the Orthodox Church was needed for the political mobilisation of the revolutionary regime and its secular project of earthly happiness as "salvation." The regime therefore attempted to control the Orthodox Church rather than eradicate it as it tried with less politically significant church bodies.

The ECMY Letter states that the church had a dual obligation of social service and proclamation of the gospel. The ECMY church officers were critical of a mindset which saw humanitarian needs as self-evident while ignoring people's spiritual needs. They were equally critical of a view that would use social services as a means to another end. The authors saw that when economic growth becomes the standard of evaluation, other values in life are neglected and material development may become a threat to those values that make life meaningful. While economic development is important, it is not the meaning and end goal, *telos*, in life. The salvation of the world is intrinsically bound up with the question of human destiny. What, if any, is the ultimate purpose of human life? Nihilists would deny any such purpose, and objective meaning in life, but that would contradict empirical evidence, because survival is not enough, as Viktor Frankl learnt during the Nazi concentration camps.[138]

Behind a one-sided materialistic view of development, the ECMY officers argued, was a view of human beings as suffering creatures, patients. Instead of a reductive anthropology, they believed that "the development of the inner man" is a prerequisite for societal development. Therefore, they argued for an "integral human development" where the spiritual and material needs are seen together. Development then becomes liberating for individuals and societies and is in line with human potential and God's purposes. Humanism needs to be open to God and a vocation to serve others for it to be humanism at all, according to these authors.

The *Maedot* gave emphasis to the Christian gospel of Jesus Christ and life as a gift from God as the foundation for social commitment. As the church is commanded to work on peace and good will among men, Christians are called to contribute to this work, thus fulfilling the mission of the church. When all Christians are unified in the witness to the gospel, they are contributing to "brotherhood

---

[138] Frankl 1986.

among peoples" and "peace of the world"[139] Therefore, all Christians in the world have a duty to work for the common good, in accordance with common sense, and with the blessing of God. The Holy Apostolic Church, instituted by Christ, is one, and the Christian faith creates an ecumenical family made up of many languages and cultures in the world. This is the Orthodox foundation for engaging in common relief work and the restoration of the historical unity of the church.[140]

Contemporary diakonia is grounded in the sacramental life of the church and the prayers for all those in need and becomes part of the apostolic diakonia – ministry – of the church.[141] The social commitments of the church are rooted in the theological foundations of the church and the spirituality of the faith which renders a "deep concern for the poor."[142] The "otherworldliness" and ascetic spirituality of the Orthodox Church could become a basis for ecumenical collaboration rather than a materialistic basis which would marginalise the church and make the state central. On this ground, the church has engaged in society in everything from relief and development works to all aspects of spiritual and cultural life without which people fail to prosper also in the economic sense. Orthodox church life and tradition have relevance to its people's engagement in aid work.[143] This is a point strengthened by academic works on the liturgical theology of the Ethiopian Orthodox Church. The liturgical celebration of the church is essential for fostering a common life and a deep sense of commitment to creation and people of all social standing.[144]

The Ethiopian Orthodox Tewahido Church has a high view of the Christian Church in light of the resurrection of Christ. It is seen by others as "otherworldliness", but the church itself sees it as a sacramental view of reality in its liturgical theology. The Ethiopian Evangelical Church Mekane Yesus has a high view of man in light of the gospel. While the authors of *the ECMY letter* used the explicit

---

[139] *Maedot* 1983, 13–14.

[140] *Maedot* 1983, 6–9.

[141] *Maedot* 1983, 26–28.

[142] *Maedot* 1983, 26–28. Cf. EOC-DICAC Commissioner Nigussu Legesse: "Thus, the realization of the Kingdom of God, through care for the needy, underprivileged and poverty stricken has always been an expression of Orthodox spirituality. Indeed the monasteries and churches were not only centres of religious activity, but also provided whatever social assistance existed in traditional society." EOC-DICAC 2009, 2.

[143] *Maedot* 1983, 21–23.

[144] *Mebratu Kiros Gebru* 2012.

natural law language,[145] speaking of the integral development of man, it should be interpreted in line with the teaching of Mekane Yesus that the free gift of the gospel is to be received in faith. This, for the church officers, is the prerequisite for the true development of men and women and their communities in which man is liberated from sin to serve his neighbour.[146]

In chapter four attention was turned from the sources of the appeal and sources of its principles to primary sources from the churches themselves. The evidence is clear that concern for the fellow man, common life in society, and relief work stem from deep roots in the living tradition of the churches. The Mekane Yesus and the Orthodox Church were keen to offer critique on the ecumenical collaboration based on their understanding of the church, the nature of man, and a sense of mission beyond relief and development. While church ministry includes a diakonia of service to the needy in society, it aims for the proclamation of the gospel, the sacramental life of the church, and the hope of resurrection.

In this chapter, the importance of the political context has been highlighted since the Derg military regime attempted to either eradicate or control the churches in its attempt to create an ideal society, based on government control of all aspects of life. This illustrates the fact that the churches and their agencies act in a socio-political context, which may not only thwart relief efforts but also threaten the very life of church communities. It also highlights that churches may organise civil society organisations and raise funding among their members. Such efforts, though valuable in themselves, would not be enough to cater for a large refugee population hosted in camps, such as in the case study. Voluntary contributions will not uphold the standards discussed in chapter three.

In the next chapter, three historical modes of ecumenical collaboration in Ethiopia will be named: *the mission model*, *the inter-church aid model*, and *the international crisis model*. With the help of these heuristic models, the aim is to show that ACT members may come to ACT Alliance with different expectations. Chapter five will therefore expand on this chapter's study of the church context, before offering a concluding analysis of the ecclesiological problem of acting together.

---

[145] Cf. Boersma 2009, 91–93 in earlier research (1.1) with de Lubac's teaching regarding man as an image bearer with a natural desire for God, lacking the ability to reach that *telos*.

[146] See Smith 2016 and 2017 on "liturgical" analysis of seemingly secular activities.

5. Ecumenical Models: For Acting Together

In this chapter, the contemporary work of ACT Alliance will be situated in a larger historical context using heuristic models based on different historical platforms of ecumenical collaboration in Ethiopia. Some of the initiatives will be named to draw attention to the fact that ecumenical bodies and collaborative schemes may be different in approach. The ecumenical models that will be sketched represent different ecumenical strategies from the mid-twentieth century (ca 1944) to the beginning of the twenty-first (2014). The contemporary ACT organisation will be compared with what will be called *the mission model* with its ideal of the integrated church, *the inter-church aid model*, and *the international crisis model*. [1]

This use of historical models may be a productive way of exploring issues of church and aid and making a comparative analysis of the ACT Ethiopia Forum and its work with earlier ecumenical initiatives. The years given below do not indicate the exact beginning and end of a collaborative platform but represent the years that a model typifies. In historical reality, the approaches are not necessarily progressing from one to another as in a paradigm, nor is it mutually exclusive entities as in contradictory propositions, but these models exist as contemporary and at times complementary approaches to ecumenical services. [2]

The chapter is built mostly on earlier literature. Since ACT Alliance and its preceding organisational forms of ACT International, and ACT Development have not been researched earlier, primary documents from the ACT Ethiopia Forum have also been used. The historical account and the subsequent discussion is rather sketchy, more to draw out different lines of argument and to discuss different approaches than to close the debate. These ecumenical approaches need to be understood in light of shifting political and religious dynamics in the region.

---

[1] Dulles 2002, 1–15, on the use of models, p. 17 on heuristic models for exploratory purposes. Brodd 2009, 319–20 on the use of explanatory vs. exploratory models in Ecclesiology.

[2] On paradigms, Bosch 2011 and Swinton 2003, 382–409.

Over the last two hundred years the religious map of modern Ethiopia has been largely rewritten. Traditional religions have retreated or gone "underground" but continue to influence people without being overtly visible. Islam has reached vast new areas, and Orthodox Christianity has expanded beyond the traditional areas of the highlands in the north. The Catholic Church has also spread in various parts of the country. The formation and growth of Evangelical Christianity in Ethiopia has given rise to a number of more established churches like *the Ethiopian Evangelical Church Mekane Yesus* (EECMY), *the Ethiopian Kale Heywet Church* (EKHC), the *Meserete Kristos Church* (MKC), and *the Ethiopian Full Gospel Believer's Church* (EFGBC). Besides these, a multitude of smaller denominations, non-denominational churches, sects and para-churches have been established following the fall of *the Derg Regime* in 1991. Several of these newer churches, but not all, relate to *the Evangelical Churches Fellowship of Ethiopia* (ECFE).[3]

The first section *The Mission Model and the Integrated Church* (1944–1974) (5.1) summarises the post-Second World War approach of integrating a holistic sense of mission with the Ethiopian Evangelical Church Mekane Yesus. *The Inter-Church Aid Model* (1965–1984) (5.2) depicts the ecumenical approach of Western Churches showing practical solidarity with the Ethiopian Orthodox Tewahido Church in consequence of a sense of unity, *koinonia*, of the Christian Church. *The International Crisis Model* (1974–1991) (5.3) outlines some of the major collaborative schemes by ecumenical agencies bringing relief to Ethiopia during conflict and military regime. *Introducing ACT in Ethiopia* (1994–2014) (5.4) outlines the first years of ACT as an ecumenical enterprise. The idea of ACT (1994–) was initiated by the ecumenical movement as a way to express the practical engagement of the churches in relief, development, and advocacy works. The final section *Comparing Historical Models With ACT Alliance* (5.5) brings together the different ecumenical approaches to a comparative discussion of the present ACT Alliance.

5.1 The Mission Model and the Integrated Church

The Mission Model (1944–1958), as initiated by foreign mission societies, was a way to express the Christian faith by service and witness. The mission movement ignited the ecumenical movement in 1905 in an attempt to reach a common Christian witness to the world. In Ethiopia, the model was characterised by holistic

---

[3] Alberto 2013; 3; Donham 1999; Egerland 2016; Eide 1997; EOC 1996; Getnet Tamene 1998, Tibebe Eshete 2009, and Østebø 1998. On EECMY see chapter four, n4.

mission, respect for the Orthodox Church, general unity among missions, and Ethiopian state coordination. The holistic mission enterprise was one of the founding blocks for church-based and state-based aid in Ethiopia.[4] The first mission societies in Ethiopia were striving to renew the Ethiopian Orthodox Church as well as to share the gospel with those who had never heard it. As the missions and the Orthodox Church failed to agree, it led to a solidarity of Evangelical Christians, the establishment of new churches, and an integration of church and mission into the ideal of the integrated church (1959–1974).[5]

Holistic Mission

The missionaries focused on health care, education, and spiritual life by building local institutions such as schools, clinics, and churches, and sharing the gospel through their lives and teaching. The idea of the missionaries was that their lives would witness the faith in Christ that they wished to share with others. The way to a better society was thought first as a personal conversion to Christ, through the reading of the scripture, the preaching of the gospel, and the example of the Christian life. A commitment to Christ as saviour and Lord would be followed by a life in service to others. The modern mission movement was inspired by revivals in the churches. For those who took part in the revivals, it led to a new sense of purpose in life. A new relationship with Christ, and the love of Christ, helped them to renew their own lives, and the life of the churches, and their societies. This led to the diaconal movement and the inner and outer mission movement.[6]

Respect for the Orthodox Church

Regarding the Ethiopian Orthodox Church, the policy was one of distributing scriptures so that people themselves may read and come to a biblical understanding of the Christian gospel. Regarding people of other faiths, the policy was one of sharing the Christian gospel and inviting them to become Christians through baptism and faith in Christ. The respect for the Orthodox Church was grounded in sharing the faith and being baptised into the Christian church.[7]

---

[4] With colonial and post-colonial ambitions of Western (Western Europe and the USA) and Eastern (Soviet Union, Cuba, and China) set in the Post-World War II period of the Cold War.

[5] Jonsson 1998, 72–77 on integration and resistance to integration. Cf. Pétursson 1991, 62-66.

[6] Grenstedt 2024, 52–54 on Karl Cederqvist and his students. On revivals Bexell, Oloph 2003.

[7] Arén (1974) asked: "What caused the Evangelical Christians to establish an indigenous church of their own, though there was of old a Christian Church in Ethiopia?" Arén 1978, 18.

General Unity Among Missions

The mission societies were united in their witness to the Christian faith. United also in their basic missional approach holistically serving in health and education with the missionary as a witness to the gospel and an example to emulate. The mission societies were divided in the confessional and national character of their respective churches and the liturgical traditions of those churches. The missionaries represented revival groups of confessional and national churches in the divided Western Christendom. There was general goodwill towards each other. The Lutheran World Federation created a Commission on World Mission (CWM) to coordinate the mission efforts of its member churches and the various Lutheran missions. In Ethiopia, a Lutheran Missions Committee (LMC) was created in 1951 as a coordinating body of the Lutheran missions. These coordinating bodies worked to collaborate for the creation of one common church and thus a common theological institution. The Mekane Yesus Theological Seminary (MYTS) was built as a common effort. Government sponsored development projects also needed coordination.[8]

Arén's lists positive factors, such as the significance of vernacular Bible-reading, spontaneous demand for spiritual reform, indigenous leadership and initiative and an openness to new ideas, general education, and female emancipation. Arén 1978, 18 and 369–70. Cf. Emmanuel Abraham 1995, 250f. These are some of the reasons why a new church was. When SEM came to Eritrea in 1866, there was no intention of proselytism among the Orthodox. The vision was to reach the non-Christian Oromo tribes with the gospel and the policy towards the Orthodox was following the lines drawn by the CMS of respecting the Orthodox Church and its traditions, and to stimulate reform through the dissemination and study of the Bible in the vernacular. Arén 1978, 167. The roads to the main tribes of the Oromo lived was closed, so the mission set out to do work at the border while waiting and planning for expeditions to the Oromo people. Arén 1978, 46. When missions from Western churches did attempt to put policies of collaboration with Eastern Orthodox Christians it often turned out to be more complex than they expected. Cf. Suriel 2017. The interaction between Orthodox and Evangelical Christians shows a complex historical interaction. SEM allowed room for flexibility in the way the missionaries implemented the work. The Swedish mission and the Evangelical Pioneers among the Orthodox did not count with the resistance among higher nobility and some higher clergy, a resistance that led to persecution and even exile among those who showed an interest in the work of the mission. Arén 1978, 166. Arén is stressing the importance of an indigenous Bible-reading movement within the Orthodox Church. The reading of the Bible gave them new "spiritual insights" and inspired them towards reform. The monks asked Lager to send them copies of the New Testament and other books. Arén 1978, 13–14. When the Tseazega community became refugees, the mission provided asylum.

[8] Grenstedt 2000, 134–35. Sæverås 1974, 76–78. Missions working with what became EECMY: CMS (1830s), SEM (1866), UPM (1919), SIM (1927), Hermannsburg Mission (1927),

Ethiopian State Coordination

The Imperial Ethiopian Government sought to drive an autonomous line of development and state-building utilising the mission agencies in the nation-building project of modern Ethiopia by the 1944 imperial mission decree. There was a coordination of the efforts of mission societies according to the pattern set by the legislation and government officials. As such, the educational and health-oriented efforts of the missions brought up the social standards in the margins of the empire and contributed to the nation-building efforts of the emperor. The missions, on their hand, had a practical collaboration in matters of contact with state authorities. Imperial policies were based on a political balancing act between different stakeholders and their interests. State coordination did not promote understanding between Orthodox church authorities and mission representatives. It also did not promote collaboration between mission societies. A political coordination such as the 1944 Mission Decree led to estrangement and hostilities between Orthodox and Evangelical Christians rather than rapprochement and understanding.[9]

Solidarity Among Evangelical Christians

Beginning of the 1940s, in the wake of a renewed nationalism, Orthodox resistance rather than acceptance of the Evangelical movement and the teachings of the missions pushed developments towards an Evangelical ecumenical solidarity and fellowship and attempts to form an Evangelical national church on the basis of the existing Evangelical fellowship.[10]

NLM (1948), DEM (1948), ALM (1957), FLM (1967) and FELM (1859). In 1960 MYTS was founded with a diploma programme. In 1971 B.Th. was offered.

[9] The imperial mission decree set the legal boundaries of the mission model between 1944 – 1974. The legal framework was set up for the mission agencies registered with the imperial government. Citizens were not bound by the mission decree. Orthodox Christians responded in different ways to the missions. While some distrusted the missionaries, others respected them, and some even joined the evangelical movement. There was a general reluctance and suspicion to the whole mission project among Orthodox leaders who perceived the missions more as a threat than as an opportunity for renewal. Partially this was grounded in earlier historical encounters with Western Christianity which had led to civil war in the 17th C. There was a will to send Orthodox priests to teach according to the teaching of the Ethiopian Orthodox Church. This initiative was not taken in collaboration with the missions but as something opposed on the societies through the channels of governmental authorities.

[10] Sæverås 1974. The Evangelical fellowship was in theological terms a *koinonia* based on one faith, one Bible, unifying experiences, and ecumenical evangelical solidarity. There was also a shared Ethiopian identity. Despite differences in culture and language, historic grievances were

The mission intent to revive Ethiopian Orthodox Christianity was on the whole not accepted by the establishment of the Ethiopian Orthodox Church. The suspicion against the missionary endeavour turned into attempts to suppress Evangelical Christians and the use of the legal system to that end. There were informal acts of practical evangelical solidarity resulting in a sense of fellowship across cultural borders. Part of the aid rendered was seeking legal redress of abuses of the law.[11]

The sustained suppression of the Evangelicals resulted in the attempt of Ethiopian Evangelical Christians to form a national church. This actualised existing differences and emerging ethical issues, such as the use of alcohol, and the practice of polygamy. There was no serious disagreement on *ethos*, but the conflict remained on the policy level. What was to be allowed among Evangelical Christians? During the attempt to form a church of their own, missionary, and denominational factors resulted in the failure to stay within one common church. Even though the attempts to form one united Ethiopian Evangelical Church (CEEC) failed, the solidarity among evangelicals would continue as an ecumenical ideal.[12]

When the attempt to stay united as a national church failed, the work on a confessional Lutheran church began among the missions.[13] It would result in the establishment of the Ethiopian Evangelical Church Mekane Yesus in 1959. In parallel, there would be a continued openness towards the Ethiopian Orthodox Church on the one hand and continued annual conferences of Evangelical Christians – beyond "Mekane Yesus" – until 1963.[14] It would not be of immediate import for church formation, but important for a continuation of a sense of unity among Evangelical Christians with practical consequences.[15] The Mekane Yesus congregation in Addis Ababa, in expectation of the forming of a common national church, received an interim membership in the Lutheran World Federation in

---

overcome. There were attempts to deal with aspects of traditional *ethos*, such as polygamy, from a Christian ethos which raised practical issues of theological, disciplinary and canonical import. This was a *koinonia*, in the more limited sense of fellowship, but not yet an *ecclesia*, lacking ecclesial features such as a unifying baptismal practice and episcopal office.

[11] Arén 1999, 45–49, 83–84, 147. Grenstedt 2024, 52.

[12] Sæverås 1974, 41–75. Grenstedt 2000.

[13] Sæverås 1974, 76f. "A Confessional Lutheran Church 1951–59." The failed attempt for a theological basis pushed into various church formations, p. 67–68.

[14] Sæverås 1974, 69–70.

[15] Ecumenical Solidarity and collaborative projects such as EGST and ECFE and the attempt of CCCE as a countermodel to the Derg's political project of national-religious unity. Grenstedt 2024, 175, 221–22.

1957. As the EECMY was instituted Jan 1959, in 1961 the church could become a full member of the federation.[16]

The Ideal of the Integrated Church

How would the newly established national church relate to the missions? The church president, Emmanuel Abraham, was raising one of many points involved:

> If the Missions were to remain separate organizations and were to continue *to be responsible to the government alone* [emphasis added] as had been the case up to that time, it would be clear that the Church would be identified with the Missions, seeing that it was mainly located in the geographical areas allotted to the Missions, and as the Synod structure of the Church was almost identical with the Mission areas. In that case, the Church would continue to be identified with the Missions and remain a somewhat diffuse organization in the eyes of the government and the public.[17]

As a fruit of the efforts of the mission societies, a national church had taken over many church responsibilities from the missions. This raised questions regarding the institutional and development work of the mission societies. As Emmanuel Abraham argued, the missions would be associated with the church, but the missions were not accountable to the church but only towards the government. After discussions, the missions and the Mekane Yesus worked towards an integration of church and mission in which the national church would lead the work, in the name of Mekane Yesus.[18]

In 1969 April 7, the so-called Integration Policy was signed by EECMY and its Mission partners. It meant that the work of the missions was to be integrated with the work of the church. All work was ultimately to be situated under the authority of the church and its leadership.[19] In the case of the Mekane Yesus, the missions

---

[16] Emmanuel Abraham 1995, 243, 256. When EECMY was registered in 1961 there was no law regulating religious institutions, the so it was registered as an association. A new "Associations Registration Regulations" were issued in 1966 and the church was to re-register to the Security Department. The Minister of Interior and the Chief of Security delayed the re-registration until Feb. 1969 when it was registered as Evangelical Church Mekane Yesus in Ethiopia. In 1979 the general assembly reverted back to the Ethiopian Evangelical Church Mekane Yesus (EECMY). Emmanuel Abraham 1995, 256–57. The EECMY would also join the WCC 1979, the AACC 1974 and the World Alliance of Reformed Churches. Emmanuel Abraham 1995, 278.

[17] Emmanuel Abraham 1995, 261. The discussion pp. 258–67.

[18] EECMY works for the integration of the work of the missions with legal aspects, financial aspects, organisational or institutional aspect, and theological aspects.

[19] This may be compared to the work of SIM. The local churches were established with the classical three selves in mind. The CMS secretary, Henry Venn, had set as aim that newly

tried to hand over too much, too quickly, to the church. This became a problem, and the general secretary Gudina Tumsa and his fellow church officers criticized the Lutheran World Federation for supporting an unbalanced aid system in which the local church was expecting to serve, without enough resources and personnel forcing the church to prioritise aid – not evangelism.[20]

The national church – earlier more a symbol of unity – now would become an administrative centre for the institutions of the church. The Mekane Yesus had been built as a "bottom up" structure with the respected leaders in Addis Ababa on the helm on a voluntary and layman basis. Now church officers would relate to the state in matters of the institutions and development programmes of the church, a matter which would change the national leadership's relationships to the parishes and synods of the church. It would no longer be mission societies in collaboration with one another, but a national church coordinating and collaborating with the mission societies. The main vehicle for this collaboration was the Committee of Mutual Christian Responsibility (CMCR).[21]

What the officers of Mekane Yesus are arguing in the text in chapter four is what here is called *the ideal of the integrated church*. It was built on the foundations of the work of the missions. The mission model had in the life of the missionaries, and by extension, the lives of Evangelical Christians integrated Christian witness and service. It can be argued that the integration in the mission model took place in each person. In the ideal of the integrated church, the Mekane Yesus were striving to keep these together organisationally, in the church organisation. Christian witness and service were the two elements that *the ECMY Letter* critiques the Lutheran World Federation for having separated in the federation as an ecumenical organisation and in the support rendered to member churches such as Mekane Yesus. The officers argued that witness and service must be kept together because of what man is. Man is holistic, with both bodily and spiritual needs, and man is an agent whose agency should not be violated.

---

established churches should be self-supporting, self-governing and self-propagating. Bevans and Schroeder 2006. The SIM as a mission agency supported the local church to be autonomous and created a parallel structure with hospitals and schools run by the mission.

[20] Bakke 1987, 224. Emmanuel Abraham 1995, 258–67. See *The ECMY Letter* 4.1.

[21] Sæverås 1974. The CMCR focus is the church with the mission agencies supporting the mission of the EECMY.

Discussion on the Mission Model

The mission movement was forwarded by free associations within the churches, organised as mission societies. Revivals within the churches had led to the idea that Christians have the freedom and obligation to spread the Christian faith. People organised themselves freely into mission societies and associations to support the cause of the mission. This led to a debate within the churches as to the appropriateness of free societies versus "church-based" mission organisations. The discussion is of principled importance because of the analogical relationship between missions and aid agencies.

5.2 The Inter-Church Aid Model

The Inter-church Aid Model (1965–1984) was a way to express "practical solidarity" in the ecumenical movement to correspond to the deeper sense of unity, *koinonia*, of the Christian Church. This was especially true of the Orthodox initiative, as part of rebuilding after the fall of the Ottoman Empire, but the motive of mutual aid among churches was there in other parts of the movement as well, in the mission movement as part of the mission, in the Life and Works movement as part of societal concern, and in the Faith and Order as an expression of Christian unity. In Ethiopia, inter-church aid was part of the Emperor's stress on nation-building and solidarity with Africa, but the patriarch also took initiatives of which refugee assistance was one. The Orthodox Church, in collaboration with ecumenical partners, started several aid initiatives on the stance of inter-church aid with refugee assistance, development works, drought relief, and intra-church aid projects.

Ecumenical Initiatives

On 10 January 1919, by the end of the First World War, as the Ottoman Empire was crumbling, the *locum tenens* of the Ecumenical Patriarchate, the Metropolitan Dorotheos of Brussa, proposed to the Holy Synod of the Church of Constantinople to invite all Christian churches to form a "league of churches" in analogy with the League of Nations proposed by the President Wilson. Mutual help between Christian churches was one of the motivating factors for Orthodox churches engaging in the movement.[22]

---

[22] Visser't Hooft 1982, 1–3. Fuchs 2008, 161–62. The Ecumenical Patriarch was invited and sent a delegation to the Lambeth Conference of 1920 inspired by the encyclical and Lambeth's "Appeal to all Christian People." Fuch 2008, 217. A report was drafted by the Theological School

The idea of mutual aid was in Stockholm in 1925 integrated with the idea "to manifest the universal character of the church." Söderblom perceived the church as the Christian spirit of the Christian nations and thus of the newly established League of Nations. Söderblom thought of the Church Catholicos – the universal church – as having three main divisions, the Orthodox Catholic, the Roman Catholic and the Evangelical Catholic. "Protestant" Churches thus conceived as Evangelical Catholic were not thought of as opposing churches to Roman churches, or to Orthodox churches. Thus, a vision of mutual aid in one united Christendom became integral to church engagements in "reconciliation, unity and peace" between the nations.[23] As the World Council of Churches was formed, inter-church aid became an integral part of the organisation from its very beginning.

Ethiopian Initiatives

Emperor Haile Selassie strove for the acceptance of Abyssinia among the European nations and to unite a liberated Africa. An Ethiopian Red Cross Society was established – a sign that Ethiopia joined "the civilised world." The emperor changed the laws to prohibit slavery[24] and applied to become a member of the League of Nations. The Ethiopian Orthodox Church became a founding member of the World Council of Churches, and the Ethiopian patriarch became one of its early presidents. As the ecumenical movement also initiated regional organisations, the church also became part of the All Africa Conference of Churches (AACC). Through its ecumenical engagement, the Orthodox Church at an early

---

of Halki under the leadership of its dean, Germanos Strenopoulos, Metropolitan of Seleukia, approved by the Holy Synod and sent out as an Encyclical in January 1920. A programme of a League of Churches was drawn up in the encyclical with eight points: a mutual understanding of Christian mission without proselytising, mutual help between Christian churches, a common establishment of Christian principles against non-Christian systems, knowledge and study of the churches, reunion of smaller Christian communions, abdication of the churches of all political questions, examinations of differences of faith and order, and union of all the churches as the final purpose. A proposal for organisation was also laid out in the encyclical.

[23] Visser't Hooft 1982, 2, 8, 13; Fuchs 2008, 162–63.

[24] The modern policies of the Emperor such as the prohibition of slavery must have upset those who benefited from the *status quo*. Cf. that the abolishment of slavery in the USA was one of the reasons for the civil war.

stage got involved in refugee assistance,[25] care of children,[26] and various forms of relief and development initiatives.[27] The patriarch instituted the parish movement with the help of assistance from the World Council of Churches and set about modernising church education and organisational structures. These developments showed that Ethiopia as a nation under the leadership of Haile Selassie worked to be part of a larger community of nations and that the church under the patriarch was willing to establish ecumenical relations with churches across the world.

An Orthodox Ecumenical Commitment

These initiatives, though some stemming from state authorities, show an Orthodox commitment to be part of the larger community of churches and nations. This is not a modern stance,[28] but the traditional default stance.[29] The Church in

---

[25] What is now the Refugee and Returnees Affairs Department (RRAD) of the Ethiopian Orthodox Church Development and Inter Church Aid Commission (EOC-DICAC) began its work as the Ethiopian Orthodox Church Inter-Church Aid and Refugee Service Committee (EOC-ICARC) in 1965. The work involved higher education, which later ended, and secondary education for South Sudanese refugees already in 1986. The refugee work was both involved in the urban refugee programme and in camp-based refugee assistance. Main areas of intervention were the provision of secondary and post-secondary education, providing vocational skill training, and schemes aiming at providing livelihoods to increase sustainability and resilience.

[26] Drought Relief: In connection with the severe drought of 1973–74, the Ethiopian Orthodox Church and the *Kinder Not Hilfe* (KNF) from Duisburg in West Germany collaborated to establish the Church Council for Child Care. The council created orphanages which served children who had become orphans due to the famine. Eshetu Mehretu "The Ethiopian Orthodox Tewahedo Church Council for Child Care" in *Maedot* 1, 1983, 43. The council work with donor agencies such as BftW, *Algemeen Diakonal Bureau*, and Tabor Society Heidelberg.

[27] EOC-DICAC was established by legal notice No. 415 in 1972 as the development wing of the EOTC. In April 2013 it was reregistered as an Ethiopian Resident Charity, license no. 1560, according to the new proclamation of Charities and Societies from 2008.

[28] EOTC is a reminder of distant times and contemporary realities. As keepers of the Christian tradition, what appears distant for the historian may yet be a living tradition.

[29] Atiya 168, 153. Ethiopian Orthodox Christians stand for generosity and tolerance as illustrated in the story of how the Ethiopian king acted when the first followers of the prophet Muhammed fled Mecca. The Kingdom of Axum received refugees from the early followers of Mohammed. The king received the refugees and listened to their plea. He initiated the first theological dialogue with Muslims recorded in history by delineating the commonalities and making a distinction between Christians and Muslims. Finally, the king did not allow their persecutors to seize the Muslims in their custody, but instead gave them refuge and allowed them to settle in the land under his rule. Atiya 1968, 147 stresses how Ethiopia survived the coming of Islam in contrast to many other Christian territories. The coming of Islam was pivotal to changes in the region.

Ethiopia has a long history of social engagement in the "Greater Ethiopia" area and has had from its early roots a public character. This was far from a model of separation of church and state. Even though there are historical examples of forceful conversions to Christianity, the main model of Orthodox witness has been one of attraction and long-term engagement with people.[30] The historical closeness of church, state and society in historical Ethiopia is important since we are dealing with contemporary refugee assistance which requires a close collaboration of churches and states.[31]

Inter-Church Aid

The Development and Inter-Church Aid Commission of the Ethiopian Orthodox Church (EOC-DICAC) was established in 1972 as the development wing of the Orthodox Church. The commission worked in areas ranging from education and health to livelihoods, relief, rehabilitation, and disaster risk reduction with support from the World Council of Churches and development partners including UN agencies, EU, USAID, and the World Bank. EOC-DICAC also obtained funds from government sources such as the Ministry of Health.[32]

EOC-DICAC also have had special projects strengthening the church and the church community. Intra-church projects would for example promote the use of antiretroviral drugs (ARTI) in rallies led by archbishops, or the patriarch, to show the compatibility of modern drugs in combating disease with the church's teaching and traditional healing practices such as the usage of Holy Water (*tsebel*). The

---

The reception of the Muslim refugees became a symbol of good relations between Christians and Muslims, retold on numerous occasions of Christian-Muslim relations. Later as Muslim influence in the region increased, relations became more strained. Arab traders eventually controlled the trade along the coastline, the ways down the Nile, and occupied the Red Sea islands. As Egypt was conquered by an Arab army in 642 AD, communications with the Byzantine Empire decreased for the church in Axum. As the armies also pushed south to conquer Nubia, they were initially not successful. A *Baqt* was established, and the military advance south was suspended until ca 1250 AD. A *Baqt* is a treaty made by an Arab ruler cf. Eng. *pact*.

[30] The Christian state tolerated Muslims to practice their faith and conflict between Christian rulers and Muslim subjects were often not religious in character, contrary to Western beliefs, as Rubenson 2009 has shown.

[31] Rubenson 2009.

[32] EOC-DICAC work on emergency relief and rehabilitation, livelihoods, environmental protection and rehabilitation, climate change adaptation and DRR, water, sanitation and hygiene, peace and reconciliation, health and nutrition, HIV/AIDS prevention and control, response to gender-based violence and traditional harmful practices, refugee and returnees support (through RRAD), education, social accountability (public service delivery).

church has also been able to mobilise and train youth through the extensive Sunday School Movement. The church aimed at developing local development programs run by the clergy through the new parish council organisation. This venture was supported by the World Council of Churches and its Commission for the Churches Participation in Development (WCC-CCPD) which signed an inter-church aid agreement with the parish council department of the church in 1976. This system was utilised in 1983 for the relief programmes supported by the World Council of Churches and other donors.[33]

Sovereignty, Modernity and Unity

During the nineteenth century and first half of the twentieth century, the rulers of Ethiopia aimed for sovereignty, modernity, and unity. To achieve those goals, the emperors drew on a strong central authority and in addition sought the support of external powers. The emperors were setting up provincial administrations, established a modern legal framework, modernised the army, worked to bring in a system of modern education, were eager to use modern technology, and attempted to nationalise and thus to control the Orthodox Church. The work of foreign mission societies, as discussed earlier, should be understood in this Ethiopian political context. Missionaries were tolerated, and at times encouraged, to reach the aim of education and modernising the vast areas under imperial control.[34]

During the rule of Emperor Haile Selassie, there was a ruse of Ethiopian nationalism, and Haile Selassie worked hard for an *autocephalous* church, freed from the authority of the Coptic Patriarchate. The Ethiopian Patriarchate thus

---

[33] *Maedot* 1984, 28.

[34] Adejumobi 2007. Levine 2000. Prunier 2015, 7–9. Tolo 1998, 109–111. Three Emperors: Tewodros II, Yohannes IV and Menelik II, restored the authority of the Emperor, attempted to reunify the church, expand the empire, and protect their interests from European colonial powers and Muslim nationalism through a conscious policy of bringing in European technology to achieve their goal of controlling the empire from the centre. Emperor Tewodros II (r. 1855–1868) aimed to restore the Solomonic dynasty and introduce peace and justice after the *Zemene Mesafint*. Yohannes IV enforced religious unity in 1874 with a unionist creed, *tewahido*, in line with the Coptic Church, while Menelik (r. 1889–1913) was expanding the empire with the help of weapons bought from Italy. Menelik also founded a new capital, Addis Ababa, installed water, electricity and telephone and established the first railway project between the capital and the coast. This was after the Berlin Conference in 1885 when the European powers had divided the African continent into zones of European national interest. In 1896, Emperor Menelik won the Battle of Adwa, curtailing the colonial ambitions of Italy, and sending a message of symbolic importance that the European powers were not unbeatable. This was one of the reasons for the Ethiopianism movement of African independent churches.

established also included both the title of *abuna* of Axum and the title of *itchege* and abbot of Debre Libanos to also secure the allegiance of the monks and nuns in the one person of the patriarch. Thus, the Emperor secured control over the church in a way not possible earlier in its history.[35] Haile Selassie also took an impression of the missionaries of his times and attempted to modernise the church in various manners establishing modern theological education, encouraging the Sunday School movement, and initiating Orthodox charity organisations.[36]

Discussion on the Inter-Church Aid Model

The Inter-Church Aid Model as a way to express "practical solidarity" was deeply rooted in the ecumenical movement.[37] As this model went beyond the mission model of voluntary service and witness into nation-building and development, there was more collaboration between church and state. In Ethiopia, the imperial regime strove to keep its sovereignty and unity while aspiring to bring about a modern society. Initiatives were taken by Haile Selassie to this end, several of which included imperial involvement in church affairs. The Orthodox Church by becoming autocephalous became more national. The reformed office of the patriarch became more tied to the imperial office. The emperor strove to balance the political and ecclesial needs. The patriarch strove to keep the public profile of the church, also in modern times. The World Council of Churches and other ecumenical actors worked with the church to find new organisational structures in a changing time.

If the Orthodox Church at times was struggling to enculturate the innovations of modernisation and were pushed by the emperor to do so, the Ethiopian Evangelical Church Mekane Yesus was born with the "DNA" of modern development. The work of the missions was built on the idea of integration of social services and the sharing of the Christian gospel. As the missionaries were building schools and clinics and shared the gospel through their lives and teaching, they inspired the people they taught to follow their example.[38]

---

[35] On the relations between church and state such as separation, the primacy of the ecclesial over temporal authorities (sacerdotalism), the subordination of ecclesial to temporal authorities (caesaropapism or Erastianism), and symphony. Bretherton 2019, 232. Cf. Tamrat 1972, 156.

[36] Atiya 1968, 166. Haile Selassie was not only inspired by missionaries but also developments in the Coptic Church in Egypt. Suriel 2017. Prunier 2015, 83.

[37] Cf. Grenstedt 2000 on "Ethiopian Evangelical Solidarity", e.g. 2000, 25–27.

[38] Arén 1974 and 1999. On "DNA" in ecclesiology, Fahlgren 2006a.

5.3 The International Crisis Model

The subsequent ecumenical approach, here called *the international crisis model* (1974–1991), gave less emphasis on the leadership and initiatives of the Ethiopian churches, Christian witness, and nation-building, and more on coordination of aid agencies for the survival of people and with the people, the churches as churches. The background was the revolutionary changes in Ethiopia, which threatened both life in society and church. I would, therefore, see the period of the Derg regime as witnessing a new model of ecumenical collaboration. I will give this model more space here because of the parallels with the ACT approach.

1960s Radical Student Movement

In the 1960s a radical student movement grew among university and high school students in Ethiopia.[39] The students viewed the world as a struggle between progressive forces and world imperialism.[40] There was in the student movement a divisive issue: the question of nationalities.[41] The new ideology of Marxism saw Ethiopia as "an aggregation of numerous ethnic liberation movements" and several groups gave priority to self-determination of nationalities. This naturally led to the

---

[39] The new educational system was struggling financially, pushing to increase the number of students without increasing the budget. The result was more graduates with lesser abilities. As the job market was unable to swallow the number of graduates, disgruntled graduates turned to a new ideology. Prunier 2015, 212. "Ethiopian intellectuals who searched for a new cultural script thought they had found it in Marxism, rather than in the vision of a liberal democracy that acknowledged both the rights of all citizens and the values of their constituent cultural traditions." Levine 2000, XVII. Adejumobi 2007. A fascinating account of the political discussion in a university setting between Marxist and Evangelical students is given in Tibebe Eshete (2009) *The Evangelical Movement in Ethiopia: Resistance and Resilience.*

[40] Whereas intellectuals of the many liberation movements in Africa were guided by "worldwide left-wing ideologies such as Pan-Arabism or Third-Worldism" in an attempt to be liberated from the colonial powers, Prunier 2015, 101, in Ethiopia, according to Harold Marcus, radical students were interested in trying out the "the theoretical egalitarianism of unproved [*sic*] Marxist-Leninist models of development", Marcus 2002, 176. Prunier 2015, 210. They wanted land reform, giving *land to the tiller* at a time when commercial agriculture was beginning to cause a rural social crisis by enclosing common pasture, limiting access to water and evicting tenants or raising their rents. During the 1960s, the costs of cultural devastation, freedom and loss of human life in the communist regimes of Russia, China and Cuba were still largely unknown by the rest of world, which made the radical movement among intellectuals possible. Marcus 2002, 176.

[41] Prunier 2015, 258. Differences of opinion on this issue polarised and split the movement.

formation of insurgent groups according to ethnicity.[42] The Eritrean Liberation Front (ELF) was established by a group of Muslim exiles in Cairo.[43] Oromo farmers and Somali herders rebelled in 1963 and 1970 in response to new taxes on land and animals.[44] The government had not undertaken social and economic measures to win the allegiance of the people in Eritrea and Bale.[45] The ambitions in Mogadishu were on a collision course with Ethiopia – refusing to sign Article 4b of the Organisation of African Unity (OAU) charter which protected the set colonial borders.[46]

The Revolution of 1974

The revolution of 1974 and subsequent events had dramatic consequences for the Orthodox Church. There was a radical disestablishment with the introduction of a draft constitution separating church and state in 1974.[47] Needing support from the Orthodox, the government tried to suppress the church leadership into submission, arresting, imprisoning, and executing the patriarch *Abuna* Theophilos in 1979.[48] There were vast degrees of nationalisation of church property and institutions. For a church dependent on income from the agrarian sector for the upkeep of buildings and the large clergy, this was a serious blow. As seen in chapter four, already in 1972, Parish councils, had been established. During the Derg regime,

---

[42] Levine 2000, XVIII. Donald Levine emphasises that the lack of a vision of unity led to this ideology. For it to function there was a need to find an "oppressor" among the people groups to be liberated from. They found this in the image of the "wicked Amhara". For Levine, on the contrary, to see Ethiopia as the sum of separate ethnic groups living in parallel societies is "simply counterfactual". Levine 2000, XIII.

[43] Marcus 2002, 174–78. Initially, the leadership saw their efforts in the light of the pan-Muslim movement. Sudan and South Yemen facilitated arms deals to the front. Marcus 2002, 178. Later, in the 1960s, nationalist agitation in the Christian highlands of Eritrea changed the perspective. Marcus 2002, 177–78.

[44] Marcus 2002, 178. The rebellions were crushed, but the people got involved with "the politics of Greater Somalia". Radio Mogadishu became a vehicle calling for both Somalis and Oromos to Muslim unity against the Amhara under the framework of Somali nationalism.

[45] Marcus 2002, 179. Haile Selassie who wanted to appear as a symbol of a free and independent Africa had allowed the establishment of local sharia courts but was unwilling to allow a renewed discussion on the role of the Muslim communities in Ethiopia. Prunier 2015, 102.

[46] The plans of a Greater Somalia included Djibouti, the Ethiopian Ogaden, and the Kenyan Northern Frontier District. Prunier 2015, 221.

[47] Eide 1996, 139.

[48] Nigussu Legesse 2014, 282.

these councils were amended to secure government control of the local church economy.[49]

For the monasteries, the nationalization hit even harder. As farmers, the monks and nuns were denied the land they had been cultivating and often no alternative was offered but begging.[50] The monastic communities had previously been self-sustaining by working their lands and had also been able to provide hospitality and care to those who were travelling, sick, elderly or living with disabilities. The impoverishment of monastic communities, which came as a result of changing policies, hostile attitudes, and the subsequent civil war, had not only had a detrimental effect on these communities but on the whole society in terms of loss of religious and cultural values and tangible support of vulnerable individuals to whom the monasteries became unable to render support.[51]

The revolution was at first welcomed by many Evangelicals who saw the possibility of a more democratic government granting religious freedom and land reform.[52] During the Ethio-Somali war, however, the regime turned to the Soviet Union and Cuba for support. *The Red Terror* showed that the Derg regime under Colonel Mengistu Haile Mariam had chosen path. Church buildings, institutions and land were nationalized and Christians like Emmanuel Abraham, *Qes* Iteffa Gobena and the Catholic *Abuna* Berhane Yesus were put in prison, while others like *Qes* Gudina Tumsa and *Abuna* Theophilos were killed in 1979.[53] Pentecostal

---

[49] These councils now made it possible for the faithful to contribute to the upkeep of churches. Particularly in urban areas this secured an economic basis for church activities and property. It also introduced tensions between the laity and the clergy in church affairs as it opened new questions of authority and structure into the Ethiopian Orthodox Church. Suriel 2017 for a discussion on tensions between the laity and the clergy in the context of the modern society.

[50] Persoon unpublished written manuscript from presentation 2006. This also touches upon the fact that other aspects of the cultural life of the church, which earlier had been supported by the royal family and the aristocracy, suffered during the new regime. Rural monasteries, churches, art, and the cultural heritage were left without protectors and benefactors. EOC-DICAC 2009, 3, the churches and monasteries were also traditional guardians of the natural environment with "protection of nature being an expression of the recognition of the sanctity of holy sites". The impoverishment of the monasteries led to an "age of ecological crisis".

[51] Bakke 1986, 87–103. The institution of begging had traditionally been used as a way to support students in particular areas of the educational system. Local boys had been supported by their community through a system asking for food during the early stages of their education.

[52] Many Evangelicals in the south, in the beginning, became important local leaders as they had experience of democratic leadership and were trusted by the local population.

[53] E.g. *Qes* Iteffa Gobena, president of EECMY, and archbishop and later cardinal of the Ethiopian Catholic Church, *Abuna* Berhane Yesus, spent three years in prison together.

churches were closed, while most Orthodox Churches, and some Mekane Yesus, remained open.

During the military regime, as Christians struggled with persecution, for being Christians, or standing up against abuse, how did the churches cope? Seminars were held to teach Christians how to understand Marxism and to be rooted in their faith.[54] Evangelical Christians created an ecumenical council, the Council for Co-operation of Churches in Ethiopia (CCCE), in 1976, but were forced to go for a smaller Evangelical fellowship resulting in the establishment of the Evangelical Churches Fellowship of Ethiopia (ECFE). The Mekane Yesus opened their doors for other Christians to worship in their churches. Many churches created power-ful underground churches. After the model in Eastern Europe and Asia, Chris-tians met in small house churches.

The Soviet Union – through its aid – wanted to see a People's Republic in Ethiopia and worked with the Derg in that direction, as now the army, and not an emperor was ruling. The Workers Party of Ethiopia was established in September 1984 to coincide with the tenth anniversary of the revolution. While preparation of a huge anniversary celebration took place, the civil war in combination with another drought had led the country into famine. In order to alleviate the famine, the regime would have to rely on Western and American aid.[55] The famine took place in the midst of civil war and in territories sympathising with the cause of the rebels.[56]

The civil war and consequent famine led several hundred thousand people to seek refuge elsewhere. Many fled to the Sudan, where they were catered by human-itarian agencies. From Sudan, many Ethiopians and Eritreans continued to Europe and North America. In 1980, the Refugee Act allowed these asylum seekers to mi-grate to the United States.[57] As with the drought in the 1970s, the famine was an important contributing factor to the downfall of the Derg regime. The churches

---

[54] The seminars at the Mekane Yesus Seminary aimed at analysing socialism and share expe-riences from other countries suffering from communism. Speakers came from LWF, e.g. Jonas Jonsson, an expert on the Chinese revolution. Eide 2000, 116-17. Gemechu Olana 2005, 85–87.

[55] Prunier 2015, 222–23. For a regime that had used famine to gain control of power, a famine under its watch was a disaster for public relations. In the midst of the famine, the government tried to relocate and resettle the starving people of Wollo and Tigray in Gambella and Gamo Gofa leading to a second disaster, when a poorly planned and implemented operation brought farmers to an unknown environment plagued by malaria without the needed support and infra-structure, leading to tension with the local communities.

[56] Prunier 2015, 223.

[57] Prunier 2015, 53.

and their relief organisations delivered aid both to government-controlled areas and non-government-held areas bringing relief items from Sudan and later on from the port in Eritrea. The Lutheran World Federation World Service and other Christian relief organisations were needed to counter the famine in 1984–1985, and that put pressure on the government to show "religious freedom."[58]

Civil War as the Context

The context of the drought of the 1980s was the civil war between the military Marxist regime of the Derg and the Marxist *guérilla* movements of the regions.[59] The church-based agencies were able to mobilise support from their constituencies, in terms of their churches, nations and states. Most of the relief came from Western governments even though the military regime in its policies and warfare was aligned with the Soviet Union and Cuba. Through Addis Ababa, relief was channelled through the churches. This made it easier for the US than it would have been if support had gone through government channels. The "civil society" grew as a result. The Ethiopian government was not willing to follow the humanitarian principles of allowing aid also to reach rebel-held territories. The war and the drought combined created a humanitarian crisis of gigantic proportions. People fleeing those territories would receive aid but also be subject to government plans of relocation to other areas. The plans had both humanitarian and political objectives: to relocate people to less densely populated areas and to remove them from the influence of the *guérillas*.

---

[58] Tibebe Eshete 2009 on EECMY 232–40, on Ethiopian Kale Heywet Church (EKHC) 240–51, on Meserete Kristos Church 253–63, and Mulu Wongel Church 263–72.

[59] The famine of 1972 could have been averted, but the systems were not in place and the governor failed in his duty to the people. So did the emperor who failed to put in place a system of governance in place of the feudal structures of old. The centralisation efforts of the imperial government had not brought prosperity to the regions. The churches set the alarm, mobilised their agencies and called for external assistance. The response came. Too late to avert the worst forms of famine but it gave alleviation for the suffering of thousands. The famine became the end of the imperial regime, but not to the unity of the regions of Ethiopia.

Ecumenical Coordination and Collaboration

This period contained several different organisations for ecumenical coordination and collaboration in what I call the international crisis model: Lutheran World Federation – World Service Ethiopia (1973–),[60] Christian Relief and Development Association (CRDA 1973–), The Joint Relief Partnership (JRP 1984–2005), The Emergency Relief Desk (ERD 1975–1992 and the informal network *Kontakt der Kontinenten* (KdK 1985–2010).[61] Among these, the Christian Relief and Development Agency was probably the most important in the 1970s while the Joint Relief Partnership filled that role in the 1980s and common organisations. The Lutheran World Federation, some organisations that are now ACT members, and the Catholic Relief Services (CRS) were among those organisations that were able to mobilise support for the Christian Relief and Development Agency and the Joint Relief Partnership.

The Christian Relief and Development Association (CRDA)

At the beginning of the famine in Wollo and Tigray, twenty representatives of churches and missions with a few additional humanitarian organisations[62] created the Christian Relief Committee in mid-1973. In September 1974 a new name was given, the Christian Relief and Development Association (CRDA) with the idea "to promote and encourage relief and development activities in Ethiopia." The government created an agency for the relief work, The Relief and Rehabilitation Commission (RRC) in August 1974 and set up an agreement with the Christian Relief and Development Association in March 1975. The members shared information and were able to receive funds and assistance through the secretariat. This mechanism for monthly allocation of funds between members in general meetings strengthened the coordination role of the Christian Relief and Development

---

[60] The church president, Emmanuel Abraham, on behalf of the Mekane Yesus Church, called upon LWF to assist in the famine 1974. In order to reach remote areas, LWF bought small aeroplanes bought for food bombing. In the second famine in 1984, LWF was able to bring 25 trucks filled with seeds for the farmers who had spent their seeds as emergency rations. When the humanitarian crisis was over, LWF followed up with development work in the same areas where they had engaged with humanitarian relief work. This was a time for large project of water works and feats of engineering to bring water to the fields.

[61] Henrich and Willemse 2015.

[62] This included Including SIM, EKHC Development Programme, and St Matthew's Anglican Church. The humanitarian agencies were Concern, Save the Children Fund-UK and Oxfam-UK. By December 1973, they were able to hire a full-time coordinator for the work.

Association.[63] In time, the association also gained the capacity to maintain vehicles, purchase seeds and provide transport services. This reduced the cost of duplication of efforts.[64] The association continued to play a role after the emergency as this statement from northern ACT members in Ethiopia shows: "CRDA has a unique valuable role to represent the NGOs and CSOs including the International NGOs. This representational role is vital in Ethiopia since the government continually attempts to limit the operational environment."[65]

The Joint Relief Partnership (JRP)

The LWF World Service Programme, which was responding to the famine in 1984, invited other church-based relief agencies in a joint appeal for Africa – the Churches' Drought Action Africa – to be able to draw funds, coordinate a better response and have a larger impact across Africa.[66] As part of the larger African response, the Joint Relief Partnership (JRP) was formed for the work in Ethiopia in 1986 with the American-based Catholic Relief Services (CRS) as the lead agency responsible for coordination and logistics and with the Ethiopian Catholic Secretariat (ECS), the Lutheran World Federation (LWF), the Ethiopian Orthodox Church (EOC-DICAC), and the Ethiopian Evangelical Church Mekane Yesus (EECMY) as operating agencies.[67]

The international members – the Catholic Relief Services and LWF World Service – made use of their donor relationships with USAID and the European Commission to acquire resources for the programme. Member agencies took the supervising responsibility for particular provinces. Within that mandate of supervision, there was flexibility for member agencies to pass on food to other agencies

---

[63] In addition to the coordination, in 1982, the CRDA was able to field its own team of four nurses to run an intensive feeding program at Ibnat.

[64] Bennett 2013, 31–39. When the association was legally registered in 1975 it had 22 members, by 1988 it had 53, 28 agencies of which were not related to churches, and the remainder were local church-based agencies, foreign missions, and church affiliated agencies. Some of the agencies: Christian Aid, Catholic Fund for Overseas Development (CAFOD) and Band Aid in the UK, Church World Service and USA for Africa in the USA, EOC-DICAC, Interchurch Coordination Committee for Development Projects (ICCO) and Catholic Organisation for Joint Financing of Development Programmes (CEBEMO) in the Netherlands, *Brot für die Weld* and *Zentralstelle fur Entwicklungshilfe* (Protestant Association for Cooperation in Development), (EZE) in Germany, DanChurchAid in Denmark and Cardinal Leger and Peace and Development in Canada.

[65] 2008 08 05 Minutes of August 5 E8 Meeting.

[66] Carter 2011, 65.

[67] By mid-1985, 29 agencies were affiliated to the partnership programme.

within that province. A standard distribution method was adapted and used by all.[68] In addition to the common relief activities, member agencies could independently work on rehabilitation and development activities. The partnership never had an independent legal status, which ensured the autonomy of the member agencies and limited the power of the secretariat.[69]

For the European Commission and the USA, the strong anti-western stance and the Marxist policies of the government were making it difficult to support the relief operations of the Relief and Rehabilitation Commission (RRC).[70] In addition, the controversial resettlement programme and the high army expenses did not make it easier for Western donor countries to wholeheartedly support the work of the commission. These are some of the reasons why during the mid-1980s era, there was a shift from supporting government relief efforts to independent humanitarian agencies. It is estimated that circa 70% of food and 50% of non-food aid was channelled through non-government organisations during 1985–1991.[71]

The Emergency Relief Desk (ERD) 1975–1992 and "KdK" (1985–2010)

During the civil war, humanitarian agencies were unable to reach rebel-held territories with humanitarian relief. A few Christian agencies, led by the Norwegian Church Aid (NCA), therefore set up a consortium, formally in the name of the Sudan Council of Churches (SCC), and collaborated with the secular relief agencies of the liberation fronts: the Eritrean Relief Agency (ERA), the Relief Society of Tigray (REST), and the Oromo Relief Agency (ORA). As mentioned earlier, this was at that time a controversial cross-border operation. It challenged humanitarian and United Nations notions of sovereignty and neutrality by operating

---

[68] The distribution method was based upon the Nutrition Intervention Programme (NIP).

[69] Bennett 2013, 37. The initial name was "Churches Drought Action Africa/Ethiopia" (CDAA/E). The Ethiopian Orthodox Church joined the group at a later stage. Bennet 2013, 38: "The JRP showed how a consortium of Northern NGOs capable of accessing the substantial food aid resources of the USA and the EC, coupled with the infrastructure of local churches, can mobilise and distribute substantial quantities of relief and rehabilitation resources."

[70] The Relief and Rehabilitation Commission (RRC) of the federal government coordinated and carried out national relief activities. In the late 1984 to early 1985, a massive volume of assistance came from Western governments in response to the famine. The commission which had a predominant position was highly centralised and many decisions were taken in Addis Ababa, rather than at the field level.

[71] Bennet 2013, 30, 60.

in areas not controlled by the government and through the use of community-based organisations (CBOs) in collaboration with the liberation fronts.[72]

As a result of the monopoly of the relief operations held by ERA and REST inside Eritrea and Tigray, the role of international NGOs was effectively as conduits between donors and ERA and REST, which the international agencies referred to as "implementing agencies" or "implementing partners."[73]

The implication of Bennett's judgement above is that transnational aid agencies empowered the liberation fronts by using the Eritrean Relief Agency and the Relief Society of Tigray as channels of distribution. The political importance was hidden by referring to these organisations as "implementing agencies", i.e. the conduit of the policies of the Christian agencies.[74]

Discussion on the International Crisis Model and the Issue of Solidarity

In the Emergency Relief Desk, there was tension between the idea of humanitarian solidarity versus political solidarity. What it shows is that what began as a relief engagement for starving communities led to extended development work, and diplomatic efforts in an attempt to secure a peaceful development. It was therefore not humanitarian work in the sense perceived as only temporary life-saving relief work without further social and political engagement in the sense of "emergency humanitarianism", i.e. humanitarian in its most limited sense.[75]

---

[72] ERD provided some 685 000 tonnes of food to ERA, REST and a small amount to the ORA 1981–1992, Bennett 2013, 30. Bennett states that ERD was formed in 1981.

[73] Bennett 2013, 29.

[74] The successful operations of the agencies behind the Emergency Relief Desk, performed in the name of the churches, but operationally in collaboration with civilian arms of the liberation fronts, gave the active Christian aid agencies a moral leverage towards the leaders of the liberation fronts once they were in the process of taking over the governmental powers in Ethiopia and Eritrea. This gave room for an engagement of "unconventional mediation effort" by the local heads of the agencies, the so-called "KdK"-group, in relation to the heads of the liberation fronts which they had come to know during the relief efforts of the civil war. The effort was informal rather than formal and Ethiopian and Eritrean churches were consciously left out of the process. The aim was to convince the new political leadership of the benefits of a peaceful agreement rather than fighting out their differences with military force. The study by Henrich and Willemse shows how the relief concern with sustained relationship with the communities led to an informal political engagement for the pursuit of long-term peace and reconciliation. Henrich and Willemse 2015.

[75] Barnett 2011, 4, 39. Barnett's distinction between what he calls "emergency humanitarianism and "alchemical humanitarianism". See (3.3, s. 169, and 173 in this thesis.)

What is also of interest to this study is the relief engagement with the communities of the liberation fronts was done without the explicit support of the Ethiopian churches, officially under the umbrella of the Sudanese churches, and therefore the personal engagement of experienced local heads of agencies were able to work diplomatically without the pursuit of support from the local churches, i.e. the Mekane Yesus and the Orthodox Church. The churches perceived that these Christian agencies understood themselves as having an independent authority from that of Ethiopian churches by working in rebel-held territories outside of the control of the Derg, establishing and working through relief wings of liberation fronts, and negotiating with the political actors of the liberation fronts without the explicit support of the churches and their leadership. The churches were at the time suppressed by the Derg regime and would see the meddling of Christian relief agencies in matters of national politics as a potential threat to the Christian communities and the churches.

The rebel leaders who were going into governmental leadership or opposition, thus had the experience of heads of relief agencies acting as diplomatic agents involved directly in political negotiations of the future Ethiopia and Eritrea. Relief did not necessarily entail only humanitarian relief, but a foothold on which a platform could be formed, not necessarily in the interest of a particular party, or in the interest of the agencies, but still a political platform. For a liberal mindset, this would not be an issue, but for those who perceive that political influence should rest in the hands of the few, it would constitute a challenge. This experience may possibly have impacted the way the leadership of the Ethiopian People's Revolutionary Democratic Front (EPRDF) interpreted the role of civil society organisations in the contested 2005 election.[76]

5.4 ACT in Ethiopia

The idea of ACT (1994–) was initiated by the ecumenical movement as a way to express the practical engagement of the churches in relief, development, and advocacy works. The idea of ACT included both the experience of a sense of international church unity achieved through the World Council of Churches and an urgency to act in the world for its healing and unity. In Ethiopia, many aid agencies who joined ACT had already collaborated for years under different constellations. It was therefore natural to join hands under this new umbrella. The end of the

---

[76] CRDA was informing communities about electoral processes.

Derg regime, and the beginning of the EPRDF, was one of rehabilitation and re-building after the devastations of the civil war.

In May 1991, the liberation fronts behind the fall of the Derg – the EPRDF – were confronted by an economy in crisis. This coalition did not include the Eritrean People's Liberation Front (EPLF) since the goal of the EPLF was to sever Eritrea from Ethiopia, and not to take part in its development. Several political parties were created on regional and ethnic basis in order to form a coalition government. Regional elections were organised, but the loose alliance was immediately challenged by the Oromo Liberation Front's (OLF) decision to leave the collaboration and take up arms.[77] The Ethiopian People's Revolutionary Democratic Front (EPRDF), which was initially dominated by the Tigrayan People's Liberation Front (TPLF), took over an economy dominated by the state. The aim of TPLF, coming from a radical Marxist movement, was to push for a revolutionary democracy where "development is first of all a political process" and all politics is dominated by the ruling party.[78] The new regime was encouraging markets, opening up trade and privatising state farms and particular state holdings, but kept key sectors such as banking, insurance, and main utilities in the control of the state. Apart from direct holdings, the regime also controlled parastatals through endowments, such as the Endowment Fund for the Rehabilitation of Tigray (EFFORT) managed by the Relief Society of Tigray (REST).[79]

ACT Ethiopia Forum

When ACT International was founded in 1995 to increase humanitarian coordination among its member agencies, the members in Ethiopia had already coordinated relief effectively under the Christian Relief and Development Association, the Joint Relief Partnership, and other collaborative schemes. In 2007, ACT Development was established to complement ACT International, and a first consultative meeting was held to establish ACT Development Ethiopia. After successive meetings, a draft memorandum was produced and a representative from Geneva was welcomed for a consultation in 2008 at Norwegian Church Aid in Addis Ababa.[80]

---

[77] Prunier 2015, 273.

[78] Prunier 2015, 360. Prunier 2015, 306 "The developmental state project is premised on the belief that a government can both be developmentally activist and also avoid the 'socially wasteful rent-seeking activities' associated with a dominant public sector."

[79] Prunier 2015, 362.

[80] Minutes of ACT-D/Ethiopia Consultative meeting Feb 13, 2008.

By that time the ACT members in Ethiopia had worked for four years to es-tablish an ACT International Forum in Ethiopia. Neither the Christian Relief and Development Association, nor the Ethiopian Catholic Church, were able to gain membership in ACT Development because each member agency of ACT had to relate to a member church of either the World Council of Churches or the Lu-theran World Federation. The reasons were ecumenical. ACT was seen as some-thing developing from the churches. For these reasons, the already established forms of ecumenical collaborations with the broader civil society (CRDA) and ec-clesial partners, such as the Ethiopian Catholic Church, did not enter formally into the new organisation of ACT.[81]

This was of concern not only for the Ethiopian church member agencies, but also for the European members of ACT, who wanted both the effectiveness of the past and a broad ecumenical basis.[82] In 2011 as ACT Alliance brought together the relief coordination of ACT International and the "livelihood-building" of ACT Development, the members of ACT in Ethiopia established the ACT Ethiopia Forum.[83]

European ACT Members: "Six Agencies Group" or "E8"

The six European ACT Agencies, which later became eight, in 2006,[84] were work-ing with 64 partners altogether, out of which only four were church partners. This

---

[81] In Ethiopia a first consultative meeting to establish an ACT Development Ethiopia was held Aug 21, 2007. Mrs Jill Hawkey from ACT Development in Geneva was welcomed to con-sultative meeting Feb 13, 2008 at NCA in Addis Ababa. CRDA's request for membership in ACT Development or observer status in ACT Development Geneva had been rejected. The rea-son was the insistence on membership in either WCC or LWF for reasons of church unity. For the same reason, the Roman Catholic Church is not a member of ACT. In Geneva, the work had begun with a planned merger of the ACT International and Development. Minutes of ACT-D/Ethiopia Consultative meeting Feb 13, 2008.

[82] "Similar challenge has been faced in the ACT Development forum membership. The local context invites widening the membership space while the Geneva guidelines limit the space for only registered members. It may be necessary to follow ACT/Geneva guidelines but we should also look at our own local context." 2008 08 05 Minutes of August 5 E8 Meeting.

[83] The forum is also called ACT Alliance Ethiopia Forum.

[84] The Six Agencies Group in 2009 invited other members of what has been called "E8", i.e. a European collaboration of ACT members, i.e. FinnChurchAid and the Church of Sweden Aid to participate even though these agencies were not registered in Ethiopia. (*Hilfswerk der Evange-lischen Kirchen Schweiz* (HEKS), also called Swiss Inter-Church Aid, was also invited. The Swiss agency was by that time represented in Ethiopia but had not joined the group. "It has been a

created uncertainties regarding how the group with its many partners would relate to the new initiative of ACT Development since a vast majority of the partners were not ACT members.[85] The work of the European group was not intended to weaken the new ACT initiatives, on the contrary. Capacity building of national ACT members was high on the agenda. One example was to introduce EOC-DICAC, EECMY-DASSC, and LWF World Service to new accountability initiatives like the Humanitarian Accountability Partnership (HAP).[86] In this context, it is also important to mention the long-standing Christian Relief and Development Association engagement of the members of the Six Agencies Group. One of the aspects of these agencies and their internal collaboration is continuing efforts to find suitable means to strengthen the work of civil society organisations and locally based aid agencies.[87]

ACT Appeals

In Ethiopia, in 2014, there were eleven member organisations in the ACT Ethiopia Forum.[88] Since the establishment of ACT, several relief appeals have been released.

---

challenge to find a balance between Europe-based criteria and local context. For instance HEKS is a member of ACT Development and it is an active player within the ACT International Forum here in Ethiopia. However, HEKS is not a member of the E8 in Europe. What will be the harm to include it in the E8 Ethiopia? The decision is that it is up to HEKS to ask for membership to the Ethiopia E8 group." 2008 08 05 Minutes of August 5 E8 Meeting.

[85] Six Agencies Group 14 April 2008 *Six Agencies Group: The Lead Agency Concept*. PPT.

[86] 2009 02 09 Eyasu email to E8 members *re* HAP training. DCA invited to training on the HAP-standard for four days, 10–14 May 2009.

[87] "Almost all E8 members (except BftW) do have partnership agreement including membership in CRDA. In fact EED, CA, and ICCO have been long term institutional donors for CRDA and it is with this role that the issue of CRDA is raised at the meeting." 2008 08 05 Minutes of August 5 E8 Meeting.

[88] Two of those are local church-based members, the Ethiopian Evangelical Church Mekane Yesus Development and Social Service Commission (EECMY-DASSC) and the Ethiopian Orthodox Church Development and Inter Church Aid Commission (EOC-DICAC). The rest are northern faith-based or church-based agencies: Christian Aid from UK (CA), Church of Sweden (CoS) from Sweden, DanChurchAid (DCA) from Denmark, The Swiss Inter-Church Aid (HEKS) from Switzerland, ICCO Cooperation (ICCO) from the Netherlands, International Orthodox Christian Charities (IOCC) from USA, Lutheran World Service World Service Ethiopia (LWF) a Geneva based humanitarian wing of the Lutheran World Federation, the Norwegian Church Aid (NCA) from Norway, and finally the Protestant Agency for Diakonie and Development (PADD) from Germany. PADD was created through the merger of Bread for the World (BftW) and EED. Internationally it also includes the humanitarian wing: *Diakonie Katastrophenhilfe* (DKH).

The last appeal with support from the WCC Emergencies Desk was in 1995 with an ACT Committee set up in Ethiopia in 1998. Between 1999 and 2003, appeals still referred to the Joint Relief Partnership (JRP), but since 2004 the connection to the partnership appears to have been lost. The funding coverage ranges from 10% (AFET41) to 75% (AFET01) of the requested budgets of the appeals.[89] The closest ACT Appeals in time before the ETH141 were the ETH111[90] and the ETH121,[91] the first concerned with drought which in 2011 hit across the Horn of Africa and the latter with refugees coming from the Republic of Sudan in 2012.

---

[89] AFET81 Draft Final Report with annex "Chronology of ACT Ethiopia appeals since 1995." ACT Appeals in Ethiopia: AFET91 (1999), AFET92 (1999), AFET01 (2000), AFET11 (2001), AFET21 (2002), AFET22 (2003), AFET41 (2004), AFET51 (2005), AFET61 (2006), AFET81 (2008), ETH111 (2011), ETH121 (2012), ETH141 (2014).

[90] There was a serious drought in the whole of the Horn of Africa in 2011. Rains started failing already in 2010, resulting in "harvest failure, decrease in water availability, deteriorating pasture conditions" and losses of livestock particularly hitting lowland areas of pastoralists and agropastoralists across several nations. 2011 07 14 ETH111 Ethiopia Drought Response. A drought situation today does not have to lead to famine or a refugee situation. Famine is a result of lack of proper response. People do not have to die of hunger. In countries like Ethiopia and Kenya, humanitarian relief was rendered in local areas, but in Somalia conflict and drought together led to people leaving the country primarily for Kenya and Ethiopia creating the largest refugee camp in the world: Dadaab in Kenya (ca half a million refugees) and large camps in Dollo Ado in Ethiopia. Drought if unattended may lead to people abandoning their homes in search for survival. Since access to water is crucial for survival, part of ACT Alliance drought response was directed towards serving refugees with water and sanitation. The same organisations simultaneously served local Ethiopian communities in drought prone areas, so that people could stay in their localities. ACT Secretariat letter 2011 08 12 ACT Response to Horn of Africa Crisis and Issues of Concern. The requesting members were EECMY-DASSC, EOC_DICAC indirectly through partnership with IOCC, LWF World Service and Christian Aid with its local partners. See 2011 07 14 ETH111 Ethiopia Drought Response.

[91] Fighting between the Sudanese Armed Forces and other Sudanese armed groups (mostly SPLM-N) in southern regions in Sudan with air attacks within the Blue Nile State of the Republic of Sudan drove a large number of Sudanese civilians to cross the border and seek shelter along the Ethiopian border to Sudan filling up Sherkole, Tongo and Bambasi refugee camps. Conflict is the main force driving refugees: many current conflicts are intrastate rather than conflicts between states. LWF World Service issued an ACT emergency appeal responding with water and sanitation services, and in longer terms with backyard gardening (as livelihood activities), tree plantation (for environmental rehabilitation), community-based literacy programme and community based psychosocial support. 2012 02 02 ACT Alert 04–2012 Emergency Assistance to Sudanese Refugees in Ethiopia,. Two resources regarding conflict are the Uppsala Conflict Database, which monitors conflicts, and the Horn of Africa Bulletin, which discusses policy issues regarding conflicts in the Horn of Africa.

Then the ETH141 appeal – the case study – was a response to the violence that erupted in the capital of South Sudan within the ruling party SPLM on December 15, 2013, developing into a full-scale civil war leading to a full-blown refugee crisis with people ending up in refugee camps both in country, internally displaced, and to Kenya, Uganda and Ethiopia.[92] In Ethiopia the LWF World Service and the Refugee Department of the Orthodox Church responded by digging latrines, providing water, setting up secondary schools and psychosocial support.[93]

After the ETH141, the Horn of Africa was suffering from yet another severe drought. How that affected the flow of refugees is beyond the scope of the thesis. As we have seen earlier – how communities will be able to cope depends to a certain amount on the political situation which brings us to the last major influx of refugees to be mentioned. Ethiopia has for many years received a steady flow of Eritrean refugees.[94] As emergency appeals are designed to give an appropriate response to sudden onset crisis, no emergency appeal was issued by ACT Alliance but several ACT members were working in the camps with Eritrean refugees rendering secondary education and community based psychosocial support.

The Lutheran World Federation (LWF), and The World Council of Churches (WCC), both aiming to restore the visible unity of the churches, and to work for peace and development, inspired northern ACT members to engage in relief and development work in Ethiopia and to form collaborative organisations such as the Christian Relief and Development Association (1973), and the LWF World Service Ethiopia (1974). During the political environment of the Derg (1974–1991) the northern church agencies used the civilian organisations of the rebel fronts in the civil war of the 1980s to bring humanitarian aid to groups beyond government control. This led to a dependency on northern government support and models of coordination and acting outside the local churches. With the engagement in ACT International (1995), The Six Agencies Group (SAG 2006),[95] ACT Development (2007), the Inter-Religious Council of Ethiopia (IRCE 2010),[96] and ACT Alliance (2011), the ACT agencies lost the financial support they had enjoyed with

---

[92] 2013 12 20 ACT Alert 48–2013 South Sudan Conflict.

[93] 2014 02 12 ACT Appeal ETH141 *Assistance to asylum seekers and refugees from South Sudan*, Feb 12, 2014, 44pp, Geneva, ACT Secretariat.

[94] People who are discontent and disillusioned by the political situation and a deteriorating economic and social situation and decides to leave Eritrea. For many, Ethiopia is not the final destination, but Europe, and some refugees are leaving Ethiopia to seek the dangerous route across the desert to reach Israel and possibly Europe in the end.

[95] Six Agencies Group *Mar 2006* MoU.

[96] NCA 2012 *ICRE Newsletter*.

the Emergency Relief Desk (ERD 1975–1992), and the Joint Relief Partnership (JRP) (1984–2005), and thus despite efforts, have so far failed to work effectively as one well-coordinated ACT Ethiopia Forum.

5.5 Comparing Historical Models and ACT Alliance

This section brings together the different ecumenical approaches to a comparative discussion of the present ACT Alliance. It will thus compare ACT Alliance with the mission model, the inter-church aid model and with the international crisis model. There are two main reasons for this. First, ACT members today act differently depending on their main approach. These approaches are coloured by the historical developments of these organisations. Discovering patterns in the past may therefore be helpful in understanding why people act the way they do today. Second, the way ACT Alliance functions in both similar and dissimilar with historical patterns. So, in order to clarify what the *action by churches together* is and entails, comparing and contrasting with the past ought to be a fruitful exercise.

ACT Comparison with the Mission Model

The mission model was initiated by foreign mission societies as a way to express Christian love (*caritas*) by service and witness. In Ethiopia, the model was initially characterised by a holistic mission, respect for the Orthodox Church, general unity among independent missions, and Ethiopian state coordination. As such, the first ideal was that of the independent mission agency whose missionaries integrated the gospel in personal life and service. In the 1940s as Orthodox resistance to the Evangelical movement pushed solidarity among Evangelical Christians. These Ethiopian Christians strove to establish one Evangelical Church with the ideal of integrating church and mission into one missionary church.

In comparison of ACT Alliance with the mission model, first of all, both are part of the ecumenical movement as a larger movement containing different ways of facilitating a sense of church unity and collaboration. Like the mission societies, the ACT agencies function as free associations with the power, capability, and decision-making, of acting. Such a capability lies within the organisation based on the mission of the organisation and the support of its constituency, and not in churches. Both ACT Alliance and Foreign missions were initiatives from the Western churches. Both these initiatives – ACT and missions – were taken up and appropriated by Orthodox Churches and other churches in the global South, e.g. when *the Ethiopian Evangelical Church Mekane Yesus International Missionary Society* (EECMY-IMS) was established in 2008.

A similarity with the modern missionary movement is cross-border operations, and the international scope of the work. Historically, the international aspect of ACT Alliance and other aid agencies is derived from the mission agencies. This feature was not there in the national Red Cross Societies from the start as each society catered for the needs of their own soldiers in the first place, and as a matter of extension, the soldiers of the opposing side of the conflict. It meant that the Red Cross Societies worked within their national borders, and not as in foreign missions, across borders. This changed, and Ethiopia was part of this as most missionaries sided with the Ethiopians and mobilised a Red Cross ambulance service during the conflict with Fascist Italy in 1936.[97] The Emperor in his nation-building sought contact with smaller countries like Sweden to counterbalance the perceived colonial interest of the United Kingdom. The work of Swedish missionaries contributed to the positive attitude of the Emperor towards Sweden, which paved the way for the 1953 decision to include Ethiopia in the new programme for Swedish technical assistance.[98] The missionary enterprise thus contributed to aid both in the form of an extension of the vision of the Red Cross Societies and bilateral state aid, in terms of technical assistance, which was not part of a colonial project.

Another contribution from the modern missionary movement, and the mission model, was the focus on medical mission and education that was brought into aid collaboration. As seen in chapter two, in refugee assistance, medical service and education are crucial parts of the assistance.[99] *The ECMY letter* emphasised that these forms of civil mission were an integral part of the missionary enterprise and not a side-step away from some kind of religious activities. From this type of social services – medical and educational – later developed new forms of project-based

---

[97] Arén 2000, 467–70. Grenstedt 2024, 88–90. Among them Dr Lambie, Dr Hylander, and Manfred Lundgren. The Swedish Red Cross Society raised funds since the statutes did not allow them to use their own funds. This was probably the first foreign intervention for the Red Cross Society, an important precedence for missions during the Second World War. Despite international law protecting the Red Cross, the ambulance was attacked and there were casualties. In 1944 Haile Selassie proclaimed a Decree on Missions giving legal status to Evangelical Missions.

[98] Grenstedt 2000, 76–81. *DECREE No. 3 of 1944.* For the challenge of British domination, Bahru Zewde 1991, 179–83; Halldin Norberg 1977, 82–85, 101–2, 233, 275–83. For Sweden, this became the first example of Swedish development assistance with personnel sent at the cost of the Ethiopian government, but also credit given in 1945 and 1946 which paved way for the 1953 decision to include Ethiopia in the new programme for Swedish technical assistance of the Central Committee for Swedish Technical Assistance to Underdeveloped Areas. Ezra Gebremedhin 2017.

[99] Secondary education is not mandatory in refugee assistance and EOC-DICAC work has contributed to the rolling out of secondary education to refugees across Ethiopia.

relief, development, and advocacy. This is still seen in the name of EECMY-DASSC as a *Development and Social Service Commission*, in which development refers to the project-based approach and social service refers to the missionary approach of running health and educational services.

A clear difference from the mission model is that ACT Alliance and many of its member agencies were not set up for the spread of the gospel, for witness, but for a different purpose. The mission model was initiated by foreign mission societies as a way to express Christian love (*caritas*) by service and witness. ACT Alliance was set up to express Christian love by service but explicitly not evangelistic witness. In this aspect, the Mekane Yesus lost the argument of *the ECMY Letter* which may indicate that modern churches in the West, as a whole, are not interested in evangelisation.[100] The main question though, is not whether or not the gospel is central, but what gospel is being proclaimed. The Mekane Yesus spoke of the gospel of Jesus Christ who came to deliver us from our sin, death, and the devil. This gospel, as seen in chapter four (4.1) was for many Ethiopians, who had never heard the Christian gospel because they lived on the outskirts of Christian Ethiopia, live-changing and led away from tribal conflicts to a life in peace and of service to neighbour.[101]

A different type of gospel is also preached in the ecumenical movement. In the good news, according to Michael Taylor: "The gospel is not about forgiving sins so much as about overcoming hunger and unjustice, putting the last and the least first and lifting the burdens of oppression." Therefore, for Taylor, "the concern about poverty is not an *implication* of the gospel as it is worked out in the life of the believer. It is the *definition* of the gospel: the point at which everything Christian has to begin."[102]

Taylor clarifies that it is not a matter of holism versus something else, but "fundamentally different understandings of that whole."[103] It is, for Taylor, not a matter of division of labour but radically different understandings of the church and

---

[100] Empirically, this is supported by the rise of the so-called "nones", the number of people in Christian nations unaffiliated with Christian churches due to the lack of Christian education and witness. This is why in ecumenical mission theology, the focus on mission fields have shifted from the non-Christian world to "the whole world", or as it is also put, the "five continents".

[101] Grenstedt 2000, 70 notes how barriers of ethnicity, status and denominationalism were overcome already in Massawa in 1972 and that "the Evangelical Pioneers transcended barriers of ethnicity and promoted communication between different ethnic groups. This meant an appreciation of other peoples' cultures and efforts to learn new languages".

[102] Taylor 1995, 43.

[103] Taylor 1995, 42.

its mission. In his vision, the poor are the "target audience", the key task of the church is "to be active and practical", with the doing being the essential. As such the church is at its core good news to the materially and politically poor, not good news to all, rich and poor. Taylor recognizes the tensions this brings between the agencies of the North and the churches in the South.[104]

Compared with reformation theology as formed by Martin Luther, such a political diakonia would be to confuse law and gospel, preaching law instead of the gospel. This social gospel is simply the moral law and its demands on every person to do good and avoid evil with an added plea to serve the stranger in need. When it is not accompanied by a gospel of deliverance from sin, it opens itself up to Christ's critique of the Pharisees, that: "They bind heavy burdens, hard to bear, and lay them on men's shoulders; but they themselves will not move them with their finger" (Matt. 23:4).[105]

So, the liberation theology from England, in this case from a representative of Christian Aid, stands over and against the reformation theology from Ethiopia.[106] If it is this social gospel that ACT is preaching, then the life of word and sacrament in the churches becomes as irrelevant as in the height of the 1960s.[107] African churches are also appropriating social forms of the gospel, such as liberation theology and prosperity gospel, but the way Taylor argues moves the initiative from the churches in the South to the agencies of the North. For the Mekane Yesus, it would entail that they engage in a holistic mission with the members of the Committee of Mutual Christian Responsibility (CMCR) and in aid with members of ACT Alliance. The point of integration becomes only at the highest

---

[104] Taylor 1995, 42–44. Cf. Jambulosi's 2021 study in earlier research (1.1), on mission theology in the WCC and the Lausanne movement, and how he, as a Zimbabwean theologian, trained in South Africa, while appreciating the stance of both sides of the ecumenical movement, sought the reconciliation between a social engagement and the church's task of evangelisation, that Taylor denies, but that Jambulosi could find in the subsequent discussion in mission theology.

[105] Foster 1998, 11, comments: "Our world is hungry for genuinely changed people." Kreeft 2003, 3 As mentioned earlier (3.2n), that "third-level morality as taught by various religious traditions goes beyond demands for justice and includes mercy."

[106] Taylor 1995. Michael Taylor led the Christian Aid from 1985–97. Here a distinction needs to be drawn between the Latin American liberation theology as taught and practiced in Roman Catholic base communities, and the appropriation and adaptation of the theology in Western academia. Boff 2002, 194–97. In Roman Catholic thought, the justice tradition runs deep, but it is embedded in the Roman sacramental life and integrated with the life of the Christian. Cf. Bevans and Schroeder 2006. The British have their justice tradition largely drawing on Reformed Theology. Cf. Foster 2000, 129–71.

[107] See chapter one, earlier research (1.1).

administrative leadership, not with the people in the church.[108] If ACT entails a top-down approach, while Mekane Yesus is built bottom-up, consequent tensions are effected in the church between church workers and aid staff in the church.[109]

The foreign missions classically worked to enable the new churches to be self-supporting, self-governing, and self-propagating and thus to hand over the torch of the mission to the churches as churches.[110] Thus the integration of the work of the missions to the new churches started in Mekane Yesus in the 1960s.[111] There were and still are tensions between foreign missions and churches as such kind of handover is not self-evident or something that comes by itself. Hence, some of the rhetoric of the ECMY Letter aims to empower an African Church in contrast to agencies that are foreign in that context. The question is how that kind of dynamics corresponds to the work and vision of ACT Alliance.

If national churches would integrate the aid work of ACT, how would that impact relief, development, and advocacy initiatives? The missions have come further than the aid sector in this regard. There are different tendencies. One trend is voices that stress the importance of local ownership of relief work and coordination. There is talk of partnership, capacity building, and resilience. The *World Humanitarian Summit* convened in Istanbul in 2016 certainly emphasised the importance of "cooperation with local communities"[112] and the plea was for "political leadership to prevent and end conflicts",[113] which implies that "the primary responsibility for conflict prevention and resolution lies with Member States and the Security Council."[114] Though the international community shares the responsibility, the primary solution lies in local and national political leadership and a commitment to peaceful political solutions.

The ACT Ethiopia Forum can, and at times, does work as a forum in which the two churches may voice concerns and opinions. Given the nature of aid work, with primary decision-making being made in New York and Geneva, and other

---

[108] Jonsson 1998.

[109] Cf. Jonsson 1998. On prosperity theology in ecumenical documents, Vähäkangas 2015.

[110] The three selves were articulated by Rev. Henry Venn CMS General Secretary 1841–72. Bevans and Schroeder 2006. These are not to be confused with Maoist political interpretation of the three selves in the communist attempt to isolate Chinese Christians.

[111] Jonsson 1998, 72–77.

[112] UN 2016 02 02 Ban Ki-Moon 2016, 16, #58, "Respect and protect humanitarian and medical mission." in "One humanity: shared responsibility."

[113] UN 2016 02 02 Ban Ki-Moon 2016, 6–12, #23–45, "Core responsibility one: political leadership to prevent and end conflicts."

[114] UN 2016 02 02 Ban Ki-Moon 2016, 8, #29.

capital cities in the West, it is a steep uphill struggle to create an equitable environment in ACT Alliance. Aid is conceptualised and practised from the political and economic centre, and it is hard for people to be heard in such a structure.[115]

A major difference is that mission agencies work with churches while ACT agencies primarily work with communities of their choice, civil society organisations, UN agencies, and government agencies. When partners to ACT agencies are organisations unlinked to churches, the church may be as irrelevant to the strategic plans of ACT agencies as in the 1960s report *A Church For Others* mentioned in chapter one. The Mekane Yesus had argued for the ideal of the integrated church, i.e. a national church would be in authority and agencies would support the church's mission as it makes decisions through its own systems of accountability. This was the second part of the development debate that Mekane Yesus lost as the aid agencies would not relinquish authority and resources to the national church. As the church lost many of its institutions to the Derg and the new project approach is more linked to the state than to churches, the influence of churches in Ethiopian society has diminished in that respect.

This brings up the question of whether the Mekane Yesus also lost the argument regarding a Christian worldview and anthropology. Is it still the case that, in the humanitarian sector, a material view of man is prevalent with corresponding catering of primarily material needs? When biological survival is the goal, the refugee camp is the solution. So the prevalence of camp-based assistance seems to indicate such a limited anthropological outlook from the humanitarian sector in general.[116]

The community-based psychosocial approach as utilised by both the LWF World Service and the Refugee Department of the Orthodox Church, however, contains a concern for families and communities, and a view to the local resources and capabilities of the populations being served. Such a contextualisation of mental health indicates a more than material view of man. There are, however, no indications that ACT agencies stress the kind of personal integration of the Christian faith that the mission model presupposed in the staff.[117]

---

[115] Anderson, Brown, and Jean 2012.

[116] See Hilhorst 2018 for a discussion on "classical humanitarianism" and "resilience humanitarianism" and how aid is not "outside of societies but are embedded in local realties" and therefore a factor in reshaping institutions in both intended and unintended ways.

[117] On the ecumenical discussion on holism, Taylor 2002, 585. Taylor 1994, 21–46.

ACT Comparison with the Inter-Church Aid Model

The inter-church aid model was a way to express practical solidarity with Orthodox Churches in the ecumenical movement to correspond to the unity (*koinonia*)
of the Christian Church. In Ethiopia, inter-church aid was part of Ethiopian initiatives on behalf of the Emperor for acceptance of Ethiopia among the European
nations and for unity and solidarity with Africa. These initiatives showed an Orthodox commitment to be part of a larger community of nations and churches.
The EOC-DICAC, established in 1972, worked on a range of areas including intra-
church projects strengthening the church and its communities.

How does ACT Alliance compare with the inter-church aid model? As with
the mission model, both ACT and inter-church aid arose from the ecumenical
movement.[118] While the initiative for inter-church aid came mainly from the Geneva and the World Council of Churches as a multi-lateral initiative, the mission
and aid agencies primarily have been working locally in one place and bilaterally
with one church or one community. Even the LWF World Service which is an
extension of the Lutheran World Federation as a communion of churches is in one
sense a multi-lateral organisation, but it still connects with one church at a time
when doing its work – in Ethiopia, the Mekane Yesus.[119]

In general, the inter-church aid model, in the sense of direct support to
churches, has been a vehicle of less financial support than the mission and aid ventures.[120] As such, the inter-church aid model, has been the less extensive approach
of the three. The question is whether ACT Alliance inherits this lower level of income from the inter-church aid model?

Did the Ethiopian Orthodox Church lose the argument of building on a foundation of Christian spirituality? If ending poverty in the world is ACT Alliance's
goal, would that not imply that rich nations take the centre stage, and churches

---

[118] Taylor 2002, 583–86. N.B. that the inter-church aid, as here treated, is narrower than what
Taylor describes as "Interchurch Aid" in the Dictionary of the Ecumenical Movement as the
three approaches, the mission model, the inter-church aid model, and the international crisis
model, and ACT would all fit into what Taylor describes. Cf. Taylor's problematization of "interchurch aid", Taylor 1995, 34. Taylor's profile, with his background in Christian Aid, would fit
better into the international crisis model than into the inter-church aid model as analysed here
for several reasons: 1) the target group for him is poverty in general, 2) the problem for him is
structural, and 3) the solution is political. See Taylor 1995.

[119] As such, the World Council of Churches preferred working with national ecumenical
councils rather than with real churches, so from a multi-lateral to another multi-lateral institution. Still, the inter-church aid was used as a multilateral vehicle for aid given to actual churches.

[120] On the round table approach, Taylor 1995, 42–45.

become marginal in society and for ACT Alliance and its member agencies? If ending poverty in the world is the controlling logic of ACT Alliance, churches, per definition, again may become irrelevant, like in the 1960s, to the vision of the agencies of the West.[121]

There are theological, ecclesiological, church-ecumenical motives involved in the inter-church aid model, like the discussions on Ethics and Ecclesiology in the 1990s that brought about the idea of ACT. The Orthodox rapprochement to the churches in the West in 1919 included both a church koinonia and practical inter-church assistance. After all, St Paul's contribution, κοινωνία, (Rom. 15:16), or assistance, διακονίαν, (Acts 11:29), or collection, λογεία, (1 Cor 16:1) to the relief aid in Jerusalem – which took the Apostle several years of focus in his ministry[122] – was backed up by a long theological argumentation on the extent to which churches in other places belong to the same body as the church in Jerusalem.[123] The importance for the early church of assisting the poor was clear as Paul and Barnabas agreed "that we should continue to remember the poor, the very thing I was eager to do." (Gal. 2:10). This had a special emphasis on the duty to support Christians in need: "do good to all people, especially to those who belong to the family of believers" (Gal. 6:10) As well as being part of "body politics", St Paul stresses that giving to others belongs to good stewardship of possessions.[124]

---

[121] Cf. Easterly 2006 *The White Man's Burden: Why the West's Efforts to Aid the Rest Have Done So Much Ill and So Little Good.*

[122] Blomberg 1999, 171, 178. Agabus, like modern forecasts of famine, predicts a famine to take place in Judea in AD 45–47, see Acts 11:27–30. As there is no indication of a common treasury, the principle of all to support according to their ability was set.

[123] Rom 15:14–29, especially vv. 26–27 with the mutuality of the church in Jerusalem, Macedonia, and Achaia sharing, κοινωνίαν, in the spiritual benefits, τοῖς πνευματικοῖς, and therefore being obligated to minister, λειτουργῆσαι, in material needs. Blomberg 1999, 188–89. 1 Cor 11–16, Blomberg 1999, 187–89. 1 Cor 16:1–4 ought to be the oldest reference to a Christian weekly Sunday collection. For Blomberg 1999, 188: "Those who eat and drink without concern for the needs of the poorer members do not recognize the nature of the church – a refuge for refugees, in which all must care for one another". Acts 2, St. Paul's teaching is not communism. He does not teach that some should work, and others support them, on the contrary, 1 Thess 2–5 and 2 Thess 3:6–15. Paul consistently challenged the Greco-Roman system of patronage with consequent welfare syndrome. Thus, for Paul, Christians ought not to become dependent but become productive citizens who are not relying on others' welfare. Blomberg 1999, 179–82 thus draws two applications to the modern world: 1) the church ought to ensure that "the genuinely needy in their midst do not suffer" and 2) still have "a concern to put as many to work as possible" regardless of societal conditions. On the conception of Acts 2:42–47 as a communist vision, Blomberg 1999, 160–167.

[124] Blomberg 1999, 178–179

ACT Comparison with the International Crisis Model

Finally, there is a need to compare ACT Alliance with the international crisis model. As with the mission model and the inter-church model, ACT Alliance is a child of the ecumenical movement, and more specifically the World Council of Churches and the Lutheran World Federation. The initiative, as before, is coming from the nations in the global north and its Western churches. So far, the *action by churches together* under the ACT umbrella has consisted mainly in collaborative ventures on an *ad hoc* basis according to need and utility, like the ETH141 appeal. These are mainly pragmatic reasons.

The main reason for this may come from the fact that the power lies in the individual agencies from the north according to their respective missions and approaches. It is not a matter of size – agencies in the global south may be as large or larger than those of the north. But it is a matter of resource mobilisation, as discussed in the end of chapter two. Therefore, ACT Alliance is more like the international crisis model; in that it is not concerned with mission (evangelisation), not concerned primarily with supporting sister churches (but some capacity building), but people in need in general.[125] As in the gospel according to Taylor, poverty and issues of structural justice seem to be the overarching concern. The picture, however, is not clear, but ambiguous and open for different interpretations.[126]

There are specific matters in the international crisis model that have formed how ACT members collaborate under ACT Alliance even though the context has changed substantially. The way that the crisis of the Derg period and the civil war with subsequent humanitarian situations were handled, I would argue set important precedents in the thinking and acting of the members of ACT. ACT agencies were used to running large-scale relief operations.[127] The relief and development wings of the Mekane Yesus and the Orthodox Church were used to running

---

[125] Cf. Christensen and Hutchison 1982, 6: "Evangelization, the proclaiming of the Gospel, was nearly always the leading announced objective in foreign missions; an objective that, as already suggested, was a matter of fundamental agreement despite theological and methodological differences. The aim of civilizing however (or of offering an alternative and allegedly better civilization), never evoked similar agreement. Some of the most prominent nineteenth-century theorists – Gustav Warneck in Germany, Rufus Anderson in the United States, to a lesser extent Henry Venn in Great Britain – considered a civilizing ideal inappropriate from Christian mission."

[126] Taylor 1995, 21–46, in particular on gospel and forgiveness of sin. Cf. Cooper 2021, 6 comments, "ideological movements can only end in failure as the system itself is full of contradiction, infighting and a lack of forgiveness and restoration that is inherent to any religious system which has any lasting impact." Cf. Kreeft 2003, 3 on third level morality. See discussion 3.2.

[127] See chapter (5:3) with special reference to CRDA and JRP.

large-scale relief operations under an ecumenical umbrella during the 1980s–90s.[128] This was to a large degree thanks to government funding and the ecumenical collaboration that made it possible. When the collaboration with ACT began – all that stopped.[129]

ACT agencies who were pleased with the way it used to work, with finances coming in according to need, and a great deal of organisational autonomy, would reasonably continue to think and act in the same way. Government funding seldom goes through the ACT system, however. Expectations based on historical performance may therefore feed impatience with ACT Alliance. In the refugee assistance to the South Sudanese, ACT Ethiopia Forum members created separate projects rather than supporting the common appeal. There were also instances in which close collaboration would make sense, but there was no earlier precedence for such a mode of working together. Still, there was progress towards collaborative ventures, such as when the LWF World Service and the refugee department of the Orthodox Church decided to work in the same camp and the same sector.

The collaboration of the Joint Relief Partnership was a broader ecumenical body than ACT Alliance since it included the Ethiopian Catholic Church, the Ethiopian Kale Heywet Church, the Ethiopian Meserete Kristos Church, and the Evangelical Churches Fellowship in Ethiopia (ECFE). From a church perspective, these Ethiopian church relations are as important as those that are aligned with the World Council of Churches. The churches were appreciated in the country for their relief efforts and the Ethiopian churches appreciated the international relief both for its impact in general and because the churches were able to participate and work together. These facts acted as a counterforce to the violent secularisation policies pursued by the concurrent Ethiopian regime.[130]

---

[128] The same is true for the LWF World Service who built up a large relief organisation, often in connection to Mekane Yesus Church properties.

[129] Carter 2011, 65. The collaboration of "JRP" continued, but under *the Joint Emergency Operation Plan* (JEOP) partners – and the seven remaining members became important in the Productive Safety Net Programme of the Ethiopian government still under the leadership of Catholic Relief Services and with *the Food for Peace* – USAID funding. In this way, the new consortium was able to continue the kind of large-scale emergency food programming, that otherwise mainly is channelled from World Food Programme through government agency. This no longer applies to the ACT members who continued under the auspices of first ACT International from 1995, and later ACT Alliance, from 2011. CRS (JEOP lead agency), CARE, World Vision, Food for the Hungry Ethiopia (FHE), Save the Children US, and UK, and REST.

[130] Violent refers to state imposition of a non-religious outlook of life and the use of legal system, police, and military to persecute Christians. Grenstedt 2024, 174–77. Eide 1996.

The international crisis model was partially a way for Christians in the political West to express their concern for the survival of people caught between natural disaster and civil war and partially a way for the governments of the political West to support people in dire need while avoiding support to a military dictatorship. The model gave less emphasis on the leadership and initiatives of Ethiopian churches, Christian witness, and nation-building, and more on coordination of aid agencies for the survival of people, and with the people, the churches. It has to be understood in the desperate situation of people dying due to political strife and negligence of human suffering and the unique abilities and networks of the Ethiopian churches and the mission agencies that Christian – and other – aid agencies could tap into and utilise to save as many people as possible.[131]

This model began with LWF World Service and the Christian Relief and Development Association in connection to the 1970s drought and subsequent revolution as radical Marxist students sought to change imperial Ethiopia into either a socialist nation or, alternatively, different socialist ethnical nations. The context of the drought of the 1980s and the civil war between the military Marxist regime of the Derg and the Marxist *guerrillas* of the regions, pushed church-based agencies to mobilise support for relief. Funding came from Western state donors as well as voluntary church contributions, and it was channelled via Addis Ababa through the churches throughout Derg control areas by the Joint Relief Partnership as coordinated by the Catholic Relief Services and the Lutheran World Federation.

As relief aid did not reach people in rebel-held territories, the Norwegian Church Aid-led consortium the Emergency Relief Desk (ERD) in the name of the Sudan Council of Churches sent aid through Sudan through the political relief agencies of the liberation fronts (ERA, REST, and ORA). Two simultaneous ideals were operative – one in a consortium channelled aid through local churches and their relief organs, and another consortium in which aid was channelled through the civil arms of the liberation fronts of the time. Neither ideal empowered Ethiopian churches, but the first gave the churches respite under a socialist regime, and allowed the churches to participate, while the second empowered the liberation fronts indirectly. The American and European Christian aid agencies were able to channel aid through the churches because the Western state donors did not want the support the Derg military regime of that time.

Rather than working through local churches – as the concept of inter-church aid relates to – the agencies worked through political entities, the civilian parts of

---

the liberation fronts of a civil war. They worked with the people who later became the national leaders of Eritrea and Ethiopia, and those who left for life in the diaspora. This started a trend in which these agencies sought and found new "secular" partners for the relief or development project they aimed to conduct. These Christian aid agencies may still work with Ethiopian church agencies, when convenient, but through other partners, they may pursue their own development goals.

ACT was initiated by the ecumenical movement to express the unity of the churches through the practical engagement of the churches in relief efforts. In Ethiopia, the aid agencies that became members of ACT had already coordinated relief effectively for years under the Christian Relief and Development Association, the Joint Relief Partnership, and other collaborative schemes.

Through its ecumenically minded membership criteria, ironically enough, ACT did not allow for the broader ecumenical models of the Christian Relief and Development Association (CRDA) and the Joint Relief Partnership (JRP), while causing uncertainties regarding the many non-church partners of the European members of the ACT Ethiopia Forum. Because ACT was tied to the World Council of Churches and the Lutheran World Federation, the Christian Relief and Development Association, as well as church partners like the Ethiopian Catholic Church and the Ethiopian Kale Heywet Church (EKHC), were not allowed to join ACT. The establishment of ACT thus led to a gradual discontinuation of the collaboration within the Joint Relief Partnership consortium and a dependency on ACT for fundraising for emergency relief, i.e. ACT Appeals. The idea of ACT Alliance as church-based, and in that sense grounded in grass root communities, here lies in tension both with the past experience of "big tent" ecumenical interchurch collaboration, and with the experiences of northern Christian agencies working with any suitable partner.

The present ACT members of the forum have institutional experience of being able to mobilise enormous funds for relief work through creative initiatives, a stubborn concern for those in need, and a willingness to collaborate across all kinds of borders. This history informs how people think and act in the ACT Ethiopia Forum. The ACT appeal system of ACT Alliance can be seen as an attempt to formalise these past experiences into a system, but it does not function well. As ACT have been unable to replace the funding lost by the discontinuation of the Joint Relief Partnership, the crisis in fundraising as shown in the ETH141 appeal has not been a one-time event but represents a trend.

LWF World Service, seem to have been, a special case in this. Like the churches, it received much funding during these years and was a celebrated agency in the country. Unlike the churches, LWF World Service, both worked on their own projects and acted as a channel to others. After the end of the civil war, LWF World Service was able to launch large development projects to rebuild the country. In the past, they kept a close relationship with Mekane Yesus while acting as an international NGO. As we saw in the case study, LWF World Service worked on the premises of the local Mekane Yesus and was thus able to set up a new office, two tents, quickly near the refugee camp. Unlike the E8 members, LWF World Service is not affiliated with one church, but with a federation of churches. The agency therefore has no exclusive church constituency to support it.[132] As such, LWF World Service is as dependent on the relief funding of the ACT appeal system as the Ethiopian church agencies.

There is also another tension between European and Ethiopian agencies. The European agencies have an international scope, so a local ACT forum is only one part of a larger international network. These agencies may have a membership in several ACT forums.[133] The Ethiopian agencies have a national scope, and the forum is their only ACT forum, though they may simultaneously be members of other organisations such as the Christian Relief and Development Association.

Discussion on Ecumenical Models

By going beyond the scope of the case study of the ETH141 ACT Appeal of refugee assistance and exploring historical ecumenical approaches, what is revealed is a complex network of relationships. Through the use of *historical models*: the mission model, the inter-church aid model, and the international church model – used for an exploratory purpose, the thesis has clarified some of the patterns.[134]

---

[132] In terms of funding, LWF World Service have been more supported by some churches, such as ELCA and CoS than others.

[133] ACT later introduced regional forums, such as one in Southern Africa, and regional offices, such as one in Nairobi, something which makes sense for European agencies who want to pursue regional issues and consolidate personal resources. It may not make the same sense for a national church, or national ACT members, however.

[134] One example of the organisational complexity is the NCA initiative in 2009 to establish an Inter-Religious Council of Ethiopia. "NCA intends to arrange a regional conference for Religious Leaders, just after Ethiopian Easter in Ethiopia. The objective is to have them together to learn from each other and to explore the possibilities for an agenda of cooperation on a broader scale." The NCA had worked some time to bring the Ethiopian Religious Leaders on Board in collaboration with the Peace and Conflict Prevention Inter-Religious Coordination Office, a government office, regarding the topic. 2009 02 20 Meeting of E8 Minutes.

One of the consequences of the way the ACT Appeal system works *de facto*, in practice, in contradistinction to *de jure*, in principle, is that nation-states and governments are seen as prime vehicles for social welfare *de jure* while *de facto* state action may be the prime vehicle for social disruption and arbitrary use of authority. As the Orthodox were arguing in chapter four, this may lead to a marginalisation of Christian churches and civil society organisations. This is relevant both concerning a) the South Sudanese state and contending parties in the conflict for political power in South Sudan and b) donor states' attempt to mitigate the suffering of ordinary people by contributing to relief and development.

There is a tension between the idea of ACT Alliance as action by churches together, on which the alliance was based, and the idea and form of tax-funded emergency relief. ACT Alliance is dependent on the good will of civil servants and the political will of foreign governments. As such the work is neither voluntary, nor rights-based, but conditioned by political will and global politics and the willingness of the conflicting parties to seek a peaceful solution. In this, there is historical continuity with the Joint Relief Partnership (JRP) (1984–2005), and the Emergency Relief Desk 1981–92), as seen in this chapter.

For the two agencies that focus on refugee assistance, LWF World Service and the refugee department of EOC-DICAC, it was more profitable working with UNHCR than with the ACT Appeal system. It was possible, though, for these ACT members to benefit from the contributions made in the ACT Appeal while relying mainly on a partnership with UNHCR.

The ACT appeal showed a lack of close collaboration among the ACT members. The appeal was raised in the name of the forum members, but by requesting members, and other members did not see it as their responsibility to raise the funds needed. This lack of close collaboration is in historical continuity with the Joint Relief Partnership. As shown in this chapter, it worked on a model of coordination by a fair distribution of funding, not close collaboration in the field. Such an approach allows for a great deal of autonomy for each agency. The main difference between the Joint Relief Partnership (JRP) and ACT Alliance is that the former was able to raise sufficient funding which latter so far has been unable to do.

ACT Alliance Informed by Ecclesiology

The main rationale, however, of ACT Alliance is based on the ecclesiological conviction that churches, not talking specifically about ACT members, are not separate entities, but share in the reality of the One, Holy Catholic and Apostolic Church of the creed, as the Orthodox Church asserts in chapter four. Since the churches are not separate realities, the ACT agencies, initiated by churches, ought not to behave as separate entities either. This ecclesiological basis distinguishes ACT Alliance from other forms of collaboration in the aid sector.[135]

The tensions mentioned above between government donor agencies and the churches show that there is a need for more research: on church-based fundraising in the churches in the North, and in the South, and on church-state dynamics on issues of aid in the global North, and the global South.

The unity in ACT Alliance between the ACT members, as aid agencies, so not talking about churches now, is seen as analogous to the unity of the churches, a unity derived from the participation in *koinonia*, the life given by the Father, through the Son, and in the Holy Spirit, one God. The rationale for this view is that, theologically speaking, the boundaries of the church are not clear from a human point of view.[136] The risk with using language derived from sacramental theology outside of the sacraments of the church is that it may bring confusion rather than clarity in language, and a mixing of human and divine matters. The point of using it is to be able to speak of God's redeeming grace outside of the physical doors of the local church building, as the Christian church, in the sense of the Christian community is spread out for the liturgy after the liturgy, the celebration of the Christian faith in loving service to the neighbour.

---

[135] See earlier research 1.1.
[136] Brodd 2005b.

6. Action by Churches Together

The purpose of this thesis is to draw attention to the ecclesial matters of aid. The aim is to analyse the ecclesiological problem of the meaning and identity of ACT Alliance as an *action by churches together*. The problem has two sides, the ecclesial and the social. The ecclesial dimension has to do with the church and more specifically what it means for churches to be working together through agencies whose identity may be ambiguous, and the social dimension has to do with the practical issues the churches collaborate on. The ecclesial side of aid is important to highlight and research since Christian aid agencies may suffer a mission drift and loss of Christian identity over time. This may cause inner secularisation in the churches endangering the moral life of Christians. This last chapter will summarise the research and discuss the main issues of the ecclesiological problem.

In an article, Brodd pays attention to the problem of the identity of Christian organisation[s], with specific reference to "church related development organisation[s]."[1] He argues a distinction between the Christian Church and such organisations needs to be drawn. Building upon that fundamental analysis, this thesis has explored and clarified the issue further by starting from a practical point of view, i.e. investigating the ACT appeal to support refugees from South Sudan in Ethiopia by ACT Alliance in 2014.

In the thesis, I am asking in what sense ACT Alliance is thought of as an *action by churches together* and what it would entail practically for the refugee assistance of ACT Alliance. If ACT Alliance is thought of as an *action by churches together*, what does it mean conceptually and what does it entail practically? The aim has been to centre on questions of ecclesial identity by studying tensions arising when the idea, *action by churches together*, is put into practice in the actual work and organisation of ACT Alliance.

In chapter two, the refugee assistance that the ACT members in Ethiopia planned to render according to the common ACT appeal ETH141 was described and

---

[1] Brodd 2005b.

analysed. Though the ACT appeal mechanism failed to raise funds and function as an effective means of coordination, all members contributed to the refugee assistance in one form or another. In chapter three, the principles on which the work was founded were analysed. The assistance was based on internationally agreed-upon standards, operational principles, and international law. In chapter four, some historical and theological reasons for the ecumenical social engagement of the Ethiopian churches were investigated. The two national churches both engaged in ecumenical collaboration but also kept a critical approach to such engagements.

Thus, the reasoning process in the thesis began from a practical point of view, following the conception of a plan to assist refugees (the ETH141 appeal), through the chequered results of the appeal as it launched and the lack of funding hampering its complete success. As the planned activities of the ACT appeal were based on contemporary international standards, these standards were also analysed to illuminate the principled thinking behind the plan. This investigation confirmed that people conceptualise the main source of protection for refugees as primarily a state responsibility. Hence the first part of the thesis started with practical concerns and challenges but transitioned into examining standards and principles.

The second part of the thesis, chapters four and five, reversed the reasoning process. Chapter four was the turning point of the thesis and involved the critical views of the churches. The idea of the state as the focus of development was problematised. The Mekane Yesus Church's emphasis on the human person stands in critique to the reduced anthropology utilised in state-led aid whereby people are reduced to objects of charity. Likewise, the Ethiopian Orthodox Church referred to the resurrection of Christ as the starting point for change and warned that the goal of all-out social change would empower the state and marginalise the church in society. In chapter five different models of ecumenical action were discussed.

This final chapter, chapter six summarises and discusses the different senses of *action by churches together* by incorporating the results of the previous chapters: *The ACT Appeal and Its Standards* (6.1), and *the Churches and Ecumenical Models* (6.2), into a discussion of *What "Action by Churches Together" Is and Is Not* (6.3) in the ETH141 appeal and its principles. In *Beyond ACT Alliance* (6.4), a further discussion will be held on church diakonia beyond humanitarian relief work by pointing to the difference between the sacramental mission of the church and the kind of ecumenical *Diakonie* that fits into ACT Alliance. In *Concluding Discussion* (6.5), last in the chapter, the general idea of the dissertation will be concluded in brief form.

6.1 The ETH141 ACT Appeal and Its Standards

The first chapter introduced the ecclesiological problem of church and aid built into ACT Alliance, the topic of the refugee crisis and assistance in Ethiopia, and the case of the ETH141 ACT Appeal. In *Earlier Research and Background to ACT Alliance* (1.1), it was stated that research on aid in general and African churches in particular may be appropriately and fruitfully conducted with theological and ecclesial questions of church and aid since African churches are both involved in and affected by aid and its potentially harmful effects. As ACT Alliance was founded in 2011, building on an earlier ecumenical relief initiative, research on the ecumenical organisation may prove rewarding as theological and ecclesiological assumptions were built into the very name of *Action by Churches Together* (ACT).

Research Problem, Questions, and Material (1.2) formulated the research problem of the meaning and identity of ACT Alliance as an *action by churches together*. The problem is closely related to the identity of Christian organisation[s], with specific reference to "church related development organisation[s]." ACT contains conceptual and practical tensions in its organisation and work. These tensions signify an unclarity of what *action by churches together* means, which this thesis has investigated through the case study of refugee assistance in Ethiopia in 2014 and by positioning the issue in a larger historical context in which two Ethiopian churches may contribute by shedding light on the problem. The thesis has asked questions about in what sense ACT Alliance is thought of as *action by churches together* and what it would entail practically for the refugee assistance of ACT Alliance.

The idea of ACT Alliance was discussed in ecumenical deliberations under the theme of ethics and ecclesiology and then instituted as ACT International, ACT Development and ACT Alliance. From the theological concept of *ecumenical diakonia, Action by Churches Together* (ACT) was by the World Council of Churches given a theological meaning expressing that the churches should act together. This was in consequence of the participating churches having a sense of growing together in *koinonia*. Common action by different churches is an effective sign to the global world of an ecclesial unity through which social action, one of several aims in the ecumenical movement, should be (an ecumenical imperative) linked to the process of uniting the churches, the primary aim of the movement.

From the operational framework of *international aid*, however, ACT Alliance was, by the ACT Secretariat in Geneva, given an operational meaning: ACT, as an ecumenical institution, was essentially formed "to ensure better coordination between churches and their related agencies around the world in their response to humanitarian situations and disasters." The operational idea of ACT Alliance was for ACT members, not churches but organisations, to act in solidarity with people in need through collaboration and coordination in relief, development, and advocacy. This gives a creative tension between two conceptions of action by churches together, one theological and one operational.

In *A Historical and Theological Approach* (1.3), it was deliberated on the historical and theological research approach of the thesis. Relief work and relief organisations have developed historically. ACT organisations are theologically motivated as can be seen from their historical development. This is ecclesiology as a study of the historical sources and processes as the church appears in history in the form of the church itself, public Christianity, and private forms of Christian life informed by the doctrine on the church. The emphasis in this research has been on the organisational and ethical aspects of ACT Alliance.

ETH141 ACT Appeal and Research Limitations (1.4) described the historical case of the South Sudanese refugee response, the ETH141 ACT Appeal, which framed the research limitations, and excluded from the study other forms of *church-in-aid*. ACT Alliance, with particular reference to its members in the ACT Ethiopia Forum, is the research subject. As a result, other forms of church life, such as *the South Sudanese church in civil crisis, the refugee church in exile, the pastoral life of the local churches* in the host communities, and in general, *the church communities in Ethiopia*, are not included in the research.

In chapter two, the ETH141 ACT Appeal to support South Sudanese refugees in Ethiopia, was analysed as a practical case study. It was a textual study of the appeal documents to identify the aims, methodologies, conditions, and challenges of the refugee assistance rendered by the ACT Ethiopia forum.

In *Emergency Preparedness* (2.2), the level of preparedness of the ACT Ethiopia Forum was discussed and the question of why churches engage with refugee assistance was brought up. ACT Alliance was initiated by member churches of the WCC and the Lutheran World Federation as an extension to previous ecumenical engagement in aid so that churches might collaborate more closely. The idea of ACT made practical sense in terms of effectiveness and efficiency through collaboration and coordination. An ACT Appeal is the work of legally separate entities: Ethiopian church-based service institutions (EECMY-DASSC and EOC-DICAC), Christian aid agencies (BftW, CA, CoS, DCA, HEKS, ICCO, IOCC, and NCA), and ecumenical aid agencies (LWF World Service and ACT Alliance). The ACT Ethiopia Forum was set up for the collaboration on relief, development, and advocacy of ACT members in Ethiopia.

The ACT Appeal system is the main instrument for fundraising in case of an emergency. When an emergency occurs, the ACT Appeal system is set in motion for the relief collaboration of ACT Members.

ACT Response to the Refugee Crisis (2.3) analysed the response in terms of examining the alert, the preliminary appeal, and the full ETH141 ACT Appeal documents in light of the events in 2014. The ACT Ethiopian Forum launched the appeal to support refugees from South Sudan. It was thus the main instrument for planning, funding, monitoring, and evaluating relief efforts. The background was rising tension within the South Sudanese government since July 2013, with an outbreak of violent clashes in Juba, on December 15, 2013, between competing factions. This had led people to seek refuge with probable scenarios of refugee influxes in the neighbouring countries.

Three ACT Ethiopia Forum members planned the appeal and sought support from the rest of the forum members, and the churches in the ACT Alliance network. The LWF World Service, and EOC-DICAC together with IOCC sought circa 3.5 million USD for services in water and sanitation, secondary education, and livelihood activities in Lietchor refugee camp, Gambella region in Western Ethiopia, using a community-based psychosocial approach. It is not surprising that LWF World Service and the refugee department of EOC-DICAC acted as service providers in the ACT appeal, given that both organisations have worked for years to support refugees in Ethiopia.

In *A Silent Crisis Is Rapidly Evolving* (2.4), I discussed the challenges that arose when the ETH141 plan was put in place such as the difficulty for the ACT Ethiopia Forum to finance the assistance, the flooding of Lietchor camp, and the consequent challenge for UNHCR and ARRA to find suitable land for refugee camps. The lack of adequate funding was the primary challenge as only a few forum members financially supported the appeal. The ETH141 appeal needed to be fully funded for the plan to lead to an adequate response to the South Sudanese refugees. The ETH141 response was thus hampered by a lack of funding from the ACT member agencies and churches. In addition, the flooding of the Baro River created a renewed crisis and the Lietchor camp was put in question.

When the refugees kept coming and the appeal failed to attract needed resources, other ACT members engaged in the refugee response by seeking government funding to make up for the lack of church funding. Bread for the World drafted "an open letter" describing what was seen as a "silent crisis" evolving without much attention from the world, as the crisis in South Sudan was not at that time the focus of international media. The need to seek alternative means of funding meant that the ACT appeal system no longer served as the main coordinating device for the refugee response, and a consortium was created as a new tool for coordination and collaboration. This challenged the ACT appeal as a functional instrument for voluntary fundraising among ecclesial constituencies. Several members created a consortium as an alternative model to the appeal to jointly raise funds and coordinate the relief efforts.

In *Funding Tension: The Ideal and the Practical* (2.5), I discussed the tension between the appeal mechanism for assistance and the practical challenges refugee assistance brings about. As the ETH141 appeal failed to attract voluntary funding, the ACT Agencies sought different strategies, to mobilise state funding, including forming a consortium. This may also indicate a weakness in the setup of ACT Alliance as only some ACT member agencies and affiliated churches are expected to raise the funding for numerous contemporaneous emergencies. The resources available do not match the need which hampers the ability to act. This may indicate a conceptual weakness in the operational interpretation of ACT as "coordination between churches and their related agencies." What is common among these issues is that it shows a tension between the ideal prescribed in ACT policies and the practical reality on the ground. There is a gap between what people want to accomplish (the ideal) and what is achieved (the practical).

Chapter three, *International Framework and Stakeholders*, identified the main framework and principles of the ETH141 ACT Appeal by a textual study of the international standards to which the ACT appeal adheres to discuss the fundamental goals and principles of the assistance. ACT Alliance is committed to setting high standards for the work of its members. Sphere, HAP, and CBPS (as a customized version of MHPSS) represent high-quality standards of relief work. These standards are set against calculated minimum survival needs – a reasonable yardstick indeed – but it raises the question of who can cater for the means of survival for a large population during a sustained conflict. This makes refugee assistance more difficult than relief assistance during a natural disaster and highlights conflict resolution.

For refugees, three solutions are typically identified, repatriation, naturalisation, and migration to a third country. All three solutions require sustained efforts from UNHCR to advocate on behalf of the refugee population and the political will of the UN Security Council and the main political stakeholders involved in the conflict. Meanwhile, the refugee camp acts, not as a place for temporary relief, but as a semi-permanent place for containing and sustaining a population at levels just above the means of survival. It is against the dilemma of the refugee camp –

that it is easier to raise long-term life-sustaining humanitarian refugee assistance than to negotiate for a sustainable peace – that the actions of ACT members should be judged. This dilemma of the refugee camp raises the question about what ethically appropriate actions could be taken to do good and not harm.

The international standards are written to protect human life and dignity. These standards represent an international framework for humanitarian relief. The framework developed as a principled moral response to crises in different contexts. ACT Alliance is committed to a principled approach based on the Christian faith seeking local solutions by local actors. At its root is what the Nigerian theologian Agbonkhianmeghe Orobator calls "the moral priority of crisis-affected people." Thus, there are two demands to be distinguished: the requirement of responsibility towards donors and host governments to show effectiveness and efficiency, and the moral demand of serving "crisis-affected people" with "bottom-up accountability." There is an inbuilt tension between a modernist conception of instrumental reason and a post-modern critique of universalism. This is an integral challenge of the humanitarian relief sector in which a few donors, UN agencies, and humanitarian agencies dominate the ecology of actors and stakeholders.

To address human conditions by the rule of law has been a main tenet of the Christian church from its very inception. In Christian thought, legality is grounded in the moral law, which is binding on all people, and conceptualised as *natural law* and incorporated in cultures and societies. Today, natural law may be expressed in international law. International law, however, may be abused for other purposes as well as used properly to promote the common good.

African Gate Keeper States and Stakeholders (3.4) dealt with the fact that *ACT Alliance* is not acting in a social and political vacuum but in a context that became more complex because of how modern African states has mimicked colonial policies of what is known as *the gate keeper state*. The main responsibility lies on the African political leadership – considered as a whole – to seek peace rather than conflict, and practical solutions rather than seeking scapegoats. The political organs of the UN, including the Security Council share the responsibility to peaceful political aims.

In *Morality, Principled Action, and the Church* (3.5), it was argued for a plausible relation between morality, legality, and church tradition. First, the ecumenical refugee assistance of ACT Alliance is a moral response to a humanitarian crisis. Second, morality as such, is assumed in the refugee response, neither argued for nor proven, but taken for granted as a given. Third, by setting up organisations, the principled matter has not changed, but the practical matter has become complex. Therefore fourth, the operational principles are essential for agencies to be able to operate ethically within a conflicted context of many stakeholders. Fifth, parents, teachers, and communities, including the moral and social teachings of the Christian churches, come into this context by providing a cultural moral framework based on the main Christian doctrines of the faith. Sixth, the work of ACT Alliance is not exhausted by refugee assistance, ACT Alliance does not exhaust the ecumenical movement, and the movement is only one expression of the life in the churches.

In the first part of the thesis, about ACT Alliance in practice, an important question was asked: If the refugee assistance of ACT Alliance, in some sense, is an *action by churches together*, what does it mean in practical terms? ACT Alliance was initiated by churches and aid agencies with the expressed intention to collaborate on matters of aid through the coordination of the secretariat. The refugee assistance to South Sudanese asylum seekers is in historical continuity with earlier Christian initiatives to assist people in need. The motive for assisting people is grounded in Christian faith and morality and, in that sense, in the life of the churches. Principles of the rule of law and accountability of power and authority are grounded in Christian thought and church teaching. The ACT members in Ethiopia discussed and published an ACT appeal in the name of the forum. Several ACT members collaborated in the appeal, and at the end of 2014, all Ethiopian forum members had contributed to the refugee assistance in one way or another.

As such, the refugee assistance of ETH141 is not an intra-church aid aimed only at church communities in need as in the inter-church aid model. Nor is it an internal affair of ACT members, but it represents a larger collaborative approach. Ethiopian church authorities are neither leading the work nor setting the principles. Instead, the work is led by UNHCR, and the principles followed are set by international bodies. Refugee assistance is not the work of volunteers but of professionals and hired staff. The work of ACT Alliance is thus a distinguishable entity of its own, separate from the life and ministry of the churches. ACT Alliance was unable to raise sufficient funding for the ETH141. Instead, the main source of funding for refugee assistance is the OECD donors, not voluntary contributions from ecclesial communities.

6.2 The Churches and Ecumenical Models

In chapter four, *Ethiopian Churches: Ecumenical Engagement*, textual studies were used to investigate how ecumenical engagement had been understood, motivated, and critiqued by Ethiopian churches. The idea of ACT Alliance as *action by churches together* was thus set in relation to views of *the Ethiopian Orthodox Tewahedo Church* and *the Ethiopian Evangelical Church Mekane Yesus* for the sake of contributing to a discussion on ecclesial engagement.

The Mekane Yesus arose from the modern mission movement's concern to serve the whole man. It means to proclaim the Christian gospel, so that people may be liberated from sin, as well as to serve bodily needs, and to show Christian compassion to neighbour. As part of the mission movement, the Mekane Yesus became a member of the Lutheran World Federation even before its formal establishment as a national church, and it kept its membership as an integral part of being a member of the Christian Church. The establishment of the Ethiopian Evangelical Church Mekane Yesus as a national church changed the Mekane Yesus' relationship with its founding mission agencies and sister churches. The Mekane Yesus argued not for a severing of ties but changed relationships. Mission agencies would no longer lead the work according to their own accords but integrate their efforts with the work of the Ethiopian church. Such an integrated mission model would be different from the previous mission approaches in which mission agencies would act independently from the church.

A Letter from Mekane Yesus 1972 (4.1) is a textual analysis of one significant text from the Ethiopian Evangelical Church Mekane Yesus, *On the Interrelation between the Proclamation of the Gospel and Human Development*, (also called *the ECMY Letter*). The church officers wrote the ECMY Letter to the Lutheran World Federation in 1972 as a critique of a donor-oriented aid model in favour of a church-led aid model. The ECMY Letter introduced the theme of holistic ministry in the teaching of the church. It presented a framework for socio-economic service with a theological critique of donor-based aid based on holistic anthropology and a sense of Ethiopian ownership in ecumenical engagement. The Mekane Yesus position is argued from the standpoint of Christian anthropology, in contrast to utilitarian (materialist) or deontological (idealist) alternatives. The Christian humanism favoured by the authors understands human nature as holistic, and the human person as naturally directed to God. God is the origin (creation) and destiny (salvation) of human persons.

The Mekane Yesus issued severe critique to "the Churches and Agencies in the West" for supporting only material development by sending a letter to the Lutheran World Federation. Based on the comparison of ecumenical models in chapter five, the letter can be said to be a critique of aid according to an approach of international development, rather than the mission approach the church was used to deal with. That is however not explicit in the letter which instead focuses on a critique of the underlying anthropology of the concurrent work of the Lutheran World Federation. A mere material development may be a threat to values that make life meaningful. In terms of anthropology, such one-sided support represented a view of human beings as patients. The Mekane Yesus saw this as a false anthropology, as man is not primarily a patient but an agent, one who acts. Humanism, for Mekane Yesus, meant that man is realising himself by reaching beyond the present state. The exclusive humanism of late modernity thus shows itself to be no humanism at all. One of its critical tones was aimed at concurrent trends within the World Council of Churches, exemplified in trends in Uppsala 1968.

Based on this critique of materialism, Mekane Yesus argued that the need should determine where and what assistance should be given. Human needs include spiritual, personal, and community needs, but donor criteria do not reflect actual human needs, but trends in Western societies. The authors of the letter further argued that service is neither a means to another end (instrumentalization), nor an end-in-itself, but it is for the true-end-in-itself. All human beings are endowed with a true end-in-itself. Service should serve that true end. Man is an agent and a whole, created for a true destiny with God. Service, thus understood, is part of the whole concern of the church.

The Ethiopian Orthodox Tewahido Church is an ancient church with its episcopacy established in the fourth century. The Ethiopian Church has thus played a foundational role in cultural and national development. During the twentieth century, Abyssinia and the Orthodox Church sought to establish good relations with the modern West and the Ecumenical movement. As such the Ethiopian Orthodox Church is a founding member of the World Council of Churches.

Passover Message 1983 from the Ethiopian Orthodox (4.2) analysed the texts of a booklet written to Ecumenical donors to showcase the church and its commitment to ecumenical collaboration in 1983. During the Derg regime (1974–1991), the Orthodox Church published the EOC *Maedot Journals* (1983–1990). These journals are rich sources containing different voices from the church during a period of political controversy. The Derg period as a transitional time between Imperial Abyssinia and Federal Democratic Ethiopia was formative for the church and its social engagements. The *Maedot* of 1983 from *the Ethiopian Orthodox Tewahido Church* (EOTC) showed the ecclesial basis for social works, and ecumenical commitments in the 1980s in the self-understanding as a church and the Christian faith in the resurrection.

According to the patriarch, *Abuna* Tekle Haimanot, the church of Christ is commanded to work for peace on earth and good will towards men. Therefore,

Christians are called upon to contribute to world peace and to fulfil this mission in the unity of the church. The theological foundation is the Christian gospel of Jesus Christ: "His incarnation, services, suffering, death and resurrection", an understanding of life as "the most sacred gift of God both in the visible and invisible world", the world as needing the blessing of peace that comes "not only from below but also from above." The peace that Christ made between God and man may therefore be extended "among the people in the world." The ecclesiological basis is "the one, Holy Apostolic Church." On this premise, the Ethiopian Orthodox Church has joined institutions, such as the World Council of Churches, to collaborate on relief work and to restore the historical unity of the church. As the church is holy and apostolic, Christians need to guard against teachings not in line with church doctrine as represented by the early ecumenical councils.

Ecumenical engagement, for the authors of the *Maedot* no. 1, 1983, is thus rooted in the theological foundations and spiritual life of the church, and its social ministry in an ecclesial understanding of reality. Contemporary diakonia is grounded in the sacramental and spiritual life of the church with its never ceasing prayers for "the sick, the oppressed, the prisoners, the refugees, the orphans, the hungry, and all the helpless." The "Apostolic Diakonia" of the *Maedot* signifies church ministry and is not limited to charitable works. This can be seen in the way the Eucharist forms "the focal point of all religious services rendered in the EOC", in which "service" is interchangeable with "diakonia." The charitable works are derived from the Eucharistic liturgy and not the other way around.

When poverty is understood based on a materialistic basis, in contrast, it changes the meaning and extension of assisting the poor with consequences for the strategy of assistance. Materialism makes the state the centre and the church the margin in such a model for assistance. Those who hold to such a material worldview see the theological foundations and the spiritual life of the church as irrelevant otherworldliness. This was seen in the revolutionary attempt in Ethiopia to forward the material development of *a New Society* without churches or mosques. The authors of the *Maedot* plead with ecumenical partners to base interventions on a Christian view of reality instead.

In *Gospel and Liturgy Form the Christian* (4.3), I discussed the notions laid forth by the church documents concerning how the Christian gospel and sacraments contribute to the ethical formation of Christians.

The Voice of the Gospel expanded on the evangelical understanding of the gospel outlined in the *ECMY Letter* to clarify the importance of the gospel. *The ECMY Letter* addresses the dilemma that man through civilized history "may know what is good and right and even want to do the right things yet he fails to achieve it." The problem is not first of all knowing what is good, but the need for something to "make man do good." Mekane Yesus forwarded the notion of sin, "the idea that all human beings are predisposed to love the wrong things or to love the right things wrongly, and as a result to do both themselves harm and others injustice."

There are different kinds of freedom depending on what one is free from. Mekane Yesus, along with the Christian tradition, give precedence to freedom from sin. The gospel is that which can liberate man from sin and enable him to love God and his neighbour. Here is the origin of the *Diakonie,* the service, that brings about ACT Alliance as a *common* concern in the ecumenical movement. Real freedom is freedom from sin that liberates man to love and therefore to serve his fellow man. When the church officers of Mekane Yesus are writing to the Lutheran World Federation asking them to reconsider their approach to service to the world, they do so with the teaching of the reformer in mind – and arguably St Paul's apostolic teaching as a foundation. This thinking does not apply to a humanitarian sector that is based on state funding, however, as it will fall on deaf ears as governments do not integrate the gospel into their legal and governmental systems, but Christians may still act according to moral principles.

The Liturgy Forms the Christian, used insights from liturgical theology to discuss the role of the historical liturgy in forming Christians to assist those on the margin of the community. The liturgical celebration of the resurrection of Christ, as the sacramental centre of Orthodox Church life, with its fasting and feasting, is thereby essential for fostering a common life. Orthodoxy in this way strives to hold together right beliefs, worship, and practice. The crucial question for the Orthodox scholar Alexander Schmemann was how to hold together the seemingly contradictory affirmations of both the goodness and the wickedness of the present state of the world. His answer is to point to the Eucharist in which the church becomes "that which she is: the sacrament of the world, the sacrament of the Kingdom." Whenever an Orthodox Christian is involved, the liturgical life of the church may be operative in that person's moral life.

In chapter five the contemporary work of ACT Alliance was set in a larger historical context by naming some historical initiatives of ecumenical collaboration in Ethiopia and drawing attention to the fact that ecumenical bodies may be very different in approach. By using heuristic models based on historical forms of ecumenical collaboration in Ethiopia the intent was to sketch ecumenical strategies from the mid-twentieth century (1944) to the beginning of the twenty-first (2014) and compare them with the contemporary example of ACT in the case study.

Models may be used as ways of understanding issues of church and aid, and the complexities of the ACT Ethiopia Forum and its work.

The first section, *the Mission Model and the Integrated Church* (5.1) summarised the post-Second World War approach of integrating a holistic sense of mission with the Ethiopian Evangelical Church Mekane Yesus led to an ideal of the integrated church (1959–1974).

The Inter-Church Aid Model (5.2) depicted the ecumenical approach of Western Churches showing practical solidarity with the Ethiopian Orthodox Tewahido Church in consequence of a sense of unity, *koinonia*, of the Christian Church. The Orthodox Church, in collaboration with ecumenical partners, started aid initiatives on the stance of inter-church aid with refugee assistance, development works, drought relief, and intra-church aid projects.

The International Crisis Model (5.3) outlined some of the major collaborative schemes by ecumenical agencies bringing relief to Ethiopia during conflict and military regime. The international crisis model gave less emphasis on the leadership and initiatives of the Ethiopian churches, Christian witness, and nation-building, and more on coordination of aid agencies for the survival of people and with the people, the churches as churches. The background was the revolutionary changes in Ethiopia which threatened both life in society and church.

This period contained several different organisations for ecumenical coordination and collaboration: LWF World Service Ethiopia (1973–), Christian Relief and Development Agency (CRDA 1973–), The Joint Relief Partnership (JRP 1984–2005), The Emergency Relief Desk (ERD 1975–1992 and the informal network *Kontakt der Kontinenten* (KdK 1985–2010). The Christian Relief and Development Agency was probably the most important common organisation in the 1970s, while the Joint Relief Partnership filled that role in the 1980s. The LWF World Service, and the Catholic Relief Services (CRS), and some organisations that are now ACT members, were among the organisations that were able to mobilise support through the Christian Relief and Development Agency and the Joint Relief Partnership.

Whereas people working under the mission model strove to integrate the work of mission with the Mekane Yesus Church – thus building up local capacities, under the international crisis model – the initiative remained with the northern aid agencies, rather than the Ethiopian churches. There was coordination more than close collaboration and attempts at integration. From the international crisis model, two working principles developed, in the first, the European agencies worked through the Ethiopian church structures. In the latter, the agencies worked through political organs of the rebel fronts (later government parties) instead. Such modalities created a precedence for the European agencies to choose which implementing agency to work through according to need, rather than working with church agencies on a principled basis.

Though the collaborative scheme of ACT Alliance took place decades later, it could be argued that the approach that the international crisis model represents resembles the contemporary picture of the ACT Ethiopia Forum. The initiative lies with the northern agencies from which the funding comes, and Ethiopian church agencies may or may not be collaborated with on a case-to-case basis rather than from a principled approach. This leads to uncertainties within the forum as no one knows who will collaborate with whom.

In the Joint Relief Partnership, there was more coordination than close collaboration as vast territories could be covered when the areas were divided up. It was difficult for the agencies to collaborate in the case study because they were not accustomed to close collaboration, as such the details had not been worked out.

The difference between the earlier inter-church aid model and the international crisis model also confirms that ACT Alliance is not operating on the presuppositions of inter-church aid. The concept of inter-church aid was fundamental in St Paul's argument for relief aid to the church in Jerusalem. Such arguments are not operative in the case study. ACT is not, in practice, mutual aid as a sign of ecclesial community. The aid is not a sign of belonging to the body of Christ. The sacramental body language St Paul uses is not practised in the ETH141 appeal.

The Mekane Yesus (1972) and the Orthodox Church (1983) expressed clear critique against the materialistic basis of aid of that time. Both the interventions in the ETH141 appeal planned by LWF World Service and DICAC included services far beyond "lifesaving" activities. This represents the long experiences of these two agencies in working with refugees – in and outside of camp settings. Perhaps this represents a shift from a materialist one-sided thinking in relief aid towards a more holistic approach. The international standards explored in chapter three do include a more comprehensive approach than simply providing basic protection from that which threatens biological life. And both LWF World Service and DICAC have been, and still are, pushing those boundaries of what counts as humanitarian relief. The community based psychosocial approach (CBPS) both agencies have adopted signals such cutting-edge thinking. At its best, such an approach encourages community participation in relief assistance.

There was, in the practical work in 2014, more room for a holistic view of man, than during the 1970s and 1980s, at the same time two things need to be stressed. First, there is still hostility from those who represent exclusive humanism against "religion" in the relief sector. It can come from donor representatives – as seen in Holmefur's study of SIDA's policy documents of SIDA in earlier research, and it can come as competition from other relief agencies who stress their "secular" identity as a means of competing for funds and contracts with "religious" agencies. The "religious" nature of "secular" agencies has not yet been discussed to such an extent as to disclose the ambiguity involved. Let alone the religiosity of secular states and donor agencies.

Second, though there is more room for "spirituality", or "religion", in a postmodern paradigm, that is not the same thing as what Mekane Yesus and the Orthodox argued for when they called for a move away from a materialist basis of ecumenical aid. The diakonia of the Christian church cannot be limited to that which fits into a conception and practice of aid. It goes beyond because the church participates in the life of the trinity through the gospel and sacramental life of the Christian Church. This type of apostolic ministry rendered in practical terms through preaching and teaching the gospel, celebrating the sacraments, and pastoral care is not the same as community based psychosocial support. Both are morally good things. Serving the neighbour in need as conceived in ACT Alliance and the care of the pastor. If the church is not coming together as *ecclesia* during the eucharist service, there is no church, and the service to the neighbour may eventually come to a halt.

As an Orthodox author argued, from "the other world", Christ comes and gives of his life to the world, generating a deep concern among the faithful for people in need. Since ACT Alliance is not serving this need – to participate in God's saving of the world – the churches must not forget this obligation. This was mentioned in chapter one as the life and ministry of the sending churches, the refugee camps, the local church communities, and the Ethiopian churches. This apostolic ministry fits the mission model, but does not fit into the international crisis model, and therefore is not part of the *action by churches together* of ACT Alliance. It does not mean that within the mission models, the apostolic ministry was mixed up with relief work. Generally, that was not the case, but the organisational approach behind the missions was broader than that of ACT Alliance. In ACT Alliance it is part of the rhetoric of its public messages – that the local churches will remain when the agencies are gone – but not an integral part of its action.

What is *the action by churches together*, as exemplified in the refugee assistance of ACT Ethiopia Forum, when it is seen in the light of the voices of Ethiopian churches and previous ecumenical approaches to collaboration? The motive for assisting people in need is grounded in Christian faith and morality and in that sense in the life of the churches. The Ethiopian churches collaborate with other churches and their agencies based on the common Christian faith and the unity of the Christian church. The Ethiopian churches critiqued their northern counterparts for neglecting the gospel and basing the ecumenical collaboration on materialistic anthropology, thus understanding the issue of need in such a way that would marginalise the churches and focus on state inventions.

The refugee assistance to South Sudanese asylum seekers is in historical continuity with earlier Christian initiatives to assist people in need. The ecumenical movement has, as a concerted effort of the churches to do their part, been a prime mover and innovator of societal concerns exemplified in mission, inter-church aid, crisis relief aid, and peace and development initiatives. Several of these approaches have been used in Ethiopia. Both the mission model and the international crisis models showed examples of closer collaborations with Ethiopian churches and more or less independent initiatives from European mission and aid agencies.

Churches are on the whole not engaged in the ACT way of thinking and working – ACT Alliance is an alliance of aid agencies – from the north and south – working under the same conditions as other aid agencies and mostly doing things in the same way as all others – from Africa nothing new under the sun – directions are still coming from the global North. If ACT Alliance is a genuine expression of the Christian Church, it is a very thin slice of the church, at least with regard to African churches.

6.3 What "Action by Churches Together" Is and Is Not

The investigation of the refugee assistance of ACT Alliance in the case of the ETH141 appeal and the international standards, in chapters two and three, identified the aims, methodologies, conditions, and principles of refugee assistance. The main content of refugee assistance has thereby been established. It is now possible to clarify to a certain extent, what refugee assistance as an *action by churches together*, is and is not in practice, which this section will cover in detail. This is helpful because in discussions of aid and development and in discussions on Christian involvement in aid, such as that of international or ecumenical diakonia, categorical mistakes are being made by people who are either uninformed about aid or the churches' involvement in aid. No one is helped by a discussion based on false factual premises. Based on chapters two and three, this subsection will state several propositions. These are the historical results of the study of ETH141. First, what the refugee assistance of ACT Alliance is, and next what it is not, in practical terms. All these statements refer to the case study of the ETH141 appeal, and there may be limited generalisability. This section will discuss and draw the main conclusions of the enquiry into ACT Alliance.

Predicated Attributes of Action by Churches Together in ETH141

Several attributes can be predicated of the refugee assistance, and therefore what the action by churches together, in the ETH141 appeal is. These positive assertions signal what *action by churches together* means in practice, i.e. in the historical case study of the ETH141 appeal. These positive statements are matters of fact, (what something is or is not), not of moral evaluation, (what ought to be). Discussion on the latter may follow afterwards.

ACT Alliance was initiated by member churches of the World Council of Churches, the Lutheran World Federation and their respective aid agencies. The initiative was taken with the expressed intention that churches should collaborate on matters of aid in a form that better corresponded to the ecclesiological dialogues of the ecumenical movement than what previous approaches to collaboration had done. This is the essence of the idea of ACT Alliance which expressed an action by churches together. It made sense from a practical point of view, based on previous experience, to work closer together and, from an ecumenical point of view, working together expressed the unity of the churches in a divided world.

The refugee assistance to South Sudanese asylum seekers is in historical continuity with Christian initiatives in the past, as Christians have time and again initiated acts of solidarity with people in need. Christian societies and associations have been performing such acts of benevolence and have been innovators of new forms of human organisation and collaboration. This includes the mobilisation of state resources for the sake of people in need in distant countries.

The motive for assisting people in need is grounded in the Christian faith and morality and, in that sense, in the life of the churches. The life of a Christian is geared towards loving God and neighbour. This latter point can be conceptualised in terms of service (*Diakonie*). This service is not for the churches but for others as a natural fruit of the life of the churches.

The notions of the rule of law and accountability of power and authority, are grounded in Christian thought, as well as in church teaching. In this sense, several main principles of the work are rooted in Christian commitments to the good of the human person and the common good.

Taken as a whole, the ecumenical movement has been one of the prime movers of innovation in societal concerns of the churches. This is exemplified in the mission model, the inter-church aid model, and the international crisis model. ACT Alliance is one such example of a Christian organisation working for an ecumenical good, in the sense of working for the common (social) good. In the case of Ethiopia, all three approaches have been at hand, together with the approach now represented by ACT Alliance.

It is an "action together" in that the ACT members in Ethiopia come together to discuss matters in one forum and publish an ACT Appeal in the name of the ACT Ethiopia forum. It is also an action together in the sense that several ACT members collaborated and that at the end of the appeal, all ACT members in Ethiopia had contributed in one way or another to the assistance of the refugees.

Attributes Not Predicated of Action by Churches Together in ETH141

There are several properties which cannot be attributed to "act." Attributes that in fact the ETH141 appeal is not. These negative assertions also contain positive elements of what it is. To repeat myself for the sake of clarification, the purpose at this point is not to offer a critique but only to state matters of fact for clarification.

Refugee assistance is not for church communities in need. It is therefore not intra-church aid, but aid offered based on the assessed needs of any community.

It is not assistance rendered only by members of ACT Alliance, but a collaborative project of several stakeholders, such as Ethiopian federal state agencies, local authorities, UN agencies, other aid agencies, as well as the refugee population and the local population in the Gambella region. The working together of ACT Alliance is therefore not a self-contained unit, but a forum for coordination and collaboration with people of good will within a larger "ecosystem."

The assistance is neither directly supervised by nor accountable to Ethiopian church authorities, even though there are some means of indirect oversight through board members. ACT Alliance, in this sense, places itself as an autonomous body in relation to the churches, but under the current system of global humanitarian governance.

The principles of the work are not set by Ethiopian churches, nor by any other church, but mainly by various international bodies of which ACT Alliance and the Lutheran World Federation are two. ACT Alliance uses their ACT forums and "communities of practice" to promote the participation of staff from among all its members in these processes of setting up standards and regulatory systems. In addition, ACT Alliance sets up its own internal international system of regulations and principles with references to other international standards.

On the operative side of the assistance, in this case in Ethiopia, it is not the work of churches in the sense of volunteer mobilisation of church communities with at least two important exceptions to this point. First, the local Mekane Yesus congregation and its synod staff collaborated with the LWF World Service by allowing them to use their compound and facilitating initial missions of assessment by operating as guides and translators to LWF staff. Second, the agencies are mobilising volunteers among the refugee population and, to some extent, among the local population. Historically, voluntary mobilisation has been vital to the success of the churches' relief work and inter-church collaboration in raising awareness and support. This aspect has not been investigated in this project.

This point is accentuated as the work is not primarily financed by volunteer contributions from church communities but through mandatory means, primarily from OECD nations as overseen by government aid agencies. This is shown in the practical application of the ACT Appeal system. The many ACT members in Ethiopia were unable to raise the funds needed from voluntary contributions of the church constituencies. This is a consequence of the fact that standards for assistance need to be kept high for an indefinite period. The refugee camp is not a solution for people, but a way of mitigating the harm caused by a political crisis. It is not an ideal, but a compromise of competing goals.

The dependency on external funding from government sources follows the dilemma of contemporary refugee assistance as conceptualised by the international community. It has consequences for how to understand the ACT appeal system, which was set up on the premise of ecclesial funding from people willing to support people in dire need. The reliance on government funding indicates a tension between aid as ecclesial and civil society-organised voluntary forms of sharing and aid as controlled by state and UN agencies.

Correlation between the Idea of ACT and its Operation

How does the work correspond with the idea of *action by churches together* as conceptualised in the ecumenical discussion? The work of ACT Alliance follows the operational meaning given by ACT Alliance rather than the theological meaning given by the ecumenical discussions that preceded its establishment. That is, there is less actual involvement of the Ethiopian churches than what was envisioned in the theological discussions on ethics and ecclesiology in the World Council of

Churches. There is also less sense of solidarity between ACT members based on the *koinonia* of the Christian churches. Common action was less motivated by a common identity and more on pragmatic grounds.

This, however, is not the whole story, as shown in the second part of the thesis. ACT Alliance is not the first attempt to work together for the churches in the ecumenical movement. Since the inception of the World Council of Churches, social action has been practised using different approaches. There is, therefore, plenty of experience within the movement. In the second part of the thesis, the views of two Ethiopian Churches and past historical experiences of ecumenical collaboration were analysed and critiqued by turning past operational approaches into heuristic models for a better understanding.

The operational meaning of *action by churches together* as "coordination between churches and their related agencies" fits better with the results in chapters two and three. However, such a conception of ACT fails to provide sufficient grounds for common action as church ecumenism. Though, in the end, all ACT Ethiopia Forum had contributed to the cause of South Sudanese refugees, the ACT Appeal as such failed as an instrument for planning and action since there was not enough willingness and ability to fund the appeal. Hence the appeal was, to a large extent, a common failure rather than common action for ACT Alliance. It can be argued that it was a result of planning for a larger appeal than the ecclesial funding could bring about, and the inability and unwillingness of northern church agencies to support the appeal rather than doing separate projects.

ACT was not intended as assistance for church communities, as intra-church aid, or set up for the spread of the Christian faith, as mission agencies. ACT is neither supervised by nor accountable to Ethiopian church authorities, though the churches do support the work. The principles of the work were not set by churches but by various international bodies of which ACT Alliance and the LWF World Service are members. The ETH141 ACT Appeal did not mobilise volunteers from church communities or integrate assistance into the life of Ethiopian churches. It was the work of legally separate entities, Ethiopian church service institutions (EECMY-DASSC and EOC-DICAC), Christian aid agencies (BftW, CA, CoS, DCA, HEKS, ICCO, IOCC, and NCA), and ecumenical aid agencies (LWF World Service and ACT Alliance).

Therefore, the work was not performed by volunteers, but by professional staff, hired to do the work required while aiming for the highest standards in the sector, but with comparably lower wages. Organisationally, this entailed the mobilisation of foreign state resources for the sake of people in need and the appropriation of a principled approach, rooted in Christian commitments to the good of the human person, the institutionalisation of the common good in society, and aligned with a Christian worldview.

The ACT Appeal system failed to raise the funds needed from voluntary contributions of church constituencies, primarily as a consequence of the fact that living standards for refugees need to be kept at a high enough standard for an indefinite period. Refugee camps are not a solution to the problems refugees are encountering, but a way of mitigating the harmful effects of a political crisis by providing for basic needs and containing refugees in designated places while waiting for a political solution.

The appeal therefore needed to be financed not by volunteer contributions, but through tax funds of OECD nations and overseen by their respective government aid agencies. The lack of voluntary contributions from churches across the world endangered the effectiveness of the relief assistance and limited its positive impact on the well-being of the refugees. This fact shows that there is tension between the idea of ACT Alliance as *action by churches together* in the sense of a relief society with the ability to respond quickly to crises across the world, based on voluntary funding from Christians across the world, and the idea and form of public-funded emergency relief grounded in international law and dependent on the good will of civil servants and foreign government support.

Practically, the ACT members discussed the refugee crisis and published an appeal, but though all forum members contributed one way or another to assist the refugees, they did not collaborate closely. In this, there is less continuity with earlier forms of ecumenical assistance such as the Committee of Mutual Christian Responsibility (CMCR), the Round Table, the Emergency Relief Desk (ERD 1975–1992), and the *Kontakt der Kontinenten* ("KdK-group" 1985–2010), and more with the (Consortium of) Christian Relief and Development Association [C]CRDA (1973–), and the Joint Relief Partnership (JRP) (1984–2005). The lack of collaboration among the ACT members is similar to the Joint Relief Partnership which was coordinated by raising sufficient funding and distributing it fairly without close collaboration in the field. By joining ACT, the members lost the financial support they had enjoyed with the Joint Relief Partnership, and the ACT Appeal system has so far been unable to compensate for the loss of funding.

The refugee assistance of ACT Alliance is an *action by churches together* in the practical sense that the ACT members in Ethiopia discussed the refugee crisis, published the ETH141 appeal, and attempted to support the appeal, mainly through technical support while expecting state financing. The appeal did not imply that churches mobilised their members for volunteer work and financial contributions, or in the sense of a well-coordinated and closely collaborative approach in the field. The ACT members failed to respond to the refugee crisis in a coordinated and collaborative way because the ACT appeal system was set up for voluntary funding, while refugee assistance requires government funding, and because the ACT members spread the attention to different countries. This was in historic continuity with an ecumenical model which focuses on international crises without grounding the work in the national churches. The idea of *action by churches together* as a voluntary funding model by churches across the world thus stands in tension with the *action by churches together* in practice which focuses on agency responses to political crises and other emergencies. The idea that some churches from the global north would be able to finance relief and development projects all across the world is impractical and leads to frustration and unreasonable expectations for all ACT members and its churches.

ACT as a Model of Ecumenical Diakonia

As an inference to the best explanation, First, I will argue for a hypothesis that would make sense of both ACT Alliance as an *action by churches together* and the tensions of the ETH141 appeal. ACT and its agencies exemplify one model of *ecumenical diakonia*, i.e. the work of *ecumenical* specialised agencies for the social good in collaboration with other stakeholders.

This kind of *ecumenical diakonie* entailed the mobilisation of external public resources and appropriation of a principled humanitarian approach for the sake of people in need, in a constrained context of conflict, which in turn brought practical challenges (practical tensions) to the ACT Ethiopia Forum as the agencies sought to meet the needs of the refugees. Such a model is less grounded in the life and ministry of the churches.

Second, tensions in refugee assistance of ETH141, as a case study of the work of ACT Alliance, first indicate superficial conflict but deep concord between the idea of *action by churches together* as formulated in ecumenical dialogues, and as supported by Ethiopian churches, and the refugee assistance as planned in the ETH141 appeal which focuses on agency responses to a political crisis and its refugee emergencies as an expression of morality and a Christian sense of serving the neighbour.

It is the Christian sense of morality which includes the service to the neighbour, even though the neighbour may be an enemy, that explains the motivation for refugee assistance. Tensions secondly indicate superficial concord and deep conflict between exclusive humanism and the churches' mission to reach every person with the gospel and the sacramental life of the church.

The context entails working with different stakeholders that may not share the mission of the church. This includes staff members of ACT agencies. As resources are constrained, the temptation for ACT Alliance is to lose the sense that their limited ACT mission is part of the larger mission of the churches as involvement in God's mission to the world to bring about its intended end through the gospel and sacramental life of the Christian Church. The churches pointed out that the Christian gospel and the "otherworldly" stance are the foundation from which the churches may participate in the good works of men, and not by adopting a materialist stance of exclusive humanism, or an alternative gospel. There is therefore ground for ACT Alliance to scrutinise its ethical basis to see whether to what extent it follows a Christian foundation.

The concord between the refugee assistance and the churches gives ground for the churches to consider the work of ACT Alliance as a real part of the churches' outreach, or a very thin slice of the church, in the sense of an organisation of genuine Christian concern for the neighbour, i.e. alliance mission. There are therefore reasons to accept Brodd's thesis that Christian organisations are part of the reality of the church.

Tensions give grounds for caution that this line of action can potentially go against the mission of the church. This understanding of *action by churches together* in the case of ETH141 enlightens the relationship between ACT Alliance and the Ethiopian Churches in this way: Tensions in the case study indicate that there is superficial conflict but deep concord between aid (the refugee assistance of the ETH141 appeal) and the church (the Ethiopian churches) because Christians are rooted in a Christian worldview with commitments to the good of the human person, but also in superficial concord and deep conflict between an exclusive humanism and the churches' mission to reach every person with the gospel and the sacramental life of the church.

6.4 Beyond ACT Alliance

There is one last topic to end the discussion with, in view of further research. It has to do with enquiries into church ministry, *church diakonia*, that go beyond humanitarian relief work: *ecumenical diakonie*. The main thrust of the thesis has been to analyse the identity and meaning of ACT Alliance as an *action by churches together,* i.e. church-based, and other Christian-based aid agencies. This was concluded with three assumptions and one main argument. This has partially been done by following the intentions and the challenges in the refugee assistance of the ETH141 ACT Appeal 2014 and partially by investigating the writings of the two Ethiopian churches and the history of ecumenical collaboration.

I have shown that the humanitarian moral argument of aid organisations is perceived as a right to humanitarian assistance – founded in international law and applied in solidarity with communities in need. The aim of the work is for the aid agencies to render services until no longer needed, and to assist the communities in rebuilding their capacity and self-sustainability. The many practical challenges – in which the ACT Appeal system was not enough to bring the resources needed – were met by the ACT Ethiopia Forum members by applying a principled humanitarian approach and by public funding through UNHCR.

Church Ministry Beyond Humanitarian Relief Work

The churches' mission goes beyond the humanitarian argument. While an aid agency exits when the mission is done, the church stays as a community, and the *church as institution* builds up not only material goods but focuses on assisting men and women to develop and grow as a church community in the likeness of Christ. The churches have pastoral responsibilities towards the community of Christians. As the church is not bound by national borders, the mission of the church extends across borders as part of its catholicity. The pastoral ministry concerns church members who are subject to pastoral care and discipline.

Different churches in Ethiopia – but particularly Mekane Yesus and the Anglican Church – have worked hard to fulfil their pastoral responsibilities serving Christians among the refugees by assisting in organising refugee churches and supporting them. This pastoral concern of the churches is protected by Human Rights, specifically within article 4 of the 1967 Protocol Relating to the Status of Refugees that was built upon and improved the original and time-limited United Nations Refugee Convention from 1951.

The Mission of Church-Based Aid Agencies

Contemporary humanitarian agencies contain something of a paradox as they are expressions of particular communities, including church communities, which in foreign territories do not appear as communities, i.e. civil society, but as agencies, as professional aid organisations. Whereas the link to their formative constituencies may be visible in their native countries, it is not in the countries of operation, in which they appear as identity-less "NGOs," symbolised by ever-present acronyms. More visible however is the bond to their respective governments. This means that when trust is low – these agencies are associated with and may be thought of as agents of foreign governments rather than an outpouring of particular communities – in our case, church communities.

For church-based and Christian-based organisations this is both true and yet there is another important aspect to consider. As one of the four marks of the Church in the Nicene Creed – *unity* is essential to the Christian Church. If the church does not appear to be one ecumenically – that in the eyes of "the world" – it does not faithfully represent the One, Holy, Apostolic, and Catholic Church. Hence, when Christian agencies appear outside of the pastoral areas of their respective local churches, if those areas are within the apostolic ministry of other parts of the Christian Church – they will be identified with the local churches. The ecumenical movement has attempted to recognise this by bringing Christian ministries under ecumenical bodies to reconcile mission initiatives with the local churches. ACT Alliance is such an ecumenical body bringing local churches and agencies of other churches together under one roof.

For foreign Christian agencies, it means that they relate to local churches since theologically they belong to the sacramental body of Christ. This gives ACT Alliance a potential edge in aid work. There are almost always local churches on the ground in the territories where ACT agencies operate. ACT publicise this as an advantage of the Alliance – that local churches are present before and after an emergency appears. This means that ACT agencies, when operating under the auspices of local churches, ought not to be reduced to "foreign agents" but also be expressions of local churches and local societies.

An example of this is the work of the World Service Department of the Lutheran World Federation. The aid agency came on the request of the Mekane Yesus – not to serve church members, but to complement the services that the local church was able to render with its own experienced and professional staff and organisation. It was the Lutheran World Federation then that also broadened the ecumenical spectrum – beyond "Lutheran" churches – to bring in Catholics and others into an even greater response to the famine during the civil war of the 1980s, as seen in chapter five.

The principled approach of humanitarian agencies is an alternative way of breaching the gap between the agencies and the communities they work with and the local governments. The ever-existing critique of the phenomenon of "INGOs" – international non-governmental organizations – shows that the respect for humanitarian agencies as principled and appreciated actors is not always at a high level. This critique may contain both warranted and unwarranted concerns.

The mission of the church is the salvation of the world by bringing people into communion with God, and it belongs to the nature of the church to be an instrument of salvation, the sacramental community which brings God's people into communion with God. The church participates in God's mission – *Missio Dei* – for the salvation of the created world since it is divinely instituted. The agent and model for this is the body of Christ. Just as Christ is fully human and fully divine, the church is both earthly and heavenly, human and divine, in as much as the people of God are human, sacramentally incorporated into the church as the sacramental presence of Jesus Christ, the body of Christ on earth.

The thesis leaves questions unanswered and areas of research to pursue. There is a need for more research in the area of funding, including voluntary funding in the countries of assistance. The imbalance of power between ACT members is intrinsically bound up with the view that some ACT members ought to pay, and others ought to do the work.

There are also questions in the intersection of morality and legality, particularly with regard to the move from natural law reasoning to a rights-based approach. This concerns the ethical grounds for Christian agencies. There are different versions of natural law, and not all are compatible with the teachings of the Christian churches. So there is room for a theological revival of natural law in the light of the sacramentality of the Christian worldview.

The thesis skimmed the surface with regard to the moral and social teaching of the two Ethiopian churches in the study. Chapter four gives reasons for more research into how people are morally formed as Christians, and reasons why Christians may fail to live moral lives. There are learning opportunities in this regard.

The churches are not only involved in aid work, but also impacted by it, such as the South Sudanese church in civil crisis, the refugee church in exile, the pastoral life of the local churches in the host communities, and in general, and the church communities in Ethiopia. These aspects are poorly known and there is a need for field studies to learn about and from these church communities.

6.5 Concluding Discussion

The purpose of the thesis is to draw attention to issues of church and aid by analysing the ecclesiological problem of meaning and identity of ACT Alliance as *action by churches together*. Earlier research has largely ignored ACT Alliance with its ecclesiological aspects. ACT Alliance was set up by an ecumenical relief initiative in 1995 as *Action by Churches Together* (ACT), for its members to act in solidarity with people in need through coordination and collaboration, and as ACT Alliance in 2011. In ecumenical theory, the idea, conceptualised as *ecumenical diakonia*, was for ACT to express *action by churches together* in consequence of a sense of churches growing together in *koinonia*. ACT Alliance as an organisation is ecclesiologically informed and this ecclesiological idea is built into its name.

However, ACT contains conceptual and practical tensions in its organisation and work. These tensions signify an ambiguity of what *action by churches together* means that this thesis investigates through the case of the ETH141 ACT Appeal to support South Sudanese refugees in Ethiopia in 2014 and by two Ethiopian churches shedding light on the problem. The concern is that Christian aid agencies may suffer a mission drift and loss of Christian identity over time. This may cause inner secularisation in the churches endangering the moral life of Christians. The thesis asks questions about what it means for the refugee assistance of ACT Alliance to be, in some sense, an *action by churches together*, with respect to the ACT Appeal and its stated principles, Ethiopian Churches and their ecclesial self-understanding, worldview, and historical collaboration.

ACT Alliance was initiated by member churches of the WCC and the Lutheran World Federation as an extension to previous ecumenical engagement in aid so that churches might collaborate more closely. The idea of ACT made practical sense in terms of effectiveness and efficiency through collaboration and coordination. An ACT Appeal is the work of legally separate entities: Ethiopian church-based service institutions (EECMY-DASSC and EOC-DICAC), Christian aid agencies (BftW, CA, CoS, DCA, HEKS, ICCO, IOCC, and NCA), and ecumenical aid agencies (LWF World Service and ACT Alliance).

As the ETH141 appeal failed to attract voluntary funding, the ACT Agencies sought different strategies, to mobilise state funding, including forming a consortium. This was in line with a principled humanitarian approach done solely for the sake of people in need, in a constrained context of conflict. ACT is supervised by and accountable, not to Ethiopian church authorities, but to government authorities, and UN agencies. The principles of the work are not set by churches but by international bodies of which ACT Alliance and LWF World Service are members.

These facts are sources of tension. However, since the ETH141 ACT Appeal was neither a mobilisation of volunteers nor an integrated part of church life and since ACT was not intended as church-to-church assistance (intra-church aid) or set up for the spread of the Christian faith (mission), these tensions are superficial. The ETH141 therefore exemplifies *action by churches together* according to *an international crisis model*, i.e. relief assistance by *ecumenical* specialised agencies for relief services with other stakeholders.

The *Maedot* of 1983 from *the Ethiopian Orthodox Tewahido Church* (EOTC) showed the ecclesial basis for social works, and ecumenical commitments in the 1980s in the self-understanding as a church and the Christian faith in the resurrection. The *ECMY letter* of 1972 from *the Ethiopian Evangelical Church Mekane Yesus* (EECMY) presented a framework for socio-economic service with a theological critique of donor-based aid based on holistic anthropology and a sense of Ethiopian ownership in ecumenical engagement. Both churches show the integral nature of the Christian faith for a commitment to the objective good of the human person according to a Christian worldview. This moral commitment is fostered by Christian teaching, worship, and the communal life of churches.

As an inference to the best explanation, the thesis has argued for an understanding that would make sense of both ACT Alliance as an *action by churches together* and the tensions of the ETH141 appeal. The ACT and its agencies exemplify one model of *ecumenical diakonia*, i.e. the work of *ecumenical* specialised agencies for the social good in collaboration with other stakeholders. Thus, the ETH141 is best understood as *an international crisis model*, in which ecumenical specialised agencies are working together with other stakeholders to render relief assistance for refugees.

In the case study of ETH141, this entailed the mobilisation of external public resources and appropriation of a principled humanitarian approach for the sake of people in need, in a constrained context of conflict, which in turn brought practical challenges (tensions) to the ACT Ethiopia Forum as the agencies sought to meet the needs of the refugees. Such a model is less grounded in the life and ministry of the churches. Tensions in refugee assistance of ETH141, as a case study of the work of ACT Alliance, therefore, first, indicate superficial conflict between the idea of action by churches together as formulated in ecumenical dialogues, and as supported by Ethiopian churches, and the refugee assistance as planned in the ETH141 appeal which focuses on agency responses to a political crisis and its refugee emergencies as an expression of morality and a Christian sense of serving the neighbour. It is the Christian sense of morality, which includes the service to the neighbour, even an enemy, that explains the motivation for refugee assistance. As such, ACT Alliance and its member organisations express Christian solidarity with people in desperate need. It is theologically grounded in Christian ethics.

The context entails working with different stakeholders that may not share the mission of the church. As resources are constrained, the temptation for ACT Alliance is to lose the sense that their limited mission is part of the larger mission of the churches as involvement in God's mission to the world to bring about its intended end through the gospel and sacramental life of the Christian Church. The churches pointed out that the Christian gospel and the "otherworldly" stance are the foundation from which the churches may participate in the good works of men, and not by adopting a materialist stance of exclusive humanism. Tensions, therefore, secondly indicate superficial concord and deep conflict between exclusive humanism and the churches' mission to reach every person with the gospel and the sacramental life in the church.

Therefore, there is ground for ACT Alliance to scrutinise its ethical and theological basis. ACT agencies speak about a rights-based approach but seem to have lost the connection to natural law and the tradition of Christian thought. Without natural law as a ground for rights, there are no rational reasons to claim rights and no directionality towards the common good. The way ACT Alliance speaks of itself in instrumental terms, there is also no room for sacramental language. Sacraments point beyond themselves towards Christ in a way humanitarian language does not. Acts without reference have effects but may confuse. So the church and its agencies may fall apart rather than being kept together because the witness and service of the church are intentionally being separated in this case study of ACT.

The concord between the refugee assistance and the churches gives ground for the churches to consider the work of ACT Alliance as a real part of the churches' outreach, or a very thin slice of the churches' mission, in the sense of an organisation of genuine Christian concern for the neighbour. Tensions give grounds for caution because this line of action can potentially go against the mission of the church. The Ethiopian churches here pointed to the role of the church in bringing the gospel and the sacramental life to Christians with significance for people in desperate need. As a supplement, ACT Alliance is useful, as a substitute, not.

This understanding of the *action by churches together* in the case of ETH141 enlightens the relationship between ACT Alliance and the Ethiopian Churches thus: tensions in the case study indicate that there is superficial conflict but deep concord between aid (the refugee assistance of the ETH141 appeal) and the church (the Ethiopian churches) as Christians are rooted in a Christian worldview with commitments to the good of the human person, but also superficial concord and deep conflict between an exclusive humanism and the churches' mission to reach every person with the gospel and its sacramental life.

This research project started with the civil conflict in South Sudan in 2014 and the response of the churches, in terms of an ACT Appeal for refugee assistance. Though the appeal ended, ACT agencies are still assisting a large number of refugees in Ethiopia and across the world. Refugee crises and migration belong to the defining features of contemporary social life. An ACT appeal – or an ACT re-sponse – will not solve the political issues that breed humanitarian crisis and mi-gration, but it may be a response for churches faithful to the gospel of Jesus Christ to pursue together ecclesiologically informed by word and sacrament.

In Ethiopia, refugee assistance continues.

Appendix A: Primary Sources to ETH141

ETH 141 Primary Sources

The list below shows the kind of written sources and communication materials available starting from the appeal documents themselves. There are the minutes of regular ACT Forum meetings, Coordination Committee meetings, minutes from regional ACT and Webex Calls, ACT consortium meetings, and security meetings. There are also situation, interim, and final reports of the requesting ACT agencies, as well as reports from monitoring visits. There are various forms of communication materials. In addition to all these documents produced specifically for the appeal, there are documents by the ACT Ethiopia Forum, and relevant policy documents from the ACT Secretariat in Geneva of relevance to the appeal. The table shows documents from 2014. The appeal continued during 2015 so more material is available on the appeal outside of the scope of the thesis, which focuses on the first year of the ETH141 appeal.

ACT Alerts and Appeals

- Alert 48:2013: Dec 20, 2013
- Preliminary Appeal: Dec 30, 2013
- Full Appeal: Feb 12, 2014
- Alert 39:2014 Sep 12, 2014
- Revised Appeal 1: Oct 21, 2014
- Revised Appeal 2: May 22, 2015

Minutes of ACT Forum Meetings

- Dec 23 (emergency), Jan 23, Feb 20, Mar 20, May 23, Jun 19, July 17, Sep 9 (emergency), Sep 18, Oct 9 (emergency), Oct 16, Nov 20 (AGM), Dec 18, Mar 19 and April 16, 2015

ACT Coordination Committee

> Dec 13, Feb 12, Apr 8, Sep 24, Nov 12

Core Group Meetings

- Jan 15, 25 and 29, Feb 7, 12 and 26, Mar 3 (awareness raising), Mar 19 and 31, Apr 2 and 30, May 15 and June 4

Consortium Meetings

- Jun 11, 16, 18, 24, and30, July 14, and 25
- MoU signing July 28

Security Meetings and Trainings

- July 15, and 25

Situation, Interim and Final Reports:

- LWF: Situation reports Jan 22, Feb 3, Feb 19, Mar 24, May 9 and Aug 1, Aug 26, Nov 28, 2014, 20 Feb 2015, and May 27 2015. Updated financial report: Jun 30, 2014. Interim Report Aug 13, 2014. Final report: Feb 2016
- IOCC and DICAC: Situation reports Jan 25, and 27, May 26, Oct 17, Jan 24, 2015
- Interim reports: Aug 17, 2014, Feb 10, 2015, 28 Aug (rev2) 2015

Regional ACT Skype and Webex Calls

- Minutes from Dec 20, 23 and 26, 2013, Jan 8, and 14, Mar 6

Other Reports and Monitoring Visits

- Christian Aid report from Gambella: Jun 17, 2014
- NCA Gambella WASH report: Jun 16, 2014
- DCA monitoring Visit: Sep 2014
- CoS monitoring visit 5–8 Oct 2014
- DKH field visit report 18 Feb 2015

Photos and Communication Material

- Lietchor camp photo by LWF

- Lietchor camp photo by PADD
- Lietchor camp photo by CoS

Relevant Forum Documents

- EPRP draft documents Oct 25, Nov 4
- LRRD group 28 Apr (proposal), 23 Sep
- ACT DRR Think Tank session Feb 13
- ACT Retreat May 22–23
- Feb 2014 Christian Aid update on returnees
- Forum members presentation

ACT Secretariat *et al.*

- ACT General Assembly 20–24 Oct 2014 docs
- ACT Strategic Plan 2011–2014
- ACT Policies – forum, emergency
- EPRP guidelines
- ACT Code of Conduct
- SCHR Certification Model Forum feedback
- CSA 70–30 Proclamation
- CHS Second Draft 16 Sep, 2014

Appendix B: ACT Ethiopia Forum Activities 2014

2013

Nov 27	ACT Ethiopia Forum visit to His Holiness *Abune* Mateos
Dec 13	ACT Ethiopia Forum Coordination Committee
Dec 19	ACT Ethiopia Forum, NCA
Dec 20	ACT Skype call on South Sudan crisis
Dec 20	ACT Alert 48:2013 South Sudan Conflict: S. Sudan, Uganda
Dec 23	ACT Ethiopia Forum emergency meeting on South Sudan crisis and Ethiopian Returnees from Saudi Arabia
Dec 26	ACT Skype meeting on South Sudan crisis
Dec 30	ETH 141 Preliminary Appeal posted 2,234,264 USD (LWF)

2014

Jan 08	ACT Alliance Webex call meeting on South Sudan crisis
Jan 9	UNHCR Donor's meeting, UNCHR Addis
Jan 14	ACT Alliance Webex call meeting on South Sudan crisis
Jan 15	ETH 141 Core Group meeting, DICAC
Jan 16	ACT Ethiopia Forum – UNHCR meeting, UNHCR
Jan 22	ETH 141 Core Group meeting, DICAC
Jan 23	ACT Ethiopia Forum meeting, NCA
Jan 29	ETH 141 Core Group meeting, DICAC
Feb 7	ETH 141 Core Group meeting, DICAC
Feb 12	ETH 141 Core Group meeting, DICAC
Feb 12	ETH141 ACT Appeal posted 2,313,966 USD (LWF, IOCC, DICAC)
Feb 14	ACT Ethiopia Forum Coordination Committee
Feb 20	ACT Ethiopia Forum, NCA
Feb 22	Farewell for Monica, Ararat Club
Feb 24	meeting with SCHR, LWF
Feb 26	ETH 141 Core Group meeting, DICAC
Mar 2	ETH 141 Core Group meeting, DICAC
Mar 3	ETH 141 raising interest and awareness, Lucy
Mar 6	ACT Alliance Webex call meeting on South Sudan crisis
Mar 13	Meeting Ms Marion Casey-Maslen, HAP International Director

Mar 11–14	Regional ACT Meeting in Nairobi (forum representatives present)
Mar 19	ETH 141 Core Group meeting, DICAC
Mar 20	ACT Ethiopia Forum, CA
Mar 28	Ms Emilie Della Cort from LWF
Apr 2	ETH 141 Core Group meeting, DICAC
Apr 9	Coordination Committee meeting
Apr 24	Meeting with HEKS director and international director
Apr 30	ETH 141 Core Group meeting, DICAC
Apr	Kemise RRF final report
May 2	HEKS reception
May 12	ACT Bob Hedley send off
May 15	ETH 141 Core Group meeting, DICAC
May 19–21	Climate Change Advocacy Training – Nairobi (forum representatives)
May 22–23	ACT Ethiopia Forum Retreat – Bonita Centre
Jun 4	ETH 141 Core Group meeting, DICAC
Jun 16	ACT Consortium meeting
Jun 18	ACT Consortium meeting
Jun 19	ACT Ethiopia Forum meeting, NCA
Jun 24	ACT Consortium meeting
Jun 30	ACT Consortium meeting
Jul 4	Regional Climate Change Skype Meeting
Jul 15–17	ACT Security Training, Mr James Davies
July 17	ACT Ethiopia Forum meeting, NCA
Jul 18	Climate Change Task Force Meeting
Jul 23	Climate Change Task Force Meeting
Jul 28	Signed MoU Partnership for S. Sudanese Refugee Response
Sep 3	Climate Change Task Force Meeting
Sep 9	ACT Ethiopia Forum emergency meeting
Sep 12	ACT Alert 39:2014: Flooding in Leitchuor Refugee Camp
Sep 18	ACT Ethiopia Forum meeting, NCA
Sep 24	Coordination Committee meeting
Oct 09	ACT Ethiopia Forum emergency meeting
Oct 16	ACT Ethiopia Forum meeting, EGST (– not completed)
Oct 21	ETH 141 Revised Appeal posted 3,639,452 USD (DASSC)
Oct 20–24	ACT Alliance General Assembly – Punto Cana (forum representative)
Nov 12	Coordination Committee meeting
Nov 20	ACT Ethiopia Forum Annual General Meeting, EOC-DICAC
Dec 18	ACT Ethiopia Forum meeting

Main issues dealt with by the Forum

Oct	SCHR proposal + 2nd Draft (Feb)
Nov	South Wollo – alert cancelled
Dec	Returnees from Saudi Arabia, DICAC ambulance, CA Task Force
Dec	Draft Proposal ACT Strategic Plan 2015–2018

Dec	Changing Development Agenda
Dec	How Disasters Disrupt Development
Dec	Introduction of a Dropbox folder for ACT Ethiopia Forum
Dec	Alert – ETH141 appeal (in regional coordination)
Feb	EPRP
Feb	Administrative assistant of the forum
Feb	DRR Joint Programming Concept Paper
Feb	ICCO consortium: Enhanced Response Capacity
Feb	Possible Amendments of the CSO proclamation
Apr	RRF Kemise final report
May	Climate Change Advocacy
May	ACT Retreat with strategic planning of the forum
May	Restructuring of the ACT Secretariat
Jun	Consortium: Partnership for South Sudanese Refugee Response

Bibliography

I. Unpublished Sources

Addis Ababa

Deposited at Torbjörn Toll's Archive, Addis Ababa
(See also ACT Ethiopia Forum's Archive at NCA in Addis Ababa)

Documents of the ACT (Alliance) Ethiopia Forum

2008 02 13 ACT meeting "Minutes of ACT – D/Ethiopia Consultative meeting."
2009 10 11 VEST Conference Bonn Presentation on ACT Ethiopia Forum 11–13 Oct 2009.
2009 12 18 ACT Alliance Ethiopia Forum MoU Dec 2009.
2010 05 27 AFET81 Draft Final Report.
2011 ACT Alliance Ethiopia Forum "2011 Mapping."
2011 07 14 ETH111 Ethiopia Drought Response Full Appeal.
2011 08 12 ACT Response to Horn of Africa Crisis and Issues of Concern (ACT Secretariat).
2011 11 23 ACT Alliance Response to Emergencies and Annexes DRAFT Nov 23, ACT Executive
    Committee Meeting Dec 13–14, 2011 Doc 8.
2012 02 02 Alert 04:2012 (ETH121) Emergency Assistance to Sudanese Refugees in Ethiopia.
2012 02 14–15 ACT Ethiopia Forum Retreat 14–15 Feb 2012. Written Notes.
2012 06 04 Brief Profile AEF Members 4 June 2012.
2012 06 04 ETH111 Working Group 4 June 2012.
2012 08 30 HAP Working Group of Member Agencies in Ethiopia ToR, Revision 1.
2012 12 20 ACT Alliance Ethiopia Forum MoU Dec 2012.
2012 12 31 NCA-E ACT Ethiopia Forum Appeal Coordination Financial Statement Dec 31, 2012.
2012 12 31 NCA-E ACT Ethiopia Forum Financial Statement Dec 31, 2012.
2013 01 17 ACT Ethiopia Forum AGM 17 Jan 2013. 3p.
2013 02 11 EECMY News Release 11 Feb 2013.
2013 06 20 ETH121 Final Narrative Report.
2013 09 10 SCHR Proposed Certification Model: "Professionalising the Sector: A Proposed
    Certification Model for Humanitarian Organisations. Draft for Discussion. Version 1.0."
2013 09 19 ACT Ethiopia Forum Meeting 19 Sep 2013 Minutes.
2013 11 04 ACT Secretariat "ACT Strategic Plan 2015–2018 framework for Member consultation."
2013 11 06 ACT Ethiopia Forum "SCHR certification model feedback" Nov 15.
2013 11 21 ACT Ethiopia Forum AGM Minutes 21 Nov 2013.
2013 12 13 AEF Coordination Committee Agenda 13 Dec 2013.

2013 12 19 ACT Ethiopia Forum Minutes 19 Dec 2013.

2013 12 20 ACT Skype Call on South Sudan Notes 20 Dec 2013.

2013 12 20 Alert 48:2013 South Sudan Conflict 20 Dec 2013.

2013 12 20 South Sudan Forum Skype Meeting Notes 20 Dec 2013.

2013 12 23 ACT Ethiopia Forum Emergency Meeting Regarding South Sudan.

2013 12 23 ACT Skype Call South Sudan Crisis Notes 23 Dec 2013.

2013 12 26 ACT Skype Call South Sudan Crisis Notes 26 Dec 2013.

2013 12 27 "South Sudan Refugee Crisis ACT Ethiopia Forum Preliminary Appeal," 1 "FIRST DRAFT," 2 "REVISED FIRST DRAFT," 3 "SGE Comments on REVISED FIRST DRAFT," 4 "SECOND DRAFT," 5 "SECOND DRAFT Draft 3": all dated Dec 27, 2013.

2013 12 30 ETH141 South Sudanese Refugees Preliminary Appeal 30 Dec.

2013 12 30 ACT Skype meeting on South Sudan 30 Dec 2013. Written notes.

2013 12 30 KEN141 South Sudanese Refugees Preliminary Appeal 30 Dec.

2013 12 30 UGA141 South Sudanese Refugees Preliminary Appeal 30 Dec.

2014 01 03 Eberhard Hitzler Email to Arie den Toom on Security Update 3 Jan, 2014.

2014 01 06 SSD141 South Sudan Conflict Preliminary Appeal.

2014 01 22 ACT Webex call on South Sudan Notes 22 Jan 2014.

2014 02 12 ETH141 Asylum Seekers South Sudan 12 Feb 2014.

2014 04 09 ACT Ethiopia Forum "A Silent Crisis is Rapidly Evolving."

2014 06 19 James Davies ACT Security Course Overview.

2014 07 25 "Security meeting ACT Ethiopia Forum 25 July 2014."

2014 07 25 "James Davies about Draft ACT Security Report."

2014 07 29 PSSRR MoU DCA, EOC DICAC, IOCC, LWF DWS, NCA.

2014 10 21 ETH141 Revision 1 Ethiopia Refugees from South Sudan.

2014 11 17 ACT Ethiopia Forum Annual Report 2014 Nov 17.

2014 11 24 "Amendment to 30–70 Guidelines. 24 Nov 2014."

2014 11 24 ACT Ethiopia Forum Activities 2014.

2015 04 27 LWF Request for Extension and Revision ETH141.

2015 07 LWF Uganda Situation Report July 2015.

2016 02 LWF ETH141 Final Narrative Report Feb 2016.

2017 01 23 ACT Ethiopia Forum Annual Report to ACT Geneva.

Documents of the Ethiopian Evangelical Church Mekane Yesus

Also Deposited at the EECMY Archive. Addis Ababa.

ECMY. 2007. (1972) "On the Interrelation Between Proclamation of the Gospel and Human Development" (*the ECMY Letter*). Pages 85–98 in *Witness and Discipleship: Leadership of the Church in Multi-Ethnic Ethiopia in a Time of Revolution.* 2nd ed. Edited by Paul E. Hoffman. Hamburg: WDL-Publishers.

ECMY. 2007. (1975) "Pastoral Letter: The Evangelical Church Mekane Yesus in the Ethiopian Revolution" (*the Pastoral Letter*). Pages 81–84 in *Witness and Discipleship: Leadership of the Church in Multi-Ethnic Ethiopia in a Time of Revolution.* 2nd ed. Edited by Paul E. Hoffman. Hamburg: WDL-Publishers.

ECMY. 2007. (1975) "Memorandum to the Church President Regarding Some Issues" (*the Memorandum*). Pages 55–76 in *Witness and Discipleship: Leadership of the Church in Multi-Ethnic Ethiopia in a Time of Revolution.* 2nd ed. Edited by Paul E. Hoffman. Hamburg: WDL-Publishers.

ECMY. 2007. (1978) "The Role of a Christian in a Given Society" (*the Role of a Christian*). Pages 1–12 in *Witness and Discipleship: Leadership of the Church in Multi-Ethnic Ethiopia in a Time of Revolution*. 2nd ed. Edited by Paul E. Hoffman. Hamburg: WDL-Publishers.

EECMY. 2010. Letter to Archbishop Anders, Church of Sweden "Calling on the Church of Sweden to reconsider its decision pertaining to the 'rite for the blessing and ordaining of registered homosexual partnership'." Dec, 24, 2010, Rev. Dr. Wakseyoum Idosa, Church President EECMY.

EECMY-DASSC *EECMY-DASSC-NCES BO Staff Code of Conduct*.

EECMY-DASSC Annual Reports.

Documents of the Ethiopian Orthodox Tewahido Church

EOC-DICAC. *Maedot Journal* (1983–1990).

EOC-DICAC. May 1992. *Ethiopian Orthodox Church Development and Inter-Church AID Department (EOC-DICAC)*.

EOC-DICAC. Aug 10, 2005. *EOC DICAC Final Brochure-1*.

EOC DICAC. 2005. "Ethiopian Orthodox Church Development and Inter Church Aid Commission (EOC-DICAC)" in *Gender and Development Division Ladder Newsletter* Sep 2005 Vol 1:1.

EOC DICAC. 2008. *The Ethiopian Orthodox Church in Development/ 36 years in Action*. Development and Inter-Church Aid Commission Millennium Committee.

EOC-DICAC. Jan 2009. *EOC-DICAC: Success Stories, Round Table and Bilateral Partners*.

EOC DICAC. 2013. *Developmental Bible*.

EOC-DICAC Annual Reports.

Documents of the Six Agencies Group (SAG)

Six Agencies Group *Mar 2006 Cooperation between the Six Agencies Group* (BftW, CA, DCA, EED, ICCO, NCA) Memorandum of Understanding (MoU) Signed *MoU* Mar/Apr 2006.

Six Agencies Group 14 *April 2008 Six Agencies Group: The Lead Agency Concept*.

Six Agencies Group 2008 08 05 Minutes of August 5 E8 Meeting.

Six Agencies Group 2008 *Draft Revised MoU: Cooperation between Six Agencies Group (BftW, CA, DCA, EED, ICCO, NCA) in Ethiopia*. 2008 10 16.

International Standards, Reports, and Internal Publications

APRODEV 2008. *Rights-based development from a faith-based perspective: Joint Position Paper Rights and Development Group*. Approved by APRODEV AGM June 2008.

Church of Sweden (*n.d.*) *Community Based Psychosocial Support Training Manual*. Uppsala: Church of Sweden.

HAP 2010. *The 2010 HAP Standard in Accountability and Quality Management*. 2nd ed. Geneva: HAP International.

HAP 2011. *The 2011 Humanitarian Accountability Report*, Geneva: HAP International.

HAP 2013. *Guide to the 2010 HAP Standard in Accountability and Quality Management*, Geneva: HAP International.

ICRC 1994. *The Code of Conduct for the International Red Cross and Red Crescent Movement and NGOs in Disaster Relief*.

IASC 2007. *IASC Guidelines on Mental Health and Psychosocial Support in Emergency Settings*, Geneva: Inter-Agency Standing Committee.

NCA 2012 *IRCE Newsletter Update on National and Regional Dialogue Forums with Religious Institutions on Peace and Development.*

Sphere Project 2011. *Humanitarian Charter and Minimum Standards in Humanitarian Response*. 3rd ed. Rugby: Practical Action Publishing.

Sphere Association 2018. 4th ed. *The Sphere Handbook: Humanitarian Charter and Minimum Standards in Humanitarian Response*, Rugby: Practical Action Publishing.

Documents of the ACT Secretariat, Geneva

Also Deposited at ACT Secretariat. Geneva.

ACT Alliance. "Steps in an ACT emergency response."

ACT Alliance. 2009. "Procedure for Funding the Unified ACT Alliance Updated Oct 2009."

ACT Alliance 2010. *the ACT Alliance Guidelines for Complaints Handling and Investigations.*

ACT Alliance 2011a. *ACT Alliance Code of Conduct: For the prevention of sexual exploitation and abuse, fraud and corruption and abuse of power.*

ACT Alliance 2011b *Response to an Emergency: Policy, Guidelines and Tools, and Annexes*, Dec 2011. Executive Committee Meeting, Bossey 2011 12 13-14.

ACT Alliance 2011c. *the ACT Alliance Guidelines for the Prevention of Sexual Exploitation and Abuse.*

ACT Alliance 2012. *ACT Policy on Response to an Emergency.*

Documents of the LWF World Service Ethiopia Programme

Also deposited at LWF World Service Ethiopia Programme. Addis Ababa.

LWF *The Code of Conduct for the Lutheran World Federation.*

LWF World Service Ethiopia Programme Annual Reports.

Documents of the UN and UNHCR, Geneva

Also deposited at UNHCR. Geneva.

UNHCR 1992 "An Introduction to the International Protection of Refugees."

UNHCR "Introduction," a training manual.

UNHCR 2009 Global Appeal 2009 Update

UNHCR 2014 07 22 Policy on Alternatives to Camps. UNHCR/HCP/2014/9

2016 02 02 Ban Ki-Moon 2016 "One humanity: shared responsibility English Report of the Secretary-General for the World Humanitarian Summit." A/70/709 Distr.

UNHCR Infographics-Ethiopia as of 28 February 2017.

UNHCR 2018 07 25 "2017 Year-End Report GR2017-Ethiopia-eng-2. "

UNHCR 2019 "UNHCR in 2019: Overview Mission."

UNHCR 2023 Partners in Gambella Region, January 2023 by UNHCR SO Gambella Program Unit, 13 Jan. 2023.

II. Interviews

Rev. Roger Kay, Rector, St Matthew's Anglican Church, AA 11 June 2019, written notes.

Rev. Mark Deng, Pastor, St Matthew's Anglican Church, AA 11 June 2019, written notes.

Rev. Dr. Jossi Jacob, 10 June 2019, Dean, AA Holy Trinity College written notes.

Mr Berhanu Yismaw, CoS Relief Officer, 3 May 2018, written notes.

Mr Bob Hedley, Bread for the World, email and telephone conversation 15 May 2018, written notes.

Mr Mengistie Tegenie, NCA reproductive health officer, 12 April 2018, written notes.

Mr Samuel Tenna Gashaw, ACT Coordinator, 12 April 2018, written notes.

Mrs Kidist, NCA Program Head, 12 April 2018, written notes.

Mr Eivind Aalborg, NCA Country Rep, 12 April 2018, written notes.

Mr Tesfaye Negash, NCA, Finance and Adm, 12 April 2018, written notes.

Ms Cecilie Winther, DCA Country Director, 12 April 2018, written notes.

Mr Yitna Tekalign, CA Country Director, 12 April 2018, written notes.

Mr Fisseha Kebede, CA Program Coordinator, 12 April 2018, written notes.

III. Published Sources

Ethiopian and Eritrean names do not include family names, but consist of a personal name and father's name. Thus, these authors will be listed according to their personal name.

Abass, Ademola. 2012. *Complete International Law: Text, Cases, and Materials.* Oxford: Oxford University Press.

Abate Gobena. 2023. *Sanctity and Environment in Ethiopian Hagiography The Case of Gedle Gebre Menfes Qiddus.* Dissertationes Theologicae Holmienses 4. Stockholm: University College Stockholm.

Abebe Feyissa, and Rebecca Horn. 2008. "There Is More Than One Way of Dying: An Ethiopian Perspective on the Effects of Long-Term Stays in Refugee Camps." Pages 13–49 in *Refugee Rights: Ethics, Advocacy, and Africa.* Edited by David Hollenbach. Washington DC: Georgetown University Press.

Adejumobi, Saheed. 2007. *History of Ethiopia: WWII-2006.* Westport, CT: Greenwood Press.

Adler, Mortimer. 1963. *The Difference of Man and the Difference It Makes.* New York: Fordham University Press.

Ager, Alastair, and Joey Ager. 2011. "Faith and the Discourse of Secular Humanitarianism." *JRS* 24 (3): 456–72.

Aklilu Dalelo. 2003. *The Church and Socio-Economic Transformation. The Impacts of the Community Development Services of the Ethiopian Kale Heywet Church.* Bonn: Bonn University Press.

Aklilu Dalelo, and Till Stellmacher. 2012. *Faith Based Organisations in Ethiopia. The Contribution of the Kale Heywet Church.* Bonn: Bonn University Press.

Alvesson, Mats. 2003. "Methodology for Close Up Studies: Struggling with Closeness and Closure." *Higher Education* 46: 167–93.

Alvesson, Mats, and Kai Sköldberg. 2006. *Tolkning och reflektion: Vetenskapsfilosofi och kvalitativ metod.* Lund: Studentlitteratur.

An, Keon-Sang. 2015. *An Ethiopian Reading of the Bible: Biblical Interpretation of the Ethiopian Orthodox Tewahido Church.* Eugene, OR: Wipf and Stock Publishers.

Anderson, Mary B. 1999. *Do No Harm: How Aid Can Support Peace – or War.* Boulder, CO: Lynne Rienner Publishers.

Anderson, Mary B., Dayna Brown, and Isabella Jean. 2012. *Time to Listen: Hearing People on the Receiving End of International Aid*. Cambridge, MA: CDA Collaborative Learning Projects.

Anderson, Mary B., and Peter Woodrow. 1989. *Rising from the Ashes: Development Strategies in Times of Disaster*. Boulder, CO: Westview Press.

Andrea, David Joel. 2013. "A Critique of John Milbank's Theology and Social Theory." MA Thesis, Acadia University.

Arén, Gustav. 1978. *Evangelical Pioneers in Ethiopia: Origins of the Evangelical Church Mekane Yesus*. Studia Missionalia Upsaliensia 32. Stockholm: EFS-förlaget.

–. 1999. *Envoys of the Gospel in Ethiopia: In the Steps of the Evangelical Pioneers*. Stockholm: EFS-Verbum.

Arendt, Hannah. 1967. *The Origins of Totalitarianism*. 2nd ed. New York: Harper Collins Publishers.

Atiya, Aziz S. 1968. *A History of Eastern Christianity*. London: Methuen.

Axelson, Sigbert, ed. 2006. *Kristna organisationer och internationellt bistånd i det civila samhället*. Missio 21. Uppsala: SIM.

Baaz Eriksson, Maria. 2005. *The Paternalism of Partnership: A Postcolonial Reading of Identity in Development Aid*. London: Zed Books.

Bahru Zewde. 2008. *Church, State, Society: Selected Essays*. Addis Ababa: Addis Ababa University Press.

Bainton, Roland. 1960. *Christian Attitudes Toward War and Peace*. Nashville, TN: Abingdon Press.

Bakka, Jørgen F., Egil Fivelsdal, and Lars Lindkvist. 2006. *Organisationsteori: struktur – kultur – processer*. 5th ed. Malmö: Liber.

Bakke, Johnny. 1986. "Christian Ministry: Patterns and Functions within the Ethiopian Evangelical Church Mekane Yesus." Diss., Uppsala University.

–. 1987. *Christian Ministry, Patterns and Functions within the Ethiopian Evangelical Church Mekane Yesus*. Oslo: Solum.

Balisky, Paul. 2009. *Wolaitta Evangelists: A Study of Religious Innovation in Southern Ethiopia, 1937–1975*. Eugene, OR: Pickwick Publications.

Barnett, Michael. 2011. *Empire of Humanity: A History of Humanitarianism*. Ithaca, NY: Cornell University Press.

Barrow, Ondine. 1998. "Charity, Relief and Development: Christian Aid in Ethiopia, 1960s–1990s." Diss., University of London, School of Oriental and African Studies. Parkway, MI: ProQuest.

Baur, John. 1994. *2000 Years of Christianity in Africa: An African Church History*. 2nd ed. Nairobi: Pauline Publications.

Bediako, Kwame. 1999. *Theology and Identity: The Impact of Culture upon Christian Thought in the Second Century and in Modern Africa*. Oxford: Regnum.

–. 2001. "The African Renaissance and Theological Reconstruction: the Challenge of the Twenty-First Century." *Journal of African Christian Thought* 4 (2): 29–33.

Bello, Emmanuel G. 1980. *African Customary International Law*. Geneva: ICRC.

Belopopsky, Alexander, ed. 2002. *From Inter-Church Aid to Jubilee: A Brief History of Ecumenical Diakonia in the World Council of Churches*. Geneva: WCC.

Benedict XVI. 2007. *Jesus of Nazareth: From the Baptism in the Jordan to the Transfiguration*. New York: Doubleday.

–. 2023. *What Is Christianity? The Last Writings.* San Francisco, CA: Ignatius Press.

Bennett, Jon. 2013. *Meeting Needs: NGO Coordination in Practice.* New Yor71k: Earthscan.

Bernander, Gustav. 1968. *Lutheran Wartime Assistance to Tanzanian Churches 1940–1945.* Studia Missionalia Upsaliensia 9. Lund: Gleerup.

Best, Thomas F., and Martin Robra, eds. 1997 *Ecclesiology and Ethics: Ecumenical Engagement, Moral Formation and the Nature of the Church.* Geneva: WCC.

Bevans, Stephen B., and Roger P. Schroeder. 2006. *Constants in Context: A Theology of Mission for Today.* Maryknoll, NY: Orbis.

Bexell, Göran, and Carl-Henric Grenholm. 2003. *Teologisk etik: En introduktion.* Uppsala: Verbum.

Bexell, Oloph. 2003. *Sveriges kyrkohistoria: Folkväckelsens och kyrkoförnyelsens tid.* Stockholm: Verbum.

Bexell, Peter. 1997. *Kyrkan som sakrament: Henri de Lubacs fundamentalecklesiologi.* Stockholm: Brutus Östlins Bokförlag Symposion.

Biggar, Nigel. 2020. *What's Wrong with Rights.* Oxford: Oxford University Press.

–. 2023. *Colonialism: A Moral Reckoning.* Dublin: Harper-Collins Publishers.

Binns, John. 2002. *Introduction to the Christian Orthodox Churches.* Cambridge: Cambridge University Press.

–. 2017. *The Orthodox Church of Ethiopia: A History.* London: I.B. Tauris.

Bischofberger, Erwin, and Helge Brattgård. 2012. "Människovärdet i judisk-kristen tradition." Pages 81–85 in *Det svårfångade människovärdet: en debattskrift.* 2nd ed. Edited by Göran Hermerén. Etiska Vägmärken 4. Stockholm: Statens medicinsk-etiska råd.

Bischofberger, Erwin. 2012. "Från människovärde till mänskliga rättigheter." Pages 111–19 in *Det svårfångade människovärdet: en debattskrift.* 2nd ed. Edited by Göran Hermerén. Etiska Vägmärken 4. Stockholm: Statens medicinsk-etiska råd.

Björk, Gustaf. 2014. *Förändring av missionssynen? Perspektiv på Svenska kyrkans mission 1945–2000 speglad av ledning och missionärer.* Studia Missionalia Svecana 114. Uppsala University.

Blomberg, Craig L. 1999. *Neither Poverty nor Riches: A Biblical Theology of Possessions.* Nottingham: Inter-Varsity Press.

Boersma, Hans. 2009. *Nouvelle Théologie and Sacramental Ontology: A Return to Mystery.* Oxford: Oxford University Press.

Boersma, Hans, and Matthew Levering, eds. 2015. *The Oxford Handbook of Sacramental Theology.* Oxford: Oxford University Press.

Boff, Clodovis. 2002. "Church Base Communities." Pages 583–86 in *Dictionary of the Ecumenical Movement.* 2nd ed. Edited by Nicholas Lossky *et al.* Geneva: WCC.

Borgehammar, Stephan. 2007. "Vad är kyrkan?" Pages 13–33 in *Kyrkans liv: Introduktion till kyrkovetenskapen.* 3rd ed. Edited by Borgehammar, Stephan. Uppsala University.

–. 2021. "Den praktiska teologin som professionsteori." *STK* 97: 69–90.

Bornemark, Jonna. 2018. *Det omätbaras renässans: En uppgörelse med pedanternas världsherravälde.* Stockholm: Volante.

Bosch, David. 2011. *Transforming Mission: Paradigm Shifts in Theology of Mission.* 2nd ed. Maryknoll, NY: Orbis.

Braaten, Carl. 2007. "Reclaiming The Natural Law for Theological Ethics." *Journal of Lutheran Ethics* 7 (10).

–. 2010. *Because of Christ: Memoirs of a Lutheran Theologian.* Grand Rapids, MI: Eerdmans.

Bradley, James E., and Richard A. Muller. 1995. _Church History: An Introduction to Research, Reference Works, and Methods_. Grand Rapids, MI: Eerdmans.

Bretherton, Luke. 2019. _Christ and the Common Life: Political Theology and the Case for Democracy_. Grand Rapids. MI: Eerdmans.

Bria, Ion. 1978. "The Liturgy after the Liturgy." _International Review of Mission_ 67 (2): 86–90.

Brock, Sebastian P. 2010. _Det upplysta ögat: världen sedd genom den helige Efraim syriern_. Translation of _The Luminous Eye_ by Daniel Braw and Sten Hidal. Södertälje: Anastasis.

Brodd, Sven-Erik. 1989. _Pastoralteologisk praxis: Om kyrkligt liv och arbete i en urbaniserad miljö_. Stockholm: Stockholms Församlingsdelegerade.

–. 1990. _Ekumeniska Perspektiv: Föreläsningar_. KISA-rapport nr 4–5. Uppsala: Svenska kyrkans forskningsråd.

–. 1992. _Diakonatet: Från ecklesiologi till pastoral praxis_. Tro och Tanke 1992:10. Uppsala: Svenska kyrkans forskningsråd.

–. 1999. _Diakonins teologi_ 1999. Uppsala: Diakonistiftelsen Samariterhemmet.

–. 2002. "Stewardship Ecclesiology: The Church as Sacrament to the World." _IJSCC_ 2002 (2): 70–82.

–. 2005a. "Diaconia through Church History: Five Ecclesiological Models." Pages 5–36 in _The Theology of Diaconia_. Edited by Sven-Erik Brodd. Translated by Tore Bergman. Uppsala: Samariterhemmet.

–. 2005b. "Church, Organisation, and Church Organisation: Some Reflections on an Ecclesiological Dilemma." _SMT_ 93 (2): 245–63.

–. 2006. "Themes in Operative Ecclesiology." _IJSCC_ 6 (2): 124–25.

–. 2009. "Ecclesiological Research and Natural and Human Sciences: Some Observations of an Unconventional Phenomenon." _IJSCC_ 9 (4): 312–32.

–. 2015. "Ecclesiology Under Construction: A Report from a Working-Site." Pages 1–28 in _Ecclesiology in the Trenches_. Eugene, OR: Pickwick.

Bugnion, François. 2012. "Birth of an Idea: The Founding of the International Committee of the Red Cross and of the International Red Cross and Red Crescent Movement: from Solferino to the Original Geneva Convention (1859–1864)." _IRRC_ 94 (888): 1299–1338.

Cahill, Thomas. 1995. _How the Irish Saved Civilization: The Untold Story of Ireland's Heroic Role from the Fall of Rome to the Rise of Medieval Europe_. New York: Doubleday.

Cantor, David James, and Jean-François Durieux, eds. 2014. _Refuge from Inhumanity? War, Refugees and International Humanitarian Law_. Leiden: Brill.

Carter, Alix. 2011. "Joint Emergency Operation Plan NGO Response to Emergency Food Needs in Ethiopia" _Field Exchange_ 40: 65–67.

Cavanaugh, William T. 1995. "'A Fire Strong Enough to Consume the House:' The Wars of Religion and the Rise of the State." _Modern Theology_ 11 (4): 397–420.

–. 1998. _Torture and Eucharist: Theology, Politics, and the Body of Christ_. Oxford: Blackwell.

–. 2008. _Being Consumed: Economics and Christian Desire_. Grand Rapids MI: Eerdmans.

–. 2009. _The Myth of Religious Violence Secular Ideology and the Roots of Modern Conflict_. Oxford: Oxford University Press.

–. 2011. _Migrations of the Holy: God, State, and the Political Meaning of the Church_. Grand Rapids MI: Eerdmans.

Cavanaugh, William T., and Peter Manley Scott, eds. 2019. _The Wiley Blackwell Companion to Political Theology_. 2nd ed. Hoboken, NJ: Blackwell Publishing.

Chaillot, Christine. 2002. *The Ethiopian Orthodox Tewahedo Church Tradition: A Brief Introduction to Its Life and Spirituality.* Paris: Inter-Orthodox Dialogue.

Christensen, Torben, and William Hutchison. 1982. *Missionary Ideologies in the Imperialist Era: 1880–1920: Papers from the Durham Consultation 1981.* Aarhus: Förlaget Aros.

Collins, Alan, ed. 2013. *Contemporary Security Studies.* 3rd ed. Oxford: Oxford University Press.

Collins, John N. 2014. *Diakonia Studies: Critical Issues in Ministry.* Oxford: Oxford University Press.

Constantinou, Eugenia Scarvelis. 2020. *Thinking Orthodox: Understanding and Acquiring the Orthodox Christian Mind.* Chesterton, IN: Ancient Faith Publishing.

Cooper, Frederick. 2002. *Africa Since 1940: The Past of the Present.* New York: Cambridge University Press.

Cooper, Jordan. 2014. *Christification: A Lutheran Approach to Theosis.* Eugene, OR: Wipf and Stock Publishers.

–. 2018. "A Critique of the Radical Lutheran Theological Method, and Defense of the Lutheran Scholastic Method." Diss., South African Theological Seminary, Johannesburg.

–. 2021. *In Defense of the True, The Good, and The Beautiful: On the Loss of Transcendence and the Decline of the West.* Ithaca, NY: Just and Sinner Publishing.

–. 2023. *The Doctrine of God: A Defense of Classical Christian Theism.* Ithaca, NY: Weidner Institute.

Cunningham, David, S. 2008. *Christian Ethics: The End of the Law.* London: Routledge.

Dawit Olika. 2017. "Serving the Whole Person – The Case of the Ethiopian Evangelical Church Mekane Yesus (EECMY)." *Norwegian Journal of Missiology,* 4 (6): 35–44.

Dawit Wolde Giorgis. 1989. *Red Tears: War, Famine, and Revolution in Ethiopia.* Trenton, NJ: Red Sea Press.

Debela Birri. 1995. "A History of the Evangelical Church Bethel, 1919–1947." Diss., Lutheran School of Theology at Chicago.

Delkeskamp-Hayes, Corinna. 2009. "Diakonia, the State, and Ecumenical Collaboration: Theological Pitfalls." *Christian Bioethics* 15 (2): 173–98.

Deneen, Patrick J. 2018. *Why Liberalism Failed.* New Haven, CT: Yale University Press.

Deneulin, Séverine, and Masooda Banu. 2009. *Religion in Development: Rewriting the Secular Script.* London: Zed Books.

Desta Heliso. 2021. *Hope for Ethiopia.* New Haven, CT: ICCS Press.

Dulles, Avery. 1972. "The Church, The Churches, The Catholic Church." *Theological Studies* 33 (2): 199–234.

–. 2002. *Models of the Church.* New York: Doubleday.

Easterly, William. 2006. *The White Man's Burden: Why the West's Efforts to Aid the Rest Have Done So Much Ill and So Little Good.* Oxford: Oxford University Press.

Eckerdal, Erik. 2017. *Apostolic Succession in the Porvoo Common Statement: Unity through a Deeper Sense of Apostolicity.* Uppsala University.

Eckerdal, Jan. 2012. *Folkkyrkans Kropp: Einar Billings ecklesiologi i postsekulär belysning.* Skellefteå: Artos & Norma Bokförlag.

ECMY. 2007. "On the Interrelation Between Proclamation of the Gospel and Human Development." Pages 85–98 in *Witness and Discipleship: Leadership of the Church in Multi-Ethnic Ethiopia in a Time of Revolution.* 2nd ed. Edited by Paul E. Hoffman. Hamburg: WDL-Publishers.

Egerland, Erik. 2016. *Christianity, Generation and Narrative: Religious Conversion and Change in Sidama, Ethiopia, 1974–2012*. Studia Missionalia Svecana 116. Uppsala University.

Eide, Øyvind M. 1996. *Revolution and Religion in Ethiopia: A Study of Church and Politics with Special References to the Ethiopian Evangelical Church Mekane Yesus 1974–1985*. Studia Missionalia Upsaliensia 66. Uppsala University.

–. 2000. *Revolution and Religion in Ethiopia. The Growth and Persecution of the Mekane Yesus Church 1974–85*. Addis Ababa: Addis Ababa University Press.

Emmanuel Abraham. 1995. *Reminiscences of My Life*. Oslo: Lunde förlag.

Engdahl, Hans. 2006. *Theology in Conflict – Readings in Afrikaner Theology: The Theologies of F.J.M. Potgieter and B.J. Marais*. Frankfurt am Main: Lang.

Engelsviken, Tormod. 2001. "Convergence or Divergence? The Relationship between Recent Ecumenical and Evangelical Mission Documents." *SMT* 89 (2): 196–220.

EOC. 1996. *The Ethiopian Orthodox Tewahedo Church: Faith, Order of Worship and Ecumenical Relations*. Addis Ababa: Tensae.

Ers, Agnes. 2006. *I mänsklighetens namn: En etnologisk studie av ett svenskt biståndsprojekt i Rumänien*. Hedemora: Gidlunds förlag.

Esaiasson, Peter *et al*. 2012. *Metodpraktikan: Konsten att studera samhälle, individ och marknad*. Stockholm: Norstedts Juridik.

Evans-Pritchard, Edward E. 1969. *Nuer Religion*. Oxford, NY: Oxford University Press.

Ezra Gebremedhin. 1977. *Life-Giving Blessing: An Inquiry into the Eucharistic Doctrine of Cyril of Alexandria*. Studia Doctrinae Christianae Upsaliensia 17. Uppsala University.

–. 1988. "Bekännelse och mission utifrån Mekane Yesus-kyrkans historia." *STK* 88 (2): 69–75.

–. 2017. *Må detta nå Monsieur Stjärne! Krigstidskorrespondens mellan Etiopiens kejsare Haile Selassie I och en svensk missionär*. Klippan: EFS Budbäraren.

Fagerberg, David. 2018a. *Den liturgiska människan: Alexander Schmemanns vision för kyrkan, gudstjänsten och världen*. Örebro: Marcus Förlag.

–. 2018b. *Liturgy outside Liturgy: The Liturgical Theology of Fr. Alexander Schmemann*. Hong Kong: Chorabooks.

Fagerli, Beate, Leslie Nathaniel, and Tomi Karttunen, eds. 2016. *Towards Closer Unity: Communion of the Porvoo Churches 20 Years*. Porvoo Communion of Churches.

Fahlgren, Sune. 2006a. *Predikantskap och församling: sex fallstudier av en ecklesial baspraktik inom svensk frikyrklighet fram till 1960-talet*. ÖTH-rapport supplement serie 3. Örebro Teologiska Högskola.

–. 2006b. "Preaching and Preachership as Fundamental Expressions of Being Church." *IJSCC*, 6 (2): 180–99.

–. 2015. "Studying Fundamental Ecclesial Practices." Pages 87–105 in *Ecclesiology in the Trenches*. Edited by Sune Fahlgren, and Jonas Ideström. Eugene, OR: Pickwick.

Fahlgren, Sune, and Jonas Ideström eds. 2015. *Ecclesiology in the Trenches*. Eugene, OR: Pickwick.

FDRE. 1995. *The Constitution of the Federal Democratic Republic of Ethiopia*. Addis Ababa: Federal Negarit Gazeta.

Fiddian-Qasmiyeh, Elena. 2011. "Introduction: Faith-Based Humanitarianism in Contexts of Forced Displacement." *JRS* 24 (3): 429–39.

Fiddian-Qasmiyeh, Elena, and Yousif M. Qasmiyeh. 2010. "Muslim Asylum-Seekers and Refugees: Negotiating Identity, Politics and Religion in the UK." *JRS* 23 (3): 295–314.

Forrester, Duncan. 2002. "Ecclesiology and Ethics." Pages 348–49 in *Dictionary of the Ecumenical Movement*. 2nd ed. Edited by Nicholas Lossky *et al*. Geneva: WCC.

Forslund, Eskil. 1993. *The Word of God in Ethiopian Tongues: Rhetorical Features in the Preaching of the Ethiopian Evangelical Church Mekane Yesus*. Studia Missionalia Upsaliensia 58. Uppsala: Swedish Institute of Missionary Research.

Foster, Richard J. 1998. *Celebration of Discipline: The Path to Spiritual Growth*. New York: Harper Collins Publishers.

–. 2000. *Strömmar av levande vatten: Sex andliga traditioner att ösa ur*. Original title: *Streams of Living Water – Celebrating the Great Traditions of Christian Faith*. Örebro: Libris.

Fowden, Garth. 2014. *Before and after Muḥammad: The First Millennium Refocused*. Princeton, NJ: Princeton University Press.

Frankl, Viktor E. 1986. *The Doctor and the Soul: From Psychotherapy to Logotherapy*. New York: Vintage Books.

Fritsch, Emmanuel. 1999. "The Liturgical Year and the Lectionary of the Ethiopian Church: Introduction to the Temporal." *Warszawskie Studia Teologiczne* 12 (2): 71–116.

Fuchs, Lorelei F. 2008. *Koinonia and the Quest for an Ecumenical Ecclesiology: From Foundations through Dialogue to Symbolic Competence for Communionality*. Cambridge: Eerdmans.

Gaillardetz, Richard R. 2008. *Ecclesiology for a Global Church: A People Called and Sent*. Maryknoll, NY: Orbis Books.

Gemechu Olana. 2005. "A Church Under Challenge: The Socio-Economic and Political Involvement of the Ethiopian Evangelical Church Mekane Yesus (EECMY)." Diss., Humboldt University, Berlin.

George, Sam, and Miriam Adeney, eds. 2018. *Refugee Diaspora: Missions Amid the Greatest Humanitarian Crisis of our Times*. Littleton, CO: William Carey Publishing.

Getnet Tamene. 1998. "Features of the Ethiopian Orthodox Church and Clergy." *African and Asian Studies* 7: 87–104.

Gifford, Paul. 2008. "Trajectories in African Christianity." *IJSCC* 8 (4): 275–89.

Girgis, Sherif, Robert George, and Ryan T. Anderson. 2010. "What is Marriage?" *Harvard Journal of Law and Public Policy* 34 (1): 245–87.

Goulet, Denis. 2006. *Development Ethics at Work: Explorations – 1960–2002*. London: Routledge.

Grenstedt, Staffan. 2000. *Ambaricho and Shenkolla: From Local Independent Church to the Evangelical Mainstream in Ethiopia – The Origin of the Mekane Yesus Church in Kambata Hadiya*. Studia Missionalia Svecana 82. Uppsala: Swedish Institute of Missionary Research.

–. 2024. *Longstanding Relations in a Process of Change The Swedish Evangelical Mission in Ethiopia 1898–2015*. Studia Missionalia Svecana 126. Ekerö: Narin Förlag.

Gustavsson, Jacob, and Jonas Tallberg, eds. 2014. *Internationella relationer*. Lund: Studentlitteratur.

Haakonssen, Knud. 1996. *Natural Law and Moral Philosophy: From Grotius to the Scottish Enlightenment*. Cambridge: Cambridge University Press.

Halldin Norberg, Viveca. 2002. *Swedes in Haile Selassie's Ethiopia 1924–1952: A Study in Early Development Cooperation*. Studia historica Upsaliensia 92. Reprint 1977 Diss. Uppsala University.

Halldorf, Joel, 2018. *Gud: Återkomsten: Hur religionerna kom tillbaka och vad det betyder*. Örebro: Libris.

Hallencreutz, Carl F. 1981. *Kristendomens historia: Metod- och tolkningsfrågor*. Uppsala University.

HAP. 2010. *The 2010 HAP Standard in Accountability and Quality Management*. 2nd ed. Geneva: HAP International.

–. 2011. *The 2011 Humanitarian Accountability Report*. Geneva: Humanitarian Accountability Partnership International.

Harmless, William. 2004. *Desert Christians: An Introduction to the Literature of Early Monasticism*. Oxford: Oxford University Press.

Harrison, Peter, and Jon H. Roberts, eds. 2019. *Science Without God? Rethinking the History of Scientific Naturalism*. Oxford: Oxford University Press.

Haustein, Jörg. 2009a. "Navigating Political Revolutions: Ethiopia's Churches during and after the Mengistu Regime" Pages 117–36 in *Fallling Walls: The Year 1989/1990 as a Turning Point in the History of World Christianity; Einstürzende Mauern: Das Jahr 1989/1990 als Epochenjahr in der Geschichte des Weltchristentums*. Edited by Klaus Koschorke. Studien zur Außereuropäischen Christentumsgeschichte 15. Wiesbaden: Harrassowitz.

Henrich, Laban, and Jacques Willemse. 2015. *The Churches and Political Conflict in the Horn of Africa: An Unconventional Mediation Effort*. Dialogue Documentation. Berlin: Brot für die Welt.

Hildebrand, Dietrich. 2019 (1955). *Morality and Situation Ethics*. 2nd ed. Steubenville, OH: Hildebrand Press.

–. 2020 (1953). *Ethics*. 2nd ed. Steubenville, OH: Hildebrand Press.

Hilhorst, Dorothea. 2018. "Classical Humanitarianism and Resilience Humanitarianism Making Sense of Two Brands of Humanitarian Actions." *Journal of International Humanitarian Action*, 3 (15): 1–12.

Hillbom, Ellen, and Erik Green. 2010. *Afrika: En kontinents ekonomiska och sociala historia*, Stockholm: SNS förlag.

Hjälm, Michael. 2011. *Liberation of the Ecclesia: The Unfinished Project of Liturgical Theology*. Diss., Uppsala University.

Hoffman, Stefan-Ludwig ed. 2011. *Human Rights in the Twentieth Century*. New York: Cambridge University Press.

Hollenbach, David, ed. 2008. *Refugee Rights: Ethics, Advocacy, and Africa*. Washington DC: Georgetown University Press.

Hollenbach, David 2008 "Introduction: Human Rights as an Ethical Framework for Advocacy." Pages 1–12 in *Refugee Rights: Ethics, Advocacy, and Africa*. Edited by David Hollenbach. Washington DC: Georgetown University Press.

Holmefur, Niklas. 2016. *Den osynliga religionen: Analys av policy for svensk utvecklingspolitik 2010-2014*. Studia Missionalia Svecana 117. Uppsala University.

Hopgood, Stephen. 2013. *The Endtimes of Human Rights*. Ithaca, NY: Cornell University Press.

Horn, Rebecca, Djoen Besselink, and Marian Tankink. 2016. "Introduction to *Special Section*: Mainstreaming Psychosocial Approaches and Principles into *'Other'* Sectors." *Intervention* 14 (3): 207–10.

Hovil, Lucy. 2016. *Refugees, Conflict and the Search for Belonging*. London: Macmillan.

Hovorun, Cyril. 2017. *Scaffolds of the Church: Towards Poststructural Ecclesiology*. Eugene, OR: Cascade Books.

–. 2023. "Values and Secularism." Pages 277–304 in *Religious Freedom and Other Human Rights: Threats and Trends*. Edited by Weronika Kudla, Tomasz Huzarek, and Maciej Duda. Pelplin: Bernardium Publishing House.

Howard, Thomas. 1969 (reprint 2001). *Chance or the Dance? A Critique of Modern Secularism*, San Francisco, CA: Ignatius Press.

Howell, Leon. 1982. *Acting in Faith: The World Council of Churches since 1975*. Geneva: WCC.

Hugman, Richard, Linda Bartolomei, and Eileen Pittaway *et al.* 2011. "Human Agency and the Meaning of Informed Consent: Reflections on Research with Refugees." *JRS* 24 (4): 655–71.

Hull, Timothy. 2020. *Faith and Modern Thought: The Modern Philosophers for Understanding Modern Theology.* Eugene, OR: Cascade Books.

Hutchinson, John F. 1996. *Champions Of Charity: War And The Rise Of The Red Cross.* Boulder, CO: Westview Press.

IASC. 2007. *IASC Guidelines on Mental Health and Psychosocial Support in Emergency Settings.* Geneva: IASC.

Ideström, Jonas. 2009. *Lokal kyrklig identitet: En studie av implicit ecklesiologi med exemplet Svenska kyrkan i Flemingsberg.* Bibliotheca Theologiae Practicae 85. Skellefteå: Artos & Norma.

–. 2015. "Implicit Ecclesiology and Local Church Identity: Dealing with Dilemmas of Empirical Ecclesiology." Pages 121–138 in *Ecclesiology in the Trenches.* Eugene, OR: Pickwick.

Insole, Christopher. 2004. "Against Radical Orthodoxy: The Dangers of Overcoming Political Liberalism." *Modern Theology* 20 (2): 213–41.

–. 2006a. *The Realist Hope: A Critique of Anti-Realist Approaches in Contemporary Philosophical Theology.* Heythrop Studies in Contemporary Philosophy, Religion, & Theology. Aldershot: Ashgate.

–. 2006b. "Discerning the Theopolitical: A Response to Cavanaugh's Reimagining of Political Space. *Political Theology* 7 (3): 323–35.

–. 2019. "Kant, Divinity and Autonomy." *Studies in Christian Ethics* 32 (4): 470–84.

Isichei, Elizabeth. 1995. *A History of Christianity in Africa: From Antiquity to the Present,* Grand Rapids, MI: Eerdmans.

Iván, Júlia. 2017. "Where Do State Responsibilities Begin and End? Border Exclusions and State Responsibility." Pages 47–67 in *States, the Law and Access to Refugee Protection: Fortresses and Fairness.* Edited by Maria O'Sullivan and Dallal Stevens. Oxford: Hart Publishing.

Jacobs, Alan. 2018. *The Year of Our Lord 1943: Christian Humanism in an Age of Crisis.* New York: Oxford University Press.

Jambulosi, Mavuto. 2021. "What Does Athens 2005 Have To Do With Cape Town 2010: A Critical Comparison of Mission Theologies of the Commission for World Mission and Evangelism and of the Lausanne Movement on Social Responsibility." Diss., University of Western Cape.

Jenkins, Philip. 2002. *The Next Christendom: The Coming of Global Christianity.* Oxford: Oxford: University Press.

Jocic, Andreas. 2012. "Faith Is Never Alone: An Enquiry Into the Union-With-Christ Motif of the Finnish Luther Research, With a Subsequent Discussion Following Their Critique of Modern Protestant Theology." MA Thesis, Department of Literature, History of Ideas, and Religion, University of Gothenburg.

Johnson, Hilde F. 2016. *South Sudan: The Untold Story from Independence to the Civil War.* London: Tauris.

Joint Commission for Refugees of the Burundi and Tanzania Episcopal Conferences. 2008. "The Presence of the Burundian Refugees in Western Tanzania: Ethical Responsibilities as a Framework for Advocacy." Pages 53–63 in *Refugee Rights: Ethics, Advocacy, and Africa.* Edited by David Hollenbach. Georgetown University Press.

Jonsson, Eskil. 1998. *Narrow Management, the Quest for Unity In Diversity, the Case of the Ethiopian Evangelical Church Mekane Yesus With Her Relations to Various Co-Operating Partners.* Uppsala University.

Kalaitzidis, Pantelis. 2016. "Baptismal and Ethnocultural Community: A Case Study of Greek Orthodoxy." Pages 141–67 in *Beyond the Borders of Baptism Catholicity, Allegiances, and Lived Identities.* Edited by Michael Budde. Eugene, OR: Wipf and Stock.

Kalaitzidis, Pantelis. 2014. "Theological, Historical, and Cultural Reasons For Anti-Ecumenical Movements in Eastern Orthodoxy." Pages 134–53 in *Orthodox Handbook on Ecumenism: Resources for Theological Education.* Edited by Pantelis Kalaitzidis *et al.* Oxford: Regnum.

Kant, Immanuel. 2011. *Groundwork of the Metaphysics of Morals: A German-English Edition.* Edited and translated by Mary Gregor and Jens Timmermann. New York: Cambridge University Press.

Karltun, Stina. 2021. "Utrymme för handling: Svenska kyrkan och medmänsklighet kring 1986." MA Thesis. Uppsala University.

Kilby, Karen. 2000. "Perichoresis and Projection: Problems with Social Doctrines of the Trinity." *New Blackfriars* 81 (957): 432–45.

Kirk, Andrew J. 1999. *What is Mission? Theological Explorations.* London: Darton, Longman and Todd.

Korff, Valeska P. *et al.* 2015. "The Impact of Humanitarian Context Conditions and Individual Characteristics on Aid Worker Retention." *Disasters* 39 (3): 522–45.

Koterski, Joseph. 2002. *Natural Law and Human Nature.* Chantilly, VA: The Great Courses.

Kreeft, Peter, and Fr. Ronald Tacelli. 2009. *Handbook of Catholic Apologetics.* San Francisco, CA: Ignatius Press.

Kreeft, Peter. 2003. *Ethics: The History of Moral Thought and Ethics.* Landover, MD: Recorded Books.

–. 2014. *Socratic Logic: A Logic Text Using Socratic Method, Platonic Questions, and Aristotelian Principles.* South Bend, IN: St Augustine's Press.

–. 2021. *How to Destroy Western Civilisation: And Other Ideas from the Cultural Abyss.* San Francisco, CA: Ignatius Press.

Kvale, Steinar. 1997. *Den kvalitativa forskningsintervjun.* Lund: Studentlitteratur.

Launhardt, Johannes. 2004. *Evangelicals in Addis Ababa (1919–1991), With Special Reference to the Ethiopian Church Mekane Yesus and the Addis Ababa Synod.* Münster: LIT Verlag.

LenkaBula, Puleng. 2008. "The Shift of Gravity of the Church to Sub-Saharan Africa: Theological and Ecclesiological Implications for Women." *IJSCC* 8 (4): 290–304.

Lennox, John. 2019. *Can Science Explain Everything?* Surrey: Good News Publishers.

Levine, Donald N. 1965. *Wax and Gold.* Chicago: University of Chicago Press.

–. 2000. *Greater Ethiopia: The Evolution of a Multiethnic Society.* 2nd ed. Chicago: University of Chicago Press.

Lewis, Clive S. 1970. "Bulverism." In *God in the Dock: Essays on Theology and Ethics.* Edited by Walter Hooper. New York: Harper Collins Publishers.

–. 2001. (1947). *The Abolition Of Man: Or Reflections on Education with Special Reference to the Teaching of English in Upper Forms of Schools.* 2nd ed. New York: HarperOne.

Liederbach, Mark. 2008. "Natural Law and the Problem of Postmodern Epistemology." *Liberty University Law Review* 2 (3): 781–96.

Lossky, Nicholas *et al.*, eds. 2002. *Dictionary of the Ecumenical Movement.* 2nd ed. Geneva: WCC.

Lossky, Vladimir. 1976. *The Mystical Theology of the Eastern Church.* Crestwood, New York: St Vladimir's Seminary Press.

Lundström, Klas. 2006. *Gospel and Culture in the World Council of Churches and the Lausanne Movement with Particular Focus on the Period 1973–1996.* Studia Missionalia Svecana 103. Uppsala University.

Luopajärvi, Katja. 2003. "Is There an Obligation on States to Accept International Humanitarian Assistance to Internally Displaced Persons under International Law?" *IJRL* 15 (4): 678–714.

Luther, Martin. 1999. *Luther's Works: Vol. 31: Career of the Reformer I. Edited* by Jaroslav J. Pelikan, Hilton C. Oswald, and Helmut T. Lehmann. Philadelphia: Fortress Press.

Lönneborg, Olof. 2006. "Civil Society – ett civilisationsprojekt: En studie om det civila samhället och kyrkornas roll." Pages 11–72 in *Kristna organisationer och internationellt bistånd i det civila samhället.* Edited by Sigbert Axelson *et al.* Uppsala: SIM.

Mahoney, Daniel J. 2018. *The Idol of Our Age: How the Religion of Humanity Subverts Christianity.* New York: Encounter Books.

Mannion, Gerard. 2015. "Foreword." Pages ix–xiv in *Ecclesiology in the Trenches.* Eugene, OR: Pickwick.

Marcus, Harold G. 2002. *A History of Ethiopia.* Berkeley CA: University of California Press.

Marius, Richard, and Melvin E. Page. 2010. *A Short Guide to Writing About History.* 2nd ed. New York: Longman.

Marshall, Katherine, and Marisa Van Saanen. 2007. *Development and Faith: Where Mind, Heart and Soul Work Together.* Washington DC: World Bank.

McGrath, Alister. 2005. *The Twilight of Atheism: The Rise and Fall of Disbelief in the Modern World.* London: Ebury Publishing.

–. 2017. *Re-Imagining Nature: The Promise of a Christian Natural Theology.* Chichester: John Wiley & Sons.

Mebratu Kiros Gebru. 2012. "Liturgical Cosmology: The Theological and Sacramental Dimensions of Creation in The Ethiopian Liturgy." Diss., University of St. Michael's College and University of Toronto.

Melketsedek, *Abune.* 1997. *The Teaching of the Ethiopian Orthodox Church.* Danville CA: Alem Publishers.

Mengistu Gobezie Worku. 2018. *The Church of Yimrhane Kristos: An Archeological Investigation.* Lund University.

Meredith, Martin. 1998. *The Fate of Africa From the Hopes of Freedom to the Heart of Despair: A History of Fifty Years of Independence,* New York: Public Affairs.

Mertus, Julie A. 2009. *The United Nations and Humans Rights: A Guide for a New Era.* 2nd ed. Oxford: Routledge.

Meyer, Stephen C. 2021. *Return of the God Hypothesis: Three Scientific Discoveries that Reveal the Mind Behind the Universe.* New York: Harper Collins Publishers.

Milbank, John. 2006. *Theology and Social Theory Beyond Secular Reason.* 2nd ed. Oxford: Blackwell.

Milevsky, Jonathan L. 2017. "The Seven Laws of Noah or Novak: An Analysis of David Novak's Accounts of Natural Law." Diss., McMaster University, Hamilton.

Milner, James. 2014. "Introduction: Understanding Global Refugee Policy." *JRS* 27 (4): 477–94.

Misgana Mathewos 2010. "Gudina Tumsa's Hermeneutical Interpretation of the Bible from Global and Ethiopian/African Perspectives." *SMT* 98 (2): 193–209.

Murray, Rachel. 2004. *Human Rights in Africa: From the OAU to the African Union*, Cambridge: Cambridge University Press.

Narayan, Deepa, Robert Chambers, Meera K. Shah, and Patti Petesch. 2000. *Voices of the Poor: Crying Out for Change*. New York: Oxford University Press.

Negussie, Andre Domnic. 2010. *The Fetha Nagast and its Ecclesiology: Implications in Ethiopian Catholic Church Today*. Bern: Peter Lang.

Nigussu Legesse. 2014. "Catholicos Abune Paulos I." Pages 281–84 in *Orthodox Handbook on Ecumenism: Resources for Theological Education*. Edited by Pantelis Kalaitzidis. Oxford: Regnum.

Nilsson, Bengt. 2008. *Sveriges Afrikanska Krig*. Stockholm: Timbro Förlag.

–. 2017. *I tyst samförstånd: Sverige och Sovjet i kalla krigets Afrika*. Uppsala: Ethno Press.

Nolan, Riall. 2002. *Development Anthropology: Encounters in the Real World*. Boulder, CO: Westview Press.

Nordquist, Kjell-Åke. 1998. "From 'Just War' to Justified Intervention: A Theory of International Responsibility." Lic. Diss., Uppsala University.

Nordstokke, Kjell 2008. "International Diakonia." Pages 103–14 in *Mission to the World: Communicating the Gospel in the 21st Century. Edited* by Tormod Engelsviken *et al.*, Oxford: Regnum Books International.

Norris, Pippa, and Ronald Inglehart. 2011. *Sacred and Secular: Religion and Politics Worldwide*. Cambridge Studies in Social Theory, Religion, and Politics. Cambridge: Cambridge University Press.

Novak, Michael. 1999. "Human Dignity, Human Rights." *First Things* 97: 39–42.

Nygren, Anders. 1945. "Religiös eller kristen?" Pages 9–21 in *Den nya kyrkosynen: En samling föredrag*, Yngve Brilioth, Anton Fridrichsen, Ivar Hylander *et al.* Lund: C.W.K. Gleerups förlag.

Nyholm, Sven. 2015. "Kant's Universal Law Formula Revisited." *Metaphilosophy* 46 (2): 280–299.

Okure, Teresa, and Hans Engdahl. 2008. "Guest Editorial: Ecclesiology in Africa." *IJSCC* 8 (4): 271–74.

Öljarstrand, Anneli. 2011. "Den mångtydiga församlingen: Organisering, roller och relationer i spänningen mellan sekularisering och desekularisering." Mid Sweden University Doctoral Thesis 111. Östersund: Mid Sweden University.

Olofsson, Folke. 2015. *Credo: En personlig kristen tro. Del 2: Sonen*. Skellefteå: Artos.

Onsrud, Line. M. 1999. "East Africa Pentecostal Churches: A Study of 'Self-Historisation' as Contextualisation." *SMT* 87 (2): 419–46.

Orobator, Agbonkhianmeghe Emmanuel 2008 "Key Ethical Issues in the Practices and Policies of Refugee-Serving NGOs and Churches." Pages 225–44 in *Refugee Rights: Ethics, Advocacy, and Africa*. Edited by David Hollenbach. Washington D.C.: Georgetown University Press.

Østebø, Terje. 1998. "Creating a New Identity: The Position of Ethiopian Muslims in Contemporary Perspective" *SMT* 86 (3): 423–54.

O'Sullivan, Maria, and Dallal Stevens. 2017. "Access to Refugee Protection: Key Concepts and Contemporary Challenges." Pages 3–28 in *States, the Law and Access to Refugee Protection: Fortresses and Fairness*. Edited by Maria O'Sullivan and Dallal Stevens. Oxford: Hart Publishing.

Padilha, Anivaldo. 1994. "Diakonia in Latin America. Our Answers Should Change the Questions." *Ecumenical Review* 46: 287–91.

Pakaluk, Michael. 2002. "A Defence of Scottish Common Sense." *Philosophical Quarterly* 52 (209): 564–81.

Paulos Yohannes. 1998. "Filsata: The Feast of the Assumption of the Virgin Mary and the Mariological Tradition of the Ethiopian Orthodox Tewahedo Church." Diss., Princeton Theological Seminary.

Perry, Alex. 2014. *Clooney's War: South Sudan, Humanitarian Failure and Celebrity.* London: Newsweek Insights.

Pétursson, Pétur. 1991. *Missionsmål och missionsideologier.* Tro och Tanke 1991:8. Uppsala: Tro & Tanke.

Pinaud, Clémence. 2021. *War and Genocide in South Sudan.* Ithaca, NY: Cornell University Press.

Plantinga, Alvin. 2011. *Where the Conflict Really Lies.* New York: Oxford University Press.

Pluckrose, Helen, and James Lindsay. 2020. *Cynical Theories: How Activist Scholarship Made Everything About Race, Gender, and Identity – and Why This Harms Everybody.* Durham, NC: Pitchstone Publishing.

Prunier, Gérard, and Èloi Ficquet, eds. 2015. *Understanding Contemporary Ethiopia: Monarchy, Revolution and the Legacy of Meles Zenawi.* London: Hurst & Company.

Ratzinger, Joseph. 1996. *Called to Communion: Understanding the Church Today,* San Francisco, CA: Ignatius Press.

–. 1997. *Kallad till gemenskap: Att förstå kyrkan idag,* Stockholm: Catholica.

RCC. 1964a. "Lumen Gentium." Pages 5–75 in *Acta Apostolicae Sedis. Commentarium Officiale.* 1965 (57). English translation: Pages 849–900 in *Decrees of the Ecumenical Councils.* 1990. Edited by Norman P. Tanner. London: Sheed & Ward.

–. 1964b. "Unitatis Redintegratio." Pages 90–112 in *Acta Apostolicae Sedis. Commentarium Officiale.* 1965 (57). English translation: Pages 908–20 in *Decrees of the Ecumenical Councils.* 1990. Edited by Norman P. Tanner. London: Sheed & Ward.

Robra, Martin 1994 "Schlüsselbegriffe ökumenischer Diakonie." *Zeitschrift für Evangelische Ethik,* 38: 280–99.

Rodopoulos, Panteleimon. 2007. *An Overview of Orthodox Canon Law.* Rollinsford: Orthodox Theological Library.

Rubenson, Samuel. 2009. "A Christian Island? The Impact of Colonialism on the Perceptions of Islam and Christianity in Nineteenth Century Ethiopia." Pages 117–26 in *The Fuzzy Logic of Encounter: New Perspectives on Cultural Contact.* Edited by Sünne Juterczenka and Gesa Mackenthun. Münster: Waxmann.

–. 2013. "To Tell the Truth: Fact and Fiction in Early Monastic Sources." *Cistercian Studies Quarterly* 48 (3): 317–24.

Ryman, Björn. 1997. *Lutherhjälpens första 50 år: Medmänniskan till tjänst.* Stockholm: Verbum.

Sæverås, Olav 1974. *On Church-Mission Relations in Ethiopia 1944–1969: With Special Reference to the Evangelical Mekane Yesus and the Lutheran Missions.* Drammen: Lunde förlag.

Salomon, Kim. 1991. *Refugees in the Cold War: Toward a New International Refugee Regime in the Early Postwar Era.* Lund: Lund University Press.

Sanneh, Lamin, ed. 2011. *Accra Charter of Religious Freedom and Citizenship.* Oxford: Oxford Studies.

Schmemann, Alexander. 1973. *For the Life of the World.* 2nd ed. Crestwood, NY: St Vladimir's Seminary Press.

–. 1979. *Church World Mission.* Crestwood, NY: St. Vladimir's Seminary Press.

Seblewengel Daniel. 2019. *Perception and Identity: A Study of the Relationship between the Ethiopian Orthodox Church and Evangelical Churches in Ethiopia.* Carslie: Langham Publishing.

Shapiro, Daniel. 2007. *Is the Welfare State Justified?* New York: Cambridge University Press.

Shivute, Tomas. 1980. *The Theology of Mission in the International Mission Council from Edinburgh to New Delhi.* Helsinki: Finnish Society for Missiology and Ecumenics.

Shrier, Abigail. 2020. *Irreversible Damage: The Transgender Craze Seducing Our Daughters.* Washington, DC: Regnery Publishing.

Singer, Peter. 1972. "Famine, Affluence, and Morality." *Philosophy and Public Affairs* 1 (3): 229–43.

Sjöström, Lennart, ed. 2019. *Innan murarna föll: Svenska kyrkan under kalla kriget.* Skellefteå: Artos & Norma Bokförlag.

Slim, Hugo. 2015. *Humanitarian Ethics: A Guide to the Morality of Aid in War and Disaster.* New York: Oxford University Press.

Smith, James K. A. 2016. *You Are What You Love – the Spiritual Power of Habit.* Grand Rapids, MI: Baker.

–. 2017. *Awaiting the King: Reforming Public Theology.* Grand Rapids, MI: Baker.

Sphere Association. 2018. *The Sphere Handbook: Humanitarian Charter and Minimum Standards in Humanitarian Response.* 4th ed. Rugby: Practical Action Publishing.

Sphere Project. 2011. *Humanitarian Charter and Minimum Standards in Humanitarian Response.* 3rd ed. Northampton: Belmont.

Staples, Peter. 2002. "Catholicity." Pages 151–54 in *Dictionary of the Ecumenical Movement.* 2nd ed. Edited by Nicholas Lossky *et al.* Geneva: WCC.

Starr, James. 2000. *Sharers in Divine Nature: 2 Peter 1:4 in Its Hellenistic Context.* Coniectanea Biblica New Testament Series 33. Stockholm: Almqvist & Wiksell.

Stott, John R.W. 1975. *Christian Mission In the Modern World.* London: Falcon.

Sundeen, Johan. 2017. *68-Kyrkan: Svensk kristen vänsters möten med marxismen 1965–1989.* Stockholm: Bladh by Bladh.

Sundkler, Bengt, and Christopher Steed. 2000. *A History of the Church in Africa.* Cambridge: Cambridge University Press.

Sundqvist, Josephine. 2017. *Beyond an Instrumental Approach to Religion and Development – Challenges for Church-Based Healthcare in Tanzania.* Acta Universitatis Upsaliensis. Studies in Religion and Society 16. Uppsala University.

Suriel, Bishop. 2017. *Habib Girgis: Coptic Orthodox Educator and a Light in the Darkness.* Yonkers, NY: St Vladimir's Seminary Press.

Svartvik, Jesper. 2018. *Bibeltolkningens bakgator: synen på judar, slavar och homosexuella i historia och nutid.* Stockholm: Verbum.

Svenungsson, Jayne. 2014. *Den gudomliga historien: Profetism, messianism och andens utveckling.* Göteborg: Glänta.

Swanson, Mark. 2010. *The Coptic Papacy in Islamic Egypt 641–1517,* Cairo: American University in Cairo Press.

Swinton, John. 2003. "What is Practical Theology?" Pages 379–410 in *A Companion to Religious Studies and Theology.* Edited by Helen K. Bond, Seth D. Kunin, and Francesca Aran Murphy. Edinburgh: Edinburgh University Press.

Tadesse Tamrat. 1972. *Church and State in Ethiopia 1270–1527.* Oxford: Clarendon Press.

Taylor, Charles. 2007 *A Secular Age*. Cambridge, MA: Harvard University Press.

Taylor, Michael. 2002. "InterChurch Aid." Pages 583–86 in *Dictionary of the Ecumenical Movement*. 2nd ed. Edited by Nicholas Lossky *et al*. Geneva: WCC.

–. 1995. *Not Angels but Agencies: The Ecumenical Response to Poverty – A Primer*. Geneva: WCC.

Temesgen Shibru Galla. 2011. "The Mission Thinking of the Ethiopian Evangelical Church Mekane Yesus." MTh Thesis, MF Norwegian School of Theology.

Tergel, Alf. 1983. *Kyrkan och kapitalismens kris*. Stockholm: Verbum.

–. 1994. *Från Jesus till Moder Teresa: Kristenhetens historia*. Stockholm: Verbum.

–. 1998. *De mänskliga rättigheterna och Kyrkornas världsråd*. Tro och Tanke 1998:5. Uppsala: Tro & Tanke.

Terry, Fiona. 2002. *The Paradox of Humanitarian Action: Condemned to Repeat?* London: Cornell University Press.

Tibebe Eshete. 2009. *The Evangelical Movement in Ethiopia: Resistance and Resilience*. Waco, TX: Baylor University Press.

Toll, Torbjörn. 2014. "An Ecclesiological Reading of a Strategic Plan: Addis Ababa Evangelical Church Mekane Yesus Strategic Plan (2011–2015)." MA Thesis, Uppsala University.

Tolo, Arne. 1998. *Sidama and Ethiopian: The Emergence of the Mekane Yesus Church in Sidama*. Studia Missionalia Upsaliensia 69. Uppsala University.

Trueman, Carl R. 2020. *The Rise and Triumph of the Modern Self: Cultural Amnesia, Expressive Individualism, and the Road to Sexual Revolution*. Wheaton, IL: Crossway.

Van Beek, Huibert. 2002. "Ecumenical Sharing of Resources." Pages 382–83 in *Dictionary of the Ecumenical Movement*, 2nd ed. Edited by Nicholas Lossky *et al*. Geneva: WCC Publications.

Vial, Theodore M. 2013. *Schleiermacher: A Guide for the Perplexed*. London: Bloomsbury.

Visser't Hooft, Willem A. 1963. *No Other Name: The Choice Between Syncretism and Christian Universalism*. London: SCM Press.

–. 1982. *The Genesis and Formation of the World Council of Churches*. Geneva: WCC.

Vorgrimler, Herbert. 1992. *Sacramental Theology*. Collegeville, MN: Liturgical Press.

de Vylder, Stefan. 2013. *Utvecklingens drivkrafter: Om fattigdom, rikedom och rättvisa i världen*. 2nd ed. Stockholm: Forum Syd.

Vähäkangas, Mika. 2015. "The Economy and Money in Three Recent Mission Documents." *International Review of Mission* 104: 292–301.

de Waal, Alex. 2014. "When Kleptocracy Becomes Insolvent: Brute Causes of the Civil War in South Sudan." *African Affairs* 113 (452): 347–69.

–. 2018. *Mass Starvation: The History and Future of Famine*. Cambridge: Polity Press.

Wainwright, Geoffrey. 2002. "Lex Orandi, Lex Credendi." Pages 679–84 in *Dictionary of the Ecumenical Movement*. 2nd ed. Edited by Nicholas Lossky *et al*. Geneva: WCC.

Walker, Peter, and Daniel Maxwell. 2009. *Shaping the Humanitarian World,* Oxford: Routledge.

Walls, Andrew. 2002. "Demographics, Power and the Gospel in the 21 Century." SIL International Conference and WBTI Convention, 6 June 2002.

Ward, Michael. 2021. *After Humanity: A Guide to C.S. Lewis's The Abolition of Man*. Park Ridge, IL: Word on Fire Academics.

Watkins, Clare 1991. "Organizing the People of God: Social-Science Theories of Organization in Ecclesiology." *TS* 52: 689–711.

–. 1993. "The Church as a Special Case: Comments from Ecclesiology Concerning the Management of the Church." *MT* 9 (4): 369–84.

Wejryd, Anders. 2021. *Lutherhjälpen som försvann*. Studia Missionalia Svecana 123. Uppsala University.

White, Teresa J. 2002. "Diakonia." Pages 305–10 in *Dictionary of the Ecumenical Movement*. 2nd ed. Edited by Nicholas Lossky *et al*. Geneva: WCC.

Williams, Neil W., and Joe Saunders. 2018. "Practical Grounds for Belief: Kant and James on Religion." *European Journal of Philosophy* 26 (4): 1269–82.

Wojcichowsky, Stephen. 2013. "Breathing with Two Lungs: The Importance of Eastern Christian Studies" *Logos: A Journal of Eastern Christian Studies* 54 (3–4): 229–32.

WCC. 1952. *Intercommunion*. Faith and Order. London: SCM Press.

–. 1968. *The Church for Others and The Church for the World: A Quest for Structures for Missionary Congregations*. Geneva: WCC.

–. 1982. *Baptism, Eucharist and Ministry*. Faith and Order Paper 111. Geneva: WCC.

–. 1982. *PCR Information: Reports and Background Papers, Special Issue, Report of the Consultation on "The Churches' Involvement in Southern Africa."* Geneva: WCC.

–. 1986. *Church Kingdom World: The Church as Mystery and Prophetic Sign*. Faith and Order Paper 130. Geneva: WCC.

–. 2009. "The Nature and Mission of the Church: A Stage on the Way to a Common Statement." Faith and Order Paper 198. Geneva: WCC.

–. 2012. *Together Towards Life: Mission and Evangelism in Changing Landscapes*. Geneva: WCC.

–. 2013. *Moral Discernment in the Churches: A Study Document*. Faith and Order Paper 215. Geneva: WCC.

–. 2022. *Called to Transformation: Ecumenical Diakonia*. Geneva: WCC.

WCC, Pontifical Council for Interreligious Dialogue, and World Evangelical Alliance. 2011. *Christian Witness in a Multi-Religious World: Recommendations for Conduct*. Geneva: WCC.

Zizioulas, John, D. 1985. *Being as Communion: Studies in Personhood and the Church*. London: Darton, Longman and Todd.

Index of Ancient Literature

Hebrew Bible

Genesis

1:26   39

New Testament

Matthew

4:4   215
23:4   261
25:42–43   35

John

1:12–14   206
8:36   215
11:25   215
19:36   141

Acts

2:42–47   265
2:44–46   35
9:4–5   35
11:27–30   35, 265
11:29   265

Romans

1:21   206
7:15–20   214
8:29   206
13:8   215
15:14–29   265
15:16   265

First Corinthians

2:16   217

9:19   215
10:16   34
11–16   265
11:21   35
13:3   21
16:1   265

Galatians

2:10   266
3:27–28   35
4:4   215
6:10   266

Ephesians

1:4–10   206
1:10   29

Philippians

2: 6–7   215

First Thessalonians

2–5   265

Second Thessalonians

3:6–15   265

First Timothy

1:4   29

First Peter

2:9   30

Second Peter

1:4   221

Index of Modern Authors

Abass, Ademola 53, 168
Abate Gobena 189, 219
Abebe Feyissa 157, 186
Adejumobi, Saheed 241, 243
Adler, Mortimer 150
Ager, Alastair 18–19, 21
Aklilu Dalelo 224
Alvesson, Mats 55–56
An, Keon-Sang 189
Anderson, Mary B. 21, 77, 133, 263
Anderson, Ryan T. 80
Andrea, David J. 20
Arén, Gustav 189, 231–32, 234, 242, 259
Arendt, Hannah 166, 171
Atiya, Aziz S. 18, 141, 189, 208–9, 239, 242
Axelson, Sigbert 19

Baaz Eriksson, Maria 149
Bahru Zewde 189, 259
Bainton, Roland 149
Bakka, Jørgen F. 52
Bakke, Johnny 19, 189, 191, 193, 209, 220, 236, 245
Balisky, Paul 189, 207
Barnett, Michael 140–41, 149, 156, 161, 163, 169, 173, 251
Barrow, Ondine 35
Barth, Karl 29
Baur, John 18, 207
Bediako, Kwame 18
Bello, Emmanuel G. 167, 169
Belopopsky, Alexander 23–24, 35
Benedict XVI 27–29, 35, 153 (see Ratzinger)
Bennett, Jon 138–40, 249–51, 268

Bernander, Gustav 35
Besselink, Djoen 132
Best, Thomas F. 26, 158
Bevans, Stephen B. 30, 236, 261–62
Bexell, Göran 51, 149, 159-60
Bexell, Oloph 231
Bexell, Peter 38
Biggar, Nigel 149, 158–59, 162, 167, 172, 174, 214
Binns, John 189, 220
Bischofberger, Erwin 55, 156
Björk, Gustaf 27
Blomberg, Craig L. 21, 35, 265–66
Boersma, Hans 38–40, 199, 201, 228
Boff, Clodovis 261
Borgehammar, Stephan 34, 40, 51, 58
Bornemark, Jonna 133
Borton, John 132
Bosch, David 24, 27, 30, 220, 229
Braaten, Carl 27, 29
Bradley, James E. 57, 73, 204
Brattgård, Helge 156
Bretherton, Luke 216, 242
Bria, Ion 219
Brock, Sebastian P. 220
Brodd, Sven-Erik 23–25, 27, 30–32, 34, 36–37, 40–44, 51, 53, 222, 229, 272–73, 295
Brown, Dayna 133, 263
Bugnion, François 136

Cahill, Thomas 33
Cantor, David J. 173, 185
Carter, Alix 249, 267

Cavanaugh, William T. 22–23, 29, 34, 80, 148, 151, 153
Chaillot, Christine 189, 207
Christensen, Torben 266
Collins, Alan 140
Collins, John N. 32–33, 217
Constantinou, Eugenia S. 217
Cooper, Frederick 174
Cooper, Jordan 28–29, 221, 266
Cunningham, David, S. 149, 162, 167

Dawit Olika 189, 192
Dawit Wolde Giorgis 209–10
Debela Birri 189
Delkeskamp-Hayes, Corinna 22, 148, 159
Deneen, Patrick J. 167
Deneulin, Séverine 18
Desta Heliso 7, 217
Dulles, Avery 25, 31–32, 34, 36–37, 229
Durieux, Jean-François 173, 185

Easterly, William 175–76, 185, 225, 265
Eckerdal, Erik 50
Eckerdal, Jan 80
Egerland, Erik 230
Eide, Øyvind M. 18–19, 189, 191–93, 199, 204, 213, 230, 244, 268
Emmanuel Abraham 112, 191, 193, 232, 235–36, 245, 248
Engdahl, Hans 18, 55
Engelsviken, Tormod 18
Ers, Agnes 149
Esaiasson, Peter 52
Evans-Pritchard, Edward E. 86
Ezra Gebremedhin 189, 220, 259

Fagerberg, David 208, 219
Fagerli, Beate 50
Fahlgren, Sune 51, 242
Fiddian-Qasmiyeh, Elena 19, 22
Forrester, Duncan 24–26
Forslund, Eskil 189
Foster, Richard J. 261
Fowden, Garth 22

Frankl, Viktor E. 171, 226
Fritsch, Emmanuel 189, 217
Fuch, Lorelei F. 238

Gaillardetz, Richard R. 18
Gemechu Olana 246
George, Sam 53
Getnet Tamene 19, 189, 207, 217, 230
Gifford, Paul 18
Girgis, Sherif 80
Goulet, Denus 18, 149
Grenholm, Carl-Henric 51, 149, 159-60
Grenstedt, Staffan 18–19, 189, 194, 207, 212, 231–32, 234, 242, 259–60, 268
Gustavsson, Jacob 52

Haakonssen, Knud 149
Halldin Norberg, Viveca 212, 259
Halldorf, Joel 29
Hallencreutz, Carl F. 73
Harmless, William 189
Harrison, Peter 20
Haustein, Jörg 204, 212–13
Henrich, Laban 139, 248, 251
Hildebrand, Dietrich 149, 158, 162
Hilhorst, Dorothea 263
Hillbom, Ellen 140, 174–76, 178–79
Hjälm, Michael 210
Hollenbach, David 133–34, 149, 157
Holmefur, Niklas 19, 21–22, 287
Hopgood, Stephen 23, 148
Horn, Rebecca 132, 157, 186
Hovorun, Cyril 25, 31, 37, 141, 184
Howard, Thomas 22
Howell, Leon 186
Hugman, Richard 48
Hull, Timothy 29–30, 38
Hutchinson, John F. 154

Ideström, Jonas 51
Inglehart, Ronald 19–20
Insole, Christopher 20, 22, 30, 148–49, 161
Isichei, Elizabeth 18, 189

Iván, Júlia

Jacobs, Alan 21, 198
Jambulosi, Mavuto 27–29, 261
Jenkins, Philip 20
Jocic, Andreas 221
Johnson, Hilde F. 60, 197
Jonsson, Eskil 19, 21, 37, 44, 52, 189, 192,
    225, 231, 262

Kalaitzidis, Pantelis 201
Kant, Immanuel 154, 161
Karltun, Stina 30
Karttunen, Tomi 50
Kilby, Karen 29
Kirk, Andrew J. 30
Korff, Valeska P. 140
Koterski, Joseph 149, 164
Kreeft, Peter 21, 29, 42–43, 52, 149, 154,
    158–61, 163–64, 261, 266
Kvale, Steinar 48

Launhardt, Johannes 86, 189, 222
LenkaBula, Puleng 18
Lennox, John 20
Levine, Donald N. 241, 243–44
Lewis, C. S. 57, 160, 183–84
Liederbach, Mark 29, 149
Lindkvist, Lars 52
Lindsay, James 80
Lossky, Vladimir 220–21
Lundström, Klas 24, 34
Luopajärvi, Katja 139, 145
Luther, Martin 33, 197, 214–15

Mahoney, Daniel J. 165
Mannion, Gerard 51
Marcus, Harold G. 243–44
Marius, Richard 73
Marshall, Katherine 19
Maxwell, Daniel 126, 139–40, 150–53, 158,
    168
McGrath, Alister 20, 149, 165
Mebratu Kiros Gebru 189, 217–18, 227

Melketsedek, *Abune* 189, 217
Mengistu Gobezie Worku 189, 219
Meredith, Martin 174–75
Mertus, Julie A. 172
Meyer, Stephen C. 20
Milbank, John 20
Milevsky, Jonathan L. 149
Milner, James. 179
Misgana Mathewos. 19, 189
Muller, Richard A. 57, 73, 204
Murray, Rachel 171–72, 176–77

Narayan, Deepa 18
Nathaniel, Leslie 50
Negussie, Andre Domnic 18, 189
Nigussu Legesse 189, 195, 209, 227, 244
Nilsson, Bengt 21, 137
Nolan, Riall 149
Nordquist, Kjell-Åke 149, 151, 164, 169
Nordstokke, Kjell 18
Norris, Pippa 20
Novak, Michael 149
Nygren, Anders 35
Nyholm, Sven 154

Okure, Teresa 18
Öljarstrand, Anneli 51
Olofsson, Folke 163
Onsrud, Line 18
Orobator, Agbonkhianmeghe Emmanuel
    133–34, 184, 279
Østebø, Terje 230
O'Sullivan, Maria 129

Padilha, Anivaldo 18, 51
Pakaluk, Michael 158
Paulos Yohannes 189, 217
Perry, Alex 60
Pétursson, Pétur 231
Pinaud, Clémence 60
Plantinga, Alvin 20, 153
Pluckrose, Helen 80
Prunier, Gérard 141, 175, 241–47, 253

Ratzinger, Joseph 220 (*see* Benedict XVI)
Robra, Martin 23, 26, 35, 158
Rubenson, Samuel 207, 240
Ryman, Björn 35

Saeverås, Olav 18–19, 189, 194, 232–34, 236
Salomon, Kim 171
Sanneh, Lamin 18
Saunders, Joe 163
Schmemann, Alexander 20, 28–30, 52, 201, 208, 210, 219–21, 284
Schroeder, Roger P. 30, 236, 261–62
Seblewengel, Daniel 189, 204, 213
Shapiro, Daniel 181
Shivute, Tomas 18, 24–25
Shrier, Abigail 80
Singer, Peter 162
Sjöström, Lennart 30
Slim, Hugo 149
Smith, James K. A. 228
Staples, Peter 31
Starr, James 221
Stott, John R. W. 24
Sundeen, Johan 21, 30
Sundkler, Johan 18, 189, 207
Sundqvist, Josephine 21
Suriel, Bishop 232, 242, 245
Svartvik, Jesper 80
Svenungsson, Jayne 29
Swanson, Mark 189
Swinton, John 229

Tacelli, Ronald 52
Tadesse Tamrat 189
Tankink, Marian 132
Tanner, Mary 38

Taylor, Charles. 20–21
Taylor, Michael 18, 31, 35, 137, 260–62, 264–66
Temesgen Shibru Galla 192, 194, 216, 225
Tergel, Alf 137, 146, 152, 186
Terry, Fiona 132–33
Tibebe Eshete 19, 204, 230, 243, 247
Toll, Torbjörn 56, 112, 222
Tolo, Arne 189, 241
Trueman, Carl R. 80

Van Beek, Huibert 24
Van Saanen, Marisa 19
Visser't Hooft, Willem A. 18, 24–25, 31, 42, 186, 237–38
Vorgrimler, Herbert 38
de Vylder, Stefan 52
Vähäkangas, Mika 262

de Waal, Alex 60, 122, 268
Wainwright, Geoffrey 218
Walker, Peter 126, 133, 136–40, 146, 150–54, 157–58, 168–70
Walls, Andrew 20
Ward, Michael 152, 160
Watkins, Clare 51
Wejryd, Anders 35, 55
White, Teresa J. 24, 33
Willemse, Jacques 139, 248, 251
Williams, Neil W. 117, 163
Wojcichowsky, Stephen 17

Zizioulas, John D. 29, 132

Index of Subjects

accountability 49, 69, 72, 85, 98, 107, 113, 115, 117, 127–28, 131, 133–34, 142–48, 170, 182, 184–85, 240, 255, 263, 279–80, 289

ACT membership 73, 79, 85, 146, 254–55, 269–70

advocacy 18, 47, 53, 70, 77, 90, 115, 143, 146–47, 170, 178, 180, 186, 230, 252, 260, 262, 276

African
– borders 173, 176
– churches 15, 17–19, 41, 62, 200, 202, 241, 262, 275, 288
– gate keeper states 64, 126, 173, 279
– independent states 194, 176,
– theology 18

apostolicity 33–35, 189, 205–8, 216, 227, 272, 283–84, 287, 297

appeal mechanism 63, 69, 115–16, 118, 274, 278

Aristotle, Aristotelian 29, 37–39, 42, 158, 214

asceticism, ascetic 208–10, 218, 220, 227

association 22–24, 34, 42, 108, 128, 144–45, 222–23, 235, 237, 248–49, 253–55, 257–58, 268–70, 289, 293

autocephaly 37, 141, 241–42

autonomy 39, 53, 78, 138, 141, 212, 233, 236, 250, 267, 272, 290

baptism 33, 37, 40, 148, 217, 231, 234

belief 20, 115, 128–29, 148, 150, 152–53, 163, 175, 204, 208, 210, 216, 218–19, 240, 253, 284

bottom-up 134, 147, 236, 262, 279

boundaries 25, 140, 233, 272, 286

bread 132, 193–94, 201, 215–16

caritas 146, 258, 260 (see charity, love)

CBPS (psychosocial) 49, 85, 88, 97–99, 103–4, 106–8, 127–28, 130–32, 172, 180–1, 197, 201, 257, 277–78, 286–87

charity 33, 53, 159, 162–63, 239, 242, 274

charity organisations 33, 46–47, 71, 84–85, 208, 239, 255–56, 283

Christianity 16, 18, 20–22, 24, 28, 40, 51, 158, 162–64, 186, 189, 201, 208, 221, 230, 232–34, 238, 240, 276

colonialism 18, 64, 121, 127, 171, 174–76, 216, 231, 241, 243–44, 259, 279

community-based 106–7, 139, 142, 172, 180–81, 196–97, 201, 251, 256–57, 263, 277, 286

complaints handling 105, 107, 143–44

conflict
– emergencies 168
– prevention 263, 271
– resolution 278

congregation 27, 34, 53, 112, 193, 202, 217, 222, 234, 291

connaturality 39–40

consequentialist 155

constitution 21, 172, 216–17, 244

contingency 82, 85, 87–88

cooperation 21, 24, 52, 68, 70, 99, 110, 115, 131, 195, 246, 249, 255, 262, 271

coordinator 78–79, 84, 95, 107, 110, 114, 248

corruption 37, 49, 128, 144, 214

creed 31, 46, 137, 241, 272, 297

crisis-affected 133–34, 142, 279
cross-border 76, 139, 250, 259
cross-cutting 108, 130, 132
culture 20, 40, 56, 80, 86, 134, 136, 142,
    149, 153, 159–61, 167, 170, 186, 195,
    206, 208, 213, 218, 222, 227, 233, 260,
    279

denominationalism 25, 230, 234, 260
deontological 200, 281
dependency 21, 30, 120, 140–41, 222–25,
    244, 257, 265, 269–71, 291, 293
Diakonie 23, 33, 46, 50, 62, 215, 255, 274,
    284, 289, 294–95
donor-based 64, 178, 184, 191, 281, 300

ecclesiality 15, 59
ecclesiastical 37, 141, 204, 208
ecclesiology, ecclesiological 15–18, 21, 23,
    26, 30, 32, 34, 36, 38, 40–42, 44, 48,
    50–1, 62, 80, 158, 185–86, 190, 206,
    211, 228, 229, 242, 265, 272–73, 275–
    76, 283, 289, 291, 298–99, 302
ecumenical
– agencies 65, 223, 230, 285
– approaches 65, 229–30, 243, 258, 270,
    285, 288
– collaboration 51, 59, 62, 64–65, 191–92,
    225, 227–29, 243, 254, 267, 274, 282,
    284, 288, 292, 296
– commitments 62, 202, 206, 225, 239,
    282, 300
– diakonia 15, 17, 23–24, 30, 32, 35–36,
    40–41, 60, 62, 189–90, 203, 219, 225,
    275, 288, 294, 299–300
– *diakonie* 274, 294–95
– models 58, 65, 229, 269–70, 274, 280–
    81, 294
– movement 17–18, 23–26, 29, 31, 33, 35–
    36, 42, 47, 50, 58, 115, 127, 156, 184,
    186, 192, 203, 205, 207, 215, 220, 230,
    237–38, 242, 252, 258, 260–61, 264,
    266, 269, 275, 280, 282, 284, 288–90,
    292, 297

– organisation 36, 56, 236, 275
– partners 208–9, 223–24, 237, 283, 285
– theory 41, 299
ecumenism 25, 30–32, 50–51, 198, 292
efficiency 52, 134, 185, 276, 279, 299
emotivism 159
empowerment 96, 108
ethics 26, 28, 33, 51, 149–50, 158–60, 162,
    185–87, 215, 219, 265, 275, 291, 300
eucharist 33–34, 37, 207–8, 210, 221,
    283–84, 287
evangelisation 24, 34, 191, 193, 200, 236,
    260–61, 266
expatriate 53, 110, 142

faith-based 19, 36, 47, 52, 68, 70, 118, 125,
    179, 192, 255
freedom 22, 33, 131, 141, 157, 161–62, 167,
    172, 178, 197, 207, 212, 214–17, 221,
    237, 243, 245, 247, 284
fundraising 114–15, 117–18, 120, 269–70,
    272, 277–78

gender 20, 108, 130, 135, 203
Gnosticism 220–21
governance 120, 125, 247, 290

human
– dignity 156, 163, 196
– flourishing 159, 167
– nature 20, 39, 150, 152, 154, 159, 163,
    200–201, 281, 324
– person 59, 132, 156–57, 199–201, 216,
    274, 281, 290, 293, 295, 300–301
– rights 18, 23, 50, 56, 62, 64, 126, 129,
    137, 140, 146, 157, 163–64, 166–67,
    169–70, 172–73, 184, 199, 296
humanism 19–21, 198–200, 216, 226,
    281–82, 287, 295, 301
– exclusive humanism 20, 198–99, 216,
    282, 287, 295, 301
humanitarian
– access 168
– accountability 14, 127–28, 142, 255

– agencies 116, 125–26, 129, 132–34, 137, 139–40, 144–45, 155, 172, 178, 246, 248, 250, 279, 296–98
– approach 4, 170, 294, 296, 299–300
– argument 64, 126, 149–50, 154, 156–57, 159, 173, 296
– charter 49, 107, 127–28, 130, 134, 144–45, 182
– civil–military dialogue 138
– governance 120, 125, 290
– imperative 64, 126, 129, 138, 154–55
– law 50, 64, 126, 156, 160, 166–68, 170, 172–73, 180
– principles 120, 132, 139–40, 143, 148, 169, 173, 180–81, 247
– standards 13–14, 107, 128, 144–45, 170
humanitarianism 19, 23, 140–41, 151, 163, 168–70, 173, 251, 263
humanity 129, 134–35, 138, 154–55, 160
humanity, concept of 21, 136, 140, 154–56, 160–3, 165, 169, 171, 180, 184

identity 15, 21, 34–36, 41, 44–45, 50, 68, 80, 115–16, 120–21, 142, 182, 233, 273, 275, 287, 292, 295, 298–99
ideology 19, 42, 52, 137, 171, 199, 208, 243–44
impartiality 134–35, 138, 182, 185, 201
independence 116, 120, 129, 134, 137–41, 148, 168–69, 182, 185
institutionalisation 78, 127, 170, 223, 293
inter-church aid model 11–12, 65, 228–30, 237, 242, 258, 264–65, 271, 280, 285–86, 290
international crisis model 65, 224, 228–30, 243, 248, 251, 258, 264, 266–68, 285–88, 290
Islam 18, 22, 164, 230, 239

justice 26, 28, 40, 62, 116, 121, 135, 137, 158–59, 186, 206, 214, 221, 241, 261, 266

Kantian ethics 29–30, 122, 126, 154–55, 157, 160–61, 163–65

law-based 64, 126, 165–67
legality 64, 78, 127, 162, 279, 298
liberation 24, 26–28, 35, 90, 137, 139, 174, 176, 197–98, 243–44, 250–53, 261–62, 268–69
liberty 167, 176, 216
lifesaving 112, 251, 278, 286
liturgy 64, 191, 208–11, 213, 217–221, 272, 283–84
livelihood 85, 88, 94, 98–99, 102–4, 108, 112, 116, 119–20, 131, 156, 218, 239–40, 254, 256, 277
long-term 16, 52, 76, 88, 93–94, 113, 140, 142, 156–57, 186, 225, 240, 251, 278
love 33, 36, 135, 205, 213–15, 231, 258, 260, 284

management 49, 96, 107, 128, 133, 142–44, 192
mandate 25, 97, 99, 145, 168, 170, 179, 181, 249
Marxism 18, 160, 192, 203, 209, 211, 243, 246–247, 250, 253, 268
materialism 19, 158, 163–64, 195–96, 200, 209, 211, 226–27, 281–83, 286–88, 295, 301
metaphysics 38, 161, 165
mission
– agency 36, 42, 86, 194, 223–24, 233, 236, 258–59, 263, 268, 281, 292
– decree 233
– model 65, 191, 224, 228–30, 233, 236–37, 242, 258–60, 264, 266, 271, 281, 285, 287–88, 290
– movement 23–24, 156, 230–31, 237, 281
monasteries 23, 207, 209, 227, 245
monastic 189, 207–8, 223, 245
morality 21, 29, 32, 64, 80, 126–27, 149, 152, 154, 157–65, 182–84, 210, 217–18, 261, 266, 279–80, 288–89, 294, 298, 300

Muslim 22, 163–64, 211–12, 239–41, 244
mystery 25, 28, 34–35, 38, 40, 210, 220
mysticism 220

nation-building 233, 237, 242–43, 259,
    268, 285
nation-state 22, 151, 171, 176, 186, 271
natural disaster 70, 117, 120, 168, 268, 278
natural law 29, 32, 42, 63–64, 126, 159–
    60, 162, 164, 184, 186, 199, 228, 279,
    298, 301
naturalism 20, 39–40, 153, 216
neighbour 21, 32–33, 148, 213–15, 228,
    260, 272, 281, 284, 287, 289, 294–95,
    300–301
neutrality 134–39, 142, 148, 168, 250

obligation 35, 51, 111, 121, 129, 149, 164,
    166, 173, 183, 193–94, 226, 237, 287
ontology 40, 148, 150, 152, 155, 158, 163,
    202
oppression 28, 160, 169, 182, 207, 214,
    244, 260, 283
otherworldly 208, 220, 227–28, 283, 295,
    301
ownership 4, 79, 113, 195, 262, 281, 300

paradox 21, 39–40, 175, 215–16, 296
parish 61–62, 148, 205, 212, 223, 236, 239,
    241, 244
parousia 28, 30
participatory 77, 117, 129, 151, 172, 212
patriarch 31, 184, 203, 205–6, 208, 210–
    13, 220, 237–40, 242, 244, 282
persecution 212, 232, 239, 246, 268
personalism 199–200
philosophy 21, 39, 150, 152, 154, 160–61,
    200, 211
phronema 211, 217
piety 24, 40, 136, 194, 200, 217
positivism 159–60, 162

prejudice 55, 149, 212
private 22, 34, 40, 51, 53, 138, 144, 168,
    175, 181, 187, 253, 276

quasi-religion 153

religion 19–21, 28, 35, 40, 135, 150, 152–53,
    158–59, 163, 165, 167, 182, 192, 209,
    211–13, 217, 221, 287
repatriation 166, 171, 176, 278
resettlement 177, 250
revolution 11, 14, 29, 141, 165, 169, 190–
    92, 203, 212, 217, 222–23, 226, 243–
    46, 253, 268, 283, 285
rights-based 36, 102, 129, 199, 271, 298

sacramentality 25, 34, 36–38, 207, 210,
    221, 261, 272, 283–84, 287, 298
scientism 20, 153
secularism 19–20, 28–29, 39–40, 52, 216,
    221
secularity 216
suffering, alleviation of 121–22, 129, 135,
    154–56, 159, 162, 170, 209, 246–47

Theism 153, 163–65
theosis 208, 221
transparency 105, 133, 143, 147, 181

utilitarian 129, 154–55, 157, 160, 196–97,
    200, 219, 281
utopia 28–29

virtues 158, 214, 218
volunteer 136, 138, 143–44, 162, 222, 280,
    291–94, 299
vulnerability 94, 130–31

wellbeing 56, 96, 103–4, 149, 213, 218,
    222, 293
worship 61, 152, 218–19, 246, 284, 300

Dissertationes Theologicae Holmienses

1. Eurell, John-Christian. *Peter's Legacy in Early Christianity: The Appropriation and Use of Peter's Authority in the First Three Centuries.* DTH 1. Stockholm: Enskilda Högskolan Stockholm, 2021.

2. Mannerfelt, Frida. *Co-preaching: The Practice of Preaching in Digital Culture and Spaces.* DTH 2. Stockholm: Enskilda Högskolan Stockholm, 2023.

3. Appelfeldt, Joel. *Dopet som hantverk: Gudstjänstkreativitet och liturgisk taktik i Svenska kyrkan och Equmeniakyrkan.* DTH 3. Skellefteå: Artos Academic, 2023.

4. Gobena, Abate. *Sanctity and Environment in Ethiopian Hagiography: The Case of Gedle Gebre Menfes Qiddus.* DTH 4. Stockholm: Enskilda Högskolan Stockholm, 2023.

5. Lockneus, Elin. *Kyrkbänksteologi.* DTH 5. Skellefteå: Artos Academic, 2023.

6. Asserhed, Björn. *Gardens in the Wasteland: Christian Formation in Three Swedish Church Plants.* DTH 6. Stockholm: Enskilda Högskolan Stockholm, 2024.

7. Hallonsten, Simon. *Online Small Groups as Sites of Teaching: An Action Research Dissertation into Christian Religious Education in the Church of Sweden.* Stockholm: Enskilda Högskolan Stockholm, 2024.

8. Plantin, Lisa. *Birth Metaphors in the Book of Job: A Blending Theory Analysis.* DTH 8. Stockholm: Enskilda Högskolan Stockholm, 2024.

9. Nõmmik, Aldar. *Robes, Romans, and Rituals in First Corinthians: Paul and the Conflict over Head-Coverings.* DTH 9. Stockholm: Enskilda Högskolan Stockholm, 2025.

10. Toll, Torbjörn. *ACT Alliance and the Refugee Crisis: Ecclesiology and Tensions in Refugee Assistance.* DHT 10. Stockholm: Enskilda Högskolan Stockholm, 2025.